This wax impression, bearing the abbreviated name of Jesus
encircled by the inscription
"The seal of the Superior of the Society of Jesus"
(SIGILLVM PREPOSITI SOCIETATIS IESV),
was made from the seal used
by St. Ignatius when he was the first general
of the order, 1541-1556.
The medieval spelling of *prepositi* is noteworthy.
This same seal was also used by St. Ignatius' earlier successors
and by General Congregations II-XI (1565-1661),
XIII (1687), and XV-XIX (1706-1758).
St. Ignatius' secretary, Juan de Polanco, used it
upon the official text of the *General Examen* on October 9, 1558,
and Lorenzo Maggio, Secretary of the Society, put it
upon the ameliorated text
of the *Constituciones de la Compañía de Jesús*
which was approved by General Congregation V (1593-1594).
In the series of volumes,
Monumenta Historica Societatis Iesu,
there are interesting facsimiles
in *Constitutiones Societatis Jesu*, Volume II, pages 123 and 727,
and *Fontes Narrativi*, Volume I, on the title page.
The photograph was take
by the Reverend Algimantas Ke
The seal itself is now preserved in the Jes

THE CONSTITUTIONS

OF THE

SOCIETY OF JESUS

SAINT IGNATIUS OF LOYOLA

THE CONSTITUTIONS
OF THE
SOCIETY OF JESUS

Translated,

with an Introduction and a Commentary,

by

GEORGE E. GANSS, S.J.

THE INSTITUTE OF JESUIT SOURCES

St. Louis, 1970

IMPRIMI POTEST: Very Reverend Peter Arrupe, S.J.
General of the Society of Jesus
August 30, 1969

IMPRIMATUR: John J. Cardinal Carberry
Archbishop of St. Louis
September 22, 1969

©1970   The Institute of Jesuit Sources
St. Louis University, Fusz Memorial
3700 West Pine Blvd.
St. Louis, Missouri 63108

Library of Congress Catalog Card Number: 72-108258

TO VERY REVEREND FATHER PETER ARRUPE

WITH DEEP RESPECT AND ESTEEM

Published through the aid of funds

donated by the late Mr. James L. Monaghan

of Milwaukee, Wisconsin,

1867-1963,

in memory of his brother,

Reverend Edward V. Monaghan, S.J.,

1879-1922.

CONTENTS

Part two   THE CONSTITUTIONS
OF THE SOCIETY OF JESUS

The Documents, translated from the official texts

Document 1   THE FORMULA OF THE INSTITUTE
of the Society of Jesus

Part three   R E F E R E N C E   M A T T E R — *See next page*

Part three   REFERENCE MATTER

ILLUSTRATIONS

THE CONSTITUTIONS
OF THE
SOCIETY OF JESUS

Part one

Introduction

THE LIFE-GIVING SPIRIT WITHIN

ST. IGNATIUS' CONSTITUTIONS

I

The book entitled *Constitutions of the Society of Jesus*, composed by St. Ignatius of Loyola (1491-1556) chiefly during the last nine years of his life and published two years after his death, is one mature expression, among others, of his overall outlook on life. He had a world view which led him to an intense desire to be associated intimately with Christ and to cooperate with Him in achieving God's slowly unfolding plan of creation and redemption. Ignatius hoped through all his activities to bring greater praise or glory to God than that which would have accrued to Him without them. His desire to be associated with Christ did not refer merely to the Jesus who lived and taught in Judaea. It was focused also and prominently upon the Savior whom Ignatius saw at La Storta, that is, on the glorified Christ who was still present in the Church as His mystical body and in the pope as its head on earth. Under a guiding Providence that desire arose in Ignatius' heart at one moment in the long history of salvation; and it was the wellspring of everything which he thought, said, did, or wrote. That desire to cooperate with Christ in bringing greater glory to

St. Ignatius'
position in
the history
of salvation

God can well be said to be the spirit or predominant trend of his thought; and it pulsates through his Constitutions.

A. *A genetic study of Ignatius' world view*

Ignatius' life has been recounted in so many places that there is no need to repeat it here. But for our purpose of understanding the spirit as well as the letter of his Constitutions, it will be helpful to sketch his intellectual and spiritual biography. His view of the universe and of man's place in it was formed gradually in a process of many years. A study of the successive stages in that process can reveal how God Himself molded Ignatius' world view and thereby fashioned him into an effective instrument of His divine purposes. Ignatius' own part was one of wholehearted cooperation.

The use of a genetic approach such as this brings many concurrent benefits. First, it shows the gradual growth of Ignatius' own spirituality which the Society of Jesus has continually endeavored to adapt to new circumstances in succeeding eras after his death. Second, it enables us to see Ignatius' place in the unfolding history of salvation, and specifically in the important transitional period of the Reformation and the Council of Trent. Third, it harmonizes well with many healthy trends of modern scholarship which are clearly reflected in the documents of Vatican Council II.

B. *Vatican Council II on return to the sources*

On various occasions the Council has urged members of religious institutes, in their work of renewal, (1) to return continually to the sources of all Christian life, such as Scripture and Tradition, and (2) to study the original inspiration of their respective founders; for it is thus that they can both retain what is solid in the traditions of the past and also put themselves into position for a sound adaptation of those sources and that inspiration to the changed conditions of modern times.[1] Furthermore, both the Council and General Congregation XXXI of the Society of Jesus have also recommended that the training of seminarians be integrated around God's redemptive plan (called by St. Paul [Eph. 1:9, 3:1-11; Rom. 16:25] "the mystery of Christ") in the his-

For the ABBREVIATIONS USED THROUGHOUT THIS BOOK, see the list on pages 358-362 below.

1 See Vatican Council II, on the "Adaptation and Renewal of Religious Life," no. 2; Paul VI, Motu Proprio "Ecclesiae Sanctae," nos. 16, §§1-3, 17, 19, in *Acta Apostolicae Sedis*, LVIII (1966), 777-778 (abbreviated hereafter as *AAS*); address to Religious, May 24, 1964, in *AAS*, LVI (1964), 569.

tory of salvation.[2] Many of the best insights of modern theology
have been gained by projecting individual doctrines against that
wider background of the history of salvation and studying their
gradual genesis in it. By viewing Ignatius and his Constitutions[3]
against that same background we too can, in similar manner,
gain a perspective which brings us a deeper understanding of
him and of them. Such perspective must take in three important
elements: the deposit of faith, evolution of doctrine, and schools
of spirituality within the Church.[4] Among Catholics these three
factors are widely accepted in substance. There is naturally some
disagreement about details, especially in these days when much
emphasis in theological study is being shifted from being to process, from the state of a doctrine in one period to its development
in history.

c. *The deposit of faith, doctrinal evolution, and schools of spirituality*

As the centuries passed after mankind's fall in Adam, God used
different means to guide His people to achieve closer union with
Himself through love and the practice of their faith. He revealed
Himself to them in a progressive manner through His deeds and
words. Although He revealed His truth more fully, He did not
change His earlier revealed doctrine. However, to make this body
of truth more easily intelligible, acceptable, and profitable to the
people in successive eras of their cultural evolution, He varied
the manner of expressing it. He also inspired changes in the laws
regulating worship and disciplinary practice. Through Christ He
revealed the Trinity and Incarnation. He closed His public revelation, the deposit of faith which He entrusted to the Church,
with the death of the last apostle. The Church too preserves the
substance of this deposit unchanged but varies the manner of
expressing it in accordance with new cultural needs. She may,
for example, stress one aspect more in one era than in another, or
explicitly affirm truths implicitly contained in the deposit, or express the old truths in new terms such as those of Greek philosophy.

Christian spirituality is the application of relevant elements in
the deposit of faith to the guidance of men toward spiritual per-

2 Vatican Council II, on "Priestly Formation," no. 14; *Decreta Congregationis Generalis XXXI Societatis Iesu* (Rome, 1967), Decree 9, "The Training of the Scholastics Especially in Studies," no. 20; Decree 8, "The Spiritual Formation of Jesuits," nos. 9, 21.
3 On the terms constitution, constitutions, Constitutions, *Constitutions*, and the stylistic dis-
tinctions between them, see supplementary Note C in the Reference matter below, p. 356.
4 See Vatican Council II, on "Divine Revelation," nos. 10, 25; also, the references in foot-
note 1 above; J. de Guibert, *The Jesuits: Their Spiritual Doctrine and Practice* (Chicago, 1964), pp. 1-12 (abbreviated hereafter as *DeGuiJes*); G. E. Ganss, "Ignatian Research

fection, that rich development of their persons which flowers into correspondingly greater insight and joy in the beatific vision. Every Catholic or group of Catholics seeking perfection accepts the entire deposit of faith. But throughout history different persons or groups have emphasized different elements in that body of life-giving truths. Because of the need to come to grips with varying needs or opportunities in different eras; because of the varying personalities and temperaments of men or women; because of varying levels of education in diverse epochs or places; because, above all, of the formative influence which the Holy Spirit exerts through the distribution of His graces, one person or group has drawn more inspiration from one aspect of God's revelation and another from another. Thus it arose that, in age after age, it was God who took a cooperative man or woman and molded him into the personality of a Benedict, a Francis of Assisi, a Dominic, an Ignatius, a Theresa, or a Francis de Sales, and gave him a message of value for his own age and for later eras. Thence too arose the schools of spirituality in the Church. Each school draws something today from the rest and cooperates with them but also retains its own characteristics and emphases. Thence too we see why the Church in the era of Vatican Council II has been urging religious institutes to restudy and reapply the inspiration of their respective founders. Thence finally we see that Ignatian spirituality is simply Christian spirituality with emphasis on those elements in the deposit of faith which Ignatius stressed. His emphasis arose from an outlook marvelously dynamic both for total dedication of one's entire self to God and for energetic apostolic fruitfulness.

D. *The Constitutions viewed in this perspective*

When seen in perspective from that point of vantage, Ignatius' Constitutions are recognized as one of the more important developments within the gradually unfolding history of salvation. Although they are not a theoretical exposition of spirituality or of the religious life, they nevertheless clearly reflect the spiritual outlook from which they sprang. Ignatius could have made them a code which merely expressed his statutes but gave little or no indication of the reasonings which led to their formulation—a procedure followed in many a modern code. Instead, as was natural for a leader such as he was—one who knew how to motivate and

and the Dialogue with the Contemporary American Mind," *Woodstock Letters,* XCIII (1964), 141-164, esp. 142-144 (abbreviated hereafter as *WL*). The present chapter is much indebted to *DeGuiJes* and to Hugo Rahner, *The Spirituality of St. Ignatius Loyola* (Westminster, 1953, and Chicago, 1968, in the Loyola University Press reprints).

inspire others no less than to govern them—he wove his reasons into the fabric of his text. They are sometimes explicitly stated, sometimes perceptible only a little below the surface, and sometimes merely insinuated by delicate nuances and overtones, such as his reverent use of "God our Lord" (*Dios nuestro Señor*)—a phrase which is often a worshipful reference to the human Christ rather than to the other divine persons. By this procedure of inserting reasons Ignatius made his statutes more inspirational, because they are readily seen as means to his end: loving and effective cooperation with Christ toward achievement of the redemptive plan, unto greater praise or glory from men to God.

1. *The spirit and the letter*

Yet even so, some readers have seen in these Constitutions only a dry legal code. Others, in contrast, have found them powerfully motivating toward energetic service to God and their fellowmen. The one group grasps the letter alone and the other the spirit as well. The probable reason for this difference of reaction is that the one group approaches the text without and the other with the key to its life-giving spirit. That key is a knowledge of Ignatius' world view, which included his distinctive and personalized concept of God's redemptive plan. Just as that world view was Ignatius' framework of reference in composing the Constitutions, so should it be our framework of reference for interpreting the details.

E. *Ignatius' distinctive concept of God's redemptive plan*

His concept, with its distinctive characteristics and nuances whereby he habitually saw things in perspective as parts of a whole, arose chiefly from the vivid insights he received through infused contemplation[5] at Manresa and later. In fact, it ever remained the warm apperception of the mystic more than the organized and coldly reasoned exposition of speculative theologians, even though he did put an academic foundation beneath it during his studies at the universities of Alcalá and Paris. The end result was that his enthusiasm gained from mystic contemplation, built upon the natural foundation of his chivalrous temperament and united to his habits of careful reasoning and experienced practical judgment, gave rise to the optimistic and contagious attitudes by which he attracted and stimulated so many followers through his message of service through love.

---

5 The terms infused contemplation and mysticism are here used in their technical meanings: a loving gaze on God, or something pertaining to Him, which God produces in a man with his cooperation, and which is above what the human intellect, will, or other faculties can produce by their own powers. See, e.g., *DeGuiJes*, pp. 606-607.

1. *The glory, praise, and service of God*

Glory or praise given by men to God because of His radiant and saving power was a pivotal point in Ignatius' thought, as is well known. He habitually made all his decisions, great or small, by applying his one norm: Which procedure is in the long run likely to issue in greater praise to God? Two other concepts closely related to that of glory to God are also pivotal points: the service to God and the service to one's fellowmen by which glorification of God is furthered. In Ignatius' usage, "glory," "praise," and "honor" to God are synonyms. They occur some 133 times in his Constitutions and accompanying General Examen, often in close relationship to "the service of God," which appears some 140 times.[6]

2. *Their context in God's plan of creation and redemption*

For Ignatius, however, the phrases "glory to God" and "service to Him" carried rich connotations which we can grasp only by fitting them into their larger context in his own concept of the divine plan in creating man and, after his fall from grace, in redeeming him through His Incarnate Son, Jesus Christ as mediator. That divine plan first came to Ignatius' mind as the heritage of Christian tradition, then clothed in sixteenth-century trappings. A bird's-eye view of the long process by which that tradition itself had been gradually formed and transmitted to successive generations previous to 1520 will aid us to understand Ignatius, his world view, his Constitutions, and the role allotted to him by Providence in the evolving history of salvation.

II

Doctrinal evolution in the history of salvation before Ignatius' birth

A. *The redemptive plan in God's revelation*

God communicated Himself to man first by creating him and then by His many successive interventions in history, such as His deliverance of the Israelites from Egypt and His covenants with them. Through the mystical experiences which He granted to His inspired prophets and writers from Moses to St. John, His communication of Self received conceptualized expression. Many men responded to Him by acts of faith through which they committed their entire persons to Him and lived according to His word. The

---

6 See *DeGuiJes*, pp. 84, 146, 649; cf. *Constitutions*, [616, 633] (abbreviated hereafter as *Cons*).

biblical writers, too, recorded His word which took on an ever increasing fullness.

One after another they wrote how God made the world and then made man to His own image as an intelligent being (Gen. 1:1, 27); how God created to reveal His own glory or power (Isa. 43:7; Rom. 1:21) which stimulated men to praise Him (Ps. 28:1; Luke 2:9, 14); how, after Adam lost supernatural life or grace for himself and his descendants (Rom. 5:19), "God so loved the world that he gave his only-begotten Son, that those who believe in him may not perish, but may have life everlasting" and "have it more abundantly" (John 3:16, 10:10); how men may merit increased vitality of this life and proportionally greater joy in heaven by their good works (Matt. 6:20, 25:35) done here and by receiving the sacraments (John 6:54-59; 2 Tim. 1:6); how Christ, after His Passion, Resurrection, and Ascension would send the Holy Spirit who would guide the apostles and their successors to "all the truth" (John 16:13, 17:20-23), thus bringing the Church to a constantly deepening insight into God's entire revelation and its applications to emerging circumstances; how the glorified Christ lives on in His mystical body (Acts 9:5); how God was indeed worthy of praise or glory from men, for "from him and through him and unto him are all things. To him be glory forever" (Rom. 11:36).

In the centuries after Christ that revelation of God was contained and continued in the liturgy which brought men into life-giving encounter with God. This deposit of faith was also assimilated by men in their prayer and study. It was formulated anew, in a manner particularly adapted to their respective cultural eras, by the Fathers, theologians, and doctors such as Augustine, Peter Lombard, and Thomas Aquinas. It was spread to others by the witness of saints such as Benedict, Cyril, Methodius, Francis, and Dominic; by devotional writings like the *Life of Christ* by Ludolph the Carthusian, the *Golden Legend* of Jacobus de Voragine, or the *Following of Christ* attributed to Thomas a Kempis; and by the example of the ordinary faithful such as Ignatius' own neighbors at Loyola.

Thanks to the medieval theologians who used Greek philosophy to explain God's revelation, by the 1500's men had at hand a vast synthesis from which they could cull guiding truths and incorporate them into their personal philosophies of life. Some of these truths are particularly relevant here because they are the background of Ignatius' own thought. In fact, when taken in their entirety, they comprise a necessary framework for the interpretation of his Constitutions or other works. Many of his phrases or statements which seem dull at first sight will glow with new meaning when they are fitted into their proper place in that framework.

B. *God's plan in St. Thomas' synthesis*

Most useful for our purposes is St. Thomas Aquinas' synthetic view of God's plan of creation and redemption, which can be succinctly summarized as follows.

The problem to be answered is: Can God create beings other than Himself, such as men? At first sight it seems that He cannot. He is eternally and infinitely happy in Himself and cannot have His happiness increased. Therefore if He should create a finite man, He the infinite being would be operating for the sake of a finite good, man. This seems to be inconsistent with right order, for only an infinite good can be the worthy objective of an infinite will. If God operates outside Himself He must operate for the sake of Himself (*Summa theologiae*, I, Q. 19, a. 2, objection 1).

But solution of this apparent difficulty is found in the plan of creation which God used. He who is infinitely powerful and happy is also infinitely good; and goodness tends to communicate and diffuse itself. Thus God freely chose from eternity to possess His life and happiness not merely as it was in itself but also as something shared with other intellectual beings, that is, with the angels and men whom He would empower to know Him, to love Him, to praise Him, and to be completely satisfied or happy themselves by these acts of knowing, loving, and praising Him. Thus He "both wills Himself to be, and other beings also, yet He wills Himself as the end but the other beings as ordered to that end" (*ibid.*, I, Q. 19, a. 2). That is, He created not to increase His own goodness but to communicate it and have it shared and glorified. "God seeks His glory not for His own sake" as though the glory were something He needed from men or which increased His own happiness, "but for us," insofar as while operating for His own goodness He simultaneously gives us the opportunity to glorify Him and to be happy by doing it (*ibid.*, II-II, Q. 132, a. 1, ad 1). After Adam lost the supernatural life God gave him, God again made it available to men through the redemptive death and resurrection of His Son (*ibid.*, III, Q. 26-49). The more a man merits by serving God here below the greater will be his capacity or ability in heaven to enjoy Him by praising Him. In this heavenly beatitude, a person will know, love, and praise or enjoy God more perfectly in proportion to the charity he has practiced on earth (*ibid.*, I-II, Q. 114, a. 4 and a. 8). Moreover, since man is a social being, here below he should be a functioning member of the Church, Christ's mystical body (*ibid.*, III, Q. 8, a. 1) and of the society in which he lives (*ibid.*, I-II, Q. 4, a. 8; II-II, Q. 40, a. 2).

Ignatius' inheritance: his personalized concept of God's plan of creation and redemption

1. *Political and social background of Ignatius' thought*

How did Ignatius assimilate this heritage of Christian traditional thought in the expanding world of the early 1500's? That was the era when feudalistic dukedoms were becoming insufficient to themselves and yielding place to powerful central governments which were arising. Monarchs were growing strong by uniting centrifugal provinces into nations, as Ferdinand (1452-1516) and Isabella (1474-1504) strove to do in Spain. In the new world, Spain was enlarging her newly found empire and hoping to convert the natives in it to Christianity. She was also developing a system of centralized government for it by control of a king whose powers descended through a viceroy in many a far-flung province or region such as Navarre, Catalonia, Peru, or Mexico. Not far different was to be the system of government which Ignatius devised for his new supranational apostolic order which he intended to give service anywhere on earth. The authority which a superior general held under the pope in Rome would descend through a provincial superior into its respective provinces. Yet within this monarchic structure, Ignatius was going to include democratic functions and processes to a degree truly surprising for his era, that of absolute monarchs.

In northern Europe, religious unity was cracking. Southern Europe was still one in faith; but there, as in the north, the people's ignorance of that faith and the consequent neglect of practice were appalling. The Church, in need of reform "in head and members," was full of abuses, most of which stemmed from the ignorance or avarice of the clergy, and from pluralism of benefices, the system by which one bishop received the revenues of several sees from which in many a case he was almost always absent. In Corsica in 1552, none of the bishops of the island had been there for sixty years. Many of the priests did not correctly know the formula of consecration in the Mass and earned their living as laborers. It was almost unheard of that parish priests should preach. Many people did not know how to recite the Our Father or Hail Mary, and superstitions, hatreds, and immorality were rife among them.[7] At Ingolstadt all the men had ceased to attend Mass. Scarcely one tenth of Austria could still be called Catholic, and in Bohemia only four percent of the people were practicing their faith. In the diocese of Passau there were 254 parishes without even one priest to minister to them.[8] The need of moral and administrative reforms along with doctrinal stabilization called for an Ecumenical Council within the Church. Beginning in May, 1537, Pope Paul III strove hard to convoke one. But time and again his efforts were frustrated for nearly a decade by quarrels among Catholic kings, difficulties of travel through countries at war, and other indifference or opposition within the Church. At last thirty-four prelates with the right to vote managed to assemble at Trent and opened the Council on December 13, 1545. Their number rose to sixty-six in Session IV of the Council in 1546.[9] Among the people at large illiteracy was almost as widespread as compulsory education in Europe or the United States today. Probably less than five percent of the adults received education equivalent to that of seven-year-olds today. On the natural level, Ignatius' alertness to these circumstances and his desire to meet the needs of the Church were to play a large part in the formation of his views.

A. *The gradual formation of Ignatius' world view in the 1500's*

The process by which he assimilated God's revelation as handed on by the Church amid those circumstances of the 1500's was gradual, distinctive, and impressive. Especially from 1520 until his death in 1556, it combined resources drawn from the natural foundation of his chivalrous and practical character, from the all-controlling graces of infused contemplation as striking as those of an Augustine or Theresa of Ávila, from his academic studies in the foremost universities of the era in Alcalá, Salamanca, and Paris, and from his own experience in widespread travel, in training men, and in founding as well as governing an apostolic religious order. This process by which his outlook was formed ranks among the most fascinating accounts of the growth of a great saint's personal interior life. It is a tale that might rival Augustine's *Confessions* if it had been written with equal literary charm.

The steps by which his extraordinary interior life was formed and the chief characteristics of his mysticism have been treated

7 L. von Pastor, *History of the Popes* (St. Louis, 1924), XIII, 194-195; Tacchi Venturi, *Storia della Compagnia di Gesù in Italia* (Rome, 1950), I, 27-59; Ganss, *St. Ignatius' Idea of a Jesuit University* (Milwaukee, 1956), p. 323 (abbreviated hereafter as *IdeaJesUn*).
8 J. Brodrick, *St. Peter Canisius* (New York, 1935, and Chicago, 1962), pp. 132, 144, 654-655; *IdeaJesUn*, p. 322.
9 Pastor, *History*, XII, 242, 254, 267; cf. *New Catholic Encyclopedia* (New York, 1967),

extensively by many competent scholars.[10] Therefore only the particularly relevant details will be recalled here, in a compressed sketch based chiefly on Ignatius' own *Autobiography*.

1. *At Loyola, 1521*

While recovering from his wounds at the age of thirty at Loyola in 1521, he read two books: the *Life of Christ* by the Carthusian Ludolph of Saxony (d. 1370) in the Spanish translation of the Franciscan Ambrosio de Montesinos, and the *Flos sanctorum*, a Spanish version of the short lives of the saints, *Legenda aurea*, written by the Dominican Jacobus de Voragine (d. 1298) and containing a preface by the Cistercian, Fray Gauberto Vagad. Thus God's stimulus to conversion from worldliness to holy living reached Ignatius through the medieval devotional literature of the Franciscan, Carthusian, Dominican, and Cistercian schools. A scientific scholar today would scarcely turn to such devotional works as the source from which to develop his world view. Yet they were the instruments God chose to mold Ignatius; and His powerful message, like a two-edged sword came through them.

Ludolph's *Life,* expanding the *Meditationes vitae Christi* long attributed to St. Bonaventure (d. 1274), enshrined the Franciscan tradition of poverty and of love for Christ, especially in the crib and on the cross. Ever afterward Ignatius had great devotion to the human Christ, and he, like Francis, esteemed poverty as the antidote to the widespread avarice still so baneful to the Church. Ludolph presented in order meditations on the incarnation, nativity, stay in the temple, hidden life, public life, passion, resurrection, risen life, and ascension. This may well be one reason why Ignatius too later made his *Spiritual Exercises* a review of the history of salvation, that "mystery of Christ" preached by St. Paul (Eph. 1:9, 3:1-11). From Ludolph he also learned the practice of imaginatively contemplating Christ in the gospel scenes and many of the methods of praying which he taught in his *Exercises*.

Gauberto Vagad, formerly a soldier in the declining age of chivalry, told in his preface to the Spanish *Flos sanctorum* about

---

XIV, 272 (abbreviated hereafter as *NCathEnc*); *Oxford Dictionary of the Christian Church,* p. 1373 (abbreviated hereafter as *OxDCCh*).

10 A few syntheses of Ignatius' spirituality available in English and listed in the Select Bibliography, pp. 363-370, are those of Brou, Daniélou, De Guibert, A. Ellard, Gill, J. Lewis, Lippert, E. Allison Peers, Hugo Rahner. For syntheses in other languages, see I. Iparraguirre, *Orientaciones bibliográficas sobre san Ignacio,* 2nd ed. rev. (Rome, 1965), pp. 138-144, to which should now be added the recent scholarly work of J. M. Granero, *San Ignacio de Loyola: Panoramas de su vida* (Madrid, 1967), and the perceptive study of M. A. Fiorito, "Alianza bíblica y regla religiosa (Estudio histórico-salvífico de las Constituciones de la Compañía de Jesús)," *Ciencia y Fe* (Buenos Aires), XXI (1965), 3-36.

the "knights of God," the saints, who did resplendent deeds in the service of "the eternal prince, Christ Jesus," the incomparable Chief whose "ever victorious flag" these knights were following. Thus Gauberto's preface contained a fundamental idea which was to dominate the rest of Ignatius' life: to give an outstanding service to Christ, under the banner of this King who has the saints as His knights. Desire to be an outstanding knight of Christ replaced his thoughts of chivalrous service to ladies (*Autobiography*, nos. 6, 7).[11] From Jacobus' medieval hagiography Ignatius took good example, even though he poorly understood it. "St. Dominic did this, therefore, I must do it. St. Francis did this, therefore, I must do it" (no. 7). In the alternating dissatisfaction and satisfaction which he experienced from the respective thoughts of worldly and spiritual service, Ignatius "came to recognize the difference between the two spirits that moved him, the one being from the evil spirit, the other from God" (no. 8). Henceforth discernment or testing of spirits (1 John 4:1) was to have a large place in his spirituality.

He developed a habit which he never gave up, that of keeping spiritual notes. "He found much relish in those books, and it occurred to him to excerpt in brief form some of the more essential matters from the life of Christ and of the saints. So he began to write a book with much diligence . . . writing the words of Christ in red ink and those of our Lady in blue" (no. 11). Since this copybook is lost, we do not know with precision what passages he transcribed. But the following paragraph from Jacobus' life of St. Augustine may well have been among them:

> At that time, the Goths had captured Rome and the idolators and unbelievers were casting reproaches on the Christians. Therefore Augustine wrote his book, *The City of God*. In it he shows that the just are to be oppressed in this life and the wicked to flourish. He also treats of the two cities, Jerusalem and Babylon, and their kings, for Christ is the king of Jerusalem and the devil of Babylon. Two loves, he says [Book XIV, ch. 8], built these two cities for themselves; for the city of the devil has arisen from the love of self growing even to contempt of God, and the city of God from the love of God growing even to contempt of self.[12]

The ideas just cited from Gauberto's preface and Jacobus' paragraph are highly similar to key thoughts in Ignatius' meditations

---

11 The critically edited text is in *Fontes Narrativi*, I, 354-507 (abbreviated hereafter as *FN*). Henceforth in this chapter the numbers in parentheses refer to this *Autobiography* unless otherwise indicated. An English translation by W. J. Young is *St. Ignatius' Own Story as Told to Luis González de Cámara* (Chicago, 1956 and 1968).

on the Kingdom of Christ and on the Two Standards in his *Spiritual Exercises* ([91-98, 136-156])—so similar, in fact, that it is plausible to conjecture that he had entered them in the copybook which he carefully carried with him to Manresa and "which brought him many consolations" (*Autobiography*, no. 18). This plausibility is strengthened by what Nadal wrote over thirty years later about Ignatius at Manresa:

> [5]. At that time, under the guidance of our Lord, he began to treat about the interior of his soul and the diversity of the spirits, while the Lord was granting to him in all this great understanding and highly vivid perceptions of the divine mysteries and of the Church; and he even began to write but he did not persevere.
>
> [6]. There our Lord communicated the Exercises to him, thus guiding him to employ himself completely in His divine service and the salvation of souls. The Lord showed this to him through the devotion granted especially in two exercises, namely, that on the King and that on the Two Standards.[13]

2. *At Manresa, 1522*

It was at the age of thirty-one that Ignatius left Loyola, "feeling within himself a powerful urge to be serving our Lord" (no. 11). He passed the night of March 24, 1522, in a vigil of arms in the chapel of the Benedictine abbey at Montserrat. From then on he was an example of a person totally dedicated to God; and a little later he was also an apostle of such total dedication. He lived for God, to such an extent that St. Thomas' beautiful words were fully verified in him: "Charity makes us tend to God, by uniting our affections to Him, so that we live, not for ourselves, but for God" (*Summa theologiae*, II-II, Q. 17, a. 6, ad 3). God was the center and preoccupation of Ignatius' thoughts, and the object of his special love, and the beloved Person for whom he wanted to do all the little acts which make up daily living. He wanted to be bound irrevocably to God, with the bridges burnt which might lead back to another way of living in which he might have interests other than God—God and the men for whom Jesus Christ had shed His blood. One spontaneous expression of his spirit of total dedication rolled off his pen many years later: "To bind oneself more to God our Lord and to show oneself generous toward Him is to consecrate oneself completely and irrevocably to His

---

12 Jacobus de Voragine, on St. Augustine, in *Legenda aurea*, ed. T. Graesse (Breslau, 1890), p. 558. Translation mine.

13 *P. Hieronymi Nadal exhortationes in Hispania, 1554*, in *FN*, I, 306-307. The book was about the Trinity (*FN*, I, 307, fn. 11).

service, as those do who dedicate themselves to Him by vow" (*Constitutions,* [283]).

Shortly after his vigil of arms at Montserrat, Ignatius made his way to Manresa where he stayed until February, 1523. He spent much time at prayer and penance in a cave overlooking the River Cardoner and facing the lofty, sawtooth Montserrat some twenty miles away. "At this time," Ignatius states in his *Autobiography,* "God dealt with him just as a schoolmaster treats a little boy when he teaches him" (no. 27). Here it was that the Divine Master, by giving Ignatius mystical graces of the most intensive sort, shaped his world view around the divine plan in creating and redeeming man. These favors were basically illuminations in the intellect accompanied by intense experience of devotion in the will; and by way of repercussion in the imagination they produced the imperfect images by which Ignatius rather clumsily strove to describe them some thirty-three years later. An analysis of his words dictated in 1555 reveals these noteworthy features of these infused forces.

First, they focused his devotion especially on the Trinity. "He had great devotion to the Most Holy Trinity. . . . One day while he was reciting the Hours of our Lady on the steps of the same monastery,[14] his understanding began to be lifted up so that he was perceiving the Most Holy Trinity as a musical harmony from three organ keys (*en figura de tres teclas*). This was accompanied with so many tears and so much sobbing that he could not control himself" (no. 28).

Second, they gave him insights into God's plan of creation. "Another time there was represented to his understanding with great spiritual relish the manner in which God created the world. It seemed that he saw something white, out of which rays were coming, and that from this God was making light. But he did not know how to explain these things, nor did he remember well the spiritual illuminations which God impressed on his soul at that time" (no. 29).

Third, they increased his understanding of the Eucharist. "One day . . . when he was hearing Mass in the church of the monastery already mentioned, while the Body of the Lord was being raised, he saw with his inner eyes something like white rays which were coming down from above. Although he cannot explain this after so long a time, yet what he clearly perceived with his understanding was to see how Jesus Christ our Lord was present in that holy sacrament" (no. 29).

14 The monastery of the Dominicans in Manresa. See *Autobiog,* no. 23.

Fourth, they gave him new knowledge about Christ and Mary, the two mediators in the divine plan of the redemption. "When he was at prayer, he often and for a long time saw with his inner eyes the humanity of Christ. The shape which appeared to him was like a white body, not very large or very small, but he did not discern any distinction of members. He saw this many times in Manresa. . . . He has also seen our Lady in similar form, without distinguishing the members. These things which he saw confirmed him then, and gave him henceforward such great confirmation of his faith, so much so that he had often thought to himself: Even if there were no Scripture to teach us these matters of the faith, he would be determined to die for them, merely because of what he had seen" (no. 29).

Fifth, they unified and deepened all his previous knowledge, through the outstanding intellectual vision[15] which God granted him beside the River Cardoner. "The road ran along close to the river. Moving along intent on his devotion, he sat down for a while with his face toward the river which there ran deep. As he sat, the eyes of his understanding began to open, not that he might see a vision, but that he might grasp and understand many things, matters spiritual and those pertaining to the faith and learning. This took place with so great an illumination that these things appeared to be something altogether new. It is impossible to explain [now, after some thirty-three years,] the particulars which he understood at the time, although they were many, other than by stating that he received great clarity in his understanding" (no. 30).

This illumination was so great, indeed, that although Ignatius' mystical life grew constantly until his death, on no other one occasion did he ever receive illumination as intense as that one beside the Cardoner.

At Manresa he conceived his liking for the *Imitation of Christ*, from which he daily read a chapter for the rest of his life. There too he took his first steps in helping others (no. 26) and from then onward such apostolic effort took on a continually growing importance in his thought. By the time he left the little city his outlook on the divine plan, on man's place in it, and on the importance of giving glory and service to God and of helping men was formed in its essential elements. Experience, however, gradually led him to recognize the need of organizing and supplementing his knowledge by sound academic learning.

15 On the distinction between corporeal, imaginative, and intellectual visions, see *DeGuiJes*, pp. 608, 609.

3. *During the time of studies, 1524-1535*

When he returned from the Holy Land to Venice in 1524, his mind was made up "to study for a time to be able to help souls" (no. 50)—not merely by pious conversations but by a committed apostolic ministry. So at the age of thirty-three he went to Barcelona to take up Latin while still helping others according to his present capacity. From Lent of 1526 to June, 1527, he pursued the arts at Ximenes' great university in Alcalá de Henares. He "studied the logic of Soto, the physics of Albert the Great, and the Master of the Sentences. While he was at Alcalá, he also worked at giving spiritual exercises and at explaining Christian doctrine; and by this means he brought forth fruit to God's glory" (no. 57). From this we gather that his sheaf of notes for guiding others through spiritual exercises was now expanding through his experience and study. Twenty-two years later, in 1548, it became his published book, the *Spiritual Exercises*.

Here again, although we should like to know which sections of Peter Lombard Ignatius studied, we lack precise information. But it would be natural for him to seek further light on his own main interests. Consequently, two passages which are similar to his own later thought and even to his words attract our attention. The very first pages of the *Sentences* expound Augustine's view (*De doctrina christiana*, I, 3, 4): While tending toward beatitude, we should use and enjoy creatures as aids until we reach God, whom we enjoy but do not use for anything higher. Thus Peter Lombard showed all things arranged in a hierarchy of beings leading men to God (Book I, ch. 1, no. 2);[16] and precisely this was how Ignatius viewed everything, whether he learned it from Peter or not. Moreover, in the very first chapter of Book II Peter states that, in contrast with the incomplete notions of the Greeks and Aristotle, the Holy Spirit teaches that

> 3. God created the world at the beginning of time . . . Therefore we should believe that there is no other cause of created beings . . . than the goodness of the Creator. . . . His goodness is so great that He wills others to be sharers of His eternal beatitude, which, He sees, can be communicated, but in no way diminished. . . .
> 4. . . . Therefore God made the rational creature which could know the supreme good, and by knowing it love it, and by loving it possess it, and by possessing it enjoy it. . . .
> 5. Consequently, if it is asked why man or angel was created, the brief reply can be given: because of God's goodness. . . .

---

16 *Petri Lombardi Sententiarum libri quattuor* (Paris: Migne, 1853), col. 13.

6. And if it is asked for what destiny the rational creature was created, the answer is: to praise God, to serve Him, and to enjoy Him; and in all these activities the rational creature, not God, gains profit. For God, being perfect and full of all goodness, can be neither increased nor diminished. . . .

8. And just as man was made for God, that is, that he might serve God, so the world was made for man, that it might serve him. Therefore man was placed in the middle, that he might be served and in turn give service; . . . For God willed so to be served by man that by that service not God, but the man serving, might be aided; and He willed that the world should serve man, and that man might be aided by that too.[17]

Some of those sentences, in abbreviated form, may well have found their way into Ignatius' sheaf of notes and become the opening sentences of the First Principle and Foundation of his *Spiritual Exercises*, [23]. In that same paragraph we also notice another trait of his spirituality, that he clearly viewed material creatures as good. They are stepping-stones by which man can reach God by using them wisely. That Foundation was already in the *Exercises* at least as early as 1534 or 1536, though in a place earlier than its present position.[18]

Harassed by various officials and doctors, Ignatius left Alcalá in June, 1527, for Salamanca. Incurring similar difficulties there, he turned over to the examiner, Bachelor Frias, "all his papers, which were the Exercises, for examination" (no. 67). Again he was forbidden to help souls. Therefore he decided to continue his studies at Paris, which he reached in February, 1528.

There he studied humanities and philosophy until, at the age of forty-two, he passed his examination for the Licentiate in Arts on March 13, 1533, and thus opened the way to his receiving his degree of Master of Arts in April, 1534. Meanwhile he had also been winning his first permanent followers, Favre, Xavier, Salmerón, Laynez, Bobadilla, Rodrigues, Jay, Broët, and Codure, especially by guiding them through his Exercises. For about a year and a half, beginning probably close to March, 1533, he studied theology under the Dominicans on the Rue St. Jacques. Here he was fortunate to profit from the achievements of two brilliant professors who, during the preceding twenty years, had based their commentaries on St. Thomas' *Summa theologiae* in place of Peter Lombard's *Sentences*. Thus Ignatius acquired an

---

17 *Ibid.*, col. 143.
18 In the Codex Regina. See *Exercitia Spiritualia S. Ignatii*, Monumenta Historica Societatis Iesu (Madrid, 1919), pp. 570, 624 (abbreviated hereafter as *SpEx*MHSJ).

affection for St. Thomas so strong that twenty years later he too, in Rome itself, daringly prescribed St. Thomas' *Summa* rather than the *Sentences* as the basis of the lectures in theology.[19]

4. *In the school of experience, 1535-1556*

When Ignatius left Paris in April, 1535, his university studies were finished, although he studied some theology privately during his year in Venice in 1536. But he continued in the school of experience; and there he learned much in regard to himself, his work, his training of his companions, and his founding and governing an apostolic religious order. Meanwhile his mystic favors were growing continually in intensity and frequency. There is no evidence of infused contemplation during his stay at Paris, which he called "the time of distraction by study." But close to the time of his ordination at the age of forty-six in 1537, he had at Vicenza "many spiritual visions and almost habitual consolations, just the opposite of what he had had in Paris." In his journeys near Venice also "he had great supernatural visitations, such as he used to have at Manresa" (no. 95). By 1537 he confided to Laynez that "what he had received at Manresa . . . was small in comparison with what he was having" within the two years just passed.[20] This period, moreover, was followed by infused favors greater still.

In the Colloquy of his meditation on the Two Standards, Ignatius prayed God the Father, through his mediators Mary and Christ, to be placed with Christ under His banner, in order that he might lovingly imitate Him even in bearing poverty, insults, and wrongs if they would lead to greater praise and service of God (*Spiritual Exercises,* [147, 98]). While he was journeying to Rome with Favre and Laynez in 1537, he continually repeated this prayer to be closely associated with Christ. In the chapel of La Storta at the outskirts of the city God gave him a mystical answer to his prayer. This answer oriented his own spirituality and that of his followers to be one of close companionship with Christ in helping to achieve His redemptive plan by applying it to men. With extraordinary clarity Ignatius perceived that "God the Father was placing Him with His Son" (no. 96). He "saw Christ with His Cross on His shoulder, and the Father nearby who said to Him: 'I desire You to take this man as Your servant.' " Jesus in turn "said to Ignatius: 'I will that you serve Us.' And through this he [Ignatius] felt great affection for this most holy name and

19 See *IdeaJesUn*, pp. 158-160; P. Dudon, *St. Ignatius of Loyola* (Milwaukee, 1949), p. 144.
20 *Epistola P. Lainii,* in *FN*, I, 140; *DeGuiJes*, p. 33.

determined to call his congregation the Company of Jesus" (*Compañía de Jesús*).[21]

B. *His maturity at Rome, 1540-1556*

It was not long after this vision that Ignatius and his companions began to deliberate, in March, 1539, about forming themselves into a new and apostolic religious order. Their affirmative decision led them to incorporate their pattern of life (*nuestra manera de proceder* or *formula vivendi*) into a First Sketch of the Institute of the Society of Jesus. They submitted this document, also known as the Formula of the Institute, to Pope Paul III in late June or early July of 1539. After proper investigation he approved it with only minor changes and incorporated it into his bull of September 27, 1540, *Regimini militantis Ecclesiae*.[22] Thus this Formula of the Institute as contained in that bull became the Society's fundamental Rule which Ignatius, elected general on April 8, 1541, later expanded in the Constitutions which it empowered him to draw up. Thus this papally approved document, containing the Formula of the Institute, is comparable to the Rule of St. Benedict or that commonly called the Rule of St. Augustine as distinguished from the more detailed legislation found in Benedictine or Augustinian Constitutions. Ignatius was writing his Constitutions by 1544 and by October, 1547, they were his chief occupation. Experience counseled some modifications in the *formula vivendi* and they were incorporated into a new bull, *Exposcit debitum*, which Pope Julius III issued on July 21, 1550. In 1551 a quorum of professed fathers, summoned by Ignatius, gave a preliminary approval of his Constitutions as they were in text A, then almost in the final form in which he left them in the text now known as B, the Autograph. Thereupon he began their experimental promulgation, by sending Nadal in 1552 to explain them in as many houses as possible in Sicily, Spain, and Portugal. Ignatius continued to incorporate revisions until his death in 1556. The

---

21 Laynez, *Adhortationes*, in *FN*, II, 132-133. On La Storta, see also *Epistolae et Monumenta P. Hieronymi Nadal*, IV (Madrid, 1905), 678; V, 137 (abbreviated hereafter as *MonNad*); *DeGuiJes*, pp. 37, 39, 52, 589; Iparraguirre, *Orientaciones bibliográficas*, pp. 43-45.
    In 1554 Nadal used the terminology of the mystical body in explaining the vision (*FN*, I, 314); cf. *MonNad*, V, 51-52: "Christ, having arisen from the dead, and dying now no more [Rom. 6:9], still suffers in His members and constantly carries His cross, so that He said also to Paul [Acts 9:4]: 'Why do you persecute Me?' " Again in 1557 Nadal stated (*FN*, II, 10): Christ is daily suffering "afflictions and crosses in His mystical body, which is the Church; therefore a member of our Society" should propose to himself, following Christ through persecutions, to "procure the salvation of souls, in union with Christ Himself."
22 Text in *Sti. Ignatii de Loyola Constitutiones Societatis Jesu*, vol. I, *Monumenta Constitutionum praevia*, MHSJ (Rome, 1934), 34-42 (abbreviated hereafter as *ConsMHSJ*, I).

Society's official approbation came when its First General Congregation approved the Spanish text and the Latin translation in 1558.

The span of years between 1540 and 1556 is the most important in Ignatius' interior life, "because of the full maturity of his sanctity, the summit of his ascent to God, the full consciousness of his mission as founder, and the complete accomplishment of that mission."[23] These years were also the most important ones for fixing the characteristic traits of his spirituality and the subsequent spirituality of the Society.[24]

Through the vision at La Storta in late 1537 Ignatius' habitual ideas were once more reinforced and synthesized around the idea of intimate association with Christ, the Mediator through whom God's redemptive plan was carried out. His spirituality was theocentric and trinitarian, seeking always what might bring greater praise or glory to God, and simultaneously Christ-centered, aiming to cooperate intimately and loyally with Him. It should be remembered, too, that the Christ who appeared to Ignatius was the glorified Christ—not merely He who had lived in Galilee but He who was still present and functioning in and through His mystical body and His vicar, the pope. Ignatius and his followers would ever afterwards bear special devotion to this whole Christ. In no small measure Ignatius' later stress on obedience arose from his desire to secure among the members of his order effective and charitable cooperation toward apostolic success in the service of this Christ and His mystical body. The founder expected the members of his Society to love their Lord in contemplation and to manifest their love by deeds. He was singularly successful in motivating men to volunteer in the crusade for Christ's kingdom and to strive for distinguished service in it. In his view, their apostolic effectiveness was to arise from their being human instruments intimately united with God (*Constitutions,* [813]).

The end result of his God-given natural character and temperament, his infused contemplation, his university studies, and his experiences in founding and organizing the Society was a mysticism which impelled him not merely toward love of God in contemplative solitude but also toward service through love. Intense union with God within the soul was combined with a powerful orientation toward apostolic activity. Ignatius was a contemplative person in the highest stage of spiritual development whose contemplation also impelled him to engage in the works of the active

23 See *DeGuiJes,* pp. 39-44.
24 *Cons*MHSJ, I, 87, line 66. Cf. *DeGuiJes,* pp. 56, 67.

life. Thus he found and pleased God sometimes by prayer in solitude and sometimes by means of the most distracting or vexing
occupations undertaken for the love of God and his neighbor.
His ideal of apostolic spirituality was to seek and find God in all
things (*Constitutions*, [288]). In meeting the needs of his times
he gave a new orientation to religious life and developed a fresh
concept of spirituality orientated toward apostolic service. His
reason for excluding obligatory choir and some similar ceremonies
from the usage of his order was to make its members more readily
available for the demands of apostolic work, those calls or opportunities which often come at unpredictable times (*Constitutions*,
[584]). He always attributed a primacy of importance to grace
and supernatural means which unite the human instrument with
God; but he also valued natural gifts, carefully cultivated and
skillfully used. As a result, he habitually employed a balanced
union of natural and supernatural means to his objectives. Furthermore, to the enthusiastic love of Christ already present at
Manresa he added, during his years of study and later, a continually developing power of reasoning. Thus a balanced union of
the intellectual and volitional powers became perhaps the most
characteristic trait of his personal spiritual life. He united reason
and enthusiasm in the service of God.[25]

Yet it is true that these characteristics, certainly positive and
attractive, were accompanied by emphases on lowliness and the
cross which at first sight may seem somewhat negative and de-
pressing to many. Some saints have drawn their chief spiritual
sustenance from scriptural texts which prompt joy and union with
Christ, and other saints largely from passages which stress lowliness and willingness to suffer and labor for Him.[26] Ignatius is
numbered chiefly among these latter. He stresses being poor and
lowly like the poor and lowly Christ and the rendering of generous
service to Him as a means to His greater glory, no matter what
the cost. This viewpoint arose at least partially from Ludolph's
emphases in the *Life* through which Ignatius came to know Christ,
and partially too from Ignatius' own tendency to stress virtues
opposite to vices particularly prevalent and dangerous in his own
era, such as poverty against riches, humiliations against excessive
love of fame, and humility against pride (*Spiritual Exercises*, [135-
148]; *Constitutions*, [101, 265]). Living in a day when avarice,
desire of honors, pride, and neglect of duty were rampant even
among the clergy, he yearned to do what he could to make up for

---

25 See, e.g., *Cons*, [812-814]; *DeGuiJes*, pp. 73, 174-175, 595-596.
26 See *DeGuiJes*, pp. 176-181.

this great scandal by practicing the contrary virtues, which he saw as necessary means to perseverance in apostolic labor to bring about greater praise of God. Hence arose the stress on virtues of lowliness in his manner of expressing his spirituality. Sometimes the importance of these virtues so absorbed his attention that he did not then and there point out their relationship as means to the inspiring ends in his world view. Rather, he presumed that relationship as known from other sources; and one who overlooks this loses the key to accurate interpretation of his writings.

Ignatius inspired his followers by the ceaseless repetition of his inspiring ends—glory, praise, honor, and service to God, overlapping synonyms which color one another and are practically interchangeable in his writings. At the summit of his world view was the stimulating thought of bringing greater glory to God from himself and his fellowmen, both in this life and the next; and he saw everything else as means to this end.[27]

1. *His mystic prayer applied to practicalities on poverty*

Ignatius was ever eager to discern and test the spirits which were moving him, that thus he might learn the will of God and fulfill it faithfully in the least details. When a need of decisions arose, he referred them to God during his prayer, which often was mystic. Thus his mysticism had a somewhat unusual characteristic: It was prayer of infused contemplation applied to the practical decisions of daily living, a humble effort to obtain light from God on them. In this prayer he was begging for light as to which of two or more measures was likely to result in greater glory to God. Ignatius' procedure in regard to one topic is clearly revealed in his *Spiritual Diary*[28] from February 2, 1544, to February 27, 1545.

In words meant for himself alone, he recorded his prayerful deliberations about the kind of poverty his Constitutions should prescribe. Would it be more to God's glory to adopt the poverty of the mendicant orders in its strictest form and to forbid all fixed revenues, not only for the solemnly professed members and their houses but also for the sacristies and expenses of divine worship in the churches attached to their houses? Or would prescription of a poverty less stringent be more to His glory? For forty days Ignatius employed all the counsels he has given in the *Exercises* ([175-188]) for making a good election, especially those for the "second time" or occasion ([176]). Daily he noted down his interior movements and tested them. From what spirits, good or bad,

27 See *ibid.*, p. 178.
28 Text in *Cons*MHSJ, I, 86-158. On the stages of poverty in the Society, see *Cons*MHSJ, I, 35, fn. 3; A. Coemans, *Introductio in studium Instituti* (Brussels, 1937), nos. 59-62.

angels or devils, did they come? For February 2 he noted abundance of devotion and tears, with all of it inclining him more toward possessing nothing. On February 3, 4, 5, 6, and 7 he had much the same experience. He offered to God his resolution not to accept any established or permanent revenue for his churches; and he regarded the graces he received, such as those on February 10, as approbations of his resolution. He prayed, especially through his mediators Mary and Jesus, for "much light." Finally his decision became fixed through one last outpouring of light on March 12.

This one sample alone is sufficient to lead us to an important observation. Ignatius' mysticism is not readily apparent in his Constitutions, which after all are a legal code rather than the spontaneous outpourings of a mystic. But to a large extent these Constitutions are the fruit of his mystical contemplation and his natural prudence, united in a harmonious balance. To appreciate them rightly we must remember that they are the product of a mystic's mind.

Among all his writings, too, this *Spiritual Diary* is the one which most clearly reveals the nature, intensity, and chief characteristics of his infused contemplation. Predominantly focused on the Trinity whom it approaches through the mediators Mary and Christ, it is a mysticism of intense personal love of God. But it does not stop at that; it also impels the mystic toward energetic apostolic service. It has infused graces of light in the intellect (like those of St. Thomas Aquinas) and of love in the will (like those of St. Francis of Assisi), with no perceptible predominance of either type. Moreover, like the mysticism of St. Paul it influenced also the faculties of the body, such as the memory and imagination, which aid toward execution in the external order. Thus through a union of reason and enthusiasm, of the use of natural means and of the supernatural means which are supplemented by the natural, it carried Ignatius both toward union with God and toward service through love[29]—service in cooperating with Christ in the progressive achievement of God's redemptive plan as it gradually unfolded in the history of salvation.

2. *How he composed the Exercises and Constitutions*

On October 20, 1555, less than a year before Ignatius' death, his companion Da Câmara asked him "about the Exercises and the Constitutions, desiring to understand how he had composed them. He replied that the Exercises were not composed all at one

---

29 See *DeGuiJes*, pp. 50-55.

time, but that some things which he had observed in his own soul and found useful and which he thought would be useful to others, he put into writing, such as the examination of conscience. . . .

"That same day he called me before supper. He seemed to be more recollected than usual." He said that "his devotion had always gone on increasing, that is, the ease with which he found God, which was then greater than he had ever had in his life; that however often he wished, at whatever hour, he could find God. He also said he still had many visions, especially that in which he saw Christ as a sun, as mentioned above. This often happened to him, especially when he was speaking of matters of importance, and that fact brought him assurance of confirmation" (no. 99).

"He also had many visions when he said Mass, and very frequently too when he was composing the Constitutions. This he could affirm the more easily because every day he wrote what passed through his mind, and he then found this written material. He showed me a rather large bundle of collected writings and he read a goodly portion of them to me. The larger part consisted of visions which he saw in confirmation of one or another of the Constitutions, seeing now the Father, now all three persons of the Trinity, now our Lady who was interceding and sometimes giving confirmation.

"In particular he told me of the decision on which he spent forty days, saying Mass each day, and each day shedding many tears. What he was dealing with was the question as to whether our churches should possess some fixed revenues, and whether the Society could accept help from them" (no. 100).

"His method of procedure when he was composing the Constitutions was to say Mass every day, and to lay the point he was treating before God, and to pray over it. He always made his prayer and said his Mass with tears" (no. 101).

3. *His character as a leader*

By character and temperament he was a born leader. He loved people and was ever eager to converse with them, assuredly in the hope of drawing spiritual fruit. He won the affections of the followers whom he inspired and whose opinions he constantly sought before he issued commands. Thus he made them feel that they were persons as well as a part of an organization in which their opinions were valued.[30] He made much of discussion between a superior and subjects, whom he expected to be respectfully but

---

30 A striking example of group participation is found in the deliberations of Ignatius and his companions as to whether or not they should band together into a new order. Text in *Cons*MHSJ, I, 1-21, English translation by D. Maruca in *WL*, XCV (1966), 325-333.

completely frank and open. But when the consultation was done, the superior was to be the one to make the decision.[31] Sometimes he has been pictured as a stern martinet pointing ever to rules. However, if that had been his character, or if he had not been spontaneous and animated in conversation, it is hard to see how he could have inspired the affection which his followers so manifestly had for him. "Those who were in his room," wrote Nadal who knew him so intimately, "were always cheerful and laughing."[32]

4. *His literary style*

Yet when he turned to the task of putting his thoughts on paper his facility and spontaneity seemed to halt. He was a clear thinker and organizer but in writing he slowly whipped his thoughts into order, adding inserts and qualifications one after another, seemingly in fear of being misinterpreted. Such fear would have been a natural result of his experiences at Alcalá, Salamanca, Paris, and Rome, where inquisitors and examiners scrutinized his every word in eagerness to condemn him.[33] Perhaps, too, he had begun his education too late in life to become a good stylist. In any case, the result was that his sentences were often overloaded and tangled. Showing no care for beauties of form, he was intent only on giving accurate expression to his thought. His stylistic abilities and concern were far less than those of his secretary, Polanco. His writings contain treasures but often they yield them up only after ferreting study.[34] His genius lay, not in charming style like that of St. Theresa or St. Francis de Sales, nor in speculative wisdom like that of St. Thomas, but more in the practical wisdom of an apostolic organizer.

5. *His alertness to contemporary needs*

Ignatius alertly perceived the needs of the Church in his era and constantly sought means to meet them, such as evangelical poverty as an antidote to the avarice of so many ecclesiastics, or Christlike willingness to endure humiliations and lowliness as means to vanquish pride or lust for power.[35] In efforts to remedy the abuses in the Church, some men seemed to think that decrees of reform would suffice. Ignatius saw that such decrees alone would not suf-

---

31 See, e.g., *Cons,* [131, 666, 667].

32 "Qui in eius cubiculo, laetissimi semper ac risibundi," cited in *FN,* II, 121; cf. *MonNad,* IV, 662; P. Ribadeneyra, *Vita Ignatii,* I, 10, in *FN,* IV, 144-146; Brodrick, *The Origin of the Jesuits* (London, 1947), pp. 203, 205; *Ignatius . . . seine geistliche Gestalt,* ed. F. Wulf (Wurzburg, 1956), p. 27.

33 See, e.g., *Spiritual Exercises,* [22] (abbreviated hereafter as *SpEx*).

34 On Ignatius' style, see *DeGuiJes,* Index, p. 686, s.v. "Style."

35 See, e.g., *SpEx,* [142, 146, 147].

Figure 1. Rome in 1593, in the district of Ignatius' chief activity

A section reproduced from *Roma al tempo di Clemente VIII. La pianta di Roma di Antonio Tempesta del 1593, con introduzione di Francesco Ehrle,* S.J. Published by the Vatican Press in 1932.

Intersection of lines **BB** and **aa**: the Church of Santa Maria in Ara Coeli, on the Capitoline Hill, adjacent to the Forum of Ancient Rome.

B towards E, as far as the intersection with **cc**: the Via d'Ara Coeli.

CCbb: the site where Ignatius first opened the Roman College, February 22, 1551.

CCcc: the house in which Ignatius lived from 1544-1556, and in which he wrote the *Constitutions of the Society of Jesus.*

CCdd: Church of the Gesù, begun in 1568, consecrated in 1599. In 1550 the small church of Our Lady of the Way was between the house at the right and the site of the present Church.

CCff: The Roman College, built 1582-1584 by Pope Gregory XIII, was the home of the Gregorian University from 1584 to 1773, and again from 1824 to 1873.

AAee: site of the Pontifical Gregorian University, 1930 to the present. See Plate 2.

DDgg: the Pantheon of Ancient Rome, now the Church of Santa Maria Rotunda.

Line **ff**, if extended three fourths of an inch below the picture, would mark the site of the Papal University of Rome, the Sapienza.

Point **A**, at the upper right, is in the Forum of Ancient Rome, near to the Arch of Septimius Severus and the columns of the Temple of Saturn.

T. S. Marcelli

S. Maria

Collegium
Societ. Iesu

Nūciat.

S. Ma...

T. S. Mariæ superminentiam

T. S. Mariæ Rotundæ

...tica Sara

Figure 2. A detail of Figure 1

The Roman College, the Church of the Gesù, and the site of the house in which St. Ignatius wrote the Constitutions of the Society of Jesus.

fice; rather, that successful reform must begin through a renewal of genuine Christian spirit within the Church's members. To produce such genuine men of the Church was the central objective for which he devised his Exercises, mobilized his Society, and composed his Constitutions. In all this work, his zeal was strong to "think rightly within the Church Militant"[36] and to lead others to do the same. He had an unshakable determination to adhere to the ecclesiastical authority of the preceding centuries, which he was convinced was from God in spite of its all too manifest human defects. But coupled with this reverence for the traditions of the past was an equally great ability to test and discern in them what was of perennial value, courage to reject what had become obsolete or irrelevant, and courageous initiative to devise original measures to meet the contemporary circumstances. Hence, his interest in the past sprang chiefly from his desire to improve the present; and in the turbulent period of transition in which he lived, he was extraordinarily fitted to be a link between the past and the future, by preserving the healthy trunk of sound traditions and grafting to it new branches, the ideas and practices which his creative ability contrived. He had inventive genius which might have impelled him to excesses; but it was kept under disciplined control by his single-minded desire of choosing the course or alternative which seemed likely to bring the greater glory to God.

He was an innovator in the form of religious life; and in his Constitutions he manifested his practical wisdom, by devising new measures to meet the needs of his era and by constantly stressing the need of adaptation to circumstances of persons, places, and time. Inevitably his single constitutions were culturally conditioned by the concepts and customs characteristic of religious life in the sixteenth century. But through his genius he provided for their adaptation to new conditions. This flexibility is one more reason why his Constitutions still retain their inspirational vitality today.

IV

Conclusion— his contemplative prayer as a source of new insights into the deposit of faith

Through the mystical experiences which God gave to His inspired writers such as Isaiah or St. Paul, God gradually increased the volume of His revealed truth. Through the roughly similar mystical experiences which he gave to later saints such as Augustine, Benedict, Francis, Ignatius, John of the Cross, Theresa of Ávila, and many others, God did not increase the content of that deposit of faith destined for all men. But He did guide these

36 SpEx, [352].

saints and their followers to constantly deepening insights and applications of that revelation which were of great and providential value to the Church in meeting the opportunities or needs of successive eras.

It was in this way that God led Ignatius to a world view centered about the divine plan of creation and redemption. He also inspired in him the ardent desire to be intimately associated with Christ and His vicar in achieving that plan in the history of salvation, to bring greater praise to God and happiness to men. The content of his world view was virtually coterminous with the deposit of faith.

Christian spirituality is the application of the deposit of faith to the guidance of men toward the richest fulfillment of their Christian personalities here and hereafter. This spirituality naturally undergoes a doctrinal evolution parallel to that of the deposit itself. In this era of Vatican Council II the Church is adjusting its spiritual doctrine and practice to the mentality of modern man. Since Ignatian spirituality is simply Christian spirituality with emphasis on those elements which Ignatius stressed, it can and should receive into itself practically all the dogmatic evolution and new emphases which the Church is giving to the deposit of faith as she applies it in guiding men toward perfection in the modern world.

In his Spiritual Exercises, Ignatius applied his world view to the direction of individuals whom he hoped to aid to discover God's will and fulfill it energetically as loyal members of the Church, the people of God. In the Constitutions, he applied that same world view to the government and stimulation of an apostolic religious order, in the hope that its members might lovingly and vigorously associate themselves with Christ in the progressive achievement of His redemptive plan, by working for the application of the fruits of His sacrificial death to the souls of men in order to bring greater glory to God.

Ignatius saw each single statement, directive, or prescription of his Constitutions as a means toward that goal. For in the hierarchy of values contained in the world view which was his framework of reference, all things—material goods or evangelical poverty, work or restoring repose, humility, study, sacrifice of self for others, the practices inculcated in the Exercises and Constitutions, and even prayer itself, all were means toward bringing the greatest possible glory to God, Ignatius' supreme but simple end which drew everything else to a head in ordered arrangement under itself. If we use this same framework of reference of his, we can grasp the spirit within his Constitutions as well as the letter.

TECHNICAL INTRODUCTION ON THE

CONSTITUTIONS OF THE

SOCIETY OF JESUS

I

General description

The present chapter aims to present a somewhat technical in-troduction to some details of historical background and terminology which seem necessary for accurate understanding of Ignatius' Constitutions and which, at least in many instances, are un-wittingly overlooked.

The work entitled *Constitutions of the Society of Jesus* (*Constituciones de la Compañía de Jesús*) is the collection of statutes or ordinances composed by St. Ignatius of Loyola for the inspiration and government of the religious institute he founded. As the result of a long-standing usage which dates from the first printed edition of 1558-1559,[1] the term Constitutions as found in the title of the present book is employed in a comprehensive sense to designate four separate treatises which he left, still in manuscript, at his death in 1556: the General Examen, the authoritative explanations of it entitled Declarations on the Examen, the Constitutions

1 See *Cons*MHSJ, I, viii. The Prolegomena in *Cons*MHSJ, I, II, and III are excellent and extensive treatments by a highly competent editor, Arturo Codina, of virtually all matters pertaining to the Examen, Constitutions, and Declarations.

of the Society of Jesus, and the Declarations on the Constitutions. Frequently, however, the term Constitutions is also used in a more restricted sense, which the context usually makes obvious, to designate the third of these four treatises, which is the pivot about which the other three revolve.

The four treatises were grouped in the order given above in the manuscript of 1556 which has since been named text B, the Autograph. They severally complement one another and have equal juridical value. The Constitutions presuppose the Examen and vice versa; and by Ignatius' explicit statement the Declarations have equal authority with the Constitutions.[2] These four treatises received their binding force within the Society through the approval of its highest legislative body, the general congregation, which assembled for the first time in 1558 to elect a general as Ignatius' successor.

A. *The Formula of the Institute*

Nevertheless, the collection of the four documents just mentioned is not the basic rule or fundamental code of legislation in the Society of Jesus. The supreme authority and dignity belongs to the papal document commonly called the Formula of the Institute. This Formula consists of the "five chapters" (*Quinque capitula*) found in paragraphs [3-8] of the bull of Paul III, *Regimini militantis Ecclesiae* of 1540 and, in slightly revised form, in paragraphs [3-6] of the bull of Julius III, *Exposcit debitum* of 1550. The Formula first arose from the deliberations of Ignatius and his companions in 1539 as the First Sketch of the Institute of the Society of Jesus (*Prima Societatis Jesu Instituti Summa*). It contained five paragraphs (*capitula*) and, after minor revisions, was encased in the two papal bulls within an introduction and concluding approval.[3] The Formula established the fundamental structure of the new order and authorized its general to establish, with advice from his companions, more detailed statutes or determinations called constitutions. In modern editions of Ignatius' Constitutions, the present one included, the Formula is fittingly printed as a kind of preface to them.

B. *The General Examen*

The General Examen (*Primero examen y general*)[4] or means of investigation is a conspectus intended to give to one deliber-

---

2 *Cons*, [136, 548]. See also Coemans, *Introductio*, nos. 71-82; *EpitInstSJ*, 6. Text B, the Autograph, has been published in a photographic edition: *Constituciones de la Compañía de Jesús y sus Declaraciones. Reproducción fototípica del original* (Rome, 1908).
3 The complete texts of the *Prima Societatis Jesu Instituti Summa*, *Regimini militantis Ec-*

ating about entrance into the Society a summary but accurate knowledge of its Institute, that is, of its manner of living and the documents in which that life is authoritatively set forth and sanctioned. This Examen was also a manual which aided an examiner or counselor who explained it, and who could if he wished leave it with the candidate for leisurely pondering while he was still a guest in a house of first probation (*General Examen,* [2] and *Constitutions,* [190-203]). It was composed probably about 1546 and fills forty-eight pages (folios 2r through 26v) of the manuscript, text B. If taken strictly, the title of General Examen applies only to Chapters 1-4, for Chapters 5-8 are particularized Examens for distinct classes of applicants.

c. *The Declarations on the Examen*

The Declarations on the Examen, ten pages (folios 28r through 33v), is a collection of authoritative explanations of the related phrases or passages of the Examen. The fuller description of the Declarations on the Constitutions, given just below, applies also here.

d. *The Constitutions of the Society of Jesus*

The Constitutions of the Society of Jesus, eighty pages (folios 28r through 99v), is the main body or core of the statutes which expand, apply, and further determine the provisions contained in the papally approved Formula of the Institute. About to treat of things to be done, Ignatius showed himself aware of two possible procedures (*Constitutions,* [135-137]). He could write according to the order of logical thought, which first sets forth the end and then treats the means to attain it, or according to the order of execution, which treats step by step the means to attain the end and then sets forth the end or finished product as a kind of résumé. He chose this latter procedure and divided his Constitutions into ten parts. In a loosely chronological order he treated first of the individual members, their admission, formation, definitive incorporation into the Society, and application to its work (Parts I-VII), then of their relations among themselves and with their head or superior general (Part VIII), then of the general himself (Part IX), and lastly of the body of the Society as a whole and of its preservation and development (Part X).[5]

---

clesiae, and *Exposcit debitum,* with the paragraph numbers aptly inserted by Codina, are found in *Cons*MHSJ, I, 14-21, 24-32, 373-383.
4 See *Cons*MHSJ, I, xiii, xiv; II, vi-xxvii.
5 *Cons,* [137]. Cf. Coemans, *Introductio,* nos. 78-83.

This order was practical but it entailed overlappings and repetitions, since by it Ignatius focused his attention somewhat more upon situations than upon the topic which was being adjusted to them. For any topic, such as prayer or obedience, he had a comprehensive mental concept; but from this concept he drew merely what was appropriate for each situation. Consequently he did not aim to present a complete and well-rounded treatment of the topic in any one place. Hence it is that in the Constitutions he presupposes what is in the Examen and vice versa. To get his complete concept of virtually any topic, one must collate several scattered passages which touch on it. For example, the end of the Society is directly and perhaps most clearly stated in *Examen*, [3] and is touched upon, applied, and enriched rather than explicitly repeated in the *Constitutions*, [156, 163, 258, 307, 308, 446, 586, 603, 813]. Treatment of a topic may be adjusted in one place to a candidate first learning some precepts and in another to a superior whose duty it is to enforce them, as can be seen in *Examen* [53-59] and *Constitutions*, [254-259]. Occasionally Ignatius himself explicitly refers the reader of the Constitutions to the Examen for a fuller treatment, for example, in *Constitutions*, [256] and *Examen*, [91-97]. Cross-references to related passages are given in many modern editions, the present one included.

In this procedure adjusted to the order of execution we observe the eminently practical character of Ignatius. His major aim was not to write a set of abstract principles in a logically organized treatise. Rather, he was striving to compose a practical manual to guide the superiors and members of his order toward coordinated action in applying his and their principles, already known from some other source such as the Spiritual Exercises, by deciding what they think will lead to greater glory to God in a given situation.

E. *The Declarations on the Constitutions*

The Declarations on the Constitutions, ninety-eight pages (folios 100r through 149v) in the manuscript, is a document whose nature emerges clearly from Ignatius' own statements in its Proemium (*Constitutions*, [136]). He desired the Constitutions to consist of statutes of greater permanency and of more universal application throughout the whole Society, brief enough for handy use by all its members, and such that they could be shown also to externs when expedient. The Declarations, having equal binding force with the Constitutions, were to descend more to details, by giving, especially to superiors, particular applications or explanations; and often a Declaration might turn out to be longer than the passage it explained. Each Declaration is referred to its proper passage by a capital letter such as A, B, C. In résumé, a Declaration is Ignatius' own authoritative explanation of a point in the Constitutions.

F. *The arrangement in modern editions*

Ignatius' four treatises first appeared in print in the Latin translation of his original Spanish. The first book, containing the *Examen generale* and the *Constitutiones,* became available in 1558 and the second, the still separated *Declarationes,* in 1559.[6] In a second edition of the Latin text under St. Francis Borgia in 1570, the Declarations were not printed as separate treatises but were inserted below the passages they explained, so that the Examen, Constitutions, and Declarations made up one unified volume. This practice was followed in most subsequent editions. In the edition issued at Rome in 1949, *Societatis Iesu Constitutiones et Epitomes Instituti,* each successive paragraph of the four original treatises was given a number, encased in square brackets. Thus the more cumbersome ancient references, such as *Constitutions,* Part IV, Chapter xiii, Number 2, Declaration A, lengthy even in its abbreviation as *Cons,* P. 4, c. 13, n. 2, A, can be cited simply as *Cons,* [455]. This system, now widely adopted, is used throughout the present book.

II

Some important terminology

Any treatment touching upon the juridical structure of a religious order necessarily employs many words which are used sometimes with highly technical meanings and sometimes loosely, or even as interchangeable synonyms. These words vex some readers, especially beginners or others whose ordinary work does not keep the memory fresh on the details at issue. Among such terms may be instanced institute, order, congregation, rule and rules, constitution, constitutions, Constitutions, and *Constitutions,* statutes, precepts, ordinances, decrees, customs, and the like. Each of these terms has been used with new and different meanings in succeeding eras, and in any given era sometimes technically and sometimes unheedingly or even erroneously. Frequently a later meaning has been read into an earlier word, context, or document where it distorts the sense. For precise work in a particular treatise or context, help must be sought from historical

6 See *Cons*MHSJ, I, xvii.

dictionaries or commentaries.[7] The aim here is to give the heart of the matter necessary to understand accurately the early Jesuit documents of Ignatius' era, in a manner suited especially for beginners.

A. *A Rule*

Already in the fifth century Salvian used the word *religio* to signify monastic or religious life. His *religionem profiteri* (*Ad ecclesiam*, 2, 11) meant "to declare oneself a monk." In medieval writers *religio* was frequently used with the meaning of "a religious institute," as can be seen in St. Thomas' *Summa theologiae* (for example, in II-II, Q. 185, a. 4; Q. 186, aa. 1-7).

Early in the history of religious life, the word Rule was used as a title to mean the fundamental code of statutes for directing and governing the members of a given religious institute, as can be seen in the title of St. Benedict's Rule for Monks (*Regula monachorum*).

This meaning of the term arose through a natural evolution. Already in Cicero's day, *regula* had among its many meanings that of a rule or norm for action or conduct. Hence in early monasticism too, any statute or precept was often called a rule (*regula*); and a compilation of such statutes might be entitled Rules (*Regulae*) or even a Rule (*Regula*) in a collective sense. Thus arose such titles as the Rule of St. Pachomius.[8] From among many such ancient compilations termed a Rule, four attained a preeminence in the Church by the end of the thirteenth century: the Rule of St. Basil (d. 379?), of St. Augustine[9] (d. 430), of St. Benedict (d. 543?), and of St. Francis of Assisi (d. 1226). In 1214 the fourth Council of the Lateran, confirmed by Innocent III, and again in 1274 the Council of Lyons, confirmed by Gregory X, fearing a multiplication of religious institutes, enacted a decree which required future founders of religious institutes to adopt one of these four established Rules.[10]

---

7 A few examples are: *Dictionnaire de droit canonique* (Paris, 1935-   ); A. Blaise, *Dictionnaire Latin-Français des auteurs chrétiens* (Strasbourg, 1954); C. de Carlo, M.I., *Jus religiosorum* (Tournai, 1950); P. Maroto, C.M.F., *Regulae et particulares constitutiones singularum Religionum ex iure Decretalium usque ad codicem* (Rome, 1932); the *New Catholic Encyclopedia; the Oxford English Dictionary*, 13 vols. (London, 1933); L. R. Ravasi, C.P., *De regulis et constitutionibus religiosorum* (Tournai, 1958); T. Schaefer, O.F.M.Cap., *De religiosis: ad normam Codicis Iuris Canonici* (Rome, 1947). *Tesoro de la lengua castellana, o española* (Madrid, 1611, reprinted in Barcelona, 1944), by the first great lexicographer of Spanish, Sebastián de Covarrubias Horozco, is especially valuable for work with Ignatius' Spanish texts because it reveals the sixteenth-century meanings and nuances.

8 Text in PL 23, 49.

9 This Rule was originally compiled about 1050 from Augustine's Letter 211 and other writings. See *NCathEnc*, I, 1059-1060.

B. *Constitutions*

Especially after the jurist Gaius (ca. 180), the Latin word *constitutio* often meant a decree, statute, regulation, edict, or order. Hence as new circumstances and usages arose in monasteries, the competent authority such as a chapter enacted new statutes which further applied or determined an ancient Rule and fittingly called each such statute a constitution. Such constitutions were added to the Rule which was itself left intact. A collection of such statutes was appropriately entitled the Constitutions (*Constitutiones*). Thus, for example, St. Norbert in about 1121 added his own Constitutions of the Premonstratensians to the Rule of St. Augustine. St. Dominic (d. 1221) took that same Rule and added the Constitutions of the Order of Preachers.[11] Usually a collection of Constitutions became longer than the fundamental Rule. The Rule was regarded as permanent. In many cases it received approval from a pope and could be modified only by him, while the Constitutions could be altered by whatever lower authority had established them.

C. *The terms Rule and Constitutions after 1500*

However, as a result of an evolution already in full progress in the early 1500's and continuing until the present, great variety has arisen in the use of the terms treated above. In many instances but not all, the fundamental meanings so far given for Rule as contrasted with Constitutions were greatly changed and even reversed.

Constitutions taking the place of a Rule in the strict ancient sense first appeared, it seems, with the Carthusians (founded in 1086). They are also found among the Trinitarians (1198), the Minims of St. Francis de Paul (1454), and the Camillians (1586).[12]

In the institutes antedating 1500 in which the members lived under an ancient Rule, the vows of religion had effects which led to their being termed by canonists solemn, and the institutes themselves were termed orders in the strict sense of the term. By a solemn vow of poverty, for example, a religious gave up both ownership and independent use of possessions; by a simple vow, only independent use of them. Especially after Ignatius

10 See *DDC*, IV, col. 462; *Cons*MHSJ, I, 31; E. Fine, *Iuris Regularis* (Prato, 1909), p. 13.
11 See *DDC*, IV, col. 462; *Cons*MHSJ, II, ccxvi. The two Dominican treatises were published together in *Regula Beati Augustini [et] Constitutiones Fratrum Ordinis Praedicatorum* (Rome, 1566).
12 See Schaefer, *De religiosis*, p. 96; Carlo, *Jus religiosorum*, p. 35. To list the Society of Jesus as one of these institutes is hardly correct. See fn. 26 below.

prescribed vows termed simple for his scholastics and coadjutors whether spiritual or temporal, these somewhat less far-reaching vows were often found more practical. Many new institutes were founded in which the members took only simple vows and which were termed technically congregations. Most such congregations had as their fundamental law a collection of statutes called the Constitutions. Usually these were approved by the Holy See and were supplemented by collections of rules or customs which dealt with details of less importance and which were enacted by chapters or superiors within the institute. Hence the word rule (*regula*) was used with great frequency to mean one of these directives about a matter of less importance than a constitution. In these cases the Constitutions were approved by the Holy See and became the fundamental code of laws constituting the institute, while the book of Rules gave further and more minute determinations to this code; and thus the ancient meanings of the two terms were reversed. Sometimes the two terms, rules and constitutions, were used interchangeably. In many other instances, too, the term rule was still used in its ancient meaning of the fundamental law of an older order with solemn vows as distinguished from a modern congregation whose members take only simple vows. Great caution is necessary now to discern the precise meaning of the terms rule or constitution in any given author or context.

In 1918 the new Code of Canon Law established a terminology of its own, in which the following items are noteworthy for our purposes. The Latin term *religio* means, as it did in the writings of medieval canonists, a religious institute: a society approved by ecclesiastical authority, in which the members take public vows according to the society's laws and thus strive toward spiritual perfection (Canon 488, 1°). A vow is a deliberate promise made to God to do something better than its opposite (Canon 1307, §1). A vow is public if it is received by a legitimate superior in the name of the Church; otherwise it is private (Canon 1308, §1). An order is an institute in which solemn vows are taken by at least some of the members; a congregation, one in which only simple vows are taken (Canon 488, 2°). A clerical institute is one in which the majority of the members are or become priests; otherwise the institute is lay (*ibid.*, 4°). Religious, whether men or women (*religiosi* or *religiosae*), are persons who have taken vows in a religious institute. Religious with simple vows are those who have taken vows in a congregation; regulars, those who have taken vows in an order; sisters (*sorores*), religious women with simple vows;

nuns (*moniales*), religious women with solemn vows (*ibid.*, 7°).

The Code speaks of "rules and particular constitutions" (*regulae et particulares constitutiones*) in Canon 489 (cf. 509, §2, 1°; 593; 618, §2, 1°), but contains no mention of a Rule (*Regula*) in its ancient meaning of fundamental law of an order. Nevertheless, this omission leaves intact the status and terminology of orders which have a Rule in that ancient meaning. It also makes it evident that in the congregations of simple vows, which have all been founded since 1500, the collection of Constitutions is the fundamental law of the congregation. According to the "Norms" (*Normae*) issued by the Sacred Congregation of Religious on March 6, 1921, as guides for new congregations seeking approval, terms which apply only to orders, such as Rule (*Regula*), should not be used in the documents of congregations.[13] Hence their fundamental codes should be termed Constitutions.

D. *The terms in Jesuit documents*

When viewed against the foregoing historical background, the terminology found in the documents of the early Society of Jesus becomes easier to grasp with precision. Most of the terms, such as institute, constitution and constitutions, rule and rules, and the like, generally have the meanings which they had in the older usage before 1500. However, as is natural, there are also some usages characteristic of the period of transitional terminology in which the Society arose. This is especially true of the words rule (*regula*) and rules (*regulae*), as will soon appear.

1. *The Institute*

Ignatius often uses the word religion (*religión, religio*) in the medieval canonical sense of a religious institute (for example, in *Constitutions*, [553, 816]). He uses the term Institute of the Society to mean, first and fundamentally, the manner in which its members live and work, as contexts and synonymous phrases reveal: "el fin de nuestro Instituto y modo de proceder" (*Constitutions*, [152; see also 216, 586, 602, 603]; see also *Prima . . . Instituti Summa*, [4, 7] and *Exposcit debitum*, [1, 2, 9]). But in the course of time this manner of living was given written expression in official documents such as the papal bulls *Regimini*

---

13 *AAS*, XIII (1921), 317, no. 22, h. For brief histories of the constitutional development of religious institutes both before and after Ignatius, see R. F. Smith in *NCathEnc*, XIII, 287-294 and Carlo, *Jus religiosorum*, pp. 7-9.

and *Exposcit*, the Constitutions, and various rules. Hence Ignatius' use of the term Institute also often designates or at least connotes these documents. For example, he states that the novices "ought to see and ponder several times the bulls of the Institute of the Society, and the Constitutions and rules which should be obeyed in it" (*Examen*, [18]). Other examples can be found in [98], *Constitutions*, [134, 198, 199], and *Exposcit*, [2].

2. *The Formula of the Institute*

Already in the First Sketch of the Institute of the Society of Jesus (*Prima Societatis Jesu Instituti Summa*) of August, 1539, several almost synonymous words or phrases appear which are rather striking: a way or pattern or "formula of living in conformity with the evangelical counsels and the canonical sanctions of the fathers" (*vivendi formula evangelicis consiliis et canonicis patrum sanctionibus . . . conformis*),[14] "the observance of this our Rule" (*regulae huius nostrae observationem*),[15] "this our institute of life" (*de nostro vitae instituto*),[16] and "this pattern of life" (*hanc . . . vitae formam*).[17] Especially when thus juxtaposed, these rather synonymous phrases severally illumine one another in a manner which reveals their writers' meanings and general outlook. These "voluntarily poor priests of Christ" (*sponte pauperes Christi sacerdotes*),[18] who were somewhat afraid that acceptance of an ancient Rule would interfere with the type or scope of apostolic activities to which they felt called (*secundum scopum vocationis nostrae*) but who wished nevertheless to perpetuate their own fraternal union in friendship and charity for service to God and men—these priests desired indeed to live as clerics (*juxta commune clericorum omnium . . . debitum*)[19] but also to embrace a manner of living according to the evangelical counsels, under a Rule or Formula in a new type of religious institute for which they were seeking the pope's approval. When Paul III granted their request in 1540 by his bull *Regimini* in which all those phrases and terms remained, these priests were "clerics regular" (*clerici regulares*), priests living under a rule and similar to the Theatines or Barnabites or other new institutes of this type which were then arising in the Church.[20] Moreover,

---

14 *ConsMHSJ*, I, 18, *Prima . . . Instituti Summa*, [3].
15 *Ibid.*, I, 18, [4].
16 *Ibid.*, I, 20, [7].
17 *Ibid.*, I, 20, [8].
18 *Ibid.*, I, 15, [1].
19 *Ibid.*, I, 17, [3].
20 On these, see, e.g., Carlo, *Jus religiosorum*, p. 8; Schaefer, *De religiosis*, pp. 83, 93, 95; Pastor, *History*, XI, 515; *NCathEnc*, XII, 291-292.

through incorporation into the papal bulls, those phrases and terms became the official words of Paul III and ten years later of Julius III. After the issuance of those bulls, Ignatius and his companions had fully achieved their intention of founding a new order of priests, a clerical religious institute (*ordo clericalis*), and the Holy See had given full approval to their enterprise (*Regimini*, [9], *Exposcit*, [7]).

Hence the evidence more clearly emerges, too, that the Formula of the Institute as found in the papal bulls is the Society's fundamental inspiration and code, comparable to St. Benedict's Rule for Monks. The Formula was termed a Rule by the two popes in both bulls, as it also was by Francis Xavier.[21] Olivier Mannaerts, one of Ignatius' contemporaries, also reveals the attitude of the early Jesuits when he states about *Regimini* and *Exposcit*: "Those two bulls of the Apostolic See contain, as in a treasure house, the whole essence of our way of life, that essence which other orders call the Rule."[22] In the Constitutions Ignatius did not himself employ the term Rule in its ancient sense to designate the Formula; but the reverence with which he constantly refers back to the Formula in his Constitutions clearly shows that he regarded it and not them as the Society's basic code. Since it is a papal document, the Formula cannot be altered by any authority within the Society. Because of the statements in these and subsequent bulls, experts commonly hold that the Institute of the Society insofar as it is set forth in this Formula has papal approval "in specific form," rather than in the somewhat weaker "common form."[23]

3. The Constitutions

The Formula empowered the future general of the Society to establish more particularized Constitutions, which were to become valid by a majority vote of his associates.[24] Thus authorized, Ignatius compiled his Constitutions. Hence it is clear that they bear to the Formula or fundamental Rule the same relation as, for example, the *Constitutions of the Congregation of . . . St. Benedict of Spain and England* (Madrid, 1706)[25] bear to the

21 *Regimini*, [5], *Exposcit*, [4], in *Cons*MHSJ, I, 28, 378; *MonXav*, I, 245, 294.
22 *Exhortationes*, I, 1, no. 5, cited in Coemans, *Introductio*, no. 50.
23 See Coemans, *Introductio*, no. 50; *EpitInstSJ*, 5, §2.
24 *Regimini*, [3, 9], in *Cons*MHSJ, I, 27, 31.
25 Microfilm 1143.4 in the Pius XII Library of St. Louis University. The Spanish title is: *Constituciones de la congregación de nuestro glorioso Padre san Benito de España y Inglaterra* (Madrid, 1706).

Rule for Monks of St. Benedict.[26] Since Ignatius' Constitutions obtained their juridical force through the approval of the Society's First General Congregation in 1558, they are alterable by subsequent general congregations, provided that the change does not conflict with a higher law. General congregations have modified some statutes or provisions of Ignatius' Constitutions where there was solid reason to do so. But they have rightfully indicated such modifications only in their own decrees and thus left Ignatius' text intact.[27] This seems fitting procedure with a text which is one of the classics of religious literature and legislation. The present book too follows this example and presents a translation of Ignatius' text.

4. *Rules and ordinances*

Ignatius knew that further applications and determinations of his own Constitutions would be necessary and provided for them, terming them ordinances or rules (*ordenanzas o reglas, ordinationes vel regulae*). As we saw above, he desired constitutions to deal with matters more important, permanent, and applicable at all times and places, and ordinances or rules to treat of matters of relatively less importance and to be more readily changeable according to local circumstances (*Constitutions*, [136]).

In his Constitutions, which give his final terminology, the word rules always refers to such directives or regulations which are of less importance than a constitution. Generally this statement holds true also of most other early Jesuit documents; but one must be alert for exceptions.[28] Ignatius himself and some local superiors, such as Simão Rodrigues, composed many sets of such rules between 1540 and 1556.[29] Examples are the oldest "Rules for Scholastics" of 1540, the "Constitutions for Scholastics" at Padua in 1546, the "Rules of the Roman College" of 1551, and sets of rules for various officials, such as the minister, sacristan, buyer, cook, and other persons. In the still fluid terminology of the 1540's often little or no distinction was as yet made between a constitution and a rule; and other terms too were

---

26 It is sometimes stated that the Society of Jesus is one of the institutes which have Constitutions as their constitutive law, rather than a Rule; e.g., in *DDC*, IV, col. 462; *NCathEnc*, XII, 331; Schaefer, *De religiosis*, p. 96. However, this manner of speaking seems to be an overhasty application of the general statement (as found, e.g., in *DDC, ibid.*, or Schaefer, *ibid.*), and is unfortunate because it virtually overlooks the Formula of the Institute and its important position as a Rule which dominates the Constitutions.
27 See *Cons*MHSJ, I, xii.
28 On the term rule (*regula*) in early Jesuit documents, see *Cons*MHSJ, IV, 1°-5°.
29 These sets have been published in *Cons*MHSJ, esp. IV, *Regulae Societatis Iesu* (1540-1556), 135-310.

used interchangeably with them, such as statutes (*statuta*), cautions (*monita*), or duties (*officia*).[30] There was much revision of such rules under the early generals of the Society until the end of Aquaviva's term of office in 1615. From then on they remained fairly unchanged until General Congregation XXVII in 1923.[31] The era of Vatican Council II has naturally induced an atmosphere of more rapid change to comply with the directives for adaptation issued by the Holy Father and the Council.

5. *Additional terms after 1556*

After Ignatius' death, still other legislative regulations naturally arose and occasioned new terminology, such as the decrees and canons of general congregations, or the rules, ordinances, and instructions issued by fathers general.[32] On various occasions the chief documents pertaining at the time to the Society's corpus of still functioning laws were gathered and published. The last edition of this kind was the three-volume *Institutum Societatis Iesu* which appeared at Florence in 1892 and 1893. Subsequent documents can be found in the periodical *Acta Romana Societatis Iesu* which began publication in 1906.

III

The genesis and texts of Ignatius' Constitutions

Both the Formula and the Constitutions arose from the turn of events during the earliest two years which Ignatius and his companions spent together in Rome. Being unable to carry out their original plan of going to the Holy Land, they offered their services to Pope Paul III. Expecting soon to be separated on missions to diverse regions but desiring to perpetuate their fraternal union in charity and their work to serve God and their fellowmen, they met to deliberate[33] about "this our vocation and pattern of life" (*de hac nostra vocatione ac vivendi formula*). "Near the end of Lent," their account records, "the time was near when we were to be divided from one another and dispersed [on various missions]. We had awaited this separation even with great longing, in order to reach sooner the goal we had set

---

30 See *Cons*MHSJ, IV, 4*.
31 *Ibid.*, IV, 3*.
32 These terms will be found in *Collectio decretorum Congregationum Generalium* (Rome, 1961), nos. 2-6, and in *EpitInstSJ*, nos. 5-13. See also Coemans, *Introductio*, nos. 121-169.
33 The "Deliberation of the First Fathers" (*Deliberatio primorum Patrum*), the record of their meetings, is in *Cons*MHSJ, I, 9-14; an English translation by D. Maruca is in *WL*, XCV (1966), 325-333.

ourselves and now eagerly desired. We decided to meet together for many days before this dispersal and to hold discussions about this our vocation and pattern of life. The members
of our group came from France, Spain, Savoy, and Portugal;
and after several such sessions we found our views and opinions
divided about this state of our affairs. We had among ourselves
one single mind and determination, namely, to seek God's good
pleasure and will in every detail, according to the scope of our
vocation; but there was a diversity of opinions as to what means
would be more expedient and fruitful both for ourselves and
for all our fellow men"[34] In daily meetings from mid-March to
June 24, 1539, they systematically explored various questions.
First, was it better for them to keep themselves united through
some form of a society, or for each to go his own way in apostolic
chastity and poverty? Second, should they make a vow of obedience to one of their members, as was done in other religious
orders? If they did, they might be compelled by the pope to
live under some Rule already completely formed;[35] and this
might interfere with or even frustrate their controlling desire
of apostolic work which might require much mingling with people
and travel anywhere. On the other hand, such obedience seemed
necessary for adequate apostolic cooperation, permanence of their
group, and more vigorous, humble, and meritorious activities.
They unanimously reached affirmative answers to both questions
and sketched a few tentative statutes (*constitutiones*) for their
future "congregation or society" (*congregationem . . . vel societatem*).[36]

A. *The genesis of the Formula*

Only a little later the group elaborated the Latin document
already mentioned, the conspectus now known as the First
Sketch of the Institute of the Society of Jesus (*Prima Societatis
Jesu Instituti Summa*).[37] It is probable that Ignatius himself
wrote this document in Spanish, or at least greatly influenced
its composition, and that someone else, possibly Codure or Salmerón, translated it into stylistic Latin. It was submitted to the
pope, perhaps in August, 1539. On September 3 Cardinal Contarini wrote to Ignatius from Tivoli that he had read it to Paul
III, who was pleased with all its five articles and ordered a bull

---

34 *Cons*MHSJ, I, 1-2.
35 One reason for their fear lay in the decrees of Innocent III in 1214 and Gregory X in
   1274. See fn. 10 above.
36 *Determinationes Societatis*, in *Cons*MHSJ, I, 9-14. The terms are on p. 10.
37 Text *ibid.*, I, 14-21; see also ccv-ccviii.

to be drawn up.[38] But problems arose. Cardinal Ghinucci had difficulties, especially about the vow of special obedience to the pope. Cardinal Guidiccioni, although he thought the Sketch praiseworthy, referred to the decrees of Innocent III and Gregory X and opposed approbation of any new orders. But in time these difficulties were overcome and the First Sketch, slightly modified in form and now encased within a papal introduction and conclusion, appeared within the bull *Regimini militantis Ecclesiae*,[39] dated September 27, 1540. By it Pope Paul III officially approved the Society of Jesus and granted its members the right to compose more particularized Constitutions.[40]

B. *The gradual evolution of the texts of the Constitutions*

On March 4, 1541, the group of companions entrusted the work of composing the Constitutions to Ignatius and Codure, approximately a month before they elected Ignatius superior general on April 8 and 13. But Codure's death on August 29 left the task to Ignatius almost alone. Occupied with other business, he proceeded slowly at first, assembling or perhaps revising such collections of statutes as the document For the Foundation of Colleges (*Para fundar colegios*) which dates from 1541 and 1546,[41] gathering notes, and determining various points with his associates. There was deliberation among them in 1541, for example, as to whether the sacristies of the Society's churches could have fixed revenues, which were forbidden to the community. They decided affirmatively, in accordance with the practice then common in the mendicant orders. But Ignatius conceived doubts and, after the ponderings recorded in his *Spiritual Diary*, reversed this decision in 1545. He also worked on the Examen for candidates, of which the first draft, text *a*, was complete in 1546.[42]

1. *Polanco named secretary*

In March, 1547, he named Juan de Polanco, formerly an amanuensis for the Holy See (*scriptor apostolicus*) to be his secretary. From then on Ignatius made the Constitutions his principal occupation and the work moved steadily forward. Polanco acquainted himself with what had been done and, working closely with Ignatius, studied and excerpted both the Rule and the Constitutions of earlier institutes, including the Augustinians,

---

38 *Ibid.*, I, 21, 22; see also ccv-ccviii.
39 Text *ibid.*, I, 24-32; see also ccix-ccxi.
40 *Ibid.*, I, nos. [3, 9], on pp. 27, 31.
41 Text *Cons*MHSJ, I, 49-65; see also lxviii-lxxvi and *Cons*MHSJ, IV, 12-14.
42 See *Cons*MHSJ, II, 2.

Benedictines, Dominicans, and Franciscans.[43] From these documents he gathered and grouped ideas to be submitted to Ignatius,
who incorporated many of them. But whatever Ignatius chose he
also transformed by adjusting it to the apostolic ends and means
of his own Institute, which were something new in the Church.[44]
Thus his originality was that he changed religious life, not merely
lightly by modifying a number of its traditional observances, but
profoundly by making every element in it apostolic. Noteworthy
among Polanco's papers were "Six Lists of Problems" (*Sex du-
biorum series*) and his "Resources" (*Industriae*) in twelve parts.[45]
Account was taken of the new bulls and briefs from Paul III,
Iniunctum nobis of March 15, 1544 (which removed the restriction of the professed members to sixty), *Cum inter cunctas*
of June 3, 1545 (granting various priestly faculties), *Exponi
nobis* of June 5, 1546 (permitting the admission of coadjutors,
some of whom could be ordained to the priesthood), *Pastoralis
officii* of July 31, 1548 (approving the *Spiritual Exercises*), and
Licet debitum of October 18, 1549 (granting various privileges).[46] Then came a fresh confirmation of the Society from
Julius III, in *Exposcit debitum*[47] of July 21, 1550. This bull
repeated, with a few relatively minor modifications, omissions,
and additions dictated by ten years of experience, the substance
of *Regimini militantis Ecclesiae* of 1540. Where differences occur,
the later *Exposcit debitum* prevails and has henceforth rightly
been considered to contain the definitive Formula of the Institute.

2. *The first Spanish texts*

Between 1547 and 1550 the first complete Spanish text of the
Society's Constitutions, text *a*, was finished and contained the
division into ten Parts which remain in the final text.[48] Ignatius
summoned many of the professed members of his order to Rome
and showed them a complete and revised text of the General
Examen and the Constitutions in Spanish, text A, of 1550. Among
these consultants were Francis Borgia, Antonio Araoz, Andrés
de Oviedo, André des Freux, Diego Laynez, Nicolás Bobadilla,

43 See *Cons*MHSJ, I, clxxx-cxciv, "Algunas cosas que de la Regla y Constituciones se toman
. . ."; II, ccxv-ccxxi.
44 On Ignatius' originality in this, see *Cons*MHSJ, II, ccxv-ccxxi.
45 Texts *Cons*MHSJ, I, 268-355 and *PolCompl*, II, 719-807; cf. *Cons*MHSJ, II, clxxiv-
clxxxiii; *DeGuiJes*, p. 144; Dudon, *St. Ignatius*, pp. 288-290.
46 Texts *Institutum Societatis Jesu*, 3 vols. (Florence, 1892-1893), I, 7-21; II, 443-445 (abbreviated hereafter as *InstSJ*).
47 Text *Cons*MHSJ, I, 372-383; cf. ccxxii-ccxxv.
48 Text *Cons*MHSJ, II, 129-257.

Alfonso Salmerón, and others. They discussed the text in meet-ings lasting from early January to February 1, 1551, suggested modifications of details, and approved the work as a whole.[49]

Nevertheless, Ignatius wished to improve these Constitutions still further rather than regard them as now "closed." He desired, as his contemporaries inform us, that they should become first of all known and accepted throughout the Society; and he left their official rejection or approval to the First General Congre-gation which was to assemble to elect his successor.[50]

Ignatius appointed Nadal to explain these Constitutions and to promulgate them for experiment. Nadal visited the houses of the order in Sicily, Spain, and Portugal from June 10, 1552 to September 22, 1554, and in Germany, Austria, and Italy from February 15, 1555 to December, 1555. His procedure in each house was to assemble the community and explain the Constitu-tions for an hour daily. During his stay he also interviewed the members one by one, administered questionnaires to them, and sent reports back to Ignatius. In 1555 Ribadaneyra was sent to make similar promulgation in the Low Countries but met less success.[51] Meanwhile Ignatius himself continued to revise and perfect his text. He and Polanco revised and corrected text A and thus from it produced text B, the Autograph, on which Ignatius continued to make corrections and marginal insertions in his own hand until he died in 1556. From this text B was transcribed the text which Nadal carried on his journeys of 1552-1555 and which is designated B'.[52]

3. *The Latin translation*

It was evident that a Latin version would be needed in a worldwide order. Already in 1555 Polanco had begun a trans-lation into Latin. During the preparations for the First General Congregation of the order he hastened this version forward, probably with the aid of collaborators. Largely from Ignatius' Autograph, text B, a new Spanish text was prepared, text C, which corrected the Autograph in some details, chiefly punctua-tion and grammar.[53]

49 See *Cons*MHSJ, II, cxciv; also I, lxxvii-lxxxv, 390-396; *IdeaJesUn*, p. 285; Dudon, *St. Ignatius*, pp. 288-289.
50 *Cons*MHSJ, II, ccxxxiv-ccxxxvi.
51 *Cons*MHSJ, II, ccxxvii-ccxxxvi; Dudon, *St. Ignatius*, pp. 309-310.
52 *Cons*MHSJ, II, xv-xvii, lxxxiii-lxxxiv.
53 *Cons*MHSJ, II, 123, 726; cf. F. Roustang, in *Constitutions de la Compagnie de Jésus* (Paris, 1967), II, 35-36.

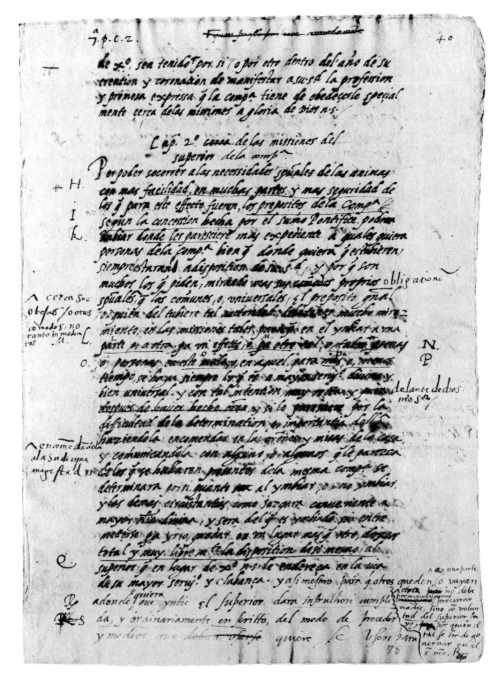

Figure 3. A page of the manuscript of text B, the Autograph

This page contains *Constituciones*, [618], from Part VII. The higher
marginal corrections are in St. Ignatius' handwriting. For a detail in the
actual size, see Figure 4 on page 272.

4. *Approval by General Congregation I*

On September 10, 1558, the Congregation approved both this text C and Polanco's Latin version; and thus Ignatius' Constitutions became binding in the Society. The Congregation further ordered that the Latin version should be printed and thus made it the official text (*versio vulgata*)[54] to be diffused throughout the multilingual provinces of the order. The printing and publication of the Latin translation occurred in 1558 and 1559. From that time on, however, the Spanish text has been taken as the norm for interpreting and correcting this vulgate Latin version. Official endeavors to produce more critically edited Spanish and Latin texts continued through the first five general congregations until 1594.

In 1581 General Congregation IV directed the preparation of a new Latin text of the General Examen and the Constitutions. This edition, called the fourth of the Latin texts, appeared in 1583 and has henceforth been the official Latin text. The Declarations were inserted, each in its proper place, within the Constitutions and Examen. The combined treatises were entitled *Constitutiones Societatis Iesu. Cum earum Declarationibus* (Rome, 1583). In 1938 this fourth edition was published anew with critical apparatus and a virtually exhaustive Introduction by Arturo Codina as Volume 65 in the series Monumenta Historica Societatis Iesu.[55]

In 1594 General Congregation V approved a new text of the Spanish, text D. This led to the first printing of the Spanish text, in an edition which also carried the Latin on opposite pages, with the title: *Constitutiones Societatis Iesu latinae et hispanicae cum earum Declarationibus* (Rome, 1606). In 1936 appeared the masterful edition which is fundamental for all present-day studies on the Constitutions, that of Arturo Codina, Volume 64 of the series Monumenta Historica Societatis Iesu: *Sancti Ignatii de Loyola Constitutiones Societatis Jesu. Tomus secundus: Textus Hispanus* (Rome, 1936). The extensive Prolegomena carry introductory studies of the highest quality. Then follow the successive texts: text *a* of 1547-1550, and after this in parallel columns texts A, B, and D, respectively of circa 1550, 1556, and 1594. Ignacio Iparraguirre edited this text anew, with more modernized punctuation, spelling, and capitalization and also with very helpful notes in *Obras completas de San Ignacio de*

---

54 Decrees 78 and 79 in *InstSJ*, II, 173; see also 205, 224, 249, 283.
55 This volume is *Cons*MHSJ, III.

Loyola (second edition; Madrid, 1963), Volume 86 in the series Biblioteca de Autores Cristianos.

The Latin translation (*versio vulgata*), although authentic, is not definitive. No translation perfectly reproduces an original and it is not surprising that Jesuits have continually expressed desires for a still more faithful Latin version. They find the official Latin version to be substantially conformed to the Spanish original, much as the Latin vulgate text of the New Testament is to the original Greek, but also to differ in accidental details. General Congregation XXIII in 1883 recommended a revision which would bring the Latin into closer conformity with Ignatius' Spanish. As a result, Juan de la Torre produced a new edition, *Constitutiones Societatis Jesu Latinae et Hispanicae cum earum Declarationibus* (Madrid, 1892), with footnotes in which he listed some 2,000 small discrepancies from the original Spanish in the Latin. In 1892 General Congregation XXIV appointed a commission to carry out the recommendation of 1883 but because of practical difficulties encountered, this work was never completed.[56]

c. *The roles of Ignatius and Polanco*

Since Ignatius and Polanco collaborated so closely in the composition of the Constitutions, the question spontaneously arises: Precisely what was the contribution of Ignatius and what of Polanco?

In attempting to answer this we must distinguish between the substance and the literary form. All the content and ideas have been at least approved formally by Ignatius, after careful scrutiny and corrections. Ignatius, too, gave the decisive answers to Polanco's doubts and problems. Moreover, the typically Ignatian ideas and inspiration of the whole are so manifestly prevalent that they prove the Constitutions to be truly his personal work. Finally, explicit testimony to this effect has come from two of his close companions. Nadal informs us that when questioned as to what Polanco had contributed to the Constitutions, Ignatius replied "that with respect to the substance of the content, there is nothing of Polanco's in the Constitutions, unless something concerning the colleges; and even that is according to his own thought." Olivier Mannaerts gives similar testimony: "Ignatius himself composed all the Constitutions and Declarations," except that in writing Part IV he obtained much light from Laynez,

---

56 See Coemans, *Breves notitiae de Instituto, historia, bibliographia Societatis* (Brussels, 1937), nos. 55-63.

Polanco, and Des Freux.[57] However, in what pertains to the form and order, Polanco's part is more important. He was the professional writer who made their style generally easy and flowing in contrast to the strong but involved and difficult style characteristic of Ignatius. He was also an extraordinarily competent and devoted secretary, an *alter ego* in this work who gave Ignatius extensive help in gathering material and discussing problems. In some instances there is evidence which enables us to discern Polanco's contribution from that of Ignatius. But these cases are relatively few.[58]

D. *Papal approbations*

The first papal approval of Ignatius' Constitutions was oral but explicit, and was occasioned by interesting circumstances. Already in the deliberations of early 1551 Bobadilla had found the Constitutions repetitious and lengthy.[59] In a moment of ill humor in 1557, while preparations were being made for General Congregation I, Bobadilla wrote to Pope Paul IV: "The Constitutions and Declarations are a labyrinth altogether confused. They are so numerous that no one, either subject or superior, can come to know them, much less to observe them."[60] The end result of his petulance was quite opposite from his expectations. Pope Paul IV ordered the Jesuits to bring to him all their documents—the papal bulls, the Constitutions, the rules, everything they had. The pope handed the papers for examination to experts whom he appointed, who studied them diligently for several months and then reported back to him. The documents were restored unchanged to the Jesuits, who took this act as equivalent to approval. Some time later, the members of the Congregation,

57 Cited in *Cons*MHSJ, II, clxiv-clxv; cf. *DeGuiJes*, pp. 145, 156.
58 For the most recent extensive study of this problem, see F. Roustang, "Sur le rôle de Polanco dans la rédaction des *Constitutiones S.J.*," *RAM*, XLII (1966), 193-202, and *Constitutions de la Compagnie de Jésus*, II, 11-128. His treatment is scholarly but questioned on important points by other experts. He argues that Ignatius' genuine thought is found in text *a* (1547-1550) rather than in the later texts A (1550) or B (1556), where it is rather disfigured by Polanco, who did not grasp it well because of his different mentality. But J. Granero in *Manresa*, XXXIX (1967), 235-244, and C. de Dalmases in *AHSJ*, XXXVI (1967), 300-306, find Roustang's opinion insufficiently proved and subject to weighty methodological, historical, and philological objections. For example, one manuscript of text *a* is written in large part in the hand of Polanco and only lightly corrected in Ignatius' handwriting, which indicates that Polanco had a much larger part in writing text *a* than Roustang allows; and in any case, while *a* is an organized accumulation of materials toward writing the Constitutions, text B expresses the last thought of the founder (*AHSJ*, XXXVI, 304, 305).
59 *Cons*MHSJ, I, 396; cf. 411, Index, s.v. "Bobadilla."
60 *MonNad*, IV, 733; cf. J.-F. Gilmont, *Les écrits spirituels des premiers Jésuites* (Rome, 1961), p. 81; Coemans, *Introductio*, no. 99.

which had just elected Laynez as general, were received in audience by Paul IV on July 6, 1558. He approved not only Laynez' election "but also this blessed Society, and all the benefits spiritual or temporal and the privileges which preceding popes or himself" had granted.[61] Subsequent noteworthy approbations in official form now published came from the Council of Trent in 1563,[62] and from Gregory XIII in the bulls *Quanto fructuosius* (February 1, 1583) and *Ascendente Domino* (May 25, 1584), which explicitly mention the *Constitutions*.[63] Modern popes too have added their confirmations of the Society's Institute, for example, Leo XIII on July 13, 1886, and Pius XI on March 12, 1933.[64] Especially noteworthy here are the words of the present Holy Father, Paul VI, in an allocution of April 21, 1969, to a group of English-speaking Jesuit provincials and superiors: "Next, we would urge you to an intimate and eager probing of the twofold thrust of your vocation, religious and apostolic; to be specific, take pains to study and implement your Constitutions, whether of recent or earlier origin, with all that sturdy and hearty perseverance which characterizes you."[65]

E. *Translations into modern languages*

The first translation of Ignatius' Constitutions into a vernacular language was one into French, made from the Latin text in great haste in the hope of defending the Society against its attackers in the French Parlement and published in Paris in 1762 with the title: *Les Constitutions des jésuites avec les déclarations*. A revised French translation, also made from the Latin, appeared in Paris in 1843. An excellent modern translation has recently been issued in La Collection Christus: Saint Ignace. *Constitutions de la Compagnie de Jésus*. Tome I: *Traduction du texte officiel, notes et index par François Courel, S.J.* Tome II: *Introduction à une lecture par François Roustang, S.J. Traduction du texte primitif par François Courel, S.J.* (Paris: Desclée de Brouwer, 1967).

In equally strange circumstances an English translation of the Constitutions, incomplete insofar as it lacked the General Ex-

61 Cited in Coemans, *Introductio*, no. 99, from Sacchini, *Historia*, II, 1, no. 89.
62 Coemans, *Introductio*, no. 100.
63 Explicit mention of the *Constitutions* is found in *InstSJ*, I, 89, 94.
64 Texts in *InstSJ*, I, 453-454; *ActRSJ*, VII (1932), 275; *Colld*, p. 351.
    For brief but comprehensive and accurate histories of the Society of Jesus, see: John F. Broderick, s.v. "Jesuits" in *NCathEnc*, VII, 898-909; William V. Bangert, *A History of the Society of Jesus* (St. Louis: The Institute of Jesuit Sources, forthcoming).
65 The entire allocution is in *The Jesuits: Year Book of the Society of Jesus, 1969-1970* (Rome, 1969), p. 87.

amen and the Declarations, appeared in London in 1838. A Protestant translator, anti-Roman as was natural at the time, happened upon a copy of the very first edition of the Constitutions in Latin, bearing the title: *Constitutiones Societatis Iesu. Anno 1558. Romae, in Aedibus Societatis Iesu. 1558.* He reprinted this Latin text, and later in his volume came another title page for the translation itself: *The Constitutions of the Society of Jesus. Printed by the Society at Rome. 1558. Rendered into English from the Latin: with an Appendix, containing the Three Bulls for the Institution, Suppression, and Restoration of the Order of Jesuits: and an Outline of the Present Condition of the Romish Church in this Kingdom. Caecum Scelus Omne. Virg. London: 1838.* The translation is accurate. But as is to be expected, the Introduction and occasional notes clearly reveal the translator's strong anti-Romish and anti-Jesuit feelings. Such opinions were then widespread and we today can perhaps best read them with a little humor, grateful that we live in more fortunate ecumenical times. The translator feared readmission of the Jesuits into England and hoped to warn his readers against them by publishing their Constitutions as the source of their unity and, in his opinion, their power of intrigue. He indicated his attitude by the summarizing epithet culled from Vergil's *Aeneid*, I, 366, which he placed on his title page: "The Whole Dark Crime." Copies of this now rare book are in the British Museum in London and in the Historical Institute of the Society of Jesus in Rome.

An Italian translation has recently become available: Sant' Ignazio di Loyola. *Costituzioni della Compagnia di Gesù. Traduzione del testo ufficiale spagnolo, note e indici a cura di Giuseppe Silvano, S.J.* (Milano: Editrice Ancora, 1969).

A translation of the Constitutions into German is in preparation. Selections from the General Examen and the Constitutions, rendered into German, have appeared in "Die Satzungen der Gesellschaft Jesu, aus dem Spanischen übersetzt und eingeleitet von Mario Schoenenberger und Robert Stalder," pages 323-412 of *Die grossen Ordensregeln*, herausgegeben von Hans Urs von Balthasar (Einsiedeln, 1961).

F. *The present translation*

The present translation is the first complete English version hitherto published of Ignatius' General Examen, Constitutions, and Declarations. It was made from the Spanish text D of 1594 as critically edited in 1936 by Father Arturo Codina, *Sancti Ignatii de Loyola Constitutiones Societatis Jesu. Tomus secun-*

dus: Textus Hispanus (Rome, 1936). The Spanish text was chosen rather than the Latin because thus the version would more fully and accurately convey Ignatius' ideas, nuances of thought, and personality, and would also be more in accord with the modern scholarly insistence on primary sources. Although an effort was made to use straightforward modern English with a reasonable flow, accuracy was regarded as still more important. Ignatius' Constitutions are principally a legal document approved by the Church and will be scrutinized for possible implications and varying interpretations. They are also the expression of a great mystic and carry important theological, ascetical, historical, and mystical implications or connotations. A freer translation might secure more pleasing readability but run the risk of losing too many nuances or inviting hasty inferences. Hence it seemed best to aim above all at fidelity to the Spanish original, by translating not word for word but idea for idea, and by rendering the shades of thought even though the original form is not necessarily retained. Hence the version does not always follow Ignatius' sentence structure. His sentences are often very long, complicated, and difficult, and were broken up or transposed when need arose. Yet an effort has been made to retain his every idea and the relations between them, and also the theological, legal, historical, ascetical, and mystical connotations or implications. The translator's hope is that the version is one which retains much of the Ignatian flavor, reveals his personality, and furnishes insight into the workings of his mind.

G. *The Commentary*

The writer's chief aim in the commentary is to give the reader quick aid toward clearer knowledge of what Ignatius stated and meant. To grasp his thought with accuracy, it is of course often necessary to study his words and phrases (for he had many highly personal usages) and to view his sentences within their literary context of the Constitutions as a whole. Beyond this, however, it is especially necessary to set his statements into the religious, cultural, and social context of his era. One must ask: What was the message which his statements carried to his contemporaries, with their background of thought and sixteenth-century attitudes? These are the steps by which a modern reader can discern the perennial substance of his thought from what is merely accidental or timely for his own era. Thus too a reader can lay the best foundation for a sound adaptation to the changed circumstances of modern times. For these purposes the writer has also added, when it seemed desirable, historical notes on the

Society's interpretations and changes of Ignatius' Constitutions as it endeavored to adapt and apply them to the evolving circumstances in successive cultural periods.

H. *Acknowledgments*

The translator bears an enormous debt of gratitude to all who have preceded and helped him in this work. The editions of Father Ignacio Iparraguirre in *Obras completas de San Ignacio de Loyola* (second edition; Madrid, 1963), Volume 86 in the series Biblioteca de Autores Cristianos, and of Fathers François Courel and François Roustang, Number 24 in La Collection Christus, have been of great aid in countless ways, and especially in preparing the notes. To mention all who have helped is impossible, although the names of many appear in footnotes throughout the book. Nevertheless, special mention is due to the late Very Reverend Father General John B. Janssens, S.J., of happy memory, and to Very Reverend John L. Swain, S.J., then his Vicar, who first gave the translator authorization and encouragement to undertake this work; also to the following Jesuit fathers for their constant encouragement and help: Fathers Leo J. Burns, Joseph P. Fisher, Linus J. Thro, and Gerald R. Sheahan; to Fathers L. Le Guen, Rafael Aguinaga, Emmanuel Casanova, and L. Schillebeeckx, all of far-off India, and Charles J. McCarthy of the Philippines, for valuable suggestions on the translation; to Father Antonio de Aldama of the Historical Institute of the Society of Jesus, Rome, for his minute and eminently helpful scrutiny of the entire work in its almost final form; and especially to our present Very Reverend Father General, Peter Arrupe, who has shown himself so warmly interested and encouraging toward bringing the project to completion. Thanks are also due to the Vatican Press for permission to reproduce sections of Antonio Tempesta's Plan of Rome in 1593, to Marquette University Press for the use of materials from the writer's *St. Ignatius' Idea of a Jesuit University*, pages 36 and 37, and to Father Hugo J. Gerleman, S.J., for his constant and highly valued help and suggestions while the book was in process of production. To all who have helped, the writer expresses his humble, deep, and sincere thanks.

Part two

The Constitutions
of the Society of Jesus

The Documents
translated
from the Official Texts

The Formula of the Institute of the Society of Jesus

The bull *Exposcit debitum*[1] of July 21, 1550,
by which Pope Julius III confirmed and amplified
the approbation first given in the bull
Regimini militantis Ecclesiae[2] of September 27, 1540.

Julius, Bishop and Servant of the Servants of God,
for a Perpetual Remembrance of the Deed.

[1]. The duty of the pastoral office, for which the Divine Majesty has chosen us in spite of our unworthiness, requires us to encourage with paternal affection any of the faithful, and especially the religious, who are advancing along the path of God's commandments for His honor and glory and the spiritual progress of their neighbors, in order that these faithful, graciously aided by the Lord's own right hand, may the more fervently pursue the reward of eternal salvation and be heartened in their holy intention.

Encouragement to the faithful, especially to religious

1 This translation is made from the text in *Cons*MHSJ, I, 373-383.
2 Text *ibid.*, I, 24-32. On the Formula of the Institute, a document previous to the Constitutions properly so called, and printed here as a preface to them, see above, pp. 36, 44-45.

Summary of previous approbations

[2]. Sometime ago our predecessor of happy memory, Pope Paul III, received information about[3] his beloved sons Ignatius of Loyola, Pierre Favre, Diego Laynez, Claude Jay, Paschase Broët, Francis Xavier, Alfonso Salmerón, Simão Rodrigues, Jean Codure, and Nicolás Bobadilla, priests of the cities and dioceses of Pamplona, Geneva, Siguenza, Toledo, Viseu, Embrun, and Palentia. They were also Masters of Arts, graduates from the University of Paris, and trained in theological studies for many years who, inspired by the Holy Spirit, had departed from their various regions and met one another some time before. They had become companions in an exemplary and religious life, renounced the attractions of this world, and dedicated their lives forever to the service of our Lord Jesus Christ and to that of the Roman pontiff, himself and his successors. They had by then praiseworthily exerted themselves in the Lord's vineyard for many years by preaching the word of God, by privately encouraging the faithful to devout meditations and to a good and blessed life, by serving in hospitals, by teaching to children and unlettered persons the saving doctrines necessary for the education of a Christian, and, in a word, by performing with much praise in whatsoever countries they journeyed, and each one according to the grace granted him by the Holy Spirit Himself, all the services of charity which pertain to the edification of souls. Therefore our predecessor approved, confirmed, and blessed their Institute, as it was comprised within a certain norm of life[4] drawn up by them in conformity with the truth of the Gospel and the sanctions of the holy Fathers, that thus the bond of charity and the unity might be preserved both among those companions themselves and among others who would desire to follow that same Institute. He took those companions themselves (whose number he then desired not to exceed sixty) under his own protection and that of the Apostolic See. Through certain letters he also granted them permission to establish Constitutions and any statutes whatsoever which

---

3 *Dudum . . . per . . . Paulum . . . praedecessorem . . . accepto:* In the curial style of the era, within passive constructions the preposition *per* sometimes had the force of *a.* The writer of 1550 constructed this long sentence by making verbal changes in *Regimini,* [2], of 1540. Thus Paul III's "Nuper . . . accepimus quod" became Julius III's "per . . . praedecessorem . . . accepto, quod . . ." and "convenerunt" became "convenerant," "dedicarunt" became "dedicaverant," and so on.

4 The phrase . . . *eorum Institutum, sub quadam vivendi formula ab ipsis edita* reveals the origin of the title "Formula of the Institute," which is more usual though less formal and official than the titles *Regimini* or *Exposcit debitum.* Other accurate translations of *formula* in this context could be: pattern, rule, method, or formula. The title Formula of the Institute, strictly taken, comprises paragraphs [3-8] of *Regimini* and [3-6] of *Exposcit,* to which these popes added their respective introductions and concluding approval.

would further the preservation and happy progress of the Society thus instituted and confirmed. A little later that same predecessor of ours learned that, with the passing of time and the help of the Holy Spirit, the spiritual harvest of souls from that Society was becoming more abundant and also that many who desired to follow its aforementioned Institute were already studying at the University of Paris and other universities of general studies. Therefore, observing the holy life of Ignatius and his previously listed companions, he granted to that Society authority to admit freely other persons who are suitable and approved according to the Society's Constitutions,[5] in any number whatsoever, and also authority to receive coadjutors, both priestly coadjutors to help in spiritual matters and lay coadjutors to give aid in temporal and domestic functions. (After completing the tests required according to the Constitutions of this Society, these coadjutors were to be allowed, for their greater devotion and merit, to pronounce the three vows of poverty, chastity, and obedience, not as solemn vows[6] but as vows by which they would be bound for whatever time the superior general of the aforementioned Society should see fit to employ them in spiritual or temporal services; and they were to share in all the good works performed in the said Society and in all the merits, equally with those who pronounced the solemn profes-

---

5 In *Iniunctum nobis,* March 14, 1544. Text in *Cons*MHSJ, I, 81-86.
6 On solemn and simple vows in modern canon law, see Introduction above, p. 42. It was in the time of the *Decretum Gratiani* (ca. 1146) that a distinction was made between solemn vows of religion (which scarcely admitted dispensation and would invalidate an attempted marriage) and vows not solemn and more easily admitting dispensation. The latter sometimes were private and at other times were more or less equivalent to the vows today termed public and simple. From then on for some centuries the Church endeavored to prevent the founding of institutes without solemn vows and to suppress those already existing. One result was that a theory became prevalent that solemn vows were essential to the religious state. In 1540 the bull *Regimini,* [3], approved solemn vows for Ignatius' new order of clerics regular. But in 1546 the brief of Paul III, *Exponi nobis,* [2], also approved Ignatius' request to admit into his order coadjutors both spiritual and temporal with vows which were not solemn (text in *Cons*MHSJ, I, 172; cf. *Exposcit,* [2, 6]), and which were termed "simple" (in *Exam,* [13; cf. 71, 119, 120] and *Cons,* [205, 533-536, 572]), as are the first vows of the scholastics (in *Exam,* [14; cf. 121] and *Cons,* [205, 533-536, 572]). This arrangement led to great controversies, in which many theologians and canonists maintained that Jesuits with simple vows of this nature were not genuinely religious. The dispute was finally settled in 1584 by Gregory XIII, who declared that such Jesuits with simple vows are truly religious and that anyone who denies this incurs automatic excommunication (see *Ascendente Domino,* in *InstSJ,* I, 96-97). From then onward institutes with simple vows continued to multiply, despite occasional discouragement from ecclesiastical officials. But the Church herself openly encouraged them during the French Revolution, when anticlerical laws recognized only institutes engaged in educational and charitable works and banned orders with solemn vows. See *NCathEnc,* XII, 328-329.

sion in the same Society.) In his apostolic kindness, our predecessor granted still further favors and privileges, to encourage and help the previously named Society in matters pertaining to the honor of God and the salvation of souls.[7]

Now, however, that everything heretofore mentioned and previously granted by our predecessor may be more fully confirmed; and also that all the matters pertaining to the Institute of the aforementioned Society may be gathered into one document which contains the sum total of the others; and further that some points which were expressed somewhat obscurely and could cause scruples and doubt may be explained more accurately by ourselves, a petition has been humbly submitted to us. It begs us to confirm the formula which now contains the aforementioned Society's Institute, expressed more accurately and clearly than before, because of the lessons learned through experience and usage, but in the same spirit. The content of that formula follows,[8] and it is this:

The new Formula

The name of the Society

The threefold vow

The end and scope of the Society

Catechesis and other ministries

[3]. [1].[9] Whoever desires to serve as a soldier of God beneath the banner of the cross in our Society, which we desire to be designated by the name of Jesus, and to serve the Lord alone and the Church, His spouse, under the Roman pontiff, the vicar of Christ on earth, should, after a solemn vow of perpetual chastity, poverty, and obedience, keep what follows in mind. He is a member of a Society founded chiefly for this purpose: to strive especially for the defense and propagation of the faith and for the progress of souls in Christian life and doctrine, by means of public preaching, lectures, and any other ministration whatsoever of the word of God, and further by means of the Spiritual Exercises, the education of children and unlettered persons in Christianity, and the spiritual consolation of Christ's faithful

7 In *Cum inter cunctas,* June 3, 1545, *Exponi nobis,* June 5, 1546, and *Licet debitum,* October 18, 1549. Texts in *Cons*MHSJ, I, 166-169, 170-173, 356-371.

8 Paragraphs [3] through [6] are the Formula of the Institute. They were originally composed by Ignatius and his companions in 1539 as the First Sketch of the Institute of the Society of Jesus (*Prima . . . Instituti Summa*), which is printed in *Cons*MHSJ, I, 16-21. The paragraphs were submitted to Pope Paul III for approval, modified only slightly in the papal curia, and incorporated into the bull *Regimini*. See Introduction above, pp. 44, 48.

9 In various editions of the bull *Exposcit,* different editors sometimes presented the entire bull and sometimes only a part of it. Hence they variously divided it into paragraphs and numbered them differently. In the present book, presenting the entire text, references are made only to the numbers in boldface type and square brackets, e.g., [3], which are those of A. Codina in *Cons*MHSJ, I, 373-383. The other numbers, in lightface type and square brackets, e.g., [1], indicate the divisions used in some other editions which omitted most of paragraphs [1, 2, 7-10], the introduction and conclusion added by the pope to the text which Ignatius had submitted. To avoid confusion of the varying references now found in different books, it seems necessary here to give both systems of numbering.

through hearing confessions and administering the other sacraments. Moreover, this Society should show itself no less useful in reconciling the estranged, in holily assisting and serving those who are found in prisons or hospitals, and indeed in performing any other works of charity, according to what will seem expedient for the glory of God and the common good. Furthermore, all these works should be carried out altogether free of charge and without accepting any salary for the labor expended in all the aforementioned activities. Still further, let any such person take care, as long as he lives, first of all to keep before his eyes God and then the nature of this Institute which he has embraced and which is, so to speak, a pathway to God; and then let him strive with all his effort to achieve this end set before him by God—each one, however, according to the grace which the Holy Spirit has given to him and according to the particular grade of his own vocation. [2]. Consequently, lest anyone should perhaps show zeal, but a zeal which is not according to knowledge, the decision about each one's grade and the selection and entire distribution of employments shall be in the power of the superior general or ordinary who at any future time is to be elected by us, or in the power of those whom this superior general may appoint under himself with that authority, in order that the proper order necessary in every well-organized community may be preserved. This superior general, with the advice of his associates, shall possess the authority to establish constitutions leading to the achievement of this end which has been proposed to us, with the majority of votes always having the right to prevail. He shall also have the authority to explain officially doubts which may arise in connection with our Institute as comprised within this Formula. The council,[10] which must necessarily be convoked to establish or change the Constitutions and for other matters of more than ordinary importance, such as the alienation or dissolution of houses and colleges once erected, should be understood (according to the explanation in our Constitutions) to be the greater part of the entire professed Society which can be summoned without grave inconvenience by the superior general. In other matters, which are of lesser importance, the same general, aided by counsel from his brethren to the extent that he will deem fitting, shall have the full right personally to order and command whatever he judges in the

Gratuity of ministries

The distribution of offices

The authority to establish constitutions

The general congregation

The authority of the superior general

10 In the Constitutions, e.g., [677, 682, 687], and in later usage this council was termed a general congregation.

Lord to pertain to the glory of God and the common good, as will be explained in the Constitutions.[11]

Obedience to the Holy Father

[4]. [3]. All who make the profession in this Society should understand at the time, and furthermore keep in mind as long as they live, that this entire Society and the individual members who make their profession in it are campaigning for God under faithful obedience to His Holiness Pope Paul III and his successors in the Roman pontificate. The Gospel does indeed teach us, and we know from the orthodox faith and firmly hold, that all of Christ's faithful are subject to the Roman pontiff as their head and as the vicar of Jesus Christ. But we have judged nevertheless that the following procedure will be supremely profitable to each of us and to any others who will pronounce the same profession in the future, for the sake of our greater devotion in obedience to the Apostolic See, of greater abnegation of our own wills, and of surer direction from the Holy Spirit. In addition to that ordinary bond of the three vows, we are to be obliged by a

The special vow of obedience to him

for missions of any kind

special vow to carry out whatever the present and future Roman pontiffs may order which pertains to the progress of souls and the propagation of the faith; and to go without subterfuge or excuse, as far as in us lies, to whatsoever provinces they may choose to send us—whether they are pleased to send us among the Turks or any other infidels, even those who live in the region called the Indies, or among any heretics whatever, or schismatics, or any of the faithful. [4]. Therefore before those who will come to us take this burden upon their shoulders, they should ponder long and seriously, as the Lord has counseled [Luke 14:30], whether they possess among their resources enough spiritual capital to complete this tower; that is, whether the Holy Spirit who moves them is offering them so much grace that with His aid they have hope of bearing the weight of this vocation. Then, after they have enlisted through the inspiration of the Lord in this militia of Christ, they ought to be prompt in carrying out this obligation which is so great, being clad for battle day and night [Eph. 6:14; 1 Peter 1:13]. [5]. However, to forestall among us any ambition of such missions or provinces, or any refusal of them, all our members should have this understanding:

Missions should not be sought by individuals

They should not either directly or through someone else carry on negotiations with the Roman pontiff about such missions, but leave all this care to God, and to the pope himself as God's vicar, and to the superior general of the Society. This general too, just

11 This is done in *Cons*, [736-765], P. 9, c. 3.

like the rest, should not treat with the said pontiff about his being sent to one region or another, unless after advice from the
Society. [6]. All should likewise vow that in all matters which
promote the observance of this Rule they will be obedient to the   *Obedience to*
one put in charge of the Society. (He should be as qualified as   *the general*
possible for this office and will be elected by a majority of the   *His election*
votes, as will be explained in the Constitutions.)[12] Moreover, he   *and power*
should possess all the authority and power over the Society
which are useful for its good administration, correction, and
government. He should issue the commands which he knows to
be opportune for achieving the end set before him by God and
the Society. In his superiorship he should be ever mindful of the   *His manner*
kindness, meekness, and charity of Christ and of the pattern set   *of governing*
by Peter and Paul,[13] a norm which both he and the aforementioned council should keep constantly in view. Assuredly,
too, because of the great utility to the order and for the sake of
the constant practice of humility which has never been sufficiently praised, the individual subjects should not only be
obliged to obey the general in all matters pertaining to the So-   *Obedience to*
ciety's Institute but also to recognize and properly venerate   *the general as*
Christ as present in him.   *to Christ*

[5]. [7]. From experience we have learned that a life removed as far as possible from all infection of avarice and as like
as possible to evangelical poverty is more gratifying,[14] more un-   *The poverty*
defiled, and more suitable for the edification of our fellowmen.
We likewise know that our Lord Jesus Christ will supply to His
servants who are seeking only the kingdom of God what is necessary for food and clothing. Therefore our members, one and
all, should vow perpetual poverty in such a manner that neither   *Its mendicant*
the professed, either as individuals or in common, nor any house   *type*
or church of theirs can acquire any civil right to any produce,
fixed revenues, or possessions[15] or to the retention of any stable
goods (except those which are proper for their own use and
habitation); but they should instead be content with whatever
is given them out of charity for the necessities of life. [8]. However, the houses which the Lord will provide are to be dedicated to labor in His vineyard and not to the pursuit of
scholastic studies; and on the other hand, it appears altogether

12 See *Cons,* [694-710].
13 The pattern of Peter and Paul can be found in 1 Peter 5:1-3; Phil. 3:17; 2 Thess. 3:7-9;
   1 Tim. 4:12; and Titus 1:7.
14 *Jucundiorem,* which could be translated "more joyful"; but it should be noted that there
   is question of deep interior joy as distinguished from mere fun.
15 *Proventus, redditus, possessiones,* used here in highly technical meanings.

proper that workers should be provided for that same vineyard from among the young men who are inclined to piety and capable of applying themselves to learning, in order that they may form a kind of seminary for the Society, including the professed Society. Consequently, to provide facilities for studies, the professed Society should be capable of possessing colleges of scholastics wherever benefactors will be moved by their devotion to build and endow them. We now petition that as soon as these colleges will have been built and endowed (but not from resources which it pertains to the Holy See to apply), they may be established through authorization from the Holy See or considered to be so established. These colleges should be capable of possessing fixed revenues, rights to rentals, or possessions[16] which are to be applied to the uses and needs of the students. The general or the Society retains the full government or superintendency over the aforementioned colleges and students; and this pertains to the choice of the rectors or governors and of the scholastics; the admission, dismissal, reception, and exclusion of the same; the enactment of statutes; the arrangement, instruction, edification, and correction of the scholastics; the manner of supplying them with food, clothing, and all the other necessary materials; and every other kind of government, control, and care. All this should be managed in such a way that neither may the students be able to abuse the aforementioned goods nor may the professed Society be able to convert them to its own uses, but may use them to provide for the needs of the scholastics. These students, moreover, should have such intellectual ability and moral character as to give solid hope that they will be suitable for the Society's functions after their studies are completed, and that thus at length, after their progress in spirit and learning has become manifest and after sufficient testing, they can be admitted into our Society.

Colleges with fixed revenues

for the benefit of the students

[**6**]. Since all the members should be priests, they should be obliged to recite the Divine Office according to the ordinary rite of the Church, but privately and not in common or in choir. Also, in what pertains to food, clothing, and other external things, they will follow the common and approved usage of reputable priests, so that if anything is subtracted in this regard in accordance with each one's need or desire of spiritual progress, it may be offered, as will be fitting, out of devotion and not obligation, as a reasonable service of the body to God. [**9**]. These

Private recitation of the Divine Office

---

16 *Redditus, census seu possessiones,* also used here in highly technical meanings.

are the matters which we were able to explain about our profession in a kind of sketch, through the good pleasure of our
previously mentioned sovereign pontiff Paul and of the Apostolic
See. We have now completed this explanation, in order to give
brief information both to those who ask us about our plan of life
and also to those who will later follow us if, God willing, we
shall ever have imitators along this path. By experience we have
learned that the path has many and great difficulties connected
with it. Consequently we have judged it opportune to decree
that no one should be permitted to pronounce his profession in
this Society unless his life and doctrine have been probed by *Profession*
long and exacting tests (as will be explained in the Constitu- *only after*
tions).[17] For in all truth this Institute requires men who are thor- *long testing*
oughly humble and prudent in Christ as well as conspicuous[18]
in the integrity of Christian life and learning. Moreover, some
persons will be admitted to become coadjutors either for spir- *Spiritual and*
itual or temporal concerns[19] or to become scholastics. After *temporal*
sufficient probations and the time specified in the Constitutions, *coadjutors*
these too should, for their greater devotion and merit, pronounce
their vows. But their vows will not be solemn (except in the case
of some who with permission from the superior general will be *with*
able to make three solemn vows of this kind because of their *simple vows*
devotion and personal worth). Instead, they will be vows by
which these persons are bound as long as the superior general
thinks that they should be retained in the Society, as will be
explained more fully in the Constitutions.[20] But these coadjutors and scholastics too should be admitted into this militia of

17 See *Exam*, [64-79, 127]; *Cons*, [510, 516-523, 748].
18 *Conspicuos*: In some recent research of great importance, "De graduum diversitate inter
   sacerdotes in Societate Iesu," *Archivum historicum Societatis Iesu*, XXXVII (1968), 237-
   316 (abbreviated hereafter as *AHSJ*), L. Lukács indicates that diverse interpretations of
   this word *conspicuos* played a large part in the later evolution of the diversity of grades
   among priests in the Society. Ignatius' interpretation (which this bull empowered him to
   set forth in the Constitutions) is "sufficient" theological learning, as appears below in
   Exam, [12], *Cons*, [518, 521; cf. 819], and in other writings. Nadal's interpretation is
   "outstanding" theological learning. This view of Nadal gradually prevailed, especially under the generals Mercurian (1573-1580) and Aquaviva (1581-1615), and in General
   Congregation VII (1615-1616). Thus in Ignatius' view, *conspicuos* meant that the professed were to be capable or distinguished in comparison with the general run of priests
   in the 1500's, who often had very little theological knowledge; but in Nadal's view,
   conspicuos meant that they were to be outstanding or preeminent in relation to other
   priests within the Society. On all this, see also below, [12, 511, 518, 521, 819] with the
   fnn., and supplementary Note B in the Reference matter, pp. 349-356.
19 Although the Society was founded and approved as a clerical institute in 1540, Ignatius
   gradually found it expedient to add both lay and priestly coadjutors to its membership.
   This step was approved in the brief of June 5, 1546, *Exponi nobis*. Text in *ConsMHSJ*, I,
   170-173.
20 See *Exam*, [119], *Cons*, [204, 535-536].

Jesus Christ only after they have been diligently examined and found suitable for that same end of the Society. And may Christ deign to be favorable to these our tender beginnings, to the glory of God the Father, to whom alone be glory and honor forever. Amen.

The Pope's approbation of the Formula of the Institute

[7]. Wherefore we have considered that in the aforementioned Society and its praiseworthy institutes, and in the exemplary life and practices of Ignatius and other previously mentioned companions, there is nothing which is not pious and holy; that everything, instead, tends toward the salvation of their own souls and that of the other faithful, and to the exaltation of the faith. By the series of these present letters and toward their precisely intended effect, we absolve those previously mentioned companions and their coadjutors as well as the scholastics of the same Society from any sentences whatsoever of excommunication, suspension, or interdict, and from any other ecclesiastical sentences, censures, or penalties, whether these have been imposed by the law itself or by any person on whatsoever occasion or for whatsoever reason, if those companions should in any way be bound by any such penalties, and we regard them as persons thus absolved, and take them under our protection and that of the Holy See. Because of our own desire and our certain knowledge, by our apostolic authority and the content of this present letter, we forever approve and confirm the founding and organizing of the Society, and the extension of that number of its members, of the acceptance and admission of coadjutors, and its privileges one and all, immunities, exemptions, and liberties both to establish and alter statutes and ordinances, and any other indults which our predecessor and this Apostolic See thereby granted to the Society and its general and also confirmed, in whatsoever tenor and forms. We also approve and confirm any letters additionally drawn up, whether under the seal of lead or in the form of a brief, and whatever is contained in them or follows from them. We further declare all these measures to be confirmed in perpetuity; and we supply for any and all defects whether of law or of fact, if any such found their way into them. Still further, we decree and declare that those measures one and all shall obtain the strength of unshaken firmness and be inviolably observed; and that this is the manner in which they ought to be judged, interpreted, and decided by any judges and commissaries, no matter what authority they exercise (and any faculty and authority whatsoever to judge and interpret otherwise is abrogated); also, that if any attempt

to the contrary should be made, either deliberately or in ignorance, by any persons whomsoever endowed with no matter
what power, that attempt is null and void.

[8]. Therefore to one and all of our venerable brothers the
patriarchs, archbishops, and bishops, and to our beloved sons
the abbots, priors, and other persons constituted in ecclesiastical
dignity, through these apostolic writings we give command in
order that they and anyone of them may give, directly or
through one or several others, the assistance of an efficacious
rampart of defense to the general and the Society mentioned in
the foregoing documents; that they may by our authority cause
the aforementioned and present letters to obtain their full effect
and to be observed inviolably by all; and that they may permit
no one to be in any way troublesome in regard to their content.
They should check any who contradict or rebel, by employing
ecclesiastical censures and other opportune remedies, by ignor-
ing any appeal, and by increasing the aforementioned censures
even many times through the holding of the legitimate trials
which should be held in such matters; and even by invoking, if
need be, the aid of the secular arm for this purpose.

[9]. This approval is not obstructed, either by the constitutions and ordinances, one and all, which our predecessor willed
in previous documents to have no obstructive effect, or by any
other contrary consideration, or even if some indult was granted
to some persons, in common or as individuals, to the effect that
they cannot be interdicted, suspended, or excommunicated
through apostolic letters which do not make full and explicit
mention of an indult of this kind, and that word for word.

[10]. Therefore let no man whatsoever have the license to
infringe this statement of our absolution, reception, approval,
confirmation, addition, completion, decree, declaration, and
command, or to work against it by any rash presumption. If
anyone should presume to attempt this, let him know that he
will incur the wrath of Almighty God and His holy apostles
Peter and Paul.

Given at Rome, at St. Peter's, on July 21, in the year of the
Incarnation 1550, in the first year of our pontificate.

F. de Mendoza   Federico Cardinal Cezi

The General Examen
and its Declarations

The First and General Examen[1]
which should be proposed [A] to all
who request admission
into the Society of Jesus

Chapter 1
The Institute of the Society of Jesus
and the diversity of its members

[1]—1. This least congregation,[2] which at its earliest founda-

---

1 When taken strictly, Ignatius' title of "General" Examen applies only to Chapters 1 through 4. Chapters 5 through 8 are particularized examens for specific classes of applicants.

2 According to Laynez (*FN*, II, 131-133), Ignatius customarily called the Society "least" for three reasons: its weak human foundation, humility, and its late origin in the history of the Church. St. Francis of Assisi had called his friars *Minori* and St. Francis de Paul had named his *Minimi*; and thus Ignatius called his Society *minima.*

   Congregación, used here as a synonym for Ignatius' cherished title of *Compañía* which will occur immediately, does not connote the modern distinction of Canon 488, 2°: a congregation is a religious institute in which the members take simple vows, and an order one in which some members take solemn vows. In this modern canonical sense, the Society of Jesus is an order, since its professed members take solemn vows

tion was named the Society[3] of Jesus[4] by the Holy See, was first approved by Pope Paul III, of happy memory, in the year 1540.[5] Later it was confirmed by the same Holy Father in 1543[6] and by his successor Julius III in 1550.[7] On other occasions too it is mentioned in different briefs and apostolic letters which grant it various favors and thereby presuppose high approval and confirmation of it.

[2]—A. *This Examen is usually proposed to all after they*
a) 146, 198, 199 *enter the house[8] of the first[9] probation.[a] Nevertheless, if in*
some particular case discretion should suggest that another and

(*Regimini*, [3]; *Exposcit*, [3, 6]; *Cons*, [524-530]). See Introduction above, p. 42, and fn. 6 on *Exposcit*, [2] above.

3 *Compañía de Jesús*, or *Societas Iesu* in the Latin translation of 1558, is the title to which Ignatius clung tenaciously after the vision at La Storta in 1537 through which he was assured of his close association with Christ. When he wrote the title here in ca. 1546 and left it unaltered until 1556, its basic meaning for him and his followers was an organized group which has Jesus as its head and is completely at His service (see, e.g., *EppIgn*, I, 116; *FN*, I, 204, 314; II, 10, 133-134, 310, 377, 595-597; *DeGuiJes*, pp. 38, 42; Granero, *San Ignacio*, p. 175). However, the title carries many connotations and overtones. It received different interpretations and emphases, supplementary rather than exclusive, from Ignatius' companions even in his lifetime, as well as misinterpretations from his opponents. This title has been so much discussed that it can scarcely be treated adequately in a footnote. See the supplementary Note A, pp. 345-349 below.

4 For the various spiritual meanings of this title, see J. Iturrioz, "*Compañía de Jesús*. Sentido histórico y ascético de este nombre," *Manresa*, XXVII (1955), 45-53; M. Giuliani, "Compagnons de Jésus," *Christus*, no. 6 (1959), 221-239; T. Baumann, "Compagnie de Jésus. Origine et sens primitif de ce nom," *RAM*, XXXVII (1961), 47-60; Granero, *San Ignacio*, pp. 72-73, 84, 89, 175; and supplementary Note A in the Reference matter, below, pp. 345-349.

5 In Paul III's bull of September 27, 1540, *Regimini militantis Ecclesiae*, which restricted the number of members to sixty. He had given an oral approval earlier at Tivoli on September 3, 1539 (*Cons*MHSJ, I, 22).

6 In the bull *Iniunctum nobis*, found in *Cons*MHSJ, I, 81-86, which cancelled the restriction to sixty members and repeated the faculty of composing Constitutions. The bull was dated March 14 of the year of the Incarnation 1543, i.e., of the year which had begun the preceding March 25. But this was already March 14, 1544 according to the civil year which had begun January 1.

7 In the bull *Exposcit debitum*, July 21, 1550, the Formula of the Institute which is the Society's fundamental Rule. Ignatius' Constitutions are determinations of the statements in this Formula. For the text of the bull, see *Cons*MHSJ, I, 373-383, and above, pp. 63-73.

8 In the Constitutions, Ignatius used "houses" and "colleges" as technical terms. Houses (*casas, domus*) were dwellings intended chiefly for formed Jesuits who had completed their studies and were engaged in apostolic work while living exclusively on alms, whereas colleges (*colegios, collegia*) were dwellings which could possess fixed or regularly recurring revenues and were intended chiefly for students (*scolares, scholastici*) or professors (*Cons*, [289]; *Cons*MHSJ, II, cxxxviii-cxliv). Ideally, a house of first probation was to be separated from a house or college but related to it. But if necessary a portion of an existing Jesuit dwelling could be separated off and used for the first probation ([190-192]; cf. [18-20]). See also Coemans, *Introductio*, nos. 62-64, and fnn. 18 and 19 on [289, 290] below.

9 In 1541, candidates to the Society went through three periods of probation: the first, three months (six months from 1545 to about 1549) spent in the experiences of mak-

*more summary examen be proposed, or that the present text
be handed out to be read without asking for replies about its
contents, or if the knowledge possessed about some candidate is
already sufficient, it would not be necessary to conduct the
examination by means of this present text. The examiner,*[b] *how-*   b) 142
*ever, ought to discuss this with the superior and follow his
opinion. In most instances, it is before the candidates enter the
house that they will be examined about certain essential matters,
especially those which bar admission.*[c]   c) 146, 196

[3]—2. The end of this Society is to devote itself with God's
grace not only to the salvation and perfection of the members'
own souls,[10] but also with that same grace to labor strenuously

---

ing the Spiritual Exercises, visiting hospitals, and the like; the second, one year of probations, which was usually spent in studies by those who had not yet completed them;
and the third, another year spent in preaching and humble apostolic works preparatory
to final profession (*Cons*MHSJ, I, 56, 59-60, nos. 17, 18; II, cxxxviii). After experience
and experimentation, the duration and arrangement changed to those found in text B
(1556) of the Examen and Constitutions. According to it, the first probation was to last
12 to 15 days during which the candidate was a guest, examining the Society and being
examined by it ([18, 190, 191]). The second probation was to consist of two
years of spiritual training or novitiate. They led candidates who had not yet completed
their studies to (1) simple but perpetual vows of poverty, chastity, and obedience
along with the promise to enter the Society through final vows years later ([16, 336]),
and thus to (2) entrance into the colleges for intellectual training as approved scholastics
([336]); but some, e.g., priests who had completed their studies before entrance, could
be admitted right after this biennium to solemn profession ([16, 98]). The third probation, made after the completion of the studies and later called the tertianship, was a
year of spiritual formation through apostolic work and preaching, often requiring lowly
and disagreeable work as means to its success, by which the young priest proved his
willingness to do the Society's often humble work ([71, 516] with the footnotes). Thus
the years spent by an approved scholastic between the second and third probations are
a prolongation of the second probation, although they have occasionally been called a
"third probation in a wider sense" (e.g., in *Constitutiones Societatis Jesu Latinae et
Hispanicae* [Rome, 1937], p. 383).
10 "Souls," *ánimas* in Ignatius' Spanish, here means the persons, the men considered as
their entire selves. This was a frequent meaning of the word for "soul" in all the
languages of Christendom, as it was of the Latin *anima* in classical times (e.g., *Aeneid,*
xi, 24; Horace, *Satires,* i, 5, 41) and in Christian writers too. Ignatius also uses *ánima,*
soul, in contrast to *cuerpo,* the body, e.g., in [812-814].
   The use of the Latin *anima* and Spanish *ánima* to mean the living man, the self,
the person, is scriptural and occurs very frequently in the Latin Vulgate, especially in
texts frequently quoted such as Matt. 16:26; Mark 3:48, 8:36 (Cf., e.g., Gen. 2:7,
12:5, 49:6; Exod. 1:5; Acts 2:41; 1 Cor. 15:45). Hence this usage was common in
all the languages of Christian Europe throughout the Middle Ages (see, e.g., Blaise,
Dictionnaire . . . des auteurs chrétiens, s.v. "anima," 4; also, Peter Lombard's *Sentences,*
II, 1, no. 8). Awareness of this usage is a key necessary for accurate interpretation of
virtually all Christian writers on spirituality. Because of their heritage of Greek philosophy, medieval theologians and later spiritual writers regarded this, more frequently
than modern scriptural scholars, as the figure of synecdoche by which the part (*anima*)
was taken for the whole, the living man (*homo*). Even this synecdoche, however, has
a scriptural basis (Wisd. 3:1, 8:19-20). In the Spanish of the 1500's (as we gather s.v.

d) 156, 163, 258, 307, 308, 446, 586, 603, 813

in giving[11] aid[12] toward the salvation and perfection of the souls of their fellowmen.[d]

[4]—3. To achieve this end more effectively, the three vows of obedience, poverty, and chastity are taken in the Society.[e] Poverty is understood to mean that in the Society no fixed revenues[13] may be sought or possessed for the Society's living expenses or for any other purpose.[f] This holds true not only of the individual members but also of the churches or houses of the professed Society.[14] Neither may the members accept any stipend or alms for Masses, sermons, lectures, the administration of any of the sacraments, or for any other pious function among those which the Society may exercise in accordance with its Institute (even though such acceptance would be permissible for others). Such stipends or alms are customarily given in recompense for the ministries mentioned; but the Society's

e) 13, 14, 121, 527, 532, 535, 537, 540, 544, 547-581

f) 555, 561-564, 570, 572, 816

---

from the *Tesoro* [A.D. 1611] of Covarrubias, who refers to Gen. 12:5 and 14:21), *ánima* and its synonym *alma* have among their meanings "that by which we live" and are "often used for the persons." Ignatius' use of *ánima* rather than *hombre* or *homo* has occasionally been taken as evidence of exaggerated dualism or even of Neoplatonism in his thought. In the light of the pervading influence of the Latin Vulgate and its use of *anima* throughout the Middle Ages, this interpretation appears to be farfetched and groundless.

11 At first sight Ignatius may appear to propose two ends of the Society, the spiritual development of the members themselves and apostolic aid to their fellowmen. François Courel maintains convincingly that in Ignatius' concept there is in reality but one end, greater glory to God, sought by means of personal sanctification and apostolic activity. See "La fin unique de la Compagnie de Jésus," *AHSJ*, XXXV (1966), 186-211.

12 The use of *ayuda* and *ayudar* to express either spiritual progress or apostolic activity is a frequent trait of Ignatius' style. See, e.g., in [63], *para más ayudarse en su spíritu,* to help one another more in the spiritual life. Possibly Ignatius was influenced in this by the similar use of "be aided" in Peter Lombard's *Sentences,* II, 1, no. 8, cited above on p. 19.

13 *Rentas, redditus:* fixed or regularly recurring revenues to which one has a right as they come due periodically, such as annually. The sixteenth-century meaning and connotations appear in Covarrubias' definition, s.v. *renta:* "that which one collects, either from his secular estate (*hazienda temporal*) or from his benefices, from *reddendo,* because they accrue to him with them and come in anew each year." Under *beneficios,* ecclesiastical benefices, Covarrubias quotes the definition of canonists: "Beneficium dicitur quaedam benevola actio, tribuens gaudium capienti." Ecclesiastical fixed incomes are called benefices because of their being favors done and conferred by the popes.

14 In the poverty of the mendicant orders, neither their houses nor their members could own stable material goods; their financial support came either from begging or from their own work (see ch. 5 of St. Francis' Rule of 1223, in *The Writings of St. Francis of Assisi,* trans. B. Fahy [London, 1964], p. 61; *NCathEnc,* XII, 291; *Cons*MHSJ, I, 35, fn. 3). This is the form of poverty which Ignatius and his companions chose.

    Already on June 11, 1539, they reached this "determination": "That houses for our habitation or churches will be accepted, but in such a manner that no right of proprietorship is acquired over them; but rather, in such a way that those who will give us the use of them may freely take them back whenever they wish, without any contradiction from us. Even more, we should not have any right to litigation for them after they have been abandoned in whatsoever way, even against one lodging a

members may not accept them from anyone other than God
our Lord; and it is purely for His service[15] that they ought to
do all things.[g]

g) 82, 398, 478,
499, 565, 566,
640, 816

[5]—4. Furthermore, although the Society owns colleges
and houses of probation which have fixed revenues for the
living expenses of the scholastics before they enter into the
professed Society or its houses[h] [B], nevertheless, in conformity
with the bull[16] which is explained in the Constitutions, the
revenues of this kind may not be used for another purpose.
Neither the houses of the professed nor anyone of the professed
or their coadjutors may use these revenues for themselves.[i]

h) 554

i) 326, 419, 557,
763, 774, 815,
816

[6]—*B. These houses of probation are in a way branches of
the colleges; and in them those who will later be stationed in
the colleges are received and tested for a time.*[j]

j) 328

[7]—5. In addition to the three vows mentioned, the professed Society also makes an explicit vow to the sovereign pontiff[17] as the present or future vicar of Christ our Lord. This is a

complaint in a manner altogether unjust" (*Cons*MHSJ, I, xlviii, 13). This prohibition
of any right to proprietorship over stable goods was incorporated into the *Prima . . .
Instituti Summa*, [5] and *Regimini*, [6]. But experience showed the need of some
change, which came in the exception granted by *Exposcit*, [5]: Neither the professed
nor their houses or churches may "acquire any civil right to . . . stable goods (except
those which are proper for their own use and habitation)." Hence proprietorship over
such stable goods is permitted. See also Coemans, *Introductio*, nos. 59-62, and fnn. 2-7
on [553-556] below.

15 In this paragraph the candidate is informed that the professed members of the Society,
as also its houses as distinguished from colleges, are not to possess or live from fixed
revenues but to subsist on alms, though not from those alms which could be considered
stipends given in recompense for spiritual ministrations. Thus Ignatius is prescribing
gratuity of ministries, something which in his day was proper to and characteristic
of the Society. The legislation on poverty given so sketchily in [4] is filled out later,
especially in [149, 557, 560, 564, 569].

This prescription of complete gratuity of ministries could be observed in Ignatius'
day but became impossible with evolving economic circumstances. Hence the Society
received papal dispensation to accept stipends and alms for certain spiritual ministrations, on various occasions and for various circumstances, especially after 1838. For
references, see *InstSJ*, III, 656; *Colld*, no. 316.

Ignatius did not mention the topic of living from salaries or the fruit of labor,
probably because it was not important in his day. But it has become important in
recent years. General Congregation XXXI (1965-1966) issued a new decree to adapt
the practice of poverty to the changed modern conditions and submitted it for the Holy
Father's approval, which he gave. This new decree recognizes that in our day poverty
is expressed not merely by living from alms but also by living from the fruits of one's labor.

16 See the Formula of the Institute, *Exposcit debitum*, [5].

17 "Vow to the sovereign pontiff": this expression involves an ellipsis. The special vow is
a promise made to God (as the words "promitto omnipotenti Deo" in [527] clearly
show). To this promise to God is added ("insuper") another vow of special obedience

vow to go anywhere His Holiness will order,[18] whether among
the faithful or the infidels, without pleading an excuse and
k) 573, 574, 609,
610 without requesting any expenses for the journey,[k] for the sake
of matters pertaining to the worship of God and the welfare
l) 527, 529, 603,
605 of the Christian religion.[l]

m) 580 [8]—6. In other respects, for sound reasons and with attention always paid to the greater service of God, in regard to what
is exterior the manner of living[19] is ordinary.[m] It does not
contain any regular penances or austerities which are to be
practiced through obligation. But those may be taken up which
each one, with the superior's approval [C], thinks likely to be
n) 263, 300, 582 more helpful for his spiritual progress,[n] as well as those which
the superiors have authority to impose upon the members for
o) 90, 98, 269 the same purpose.[o]

[9]—C. *This decision will be left within the superior's power;
and he may delegate his authority to the confessor or other
persons when he thinks this expedient.*

to the pope (see *ibid.*). However, the promise to God is expressed "in the presence of"
or "in the hands of" the pope or his delegate. Cf. "Determinationes Societatis" of 1539,
[1], in *Cons*MHSJ, I, 10: " . . . votum obedientiae expressum ipsi summo pontifici . . .
per manus prelati Societatis . . . " See also [283] with fn. 14, [539, 603], "the vow
which the Society made [sc. to God] to obey him [sc. the pope]. . . ."
18 Such errands or tasks are the missions properly so called which are treated in *Cons,*
P. 7, c. 1, 2. Examples are the pope's sending Xavier to India in 1540 and Broet and
Salmerón to Ireland and England in 1540. The special vow of obedience to the pope
was unanimously decided upon by all the companions present in Rome in 1539
(*Cons*MHSJ, I, 10), while Broët and Rodrigues were absent, having been sent on a
mission to Siena by Paul III. This vow, and whether or not it adds something to the
common obligation of all priests and religious, has been the subject of much discussion
since Cardinal Ghinucci first raised the question shortly after September 3, 1539 (see
Coemans, *Introductio,* no. 44). At the very least the vow is an inspiring expression of
Ignatius' spirit of intense desire to be closely and cooperatively associated with the pope
as Christ's vicar. The idea of making such a vow sprang naturally from his desire to be
closely associated with Christ, and consequently with His vicar, in progressively achieving
God's redemptive plan. Assurance of that association was granted to him in the vision
at La Storta.
19 *La vida es común,* i.e., common or ordinary to the general run of men (see Covarrubias,
s.v. *común*). There is not emphasis here on the canonical concept of common life by
which religious must draw from the common supply to satisfy their material needs; that
is treated by Ignatius below in [570]. What this "ordinary life" as treated here meant
to Ignatius and his companions is clear from Nadal's commentary on this passage
(*MonNad,* V, 57-61, esp. [52] on 60; see also Laynez, in *FN,* II, 138). Ignatius at
first practiced unusual penances, wore poor clothes, and the like. But he found that
such practices repelled men and hindered greater good, his apostolic purposes, while
ordinary and familiar association, carried on in such a way that their witness as religious
was clear, fostered these men's friendship, won them, and opened them to grace. Moreover, the first companions found that fasts and penances could weaken or depress one
and impede his apostolic effectiveness (*Prima . . . Instituti Summa,* [7], in *Cons*MHSJ,
I, 20). Hence in his legislation Ignatius prescribed an ordinary manner of living as more

[10]—7. The persons who are received into this Society of Jesus, considered as a whole, are of four[p] classes[20] [D], in view *p*) 511 of the end which the Society pursues. But on the side of those who enter, all ought to be men of the fourth class which will *q*) 15, 72, 111, be described below.[q]   132

important for the Society's purposes than austerities, although he himself praised these and never abandoned penances which were not excessive.

20 For the apostolic purposes which he had in view, Ignatius established the following classes or grades of members in the Society. The "professed" are the fully formed priests who have the three solemn vows of poverty, chastity, and obedience, plus a fourth solemn vow of special obedience to the pope. The "spiritual coadjutors" are priests, in Ignatius' day of lesser learning or degrees than the professed, who are assigned to ministerial labors. The "temporal coadjutors" are the lay brothers who help in temporal or exterior matters such as cooking or gardening (*Cons*, [148, 149]). The "approved scholastics" are the Jesuit students, who upon completing their two years of novitiate, have taken their simple but perpetual vows of poverty, chastity, and obedience, along with a promise to become full members as professed or spiritual coadjutors after their studies are completed. The "indifferents" or undetermined were those who upon entering the Society left it to their superiors to decide later on whether they were to be priests or lay brothers. In modern times, applicants have been admitted as "indifferents" only with great rarity. On the classes or grades of members, see *Cons*MHSJ, II. cxxviii-cxxix; Dudon, *St. Ignatius*, pp. 292-293. See also [510, 511, 516-523], with their fnn., and the supplementary Note B in the Reference matter, below. For updating of the lay brothers' status, see General Congregation XXXI, Decree 7; also, the consensus statements from Santa Clara, Cal., *Total Development of the Jesuit Brother* (Detroit, 1969).

The recent research of Lukács, "De graduum diversitate," *AHSJ*, XXXVII (1968), 237-316, has furnished extensive new information about Ignatius' establishing two classes or grades among his priests. A brief summary of Lukács' article is this.

Ignatius knew that he could not obtain enough recruits among men already trained in theology. He also knew that many years must pass before the untrained youth he was admitting could acquire, in numbers adequate for his purposes, the sufficiency of theological learning which he desired his professed members to have. Therefore he devised an original procedure. He decided to admit some candidates who, although often already priests, had little theology or aptitude to learn it (e.g., because of age), but who could help the Society in its apostolic work by celebrating Mass, hearing confessions, catechizing, and other humble ministries. After explaining his lack and need of helpers to Pope Paul III, he received permission, in the bull *Exponi nobis* of 1546, to have such priests, whom he called spiritual coadjutors, and also lay brothers to help in temporalities. The papal brief stipulated that all these helpers were to be bound by simple vows for the time that the general judged himself to need their aid. Ignatius required his professed members to possess "sufficient" theological knowledge (*doctrina . . . suficiente*), such as could be obtained in the organized four-year curriculum he devised (*Constitutions*, [418, 518, 519]); but he was content to have the spiritual coadjutors possess, like so many priests of the era, only enough knowledge of grammar and of cases of conscience to hear confessions. It seems that he expected his institution of spiritual coadjutors to be a temporary measure. They would no longer be necessary after enough of the scholastics finished the theological studies he prescribed for them; and hence the institution itself would disappear. But exactly the opposite happened after Ignatius' death. The percentage of those priests given the vows of spiritual coadjutors rose from 8% in 1556 to 11.6% by 1565, 24.9% by 1572, and then to 46% under Mercurian as general (1573-1580). The chief reason for this surprising evolution seems to have been Nadal's interpretation of the words "men conspicuous for . . . learning" in the bulls *Regimini*, [8] and *Exposcit*, [6]. He inculcated that this meant men so "outstanding" in theology that they could teach it successfully. There are cogent arguments to show that Nadal's opinion was erroneous as an interpretation of Ignatius'

r) 520, 531, 532

[11]—D. *In addition to these four classes of members, some are accepted for solemn profession of three vows,*[r] *in conformity with the bull of Julius III.*[21]

s) 524-530

t) 308, 518, 519

u) 308, 516, 819

[12]—8. First, some are received to make the profession in the Society with four solemn vows[22] (as has been stated),[s] after they have undergone the required experiences[23] and probations. These members should possess sufficient learning,[t][24] as is explained later on in the Constitutions [518, 519], and they should be tested at length in their life and habits, in conformity with what a vocation of this kind requires.[u] Also, all of them must be priests before their profession.

[13]—9. The second class consists of those who are received to become coadjutors in the service of God and to aid the

---

writings. But it gradually prevailed, was incorporated into the policy of Mercurian and Aquaviva, and into permanent law by General Congregation VII (1615-1616). Nevertheless, the existence of the grade of spiritual coadjutors continued to cause difficulties, humiliation, and sadness in the Society. Hence the percentage of spiritual coadjutors among the priests steadily decreased until it was only 5.1% by 1773. Thus it appears that the grade of spiritual coadjutor would soon have disappeared if the Society had not been suppressed (*AHSJ*, XXXVII [1968], 237, 315-316). Further background and some documentation on this summary are given in Note B in the Reference matter, pp. 349-356 below.

21 *Exposcit,* [6].
22 On the canonical distinction between solemn and simple vows, see above, p. 41, and fn. 6 on *Exposcit,* [2]. Modern terminology often uses the term "profession" of simple vows. But in Ignatius' usage, the term profession (*profesión*) always refers to solemn vows.
23 *Experiencias y probaciones.* The Spanish *experiencia* has three important meanings: (1) a testing, (2) experience, the knowledge gained through doing or testing rather than instruction, and (3) an experiment through which such knowledge is gained, often by trial and error. In Covarrubias' sixteenth-century definition (p. 555), *esperiencia* is knowledge or information about something, gained by use, testing, and experimentation, without instruction by someone else. In Ignatius' usage of *experiencia,* the emphasis shifts according to context from one of these three meanings to another; but in whichever meaning the stress is found, the other two are usually implied or connoted and color the first. The use of a doublet, e.g., by adding the explanatory *probaciones,* often reveals test as the meaning chiefly in mind. Here, e.g., the Society tests the candidate's worthiness; and he learns by experience, some of which is experimentation. Although the idea of *experiencia* was expressed by the Latin *experientia* in the brief *Exponi nobis* of 1546 (*Cons*MHSJ, I, 171), the translators of 1558 rendered *experiencias* by the Latin *experimenta,* which in turn has sometimes been turned into English by "experiments." But no single English word seems to give a satisfactory rendering of *experiencia* in its different contexts. See also fn. 7 on [64] below, and F. Roustang in *Christus,* no. 10 (1963), 335-352; also Courel, *Constitutions,* I, fn. 3 on [64].
24 *Letras.* With great frequency Ignatius uses this word in its meaning of learning in general, e.g., in the title of Part IV of the Constitutions, or in *Cons,* [307], where it is equivalent to *doctrina.* Sometimes it specifically denotes humanistic learning of Latin and Greek, e.g., in [447, 448], but often it extends to learning in general, e.g., [518, 521]. In Covarrubias' concept (p. 763), lawyers no less than humanists were considered to be among those termed *letrados.*

Society in either spiritual or temporal matters.[v] After their experiences and probations these are to take three simple vows of obedience, poverty, and chastity, without taking the fourth vow of obedience to the pope or any other solemn vow.[w] They should be content with their grade,[x] knowing that in the eyes of our Creator and Lord those gain greater merit who with greater charity give help and service to all persons through love of His Divine Majesty, whether they serve in matters of greater moment or in others more lowly and humble.

[14]—10. The third class consists of those who are received to become scholastics,[y] [25] since they seem to have the ability and other qualifications suitable for studies. They are received that after being educated[z] they may be able to enter the Society[a] either as professed or as coadjutors, as will be judged expedient. To become approved as scholastics of the Society, these too must undergo their experiences and probations[b] and then pronounce the same three simple vows[26] of poverty, chastity, and obedience, along with a promise that they will enter the Society in one of the two manners just mentioned (as will be seen later in the Constitutions [537-541]), for the greater glory of God.[c]

[15]—11. The fourth class consists of those who are received indeterminately for whichever grade they will in time be found fit.[d] The Society does not yet determine for which of the aforementioned grades their talent is best suited. They in turn should enter as still indifferent[27] with respect to whichever of the previously mentioned grades the superior will think best. In fact all, as far as they themselves are concerned, ought to enter with a disposition of this kind, as has already been said.[e]

[16]—12. Furthermore, before anyone is admitted to profession or required according to our Institute to take the pre-

v) 112-114, 119, 522

w) 119, 533-537

x) 116-118, 148, 150, 542, 543

y) 308, 333-336, 523

z) 518

a) 121, 541

b) 121, 336

c) 121, 336, 348, 511, 537-541

d) 130

e) 10, 72, 111, 132

---

25 *Scholares.* Ignatius used this term to designate either the student members of his own order or extern students. In the Latin translation of 1558 his term was sometimes translated by the Latin *scholares* (e.g., in [326]), but usually by *scholastici.* Consequently, in time English-speaking Jesuits grew accustomed to call Jesuit seminarians scholastics.

26 The meaning and juridical evolution of the simple vow of the scholastics is extensively presented in E. Olivares, *Los votos de los escolares de la Compañía de Jesús: Su evolución jurídica* (Rome, 1961). See also fn. 6 on p. 65 above.

27 *Indiferentes: indiferencia* is a key term in Ignatius' spiritual doctrine, used here with the same technical sense it has in *SpEx,* [23]: a person who, while faced with choice between possible important procedures, still keeps himself neutral or impartial or undetermined and withholds choice because the reasons for decision are not yet clear. See also its usages in *Cons,* [33, 72, 130, 132, 633]. The term carries no connotation of unconcern. The meaning is "those undetermined," i.e., in regard to their grade.

f) 71, 98, 119, 336, 346, 514, 537, 544

g) 71, 119, 514, 516

h) 100, 514, 515

viously mentioned simple vows of a coadjutor or of a scholastic, he will have two complete years[f] of probation [E]. Furthermore, to be admitted into either of the first two grades, the professed or the formed coadjutors, the scholastics will have an additional year[28] after the completion of their studies.[g] This time may be prolonged[h] when the superior thinks it advisable.

i) 283, 544

[17]—E. *Although they have an appointed period of two years, those who desire to take their vows before the two years expire[i] are not deprived of the freedom, devotion, spiritual profit, and merit which are found in binding oneself to Christ our Lord. However, it is not expedient for them to take these vows without the superior's permission. Nor will they through taking them be admitted before the ordinary time either as professed, or as formed coadjutors, or as approved scholastics.*

j) 197, 297, 579

k) 98, 198, 199

l) 190, 191

m) 98

n) 142, 190

[18]—13. During this two-year period (in which no special habit of the Society is received [F]),[j] and before its end when they must bind themselves by vows in the Society, each one ought on several occasions to see and ponder the bulls of the Institute of the Society, and the Constitutions and rules which he must observe in it[k] [G]. The first time is when he is in the house of the first probation,[l] where those desiring to enter the Society are customarily received as guests for twelve or fifteen days that they may reflect more carefully upon their whole situation, before they enter a house or college of the Society to live and associate with the others [H]. The second time is at the end of their six months of experiences and probations.[m] The third is after another six months, and similarly afterwards until the one who is to become a professed at the end of his studies makes his profession, and the one who is to become a coadjutor takes his three vows, and the one who is to be an approved scholastic pronounces his three vows with his promise. This is done that both sides may proceed with greater clarity and knowledge in our Lord,[n] and also that the more the subjects' constancy has been tested, the more stable and firm they may be in the divine service and in their original vocation, for the glory and honor of His Divine Majesty.

[19]—F. *Although there is no specified habit, it will be left to the prudence of the one in charge of the house to decide whether he will allow the novices to go about in the same*

28 In English-speaking countries this final year of training and testing is commonly called the tertianship. On it, see [514-516] with fnn. 4 and 5.

apparel which they brought from the world or oblige them to make a change; or again, when the garments become worn, whether he will give to the novices others more suitable for their own needs and for their service of the house.

[20]—G. *It will not be necessary for the novices to see all the Constitutions, but only a set of excerpts*[29] *from them, in which they learn what they must observe,*° *unless perhaps for special reasons the superior thinks it better that all the Constitutions be shown to someone.*   o) 199

[21]—H. *The phrase "to live and associate with the others" is used because at their first entrance the candidates are kept apart from the rest for twelve or fifteen days, or even as long as twenty, in the house of the first probation, as will be seen in Part I of the Constitutions.*ᴾ   p) 190, 191

Chapter 2
Some cases about which
a candidate to the Society
should be questioned [A]

[22]—1. *Among the cases about which all candidates ought for good reasons to be questioned,*[1] *the first is this: Has the*

---

29 *Un extracto dellas:* Largely from this passage sprang the collection of excerpts from the Constitutions which is well known among Jesuits and entitled *A Summary of the Constitutions.* Already in 1553, while Ignatius was still alive, Nadal promulgated in Spain a collection of excerpts entitled "Rules Excerpted from the Examen and Part III of the Constitutions." The first words were: "The Supreme Wisdom and Goodness of God . . ." ([134]). After some four such collections had been used, the first official and printed text appeared at Rome in 1560 under Laynez, with the words on page 1: "Quaedam ex constitutionibus excerpta, quae ab omnibus observari debent." In 1590 Mercurian, complying with Decree 27 of General Congregation III, added excerpts from Parts I, II, IV-X, and published this revised text, which was again slightly revised by Aquaviva. It is in *InstSJ,* III, 3-9. See also *ConsMHSJ,* IV, 315 and Coemans, *Breves notitiae,* no. 84. In 1968, in accordance with a recommendation of General Congregation XXXI in its Decree 20, §2, Father General Peter Arrupe issued a new set of selected *Readings from the Constitutions of the Society of Jesus.* These selections are chosen from the Examen and all ten parts of the Constitutions and retain the sequence they have there.

1 The impediments to admission given here are treated in greater detail below in [163-189].

candidate separated himself from the bosom of the Holy Church by denying the faith, or by falling into errors against it in such a way that he has been condemned for some heretical proposition or declared suspect of one by public verdict [B], or by being excommunicated in infamy as a schismatic after he has spurned the authority and guidance of our holy mother the Church?[a]

a) 165-167

[23]—*A. Although the cases which follow are impediments which exclude[b] one from the Society, it is not wise to propose them as such before the truth about them has been brought to light; for the one who desires to enter could conceal the truth if he knew that these are impediments and the like. Nevertheless, it is good to advise the confessor to oblige him in conscience if he did not reply truthfully.[c]*

b) 30, 164, 176, 334

c) 34, 35

[24]—*B. It is evident that one who has been suspected of some erroneous opinion in a matter concerning the Catholic faith should not be admitted while such a suspicion lasts.*

[25]—2. The second case is that of ever having committed homicide or of having been publicly infamous because of enormous sins[d] [C].

d) 168-170

[26]—*C. This infamy bars admission in the place where it exists. But when one fell into the infamy in very distant regions and has completely brought himself back to the divine service, the infamy will not exclude him from the Society. It should, however, make the Society more cautious during the probation of such a candidate.*

[27]—3. The third case is that of having taken the habit of some religious institute of brothers or clerics, by living under obedience with them for a time, whether profession was made or not; or the case of having been a hermit with the garments of a monk.[e]

e) 171, 172

f) 40, 41, 173, 174, 217

[28]—4. The fourth case is that of being under the bond of consummated matrimony or of legitimate slavery.[f]

[29]—5. The fifth case is that of suffering from an illness from which the judgment may become confused and unsound, or that of having a notable disposition to fall into illness of this kind.[g]

g) 175

[30]—6. These cases mentioned above are impediments of

such a kind that no person with any one of them may be received into the Society.[h]

For in addition to other reasons, it appears to us in our Lord that, because of the ordinary and common weakness of many persons, those who hope to enter the Society in order to be good and faithful sowers in the Lord's field and to preach His divine word will be instruments the more apt for this purpose, the less they are marked by the first and second defects.

Similarly, candidates with the third defect are not received. For it appears to us in our Lord that every good Christian ought to be stable in his first vocation, above all when it is so holy, one in which he has abandoned all the world and dedicated himself completely to the greater service and glory of his Creator and Lord.[i] Finally, we are convinced in His Divine Majesty that in addition to the greater edification of our neighbors, the more all the professed, coadjutors, and scholastics are free from impediments of this kind and the more they are all of one color or likeness, so much the more will they be able to preserve themselves in the Lord with the help of His divine grace.

Neither is anyone received with the last two impediments. For the fourth would be detrimental to the neighbor, unless the consent of the wife or master is given and the other circumstances required by law are observed. The fifth, too, would be a notable detriment to the Society itself.

[31]—7. If an impediment of this kind is discovered in some candidate, he should not be interrogated further but should be allowed to depart in our Lord after being consoled as much as possible[j] [D]. When no such impediment is discovered, the candidate should be examined further [E] in the following manner.

[32]—*D. However, if some eminent qualifications are noticed in him, the examiner should inform the superior[k] before sending him away.*

[33]—*E. The order used in the Examen is: first, to go through that which is asked of all the candidates;[l] second, that asked especially of those who are learned;[m] third, that asked especially of those who are received to become coadjutors;[n] fourth, that asked of those who are received to become scholastics;[o] finally, that asked of those who are still indifferent.[p]*

Moreover, what pertains to the persons is taken up first,[q] and then what they must observe.[r]

h) 23, 164, 176, 334

i) 53, 238

j) 192, 225

k) 176

l) Chs. 1-4, 1-103
m) Ch. 5, 104-111
n) Ch. 6, 112-120
o) Ch. 7, 121-129
p) Ch. 8, 130-133
q) Ch. 3, 34-52
r) Ch. 4, 53-103

Chapter 3
Some questions to gain
a better knowledge of the candidate

[34]—1. Certain questions ought to be asked that the candidates may become better known; and in reply to these questions they ought with sincerity to tell the whole truth [A]. If some of these matters require secrecy, it will be guarded to the extent that reason demands and the one questioned requests. Thus, to begin with his name, he should be asked what his name is, how old he is, and in what region he was born.

a) 23

[35]—A. *The obligation to tell the truth in this examination should bind under sin,*[a] *a sin reserved to the same person to whom the candidate was obliged to reveal what he concealed, or to another who holds his place, in order to avoid the deception which could arise from the candidate's failure to open his mind sincerely to his superior. Such deception could also be the source of inconveniences and notable harm for the entire religious institute.*

[36]—2. Was the candidate born of a legitimate marriage or not? and if not, what were the circumstances?

Has he come from a family long Christian[1] or one recently converted?

Has any of his ancestors been accused or censured for errors against our Christian religion? In what manner?

Are his mother and father still alive? What are their names?

In what circumstances are they? What is their occupation and manner of living? Do they have temporal needs [B] or freedom from want? In what manner?

[37]—B. *If the parents are in present and extreme need of the candidate's aid, it is evident that such a one should not be admitted. Rarely, however, do such necessities occur.*

---

1 This question was prudent, especially in Spain in the 1500's, because among the Christian Moriscos and Jews (*cristianos nuevos*), some were partial conversions (often more or less forced) or pseudoconversions (see *CathEnc*, VIII, 36; *NCathEnc*, VII, 540). But many too were fervent Christians and sought to enter religious institutes; and it seems that the aim of Ignatius' question in [36] was not to exclude these *cristianos nuevos* but to be informative and ensure their reception of adequate counsel about the difficulties of religious life. See Eusebio Rey, "San Ignacio y el problema de los 'cristianos nuevos,'" *RazFe*, CLIII (1956), 173-204.

[38]—3. If at some time a difficulty or doubt should arise in his mind either about some debts or as to whether he is obliged to help his parents or relatives in some spiritual or corporal necessity or in some other temporal need of whatsoever kind, by visiting them or helping in some other manner, is he willing to relinquish his personal judgment and opinion and leave the matter to the conscience or judgment of the Society or of his superior to decide upon what he thinks to be just? And is the candidate willing to abide by that decision?

[39]—4. How many brothers and sisters has he, married and single? What is their occupation and manner of living?

[40]—5. Has he at any time given a promise of marriage, and in what manner [C]? Has he had or does he have any child?

[41]—C. *If he gave the promise by words immediately effective[2] in establishing the marriage, or by some equivalent procedure, he would be considered to have the fourth impediment.[b] This forbids acceptance into the Society for the one who has it, unless the conditions are present which are required for a married man to become a religious.*   b) 28, 173

[42]—6. Has he any debts or civil obligations?[c] If so, how   c) 185, 188, 217
many are they and of what kind?

[43]—7. Has he learned some manual trade? Does he know how to read and write?[3] If he does, he should be tested as to how he writes and reads, if this is not already known.

[44]—8. Has he had or does he have any illnesses, concealed or manifest, and what is their nature?[d] Especially, he should be   d) 185, 186
asked whether he has any stomach trouble or headaches or trouble from some other bodily malfunction, or whether he has

---

2 The Spanish terms are "por palabras de presente." The promise ("palabra") to marry mentioned in [40] is one pertaining to the future; but the promise in [41] is "por palabras de presente," one which immediately establishes the marriage. In the legal terminology of the time, "sponsalia de futuro" established an engagement and "sponsalia de praesenti" a ratified marriage. An example of an "equivalent procedure" is found in a marriage contracted by proxy.

3 In the 1500's, even many who lived in comfortable circumstances did not learn how to read or write. Perhaps less than 5% of the population had this ability (see *IdeaJesUn*, pp. 164-165; WL, XCIII (1964), 148). Many lay brothers in the Society in the 1500's could not read or write and consequently could make only the first week of the Exercises (Iparraguirre, *Historia de los Ejercicios*, II [Rome, 1955], 344-348).

On the previous education possessed by applicants, see also fn. 2 on [160].

a defect in some part of his body. This should be determined not merely by questioning but also by observing, insofar as this is possible.

[45]—9. Has he received any sacred orders? Is he under obligation from vows to make a pilgrimage or to do something else?

[46]—10. In matters salutary for his conscience, what procedure or tendency did he have in his early years and afterwards until the present? First, in regard to prayer, how often has he been accustomed to pray during the day and the night, at what hour, with what bodily posture, what prayers, and with what devotion or spiritual experience?

How has he conducted himself in regard to attendance at Mass, other divine functions, and sermons? In regard to good reading and the practice of honorable conversations? In regard to the meditation or pondering of spiritual things?

[47]—11. He should be asked whether he has held or holds any opinions or ideas different from those which are commonly held in the Church and among the teachers whom she has approved; and whether he is willing, if at some time he should hold any, to defer to what will be determined in the Society as to what ought to be held about such matters.e

e) 274

[48]—12. He should be asked whether in regard to any scruples or spiritual difficulties whatsoever, or in regard to whatsoever other difficulties which he has or in time may have, he will let his case be judged by others in the Society who are learned and virtuous persons [D], and whether he will follow their opinion.

[49]—D. *The choice of these persons to whom the one in such difficulties should entrust himself will belong to the superior, when the subject is content with that choice. Or the subject himself may choose them with the superior's approval. If in some case and for some good reason the superior should think that God our Lord will be better served and the one with the difficulties more helped by having one or several of those who are to judge the difficulties come from outside the Society, this can be permitted. But the choice of such persons, or at least their approval, should be left to the superior, as has been said. If the difficulties concern the superior's own person, the choice or aforementioned approval will belong to the consul-*

tors. However, no one inferior to the general or the provincial, even though he is a rector of a college or a superior of some house, may without permission from one of these place such difficulties concerning his person, or allow them to be placed, within the arbitration of others from outside the Society.

[**50**]—13. Is he determined to abandon the world and to follow the counsels of Christ our Lord?

How much time has elapsed since he made this general decision to abandon the world?

After making this decision, has he wavered in it, and to what extent? About how much time has elapsed since his desires to leave the world and follow the counsels of Christ our Lord began to come? What were the signs or motives through which they came?

[**51**]—14. Does he have a deliberate determination to live and die in the Lord with and in this Society of Jesus our Creator and Lord?ᶠ And since when? Where and through whom was he first moved to this?

f) 53, 126, 193, 511

If he says that he was not moved by any member of the Society, the examiner should proceed. If the candidate says that he was so moved (and it is granted that one could licitly and meritoriously move him thus), it would seem to be more conducive to his spiritual progress to give him a period of some time, in order that, by reflecting on the matter, he may commend himself completely to his Creator and Lord as if no member of the Society had moved him, so that he may be able to proceed with greater spiritual energies toward greater service and glory of the Divine Majesty.

[**52**]—15. If, after reflecting thus about the matter, he feels and judges that for him to enter this Society is highly expedient for greater praise and glory of God our Lord and also that he may better save and perfect his own soul by helping other souls, his neighbors; and if he asks to be admitted in our Lord into this Society with ourselves, then the examination may be carried forward.

Chapter 4
Some observances within the Society
which are more important
for the candidates to know

[53]—1. The intention of the first men who bound themselves together in this Society should be explained to the candidates. Those founders' mind was that those received into it should be persons already detached from the world and determined to serve God totally, whether in one religious institute or another;[a] and further, in conformity with this, that all those who seek admission into the Society should, before they begin to live under obedience in any house or college belonging to it, distribute all the temporal goods they might have, and renounce and dispose of those they might expect to receive.[b] Further still, the founders' intention was that the candidates should carry out this distribution first in regard to matters of debt and obligation, if any existed (and in that case provision should be made as soon as possible). In the absence of such obligations, the candidates should make the distribution in favor of pious and holy causes, according to the words, "He has scattered abroad and has given to the poor" [Ps. 111:9; 2 Cor. 9:9], and according to those of Christ, "If thou wilt be perfect, go, sell all that thou hast, and give to the poor . . . and follow me" [Matt. 19:21]— thus making that distribution according to their own devotion and casting away from themselves all hope of being able to possess those goods at any time.

[54]—2. If for some good reasons a candidate does not abandon those goods immediately, he will promise to give them all up, as was stated, with promptitude after one year from his entrance has elapsed, at whatsoever time during the remainder of the period of probation the superior will give him the order.[c] When this period has passed, the professed before their profession, and the coadjutors before their three public vows, must relinquish them in fact and distribute them to the poor, as was stated. This is done to embrace more perfectly the evangelical counsel which does not say "give to your relatives," but "to the poor";[1] and also to give to all a better example of divesting

a) 30, 283

b) 55

c) 55, 59, 254, 255, 287, 348, 571

---

1 St. Ignatius himself wrote an explanation of this paragraph but did not incorporate it into the text of the Examen or Declarations. His text is in *Cons*MHSJ, II, 42, fn. 5.

oneself of disordered love of relatives, to avoid the disadvantage of a disordered distribution which proceeds from that afore-mentioned love; and finally in order that, by closing the gate of recourse to parents and relatives and of the profitless memory of them, they may persevere in their vocation with propor-tionally greater firmness and stability.

[**55**]—3. However, if there should be doubt whether it would be more perfect to make the gift or renunciation of these goods in favor of the relatives rather than others, because of their equal or greater necessity and other just considerations, even so, since there is danger that flesh and blood may draw candi-dates to err in such a judgment, they must be content to leave this matter in the hands of one, two, or three persons of excel-lent life and learning (such as each one may choose with the superior's approval [A]), and to acquiesce in what these persons decide to be more perfect and conducive to greater glory of Christ our Lord.ᵈ

d) 59, 256

Consequently, the candidate should be asked if he is willing to dispose of his goods immediately (in the manner which has been stated),ᵉ or if he is content to be ready to make that dis-tribution when the superior will order it after the first year has passed.ᶠ

e) 53
f) 54, 59, 254, 287, 348, 571

[**56**]—A. *This should be interpreted to mean persons inside the Society, unless the superior for a just reason thinks that some of them should be externs.*

[**57**]—4. The candidates should be informed that no one after entering the house may keep money in his own possession or in that of some friend outside the house in the same region,ᵍ but rather that they should distribute this money for pious works or give it for keeping to the one in the house who has this charge. This person will put into a copybook all that each one brings,ʰ in case it may be necessary on some occasion to have this knowledge [B].

g) 254, 571

h) 200, 201

Accordingly, the candidates should be asked whether, if they have any money, they will be content to dispose of it in the manner just stated.

[**58**]—B. *If it happens that a candidate is dismissed and he has given something to the Society, it ought to be returned to him, in conformity with the declaration in Part II, Chapter 3,* [224].

[**59**]—5. If the candidates are ecclesiastics, they should like-wise be informed that once they have been incorporated into

i) 54, 55, 254,
287, 348, 571

j) 53, 254

the Society as professed or as coadjutors, they may not retain any benefices;[2] also, that during the time of probation but after its first year, as was stated above, they must dispose of them[i] whenever it will seem good to the superior. They make this disposition according to their own devotion,[j] by resigning them to him who conferred them or by applying them to pious works, or by giving them to worthy persons to whom they will be instruments for the service of God; and if one of those in probation should think that he ought to give them to relatives, this should not be done unless one, two, or three persons, as was stated above, judge this to be something more expedient and a

k) 55, 256

greater service to God our Lord.[k]

l) 197, 244, 246

[60]—6. Since communications from friends or relatives, whether oral or written, generally tend to disturb rather than help those who attend to the spiritual life,[3] especially in the beginning, the candidates should be asked whether they will be content not to communicate with such persons and not to receive or write letters, unless the superior judges otherwise in some cases;[l] also whether, during all the time they will be in the house, they will be willing to have all their letters seen, both those which are written to them and those which they send, thus leaving to him who holds this charge the care of delivering them or not,[4] as he will judge to be more expedient in our Lord.

2 The term "benefice" originally meant a grant of land for life as a reward (*beneficium*) for services. As canon law developed, the term came to imply an ecclesiastical office which prescribed certain duties or conditions ("spiritualities") for the due discharge of which it awarded certain revenues ("temporalities"). See *OxDCCh*, p. 156; *NCathEnc*, II, 305. The system was obviously subject to abuses, already rife in Ignatius' day. But he saw benefices as objects about which one should be indifferent, i.e., impartial (*SpEx*, [16, 169, 171, 178, 181]). He sought benefices not entailing curacies of souls for the support of scholastics in the colleges (see *EppIgn*, IX, 587; X, 630-631).

3 *Al spíritu.* Cf. "aprovecharse en su spíritu" below in [63]. Ignatius' use of the word "spíritu" merits attention. Sometimes it means the Holy Spirit, e.g., in [134, 414, 624, 700, 701]. Sometimes it is applied to man and his spiritual activity, to denote spiritual progress, interior help, or forward movement which result from man's cooperation with God's action [8, 60, 244, etc.]. It is often used as part of a doublet with grace [94], virtue [137, 243, 791], love or charity [547, 551], knowledge and doctrine [417, 819]. As an adjective, "spiritual" concretely and dynamically designates something by which man unites himself to God to discern and act with ever greater purity of intention, energy, and fidelity [101, 419, 671, 729, 819]. See F. Courel, *Constitutions de la Compagnie de Jésus*, I, 30.

4 Some form of control or inspection of letters, such as that directed here in [60] to novices, has been traditional in monastic legislation and in the constitutions of religious institutes (see, e.g., St. Benedict's Rule, ch. 54; also *ConsMHSJ*, II, 341, fn. 9; and cf., for modern times, Canon 611 of the Code of Canon Law of 1917). The same general tenor of legislation appears in no. 179 of the *Normae* of 1901 issued by the Sacred Congregation of Religious (see the English version in *RevRel*, XXV [1966], 388). After Vatican Council II, this prescription is being modified or omitted in many revisions of religious constitutions. See also fn. 3 on [244] below, and Courel, *Constitutions*, I, 31.

[61]—7. Everyone who enters the Society, following the counsel of Christ our Lord that "He who leaves father" and the rest [Matt. 19:29; Luke 18:30], should judge that he should leave his father, mother, brothers, sisters, and whatever he had in the world. Even more, he should consider as spoken to himself that statement: "He who does not hate his father and mother and even his own life, cannot be my disciple" [Luke 14:26].

Consequently he should endeavor to put aside all merely natural affection for his relatives and convert it into spiritual [C], by loving them only with that love which rightly ordered charity requires. He should be as one who is dead to the world and to self-love and who lives only for Christ our Lord, while having Him in place of parents, brothers, and all things.

[62]—C. *That the manner of speaking may be a help to that of thinking, there is a holy counsel that they should adopt the habit of saying, not that they have parents or brothers, but that they had them,*[5] *showing thus that they do not have what they gave up in order to have Christ in place of all things. However, this ought to be observed more by those who are in greater danger of some immoderation in natural love, as novices might often be.*

[63]—8. For the candidate's greater progress in his spiritual life and especially for his greater lowliness and humility, he should be asked whether he will be willing to have all his errors and defects, and anything else which will be noticed or known about him, manifested to his superiors by anyone who knows them outside of confession; and further, whether he along with all the others will be willing to aid in correcting and being corrected, by manifesting one another with due love and charity, to help one another more in the spiritual life,[6] especially when this will be requested of him by the superior who has charge of them for greater glory to God.

[64]—9. Furthermore, before he enters the house or college,

---

5 Ignatius himself advised disregard of this counsel if it might give offense or lead to undesirable results (*Sti. Ignatii Epistolae et Instructiones*, 12 vols. [Madrid, 1903-1911], VI, 474 [abbreviated hereafter as *EppIgn*]). A stronger expression by way of precept in an early draft of [62] was tempered to the present counsel through an observation of Salmerón (*Cons*MHSJ, II, 50, fn. 7; cf. I, 392, no. 7).

6 Fraternal admonition too was a traditional topic of legislation in religious institutes. See *Cons*MHSJ, II, 58, no. 8, with the references to *Regula S. Benedicti . . . cum Declarationibus et Constitutionibus Patrum Congregationis Casinensis* (Venice, 1723), p. 165; PL 66, col. 957, no. 36; and *Cons*MHSJ, I, 256, no. 28.

m) 71, 127, 746, 748

or after his entrance, six principal testing experiences[7] are required, in addition to many others which will be treated later.[m] These experiences may be advanced, postponed, adapted, and in some case where the superior approves, replaced by others, according to the persons, times, places, and their contingencies.

n) 277, 279

o) 98, 200

[65]–10. The first experience consists in making the Spiritual Exercises for one month or a little more or less;[n] that is to say, in the candidate's examining his conscience, thinking over his whole past life and making a general confession,[o] meditating upon his sins, contemplating[8] the events and mysteries of the life, death, resurrection, and ascension of Christ our Lord, exercising himself in praying vocally and mentally according to the capacity of the persons, according to what will be taught to him in our Lord, and so forth.

---

7 On the overlapping meanings of *experiencias*, see fn. 23 on [12] above. Already in 1539 (see *Determinationes Societatis*, [9] and *Prima . . . Instituti Summa*, [8] in *Cons*MHSJ, I, 12, 30), Ignatius foresaw that special tests would be necessary for his novices, to prepare them for a life of mingling among people. Throughout the previous history of religious life, the period of novitiate was simultaneously (1) an apprenticeship in living the life which was characteristic of the institute and which the novice would later be following in his daily life as a professed religious, and (2) a test of the novice's suitability for that life.

In the older institutes the noviceship was naturally an apprenticeship in monastic living within an enclosure or cloister. But Ignatius intended a new form of apostolic living which would be spent largely in mingling with men, e.g., in hospitals, villages, cities, or even, after one was missioned to a distant country (see [92]), among unbelievers. Hence he devised his "experiences" for his novices which would be an apprenticeship in such living out in the world, as he wrote already in 1541 in "De collegiis et domibus fundandis," no 18: "Hence one who is to be a member of our Society, in one way or another, must pass through experiences and tests of its life for a year and three months. The reason which impels us to establish greater experiences and to take more time than are customarily employed in other congregations is the following. If someone enters a well-ordered and organized monastery, he will be more separated from occasions of sin because of the cloister, tranquillity, and good order there than in our Society. It does not have that cloister, quiet, and repose, but travels from one place to another. Moreover, if one has bad habits and lacks some perfection, it suffices for him to perfect himself in a monastery so ordered and organized. But in our Society it is necessary that one be well-experienced and extensively tested before being admitted. For as he travels about later on, he must associate with men and women both good and bad. Such associations require greater strength and experiences as well as greater graces and gifts from our Creator and Lord" (Text in *Cons*MHSJ, I, 60; see also *Exam*, [82-85]; *DeGuiJes*, Index, p. 668, s.v. "Novitiate"; Courel, *Constitutions*, I, 32 and Roustang, "Expérience et conversions," in *Christus*, fasc. 10 [1963], 335-352).

8 *Meditando sus peccados, y contemplando . . . misterios*: in the earlier texts, *a* and also A (1550), the order of words was "meditando y contemplando sus peccados y . . . misterios." Ignatius changed the sequence to the present one, which is more in accord with his habitual usage and his distinction between *meditación*, prayer in which reasoning has a large part (*SpEx*, [45-54, 55, 65]), and *contemplación*, gazing on spiritual realities or events as present (*SpEx*, [101, 110, 190, etc.]), because of Salmerón's observation in 1551-1552 (see *Cons*MHSJ, III, 19, fn. 10; I, 392, no. 10; also, *Cons*, [277, 340, 343, 345, 582]). In the early monastic writings, "to meditate" meant to read

[66]—11. The second experience is to serve for another month in hospitals or one of them. The candidates take their meals or sleep in it or in them, or serve for one or several hours during the day, according to the times, places, and persons. They should help and serve all, the sick and the well, in conformity with the directions they receive, in order to lower and humble themselves more, thus giving clear proof of themselves to the effect that they are completely giving up the world with its pomps and vanities, that in everything they may serve their Creator and Lord, crucified for them.

[67]—12. The third experience is to spend another month in making a pilgrimage[9] without money and even in begging from door to door,[p] at appropriate times, for the love of God our Lord, in order to grow accustomed to discomfort in food and lodging. Thus too the candidate, through abandoning all the reliance which he could have in money or other created things, may with genuine faith and intense love place his reliance entirely in his Creator and Lord. Or further, these two months may be spent in hospitals, or in some one of them, or the two months may be used in making the pilgrimage, according to what seems better to the candidate's superior.

p) 82, 331, 569, 610

[68]—13. The fourth experience consists in the candidate's employing himself, after entrance into the house, with complete diligence and care in various low and humble offices, while giving a good example of himself in all of them.[q]

q) 83, 282, 365

[69]—14. The fifth experience is that of explaining the Christian doctrine or a part of it in public to boys and other simple persons, or of teaching it to individuals, in accordance with what the occasion offers and what seems in our Lord more profitable and suitable to the persons.

[70]—15. In a sixth experience the candidate, after having been tested and found edifying, will proceed farther by preach-

---

aloud, recite, mumble (see M. A. Fiorito, "La ley Ignaciana de la oración en la Compañía de Jesús," *Stromata* [Buenos Aires], XXIII [1967], 64, and the English translation of A. A. Jacobsmeyer, in *WL*, XCVII [1968], 203; *The Rule of St. Benedict*, ed. and trans. J. McCann [Westminster, Md., 1963], chs. 8, 48, and note 88 on p. 195).

9 On Ignatius' own use of the pilgrimage as a means of formation, see *DeGuiJes*, pp. 102-105. In referring to the earlier years of his conversion, Ignatius called himself a pilgrim (*Autobiog*, no. 15), and in 1541 he wrote: "it seems that one who does not know how to remain and walk for a day without eating and sleeping poorly because of this, could not persevere in the Society" (*ConsMHSJ*, I, 54). Cf. Courel, *Constitutions*, I, 32.

ing or hearing confessions, or by laboring in both together[10] in accordance with the times, places, and capacity of all.

r) 64

[71]—16. Before they enter the second year of their probation, which is made in the houses or colleges,[11] all must spend six months in undergoing the six experiences just mentioned,[r] and six additional months in different ones. These experiences may be gone through in whole or in part throughout the entire previously stated time of a candidate's probation, with sometimes some of the experiences and sometimes others coming earlier,[s] as seems expedient in our Lord.

s) 127, 746, 748

In the case of the scholastics, the experiences may be undergone during their studies or after their completion, according to persons, places, and times. But this must be observed in its entirety: Before the professed make their profession, and before the formed coadjutors take their three public though not solemn vows, two years of experiences and probations must be completed.[t] In the case of the scholastics, when their studies have been finished, in addition to the time of probation required to become an approved scholastic, before one of them makes profession or is admitted as a formed coadjutor, another year must be spent in passing through various probations,[u] especially those tests mentioned above [64] if he did not make them previously, and through some of them even if he did make them, for greater glory to God.[v]

t) 16, 98, 119, 336, 514, 537, 544

u) 16, 98, 119, 514, 516

v) 64, 127, 516

w) 10, 15, 111

[72]—17. During the time of these experiences and probations, no one ought to say that he is a member of the Society. Rather, when occasion arises, one who on the side of the Society has been examined to become a professed even though on his own side he entered as a candidate still indifferent[w] ought to say that he is undergoing the probationary experiences while desiring to be admitted into the Society in whatsoever manner it may desire to make use of him for God's glory. If he has been examined to become a coadjutor, he should say that he

---

10 "En todo" was thus interpreted by the translators of 1558, who used "in utroque." *En todo* can also mean "by laboring in general."

11 In other orders in the 1500's, the novitiate ordinarily lasted one year. Because he expected that in later life his men would live on missions more than in religious houses or monasteries, Ignatius gradually increased this period of apprenticeship and testing. In 1539 he required a candidate who needed no further studies to spend three months in experiences (the Spiritual Exercises, service in hospitals, and pilgrimage) and then one year in the probation which was the novitiate (*Cons*MHSJ, I, 12, no. 9). In 1541, one whose studies were not yet complete had to undergo three probations. The first consisted of three months spent in the same three probations. Then he went on to his studies in a college and made the first year of them his novitiate or second probation. Some time later he made a third probation of another year (*De collegiis fundandis*, 17,

is going through the testing experiences while desiring to be received into the Society as a coadjutor. The same method of replying is meant for the scholastics and the others who have been examined as candidates still indifferent, in conformity with the particular examen[x] which each of them undergoes.   x) 130-133

[73]—18. In regard to these probationary experiences, what follows should be diligently observed. That is to say, when someone has completed the first experience, the Exercises, he who gave them should inform the superior of what he thinks of that exercitant for the end which the Society seeks.

[74]—19. When he has finished the second experience, that of serving in hospitals, he should bring back the testimony of the directors or of the one who had charge of those who serve in that hospital, about the good reputation he established while there.

[75]—20. When he has completed the third experience, the pilgrimage, he should bring from the farthest place he reached, or from somewhere near it, testimony from one or several trustworthy persons, that he arrived there while pursuing his devotion and without a complaint from anyone.

[76]—21. After the fourth experience, his performing humble functions in the house, his testimony will be the edification which he gave to all those in that house.

[77]—22. After the fifth experience, his explaining Christian doctrine, and the sixth, that of preaching or hearing confessions, or both these tasks, if he lives in the house his testimony will be that coming from its residents and the edification received by the people where the house is. If his preaching and hearing of confessions occurred in other places distant from that town and house, he should bring testimony from those places where he stayed for a noteworthy time or from public persons (with much account made of all those who are ordinaries)[12] who

---

in *Cons*MHSJ, I, 59). From that arrangement gradually evolved both the terminology and the later practice of St. Ignatius and then of the Society after his death. On the history of the Jesuit novitiate, see *Cons*MHSJ, II, cxxxviii-cxl; *DeGuiJes*, Index, p. 668, s.v. "Novitiate"; and also fn. 7 on [64] above.

12 "Ordinaries": They are often but not always or necessarily bishops. In canon law an ordinary is a cleric legitimately appointed to an office to which is permanently attached jurisdiction or authority to rule, which he exercises in virtue of his office (Canons 196-198). Usually, an ordinary is a bishop who often is an ordinary of a place; but there are also other ordinaries such as vicars apostolic. In exempt clerical religious institutes like

establish complete assurance that he has sown God's word and fulfilled the office of confessor while employing sound doctrine and good practices and without offending anyone.

[78]—23. In addition to these testimonials, the Society can also, as far as it deems expedient, gather other reports for its greater satisfaction, to the glory of God our Lord.

[79]—24. When such testimonials about the experiences are not brought, the reason ought to be investigated with great diligence, through efforts to learn the truth about the entire matter, that better provision may be made in regard to everything which is helpful toward serving His Divine Goodness better,[y] through the help of His divine grace.

y) 214

[80]—25. Moreover, after one is in the house he should not go out of it without permission.[z] One who is not a priest should confess and receive the most Holy Sacrament every eighth day,[13] if the confessor does not think he has some impediment to Communion.[a] One who is a priest will confess at least every eighth day and will celebrate Mass more frequently. He will also carry out any other ordinances or constitutions of the house, according to what will be indicated to him in its rules.

z) 247, 248

a) 261, 278, 342, 343, 584

All the residents of the house will exercise themselves in learning the Christian doctrine.[b] Those whom its superior thinks should preach will do so;[c] but among these there will be no one of those who were admitted to become temporal coadjutors.

b) 277

c) 251, 280, 402, 814

[81]—26. If he is pleased to remain in the Society, his food, drink, clothing, shoes, and lodging will be what is characteristic of the poor;[d] and he should persuade himself that it will be what is worst in the house, for his greater abnegation and spiritual progress and to arrive at a certain equality and common norm among all. For where the Society's first members have passed through these necessities and greater bodily wants,[14] the others who come to it should endeavor, as far as they can, to reach the same point as the earlier ones, or to go farther in our Lord.

d) 296, 297, 577-581

---

the Society of Jesus, major superiors (such as provincials) are ordinaries for their own subjects (Canons 198, §1; 488, 8°). See *NCathEnc*, X, 726.

13 "Every eighth day" was unusually frequent in the 1500's; but the practice is now superseded by Canon 595, §2. On Ignatius' efforts to promote more frequent Communion in the Church, see *DeGuiJes*, pp. 374-385.

14 This allusion to the mendicant life led by St. Ignatius and his first companions probably refers to that at Venice, Vicenza, and Rome from 1537 to about 1541. See *Autobiog*, esp. chs. 10, 11.

[82]—27. Moreover, besides the other pilgrimages and probations explained above, the professed before making profession, the coadjutors before taking their vows, and (when the superior thinks it wise) the scholastics before becoming approved and pronouncing their vows with the promise mentioned above, should for the love of God our Lord beg from door to door for a period of three days at the times assigned them, thus imitating those earliest members. The purpose is that, contrary to common human opinion, they may be able in God's service and praise to humiliate themselves more and make greater spiritual progress, giving glory to His Divine Majesty.[e]   *e*) 67
Another purpose is to enable them to find themselves more disposed to do the same begging when they are so commanded, or when it is expedient or necessary for them as they travel through various regions of the world, according to what the supreme vicar of Christ our Lord may order or assign to them, or, in his place, the one who will find himself superior of the Society.[f] For our profession requires that we be prepared and   *f*) 569, 573, 574,
very much ready for whatever is enjoined upon us in our Lord   610, 625
and at whatsoever time,[g] without asking for or expecting any   *g*) 92, 304, 308,
reward in this present and transitory life, but hoping always for   588, 603, 626
that life which in its entirety is eternal, through God's supreme
mercy.[h]   *h*) 478, 565

[83]—28. But to come down to details, during the tests of humility and abnegation of oneself through the performance of lowly and humble tasks, such as working in the kitchen, cleaning the house, and all the rest of these services, one should take on more promptly those in which greater repugnance is   *i*) 68, 103, 282,
found, if one has been ordered to do them.[i]   289

[84]—29. When anyone begins to perform the services of the kitchen or to aid the cook, with great humility he must obey him in all things pertaining to his office, by showing him always complete obedience.[j] For if he should not do this, neither, it   *j*) 286
seems, would he show this obedience to any other superior, since genuine obedience considers, not the person to whom it is offered, but Him for whose sake it is offered; and if it is exercised for the sake of our Creator and Lord alone, then it is the very Lord of everything who is obeyed. In no manner, therefore, ought one to consider whether he who gives the order is the cook of the house or its superior, or one person rather than another. For, to consider the matter with sound understanding, obedience is not shown either to these persons or for their sake,

but to God alone and only for the sake of God our Creator and Lord.[15]

[85]—30. Therefore it is better that the cook should not request the one who aids him to do this or that, but that he should modestly command him by saying, "Do this" or "Do that" [D]. For if he requests him, he will seem more to be speaking as man to man; and it does not seem right and proper for a lay cook to request a priest to clean the pots and do other similar tasks. But by commanding him or saying "Do this" or "Do that," he will show more clearly that he is speaking as Christ to man, since he is commanding in His place. Thus the person who obeys ought to consider and weigh the order which comes from the cook, or from another who is his superior, as if it were coming from Christ our Lord, that he may be entirely pleasing to His Divine Majesty.

[86]—*D. To request and to command, each is good. Nevertheless, at the beginning one is aided more by being commanded than by being requested.*[16]

[87]—31. This same point of view should be taken of the other lowly offices when someone is giving help in them. It should also be applied in the same manner to the subordinate officials [E] who, receiving their authority from the superior, govern the house.[k]

k) 286, 434

[88]—*E. Such, customarily, are the minister, the subminister, or other equivalent officials in colleges.*

15 Ignatius' conviction was unusually deep to the effect that all authority is derived from God, especially through Christ, and that in the Church it descends from the pope as His vicar by delegation through a hierarchically ordered series of subordinate officials (see, e.g., [7, 547 with fn. 4, 662, 821]; *EppIgn*, IV, 680, no. 26; *LettersIgn*, p. 295). In Ignatius' Society the sequence is: the pope, the superior general, the provincial, the rector or local superior, and then the minor officials whom he appoints, such as even a cook. Thus, legitimately derived authority is the foundation which motivates a member to give religious obedience in commands which do not go beyond the delegated powers. The official is obeyed not so much as man but as the representative of Christ who is God; and thus the submission to a man in authority who is legitimately commanding is obedience to Christ. Obedience to the cook here in [85] is an example of such religious obedience shown to Christ through superiors or their delegates—an obedience traditional in religious institutes (see, e.g., St. Benedict's Rule, chs. 5, 35, 71). This thoroughly Christian notion was common in medieval culture and especially that of Spain which Ignatius absorbed in his youth. There kings too were commonly thought to rule "in the place of Christ" (*en lugar de Cristo*). This topic is treated extensively and well in a dissertation written at the Institut Catholique, Paris, but not yet published: J. C. Futrell, *Making an Apostolic Community of Love: The Role of the Superior according to St. Ignatius Loyola* (1967). See esp. pp. 1-15, 136-137, 415-423, 451-452.

16 Ignatius wrote the tempering Declaration D because of an observation of Salmerón (*ConsMHSJ*, II, 71, fn. 17; cf. I, 392, no. 13).

[89]—32. In time of illness one ought to observe obedience of great integrity not only toward his spiritual superiors that they may direct his soul, but also and with equal humility toward the physicians and infirmarians that they may care for his body; for the former work for his complete spiritual welfare and the latter for that which is corporal. Furthermore, the one who is sick should, by showing his great humility and patience, endeavor to give no less edification in the time of his illness to those who visit him and converse and deal with him than he does in the time of full health, for the greater glory to God.[1]   *l*) 272, 304, 595

[90]—33. For the surer achievement of everything hitherto stated and for the candidate's own greater spiritual progress, he should be asked whether he is willing to be entirely obedient in everything which has been stated and explained here, and to perform and fulfill all the penances which will be imposed on him for his errors and negligences, or for one thing or another.[m]   *m*) 8, 98, 269

[91]—34. Through reflection in our Lord, what follows has seemed good to us in His Divine Majesty. It is a matter of great and even extraordinary importance that the superiors should have a complete understanding of the subjects, that by means of it they may be able to direct and govern them better,[17] and while looking out for the subjects' interests guide them better into the paths of the Lord.[n]   *n*) 92, 263, 424, 551

17 The Society of Jesus arose largely out of the intimate fraternal association of Ignatius and his ten cooperative companions to whom he communicated the vision of apostolic service to which God had guided him. Especially as they worked together on apostolic projects at Venice in 1537 and Rome in 1538-1541, they lived in intimate friendship, shared their thoughts, and worked out their plans for apostolate in lengthy deliberations or dialogues through which they usually came to unanimous or nearly unanimous decisions. An outstanding and vivid example is the "Deliberation of the First Fathers" of 1539, through which they came to decide to unite permanently under obedience to form a new apostolic religious order (see above, pp. 47-48). In this group, Ignatius appears as a born leader. He desired his followers to have a habitual attitude of "indifference" in his technical sense of impartiality or suspended judgment, of which St. Peter Canisius has left an excellent example (*Beati Petri Canisii epistolae et acta,* ed. Braunsberger, I, 283, cited in English in M. Espinosa Pólit, *Perfect Obedience* [Westminster, Md., 1947], pp. 173-174). Yet even after his companions had elected him their superior general in 1541, Ignatius generally inspired them rather than commanded, by leading them in much discussion so that a subject came to desire what Ignatius had in view, even before the superior himself came to a definite decision or issued a precise order (see Ribadaneyra, *De ratione quam in gubernando tenebat Ignatius,* ch. 2, nos. 1-3, in *FN,* III, 613 and 619; Brodrick, *St. Peter Canisius,* p. 613, and also p. 619; *Petri Canisii epistolae,* I, 123-124; *MonNad,* IV, 662). From all this it appears that paragraphs [91 and 92] of the Examen well mirror Ignatius' attitudes, which are important background for understanding the spirit of his legislation on manifestation of conscience or interior dispositions (e.g., in [91, 97, 263, 424, 551]) and on obedience (e.g., in [84, 85, 102, 285, 547, 659, 765, 821]).

[92]—35. Likewise, the more completely the superiors know these subjects' interior and exterior affairs, just so much the better will they be able, with greater diligence, love, and care, to help the subjects and to guard their souls from various inconveniences and dangers which might occur later on. Further still, in conformity with our profession and manner of proceeding, we should always be ready to travel about in various regions of the world, on all occasions when the supreme pontiff or our immediate superior orders us.° To proceed without error in such missions, or in sending some persons and not others, or some for one task and others for different ones, it is not only highly but even supremely important for the superior to have complete knowledge of the inclinations and motions[18] of those who are in his charge, and to what defects or sins they have been or are more moved and inclined; that thus he may direct them better, without placing them beyond the measure of their capacity in dangers or labors greater than they could in our Lord endure with a spirit of love;[p] and also that the superior, while keeping to himself what he learns in secret, may be better able to organize and arrange what is expedient for the whole body of the Society.

o) 82, 304, 308, 588, 603, 605, 626

p) 91

[93]—36. Wherefore, whoever wishes to follow this Society in our Lord or to remain in it for His greater glory must be obliged to the following. Before he enters the first probation or after entering it, before his going through the general examination or some months later (if postponement should seem wise to the superior), in confession or in secret or in another manner which may be more pleasing or spiritually consoling to him, he must manifest his conscience[19] with great humility,

---

18 . . . *inclinaciones y mociones:* Ignatius here uses both words of this doublet in his own characteristic and technical meanings. The *inclinaciones* are the tendencies which arise naturally from oneself, like the "thoughts" in *SpEx*, [32]. The *mociones* are the spiritual experiences or interior motions within the soul which are produced by good or evil spirits and which are the object of discernment (*SpEx*, [313]; cf. *ibid.,* [6, 227, 316, 317, 330] and *Cons*, [92, 144], and [627] with fn. 6). In Ignatius' usage, *mociones* most often has this latter meaning of interior motions. Occasionally, however, it means the thoughts or inclinations which spring spontaneously from one's own mental or bodily faculties (see, e.g., *SpEx*, [182]; cf. [32]). See also J. Calveras, *Ejercicios espirituales: Directorio y documentos* (Barcelona, 1958), pp. 460-468.

 Noteworthy in *Cons*, [92] is the stress on the superior's knowing the positive side of the subject's character. In Ignatius' view, manifestation of conscience included the whole consciousness or general attitude, not merely a series of faults (as the English term "examination of conscience" too often connotes). In 1611 Covarrubias defined *conciencia* as "knowledge of one's self, certain or nearly certain knowledge of that which is in our soul, whether good or bad" (p. 346). See also [263, 551] below.

19 *Manifestar su conciencia:* manifestation of the interior state of one's soul was a common practice in religious life from the time of St. Anthony (d. 356). Until approximately

integrity, and charity, without concealing anything which is offensive to the Lord of all men.q He must give an account of q) 200 his whole past life, or at least of the more important matters, to him who is the superior of the Society, or to the one whom he assigns to the candidate from among the superiors or subjects, according to what he thinks expedient, in order that better provision may be made in the Lord for everything. Thus with His more abundant grace the candidate is helped more in spiritual progress, to the greater glory of His Divine Goodness.

[94]—37. The candidates, proceeding thus with an increase of grace and spirit and with wholehearted desires to enter this Society and persevere in it for their entire lives, will do the same thing on various other occasions, until those who are to be professed make their profession and those who hope to be formed coadjutors take their vows, in the following manner.

[95]—38. After one of the candidates has for the first time given an entire account of his life to the superior of the house, he should begin from that same day and, without repeating the past manifestation which he then made, give a second account of his life for the following six months or a little more or less, to the same superior or to another whom he has appointed. Afterwards, beginning with this second and proceeding in the same manner, every half year he will give a similar account. The last one will be given thirty days or a little more or less before those who are to be professed make their profession and the coadjutors take their vows.

[96]—39. The scholastics will proceed in the same manner,r r) 424 except that in the first account which they will give after com-

1000 it was used solely for the spiritual progress of the individual. St. Bonaventure (1221-1274) approved superiors' use of the resulting knowledge to adjust religious observances to the subject's capacities. St. Ignatius notably expanded this use of the manifestation as an instrument to further the subject's spiritual welfare, the government of the Society, and its apostolic works. His example was followed widely in other religious institutes both clerical and lay, many of which imposed the manifestation by rule. In some instances, especially of lay superiors, abuses arose which infringed upon either liberty of conscience or jurisdiction of confessors. Hence Leo XIII in 1890 forbade obligatory or elicited manifestation in lay religious institutes. In the Code of Canon Law (1918), Canon 530, §1 forbids superiors to induce or oblige manifestation, but §2 encourages subjects to filial openness with their superiors, even in regard to matters of conscience if the superiors are priests. On June 29, 1923, Pius XI renewed approval of what St. Ignatius' *Constitutions* contain on this topic (*ActRSJ*, IV [1923], 261). On the history of the manifestation, cf. D. Dee in *NCathEnc*, IX, 160-162; J. Creusen, trans. Ellis, Korth, *Religious Men and Women in the Code* (Milwaukee, 1965), nos. 128-132; F. N. Korth, *The Evolution of "Manifestation of Conscience" in Religious Rules, III-XVI Centuries* (Rome, 1949).

pleting their studies, they will begin from the last which they gave in the house from which they were sent to those studies. Or, if for some reason they have never given the account of their whole life, they will do so.

[97]—40. Thus also it seems that the formed coadjutors and professed, when they find themselves in a place where they are under obedience to some superior of the Society, should give him an account of their conscience every year or more often if the superior thinks it wise, in the manner stated and commencing from the last which they gave.[s]

s) 551, 764

[98]—41. A candidate who thinks that God our Lord gives him courage and strength in regard to all that has been said, and who judges his incorporation into this Society to be conducive to greater divine glory and more salutary for his own conscience, ought to see the bulls and Constitutions and all the rest which pertain to the Society's Institute, in the beginning and afterwards every six months, as was stated above [18]. In addition to this it is expedient for him to make a general confession[20] of his whole past life to a priest whom the superior appoints for him, because of the many benefits which this entails.[t]

t) 65, 200

But if he has made such a general confession to someone of the Society on some other occasion, for example, while making the Exercises or even without making them, it will suffice for him to begin the general confession from that other one and proceed to the point where he is; and afterwards he should receive the most holy body of Christ our Lord. In this same way, he will continue to make a general confession in the manner stated, every six months beginning from the last, thus procuring a continuous increase of integrity and virtues and intense desires in our Lord to give great service in this Society to His Divine Majesty.

u) 16, 71, 119, 336, 346, 514, 537, 544

When he has fulfilled the two years of probation,[u] and shown himself always obedient and edifying in his association with others and in various tests, and has with great humility performed the penances which will be imposed on him for his errors and negligences or defects;[v] and when he and the Society or the superior of the house are content, he will be eligible

v) 8, 90, 269

---

20 Similar recommendation that a general confession should be made to the superior or his delegate was common in the legislation of many religious institutes prior to Ignatius, as Iparraguirre points out (*Obras completas de San Ignacio*, p. 435), referring to the Brothers of the Common Life and to St. Basil, *Regulae fusius*, interr. 26, in PG 31, 986. Cf. Wernz-Vidal, *De religiosis* (Rome, 1933), no. 167.

to be incorporated into the Society. But previously he should consider the bulls and Constitutions and make the general confession, as was stated above. He should previously recollect himself for a period of one week, to make the confession better and to confirm himself in his first determination. During this time, too, he should make some of the former Exercises or some others.[21] Afterwards he will make his oblation and vows, either the solemn vows in the case of the professed or the simple vows in that of the coadjutors and scholastics, in the manner which will be explained later in the Constitutions [524-546], for greater divine glory and greater profit of his own soul.

[99]—42. They should be advised that after they have taken the aforementioned vows, according to the tenor of the bulls they may not transfer to other religious institutes[22] unless the superior of the Society grants permission.

[100]—43. However, when the time of the probation has elapsed, if the candidate is content and desires to be admitted thus as a professed or a coadjutor or a scholastic, but if there is doubt on the part of the Society about his talent or conduct, it will be safer to require him to wait another year, or whatever time will seem wise later on,[w] until both parties have become content and satisfied in our Lord.   w) 16, 514, 515

[101]—44. It is likewise highly important to bring this to the mind of those who are being examined (through their esteeming it highly and pondering it in the sight of our Creator and Lord), to how great a degree it helps and profits one in the spiritual life to abhor in its totality and not in part whatever the world loves and embraces, and to accept and desire with all possible energy whatever Christ our Lord has loved and embraced.[23] Just as the men of the world who follow the world love and seek with such great diligence honors, fame, and

---

21 This interesting phrase "or some others" shows that although Ignatius prescribed a week of spiritual exercises, they were not necessarily a repetition of the sequence of exercises presented in his book, *The Spiritual Exercises.* The making of the Spiritual Exercises annually has been obligatory in the Society since Decree 29 of General Congregation VI in 1608 (*InstSJ,* II, 302; cf. *DeGuiJes,* p. 237 and Index, p. 675, s.v. "Retreats"; Canon 571, 3°; Ganss, "The Authentic Spiritual Exercises of St. Ignatius," *Studies in the Spirituality of Jesuits,* I, no. 2 (November, 1969), esp. 8-20.
22 See *Licet debitum* of Oct. 18, 1549, no. 6, in *ConsMHSJ,* I, 361. To transfer to the Carthusians, however, remained licit according to this bull.
23 Ignatius' lofty and Christocentric doctrine in this entire passage ([101-103]) is virtually identical with that about the Three Modes of Humility in his *SpEx,* [165-167]. To be understood rightly, the affronts, abnegation, and injuries of which he speaks in either of these books must be fitted into their place in his world view, in which all creatures,

esteem for a great name on earth, as the world teaches them, so those who are progressing in the spiritual life and truly following Christ our Lord love and intensely desire everything opposite.[24] That is to say, they desire to clothe themselves with the same clothing and uniform of their Lord because of the love and reverence which He deserves, to such an extent that where there would be no offense to His Divine Majesty and no impu- tation of sin to the neighbor, they would wish to suffer injuries, false accusations, and affronts, and to be held and esteemed as fools (but without their giving any occasion for this), because of their desire to resemble and imitate in some manner our Creator and Lord Jesus Christ, by putting on His clothing and uniform, since it was for our spiritual profit that He clothed Himself as He did. For He gave us an example that in all things possible to us we might seek, through the aid of His grace, to imitate and follow Him, since He is the way which leads men to life.[25] Therefore the candidate should be asked whether he finds himself in a state of desires like these which are so salutary and fruitful for the perfection of his soul.

[102]—45. In a case where through human weakness and personal misery the candidate does not experience in himself

activities, and events are seen as means to the supreme end: greater glory to God than would have accrued to Him without a man's wise use of the means. Ignatius does not ask the candidate or exercitant to accept these virtues of lowliness for their own sake, as a too hasty reading of these texts without fitting them into his world view has led some interpreters to suppose. Rather, Ignatius hopes that a candidate or exercitant will become so eager to bring greater glory to God, and to be so like Christ in apostolic endeavor, that he will accept anything which will lead him toward these goals, whether it brings pain or pleasure, blame or praise. Magnanimous love of Christ will impel him to apostolic works in a persevering manner, and he will not abandon them merely because something unpleasant is involved. Pain and hardship are usually evil and one does not choose them for their own sake. But one will accept them or at least tolerate them as means to a higher goal he truly desires, or else he will miss that goal. Furthermore, he will even "love and intensely desire" poverty and humilia- tions, not for their own sakes, but as means to become more like to Christ by putting on "the same clothing and uniform of their Lord because of the love and reverence which He deserves." By means of that effort to bring greater glory to God and happiness to men, one will accomplish good works and gain happiness, self-fulfillment, and a sense of achievement. Ignatius' whole life is an exemplification of that outlook, and he gave it spontaneous though difficult expression here. On this passage, see *DeGuiJes*, pp. 129, 178, 536-537; H. Coathalem, *Ignatian Insights* (Taichung [Taiwan], 1961), pp. 176-183, esp. pp. 178-179; Ganss, "Ignatian and Jesuit Spirituality," *Proceedings of the [Santa Clara] Conference on the Total Development of the Jesuit Priest*, Vol. IV, *Background Papers* (St. Louis, 1967), pp. 8-11, 13, 43-48; and Introduction above, p. 33.

24 To oppose a tendency toward vices or undesirable practices by a tendency to their opposites is a prominent characteristic of Ignatius' spirituality. See, e.g., [265] below, with fn. 8; *SpEx*, [22, 142, 146, 157, 167]; and pp. 23-24 above.

25 Concrete examples in which Ignatius himself applied this spiritual doctrine of his are found, as Iparraguirre points out (*Obras completas de San Ignacio*, p. 437), in *EppIgn*,

such ardent desires in our Lord, he should be asked whether
he has any desires to experience them. If he answers affirmatively that he does wish to have holy desires of this kind, then,
that he may the better reach them in fact, he should be questioned further: Is he determined and ready to accept and
suffer with patience, through the help of God's grace, any such
injuries, mockeries, and affronts entailed by the wearing of this
uniform of Christ our Lord, and any other affronts offered him,
whether by someone inside the house or the Society (where he
desires to obey, be humiliated, and gain eternal life) or outside
it by any persons whatsoever on earth, while returning them
not evil for evil but good for evil?

[103]—46. The better to arrive at this degree of perfection
which is so precious in the spiritual life, his chief and most
earnest endeavor should be to seek in our Lord his greater   *x*) 83, 117, 289
abnegation[x] and continual mortification in all things possible;[26]
and our endeavor should be to help him in those things to the
extent that our Lord gives us His grace, for His greater praise
and glory.

I, 86-88, to Isabel Roser, English partially, in *LettersIgn*, p. 11; *EppIgn*, I, 296-298,
to King John of Portugal, in *LettersIgn*, pp. 80-81; *EppIgn*, VII, 446-447, to Michael
Nobrega, in *LettersIgn*, pp. 350-352; *EppIgn*, VIII, 452-453; IX, 382-384, 450.

26 In Ignatius' world view, this continual mortification too is a means which should
not be changed into an end and lead to loss of a greater good by one sincerely
seeking what will bring greater glory to God. As he wrote to Casanova in 1556:
". . . at times, there will be more merit in taking some honest bodily recreation in
order to remain active for a long period in God's service than in repressing oneself"
(*EppIgn*, XII, 151; *LettersIgn*, p. 435).

[Particularized Examens]¹

Chapter 5
Another Examen, somewhat more
particularized, for the educated,
the spiritual coadjutors,
and the scholastics

[**104**]—1. That better knowledge and understanding of candidates of this kind may be gained, these questions should be
put to each one. Where did he study? In which faculty? What
authors and what doctrine? How long? In his own opinion,
how has he progressed? And especially, what facility has he in
the Latin language?

[**105**]—2. Has he received a degree in the liberal arts, or in
theology, or canon law, or another faculty?

[**106**]—3. Does he think he has a memory to grasp and retain what he studies?ᵃ

a) 155

---

1 Here begin the particularized examens to which the title General Examen does not fully
apply. See fn. 1 on [1] above.

Does he think that his intellect enables him to penetrate
quickly and well what he studies?[b]   b) 154
Does he find in himself a natural or spontaneous inclination
to studies?

[107]—4. Does he think that the study was injuring his bodily
health?
Does he feel that he has the spiritual and bodily strength to
bear the labors required in the Society, in studies during their
time and in the Lord's vineyard when the time comes to work   c) 44, 185, 213,
in it?[c]   216

[108]—5. If he is a priest, has he had experience in hearing
confessions, or preaching, or other means of helping his neighbor?

[109]—6. To fulfill the function of sowing and dispensing the
divine word and of attending to the spiritual aid of the neighbors, it is expedient to possess a sufficiency of sound learning;
and for the students too to give some proof of their progress
in what they have studied. Therefore all will be examined
through their delivering a lecture about each branch of learning
which they have studied;[d] and afterwards before leaving the   d) 198
first probation, and later upon entrance into the second if so
ordered, each one will deliver an exhortation, as will be seen
later.

[110]—7. Likewise, when a candidate is a priest, or when
he becomes one, he should be advised that he should not hear
confessions inside or outside the house, or administer any sacraments, without a special examination, edification, and permission from his superior, during all the time of his probation.
Neither ought he to celebrate in public before he has done
so privately before one or several residents of the house. He
should also be told to conform his manner of saying Mass[2] to
that of the Society's members among whom he is living and to
the edification of those who are to hear him.[e]   e) 401, 671

---

2 In Ignatius' time, much variety in the ceremonies of the Mass existed within the Latin rite.
He desired to unify these ceremonies within the Society by having his priests conform to
the Society's "manner of saying Mass." The variety was terminated by Pope Pius V's reform
of the Missal in 1570, to which the Jesuits, like other priests, were obliged to conform.
See Iparraguirre, *Obras completas de San Ignacio*, p. 439; NCathEnc, XI, 397; and
[401] below.

[111]—8. For a greater humility and perfection of the learned, the spiritual coadjutors, and the scholastics, if there should be a doubt as to whether one of those who will enter the Society is suitable to make profession in it, or to become a spiritual coadjutor, or a scholastic in it, a question should be put to him. It presupposes that it is much better and more perfect for the subject to let himself be judged and governed by the Society, since the Society will know no less than he what is required to live in it; and also that greater humility and perfection will be imputed to him and he will show a greater love and confidence toward those who are to govern him.

Such a candidate should be asked whether he will leave his own opinion and judgment in the hands of the Society or its superior, in order to do that which the superior will tell him, that is, that he should become either a member of the Society which is thus professed and bound to the vicar of Christ our Lord, or a coadjutor in it, or a scholastic carrying on his studies in it.

He should be interrogated further as follows. If the superior should wish to keep him perpetually only as a coadjutor in the external affairs of the Society (as one occupied with the salvation of his own soul), is he ready to be employed in low and humble offices and to spend all the days of his life for the benefit and aid of the Society, meanwhile believing that by serving it he is serving his Creator and Lord, since he does all things because of the love and reverence due to Him?[f]

f) 10, 15, 72, 132

Chapter 6
Another Examen,
for coadjutors alone

[112]—1. To give a better understanding to each one of these coadjutors, what was touched on earlier should be further explained, namely, that both spiritual coadjutors and temporal coadjutors are received into this Society.[a] The spiritual coadjutors are priests and possess a sufficiency of learning to help in spiritual matters.[b] The temporal coadjutors do not receive

a) 13, 522, 533-537

b) 113, 153

sacred orders and, whether they possess learning or not, can
help in the necessary exterior matters.ᶜ   *c*) 114, 148

[113]—2. It is more appropriate for the spiritual coadjutors
to aid the Society by hearing confessions, giving exhortations,
and teaching Christian doctrine or other branches of study. The
same favors may be given to them as to the professed for the
aid of souls.

[114]—3. It is more appropriate for the temporal coadjutors
to exercise themselves in all the low and humble services which
are enjoined upon them,ᵈ although they may be employed in   *d*) 132, 148, 149,
more important matters in accordance with the talent God gave   305, 306, 364,
them. They should believe that by aiding the Society in order   433
that it may the better attend to the salvation of souls,ᵉ they are   *e*) 149, 364
serving the same Lord of all, since they are giving this aid out
of love and reverence for His Divine Self. They ought therefore to be prompt in carrying out the tasks given to them, completely and with all possible humility and charity. By this they
both merit their own full reward and share in all the good works
which God our Lord deigns to work through the entire Society
for His greater service and praise; and they also share in the
indulgences and privileges granted by the Apostolic See to the
professed for the good of their souls.

[115]—4. Nevertheless, in their conversations they ought to
try to further the greater interior progress of their neighbors,
to explain what they know, and to stimulate those whom they
can to do good,ᶠ since our Lord has given care of his neighbor   *f*) 349, 648
to everyone [Eccli. 17:12].

[116]—5. If someone has been trained and examined to become a spiritual coadjutor, he ought to devote himself to the
spiritual matters which are appropriate and suitable to his first
vocation and not to seek, directly or indirectly, through himself
or someone else, to inaugurate or attempt some change from
his vocation to another, namely, from that of a spiritual coadjutor to that of a professed or scholastic or temporal coadjutor.ᵍ *g*) 542
Instead, he should with all humility and obedience proceed to
make his way along the same path, which was shown to him by
Him who knows no change and to whom no change is possible.

[117]—6. In the same manner, if someone has been examined
and trained to become a temporal coadjutor, he ought to devote himself in everything to the things which are appropriate
and suitable to his first vocation and not to seek in one way or
another to pass forward from the grade of temporal coadjutor

h) 542
to that of a spiritual coadjutor or a scholastic or a professed.[h] Neither ought he, even if he does remain in the same grade, to seek more learning than he had when he entered. But he ought with much humility to persevere in giving service in everything to his Creator and Lord in his first vocation and to endeavor to grow in the abnegation of himself and in the pursuit of the gen-
i) 83, 103, 289
uine virtues.[i]

[118]—7. Such coadjutors should also be asked whether, as something characteristic of their vocation, they will be content and at peace to serve their Creator and Lord in low and humble offices and ministries, of whatever kind they may be, for the benefit of the house and the Society; and whether they will be
j) 13, 148, 150
ready to spend all the days of their lives in those occupations,[j] believing that in this they are serving and praising their Creator and Lord, by doing all things for His divine love and reverence.

[119]—8. All the coadjutors, spiritual as well as temporal,
k) 16, 71, 336, 346, 514, 537, 544
pass through two years of experiences and probations,[k] and one year more if they have been scholastics[l] (as was explained be-
l) 16, 71, 514, 516
fore [16, 71]). If they desire to remain in the Society and the Society or its superior is satisfied, they must in conformity with
m) 13, 533-537
the bull of Julius III[1] make their oblation[m] of three public (though not solemn) vows of obedience, poverty, and chastity, as was said in the beginning. From then on they remain as formed coadjutors, either spiritual or temporal, in such a way that on their side they are perpetually obliged to live and die in our Lord in and with this Society, for greater glory to the Divine Majesty and for their own greater merit and stability [A]. Nevertheless the Society or its superior (who ought to care for the common good) may, when it is evident that help is not being received from them toward greater service of God but rather
n) 536
the opposite, dismiss them and put them out of its community;[n] and from that time they are left free in everything and with-
o) 120, 234, 536
out the obligation of any vow.[o]

[120]—A. *Their being bound on their side is good, since their stability is sought; and, as appears in the apostolic bull,[2] it is not unjust for the Society to have the liberty to dismiss them when their remaining in it is not expedient. For in that case they remain free; and an individual can more easily fail to do his duty than the Society or its general, who alone will be able*

1 In *Exposcit*, [6], above.
2 In *Exposcit*, [6], above; also in the brief of Paul III, in 1546, *Exponi nobis*, [2], in ConsMHSJ, I, 171-173.

*to dismiss; and he ought not to do it without highly sufficient reasons, as will be seen in Part II of the Constitutions.*ᵖ   p) 209-217

Chapter 7
Another Examen for scholastics.
First, before their
admission to studies [A]

[121]—1. When the scholastics have passed through the afore-mentioned experiences and probations, if they think it desirable to study in the colleges or houses of the Society in order to be sustained in them in the Lord of all men, and if the Society or its superior is likewise satisfied with them, for their greater merit and stability they must, either before they go to their studies or when they are in them, pronounce the simple vow of poverty, chastity, and obedience, along with the promise to God our Lord that upon completing their studies they will enter the Society,ᵃ understanding entrance as meaning to make profession or to become formed coadjutors in it if it is willing to admit them.ᵇ From that time on they will be considered approved scholastics of the Society.ᶜ The said Society remains free and does not oblige itself to admit them either to profession or as formed coadjutors if they have made a poor showing during their studies and if its superior should judge that their admission would not be a service to God our Lord.ᵈ In such case they are freed from their vows.ᵉ

a) 14, 336, 540

b) 14, 511, 539, 541
c) 14, 336, 523

d) 123, 539
e) 123, 234, 539

[122]—A. *This examen, as well as the one above, is given not only to those who are sent to their studies for the first time, but also to those who are continuing them, when they come to the house to transfer elsewhere.*

[123]—2. If at some time during the studies those who have shown greater inclination toward them than for another ministry in the Society give a proof or clear indication in regard to themselves; and if the Society or its superior thereby judges that they are not suitable to become truly learned, through their lack of ability or experience of ill health or other deficiencies,ᶠ

f) 212, 386, 387

they should be asked whether they will accept with resignation their leave-taking or the dismissal which will be given them, and be freed from every former promise.^g

g) 212, 234, 539

[124]—3. One who is found sufficiently capable for the studies should be asked whether he will allow himself to be directed in regard to what he should study, and how, and how long, according to what will seem best to the Society, or its superior, or to the superior of the college where he will study.^h

h) 355-357, 460, 461

[125]—4. Will he be content to live in the same manner as the others, without seeking greater superiority or advantage than the least of those living in the college, and allowing in everything the concern for his well-being to its superior?

[126]—5. Is he determined, when his studies and probations are completed, to enter the Society in order to live and die in it for greater glory to God?ⁱ

i) 51, 193, 511

[127]—6. When he has been thus examined and instructed, he may begin to get himself ready to go to his studies or to continue them. Likewise, he should prepare himself to undergo various other experiences and probations during the studies. If for some legitimate reasons and in view of some good purposes he has not gone through these experiences before he went to his studies, after completing them he must undergo all the experiences and probations explained above.^j

j) 64, 71

For the scholastics who have completed their studies

[128]—7. The scholastics who have completed their studies, before they enter the Society or any of its houses to be admitted into it for total obedience and complete common living in our Lord, should be asked in general whether they remain firm in their determination, vows, and promise which they made to God our Lord before they went to their studies, or during the studies if they had been received in the colleges.

[129]—8. Likewise, they should be questioned and examined in detail by means of the same questions and examen first used before they went to their studies.^k The purpose is that the superiors may refresh their memory and knowledge of the scho-

k) 202

lastics, and also better and more completely know their firmness and constancy, or any change if one occurred in the matters which were first asked and affirmed.

Chapter 8
Another Examen, for those
still indifferent[1]

[130]—1. For better understanding of a candidate who is to be examined as one still indifferent,[a] that both sides may proceed with greater knowledge and clarity in our Lord, he will receive this instruction and advice. At no time and in no way may he or should he seek or try to obtain, directly or indirectly, one grade rather than another in the Society [A], that of a professed or a spiritual coadjutor rather than a temporal coadjutor or a scholastic. But keeping himself open for complete humility and obedience, he ought to leave all the concern about himself, and about the office or grade for which he should be chosen, to his Creator and Lord and, in His name and for His divine love and reverence, to the same Society and its superior.

a) 15

[131]—A. *However, when something occurs constantly to these candidates as being conducive to greater glory to God our Lord, they may, after prayer, propose the matter simply to the superior and leave it entirely to his judgment, without seeking anything more thereafter.*[b]

b) 292, 543, 627

[132]—2. After he has been thus instructed, he will be asked whether he finds himself entirely indifferent, content, and ready to serve his Creator and Lord in whatever office or ministry to which the Society or its superior will assign him.[c]

c) 10, 15, 72, 111

---

1 *Para indiferentes:* see above, fnn. 20 on [10] and 27 on [15]. In practice before 1556, most candidates were accepted with a definite grade in view; but if it should turn out to be unfeasible, they were expected to be "indifferent" or willing to accept another. See, e.g., [12, 13, 14, 72, 111, 116, 117, 132]. On the indifferent, see also *InstSJ*, II, 259, 541; III, 80; *EpitInstSJ*, 28, §3; Koch, *Jesuiten-Lexikon*, s.v. "Indifferentes"; A. de Aldama, "De coadiutoribus. . . ," *AHSJ*, XXXVIII (1969), 389-430, esp. 401-402, 409.

Likewise this question should be put to him. In case the Society or its superior desires to make perpetual use of him only for low and humble offices (in which he devotes himself to the salvation of his own soul), is he ready to spend all the days of his life in such low and humble offices, for the benefit and service of the Society, while believing that in this he is serving and praising his Creator and Lord, and doing all things for His divine love and reverence?[d]

d) 114, 118

[133]—3. When he is thus entirely satisfied in our Lord with all that has been said, he can be instructed and examined about the remaining matters, by means of some or all of the aforementioned examens, according to what seems most expedient. The aim is that both sides may be content and satisfied while proceeding with greater clarity in everything, while all things are being directed and ordered toward greater service and praise of God our Lord.

The end

May God be praised

The Constitutions of the Society of Jesus and their Declarations

Constitutions
of the Society of Jesus

Preamble to the Constitutions

[134]—1. Although it must be the Supreme Wisdom and Goodness of God our Creator and Lord which will preserve, direct, and carry forward in His divine service this least Society of Jesus, just as He deigned to begin it;[a1] and although what helps most on our own part toward this end must be, more than any exterior constitution, the interior law of charity and love which the Holy Spirit writes and engraves upon hearts;[2] nevertheless, since the gentle arrangement of Divine Providence requires cooperation from His creatures, and since too the vicar

a) 812, 825

---

1 This deep conviction of Ignatius, thoroughly characteristic of his spirituality, is merely mentioned in passing here but is treated extensively below in [812-814].
2 "The interior law of charity . . . which the Holy Spirit writes . . . upon hearts . . .": This sentence seems to be above all an echo of Scripture: Rom. 2:15, "the Law written in their hearts," and 5:5, "the charity of God is poured forth in our hearts by the

of Christ our Lord has ordered this,[3] and since the examples given by the saints and reason itself teach us so in our Lord, we think it necessary that constitutions should be written to aid us to proceed better, in conformity with our Institute, along the path of divine service on which we have entered.

[135]—2. In the order of our intention, the consideration which comes first and has more weight is that about the body of the Society taken as a whole; for its union, good government, and preservation in well-being for greater divine glory are what is chiefly sought. Nevertheless, this body is composed of its members; and in the order of execution, that which takes place first is what pertains to the individual members, in the sequence of admitting them, fostering their progress, and distributing them in the vineyard of the Lord. Therefore, our treatise will deal first with these individual members,[4] through the aid which the Eternal Light[5] will deign to communicate to us for His own honor and praise [A].

Holy Spirit." The Mosaic Law is a law exterior to man (Rom. 2:12-16; cf. *ST*, I-II, Q. 90, Intro.), and like it are the constitutions of religious institutes. External law gives information but not always spiritual strength or inspiration. Such law is helpful and usually necessary for persevering and organized action or cooperation; but even so it cannot by itself make a man holy unless he cooperates from within. His own interior decision to do the good works and the impulse of God's helping grace are both necessary (Matt. 7:21; John 6:44; Eph. 2:4-10; 2 Peter 1:10; James 2:24).

By his conscience man perceives what the law requires (Rom. 2:15); and when he is impelled from within by the love and grace poured into him by the Holy Spirit and therefore carries out what the law requires, he truly pleases God and becomes holy. In the New Law, man is instructed by the evangelical precepts and impelled by grace. (See, e.g., the footnotes in *The Jerusalem Bible* on Rom. 2:12-16, 5:5, 7:7-8; cf. *ST*, I-II, Q. 90, Intro.; 92, a. 1, esp. ad 2; 98, a. 6; 106, a. 1.) In Q. 106, a. 1, St. Thomas states that "the New Law is chiefly the Holy Spirit's grace itself, which is given to those who believe in Christ." This grace is manifestly an interior or impelling force. A man who acts habitually and discreetly according to this interior law of faith, love, and grace has what Ignatius esteems so highly and recommends so often: "discreet charity," the love exercised by a person who is discreet which impels him to choose the better course. On *discreta caridad*, see fn. 2 on [582] below.

A few writers have maintained that Ignatius once hoped to have a Society without any exterior constitutions or rules. This is at variance not only with his prudence and express statement [134] about the necessity of exterior law but also with historical evidence. As soon as he and his companions decided to band together into a permanent religious order in 1539, they expressed their intention of writing constitutions to make it an effective organization. Clear texts are found in *Cons*MHSJ, I, 16, 17, 20, 21, 27, 31, 374. See also Coemans, *Introductio*, nos. 21-37.

3 On Sept. 25, 1539, Salmerón wrote to Laynez' father, John, that Paul III had already granted to the ten companions permission to compose constitutions (*EppIgn*, I, 154). This referred to the oral approbation of Sept. 3, 1539, at Tivoli.

4 On this practical procedure, see the Introduction above, pp. 37-38.

5 On the great variety of names referring to God in the Constitutions, and their connotations, cf. Courel, *Constitutions*, I, 56-57, and Iparraguirre, "Visión ignaciana de Dios," *Gregorianum*, XXXVII (1956), 366-390.

Preamble to the Declarations[6] and Annotations on the Constitutions

[136]—*The purpose of the Constitutions is to aid the body of the Society as a whole and also its individual members toward their preservation and development for the divine glory and the good of the universal Church.*[b] *Therefore these Constitutions,*   b) 746
in addition to the fact that they in their entirety and each one of them should be conducive to this purpose just stated, should have three characteristics:

First, they should be complete, to provide for all cases as far as possible.

Second, they should be clear, to give less occasion for scruples.

Third, they should be brief, as far as the completeness and clarity allow, to make it possible to retain them in the memory.

For the better realization of these three characteristics, the more universal and summary Constitutions will be easier to handle, that they may be observed inside and shown outside when expedient. But in addition to them, we have thought it wise in our Lord to compose also these Declarations and Anno-tations. They possess the same binding force as the other Constitutions,[c] *and can be instructive in greater detail to those*   c) 548
who have charge of the other members about some matters which the brevity and universality of the other Constitutions left less clear. The Constitutions and the Declarations both treat of matters which are unchangeable and ought to be observed universally; but they must be supplemented by some other ordinances which can be adapted[d] *to the times, places, and*   d) 18, 198, 395,
persons in different houses, colleges, and employments of the   396, 428, 455,
Society, although uniformity ought to be retained among all the   585, 654, 811
members as far as possible.[e] *These ordinances or rules will not*   e) 671, 821
be treated here, except by the remark that everyone ought to observe them, when he happens to be in a place where they are observed, according to the will of his superior.[7]

To return now to the subject matter treated here, the order of these Declarations will correspond to that of the Constitutions, part for part and chapter for chapter, whenever something in a chapter needs to be explained. The need will be indicated by

6 On the nature of the Declarations, see above, pp. 38-39.

7 On such rules and ordinances, see above, pp. 46-47; also Iparraguirre, *Obras completas de San Ignacio,* p. 446.

a letter in the margin[8] of the Constitutions, and corresponding to this will be the same letter in the text of the Declarations. Thus there will be an orderly procedure, through the aid of Him who as the Most Perfect and Infinite Wisdom is the beginning of all order.

Declaration on the Preamble

[137]—A. *It is usually best, especially in the order of practice, to proceed from the less perfect to the more perfect; for what is first in the order of execution is last in the order of consideration, since such planning first considers the end and then descends to the means to attain it. Therefore our procedure utilizes ten principal parts into which the whole of the Constitutions are divided.[9]*

Part I. The admission to probation for those who desire to follow our Institute.

Part II. The dismissal of those who do not seem suitable for it.

Part III. The care of those who remain and the fostering of their progress in the spiritual life and in virtue.

Part IV. The instruction in learning and other means of helping the neighbor for those who have made progress in the spiritual life and virtue.

Part V. The incorporation into the Society of those who have been thus instructed.

Part VI. What those who have been incorporated must observe in regard to themselves.

Part VII. What should be observed in regard to our fellowmen, through the distribution of the workers and their employment in the vineyard of Christ our Lord.

Part VIII. What pertains to keeping those thus distributed united with one another and with their head.[10]

Part IX. What pertains to the head and to the government which descends from him to the body.

8 In modern editions these letters are placed within the text, in accordance with contemporary style.
9 On the logical order and that of execution, see above, pp. 37-38.
10 *Cabeza:* In the Constitutions, Ignatius' fundamental image of the Society is that of a body (*cuerpo*, e.g., in [135, 137, 322, 510, 512], with the general as its head (*cabeza*, e.g., in [137, 206, 512, 655, 666, 668, 671, 820, 821]), and with members (*miembros*). This image guides his terminology. *Miembros* is the term by which he habitually and most frequently designated all those who had enrolled under the general's authority,

Part X. What pertains in general to the preservation and development of the entire body of this Society in its well-being.

This is the order which will be followed in the Constitutions and the Declarations while we keep our attention fixed on the end which all of us are seeking, the glory and praise of God our Creator and Lord.

even novices, as can be seen in [135, 233, 322, 510, 511, 655, 666, 668, 671, 821]. On four occasions ([659, 660, 661, 701]), he calls members personally known to one another and associated in a common task companions (*compañeros*). In two instances ([6, 322]), he extends *miembros* to include houses and colleges of the Society. Outside the Constitutions he often called Christ the head of the Society, e.g., in his *Spiritual Diary* for Feb. 23, 1544: ". . . Jesus . . . since He is the head of the Society" (*ConsMHSJ,* I, 104; cf. *FN,* I, 204; II, 596). See also fnn. 3 and 4 on [1] above, and the supplementary Note A in the Reference matter below.

Thus his concept of the Society and his terminology about it closely parallel his concept and terminology in respect to the Church as the mystical body of Christ. Ignatius conceives the Church as a body whose head is Christ, e.g., in his letter of Aug. 7, 1553, to the whole Society: "Since the order of charity, with which we ought to love the whole body of the Church in its head, Christ Jesus, requires that a remedy be applied especially to the member (*parti*) which is suffering from a more serious and dangerous illness, we think that . . . the aid of the Society should be bestowed with special affection on Germany, England, and the northern nations. . . ." (*EppIgn,* V, 221). In a letter remarkably indicative of his ecclesiology, written to Emperor Claude of Abyssinia Feb. 23, 1553, he also employs the terminology of the mystical body: ". . . the Church, which is one. . . . For anyone who is not united with the body of the Church will not receive from Christ our Lord, who is its head, the influx of grace which gives life to his soul and disposes him for beatitude." He quotes with approval the Council of Florence: "We define that the holy Apostolic See and the Roman pontiff have the primacy over the whole world, and that he is the successor of St. Peter, the true vicar of Christ, and the head of the whole Church. . . ." A little later he adds: ". . . it is a singular benefit to be united to the mystical body of the Catholic Church, vivified and ruled by the Holy Spirit who . . . teaches her all truth. . . ." (*EppIgn,* VIII, 463-464; *LettersIgn,* pp. 369-371).

Part I
The admission to probation

Chapter 1
The person who admits

[138]—1. The authority to admit to probation will belong to those whom the superior general of the Society thinks fit, and to the extent he thinks good. In communicating this authority he will look to what is conducive to greater service to God our Lord.ᵃ

a) 141, 736

[139]—2. When someone who seems suitable for our Institute offers himself to someone who does not have such authority to admit him, he may send this applicant to one who has it [A], or he may write to him and inform him about the applicant's qualifications and then act according to the orders which may be given him in our Lord, if this person written to can settle the matter from a distance [B].

[140]—A. *If a good applicant of this kind cannot easily be sent to the one who has the authority, anyone may, while the authority is being informed, receive the applicant on a tem-*

porary basis as his companion, when he judges this to be necessary or highly opportune, until he receives a reply to the report which he sent. Then he will act according to the order which will be given him.

[141]—B. *Those who can admit while absent are: ordinarily, the provincial superiors; extraordinarily, all those whomsoever the general or the same provincial commissions for this purpose. But the more ordinary practice will be to communicate to the rectors of colleges and the local superiors authority to receive into their house or college those present whom they judge suitable.*

b) 308, 819

c) 18, 190, 193, 196

d) 2

e) 18, 190

[142]—3. It is highly important for the divine service to make a proper selection of those who are admitted[b] and to take care to know their abilities and vocation well.[c] Therefore if the one who has the aforementioned authority does not do all that himself, he should have, among those who reside more permanently in the same place as himself, someone to aid him to know those who enter, to converse with them, and to examine them.[d] This helper should possess discernment[1] and skill in dealing with persons of such different types and temperaments, that the matter may be carried on with greater clarity and satisfaction on both sides for divine glory.[e]

[143]—4. Both he who has the authority to admit and his helper ought to know the Society's concerns and to be zealous for its good progress, so that no other consideration will be so strong as to deter him from what he judges in our Lord to be more suitable for His divine service in this Society. Therefore he should be very moderate in his desire to admit [C]. Furthermore, that he may be more free from affection when occasion for it might exist (as in the case of relatives or friends), one in whom this danger is in any way feared ought not to perform the function of examiner.[f]

f) 189

[144]—C. *Just as care should be taken to cooperate with the divine motion and vocation by endeavoring to secure in the Society an increase of workers for the holy vineyard of Christ*

---

1 *Discreción*, discernment or discretion, is a characteristic which Ignatius strongly desired and often stressed. He used this term, so typical of him, often in the Constitutions to designate a characteristic which should be present in every choice or decision. It connotes the principles of choice which Ignatius gave in his Rules for the Discernment of Spirits (*SpEx*, [313-336]). See also fnn. 27 on [15] and 2 on [134] above, and J. C. Futrell, "Ignatian Discernment," *Studies in the Spirituality of Jesuits*, II, no. 2 (April, 1970), 47-88.

*our Lord, so too should much thought be given to admit only
those who possess the qualifications required for this Institute,
for the divine glory.*

[145]—5. Whoever has this charge ought to keep in writing
whatever pertains to it [D], that he may better and with more
certainty carry out what is sought in this matter for the divine
service.[2]

[146]—*D. Wherever someone has the power of admitting,
there should be a complete text of the Examen in the languages
which are commonly found necessary, such as the vernacular of
the region where the residence is and the Latin. The Examen
is proposed to the one who seeks admission, before he enters
the house[3] to live in common with the others.*[g] *The impediments
which necessarily bar admission are also proposed even before
entrance into the first probation.*[h]

g) 2, 198, 199

h) 31, 196

*There will likewise be in writing another Examen containing
the matter which is to be proposed every six months during the
two years of probation; also another, very short, which those
can use who deal with applicants, that both sides may know
what should be known before reception into the first probation.
They ought similarly to have in writing the responsibilities of
the examiner and to see to it that what is prescribed is put into
practice.*

Chapter 2
The candidates
who should be admitted

[147]—1. To speak in general of those who should be admitted, the greater the number of natural and infused gifts[1]

---

2 Instructions on this topic, written by Ignatius himself, are found in *Cons*MHSJ, II, 734-
736 and IV, 404-410.
3 The wording here suggests the desirability of a separate section of the house, as the place
of the first probation. Cf. [18, 21, 190, 191] and *Cons*MHSJ, II, cxxxix-cxl.
1 Repeatedly Ignatius makes clear that, while he sets a higher value on supernatural gifts,
he genuinely esteems gifts of the natural order. See [733, 734, 813, 814]; and cf.
DeGuiJes, pp. 96-97, 147-148, 170, 174-175, 544-545.

someone has from God our Lord which are useful for what the Society aims at in His divine service, and the more experience the candidate has in the use of these gifts, the more suitable will he be for reception into the Society.

a) 112, 114, 305, 306, 364, 433

[148]—2. To speak in particular of those who are admitted to become coadjutors in temporal or external matters,[a] it is presupposed that they should not be more numerous than is necessary to aid the Society in occupations which the other members could not fulfill without detriment to the greater service[b] of God [A]. In regard to their souls these applicants ought to be men of good conscience, peaceful, docile, lovers of virtue and perfection, inclined to devotion, edifying for those inside and outside the house, content with the lot of Martha in the Society, well-disposed toward its Institute, and eager to help it for the glory of God our Lord[c] [B].

b) 305, 334, 428, 431, 433

c) 13, 118

d) 306, 433

[149]—A. *Such are ordinarily, in large houses, the occupations of a cook, steward, buyer, doorkeeper, infirmarian, launderer, gardener, and alms-gatherer in a place where the members live on alms; and there could be others of this kind.[d] But according to the more or fewer members in the houses or colleges, and to the greater or lesser requirements in the offices, there might or might not be need to assign full-time persons to all of these occupations. Consequently this matter should be left to the one in charge of the others. But he should be told to keep in mind the purpose which motivates the acceptance of such members into this Society, that is, the need to be aided which those have who are laboring in the Lord's vineyard or who are studying to labor in it later, that they may apply themselves to pursuits which bring greater service to God our Lord.[e]*

e) 114, 364

[150]—B. *If some applicant is perceived to have such a disposition that he is unlikely to remain satisfied while serving in external matters, because an inclination for study or the priesthood can be observed in him, it would not be wise to admit him to become a temporal coadjutor if he does not appear to have the ability to advance as far as it would be necessary.*

[151]—3. In regard to their exterior these candidates ought to have a good appearance, health, and age as well as the strength for the bodily tasks which occur in the Society. They should also have or give hope of having some good ability to help the Society.

[152]—4. In view of the end of our Institute and our manner of proceeding, we are convinced in our Lord that to admit persons who are very difficult or unserviceable to the congregation is not conducive to His greater service and praise, even though their admission would be useful to themselves.[f]

f) 184, 216

[153]—5. Those who are admitted to serve in spiritual matters should have the following qualifications, because of what a ministry of this kind requires for the help of souls.

[154]—6. In regard to the intellect, they should have sound doctrine, or ability to acquire it, and in respect to things to be done, discretion or evidence of good judgment which is necessary to acquire discretion.[g]

g) 106, 183

[155]—7. In regard to the memory, they should have aptitude to learn and faithfully retain what has been learned.[h]

h) 106, 183

[156]—8. In regard to the will, they should be desirous of all virtue and spiritual perfection, peaceful, constant, and energetic in whatever enterprise of the divine service they undertake, and zealous for the salvation of souls. For that reason they should also have an affection toward our Institute, which is directly ordered to help and dispose souls to gain their ultimate end from the hand of God our Creator and Lord.[i]

i) 3, 163, 258, 307, 446, 586, 603, 813

[157]—9. In regard to the exterior, a pleasing manner of speech,[j] so necessary for communications with one's fellowmen, is desirable.

j) 624, 814

[158]—10. They should have a good appearance by which those with whom they deal[k] are more usually edified.

k) 185, 186

[159]—11. They should have the health and strength by which they can sustain the labors of our Institute.[l]

l) 44, 107, 185, 216

[160]—12. They should be of an age suitable for what has been stated, that is, more than fourteen years for admission to probation and more than twenty-five[2] years for profession.[m]

m) 34, 185, 187

2 One day above the age of 14 or 25 suffices. Today Canon 555, §1, 1° requires a candidate to be 15 years of age before beginning his novitiate.
    The recently published research of Lukács, "De graduum diversitate," *AHSJ*, XXXVII (1968), 239-241, 311-312, has furnished new and important statistics about the

[161]—13. The extrinsic gifts of nobility, wealth, reputation, and the like, are not necessary when the others are present, just as they do not suffice if those others are lacking. But to the extent that they aid toward edification, they render more fit to be admitted those who would be fit without them because they have the other qualifications mentioned above. The more an applicant is distinguished for those qualifications the more suitable will he be for this Society unto glory of God our Lord, and the less he is distinguished by them, the less suitable [C]. But the holy unction of the Divine Wisdom will teach [1 John 2:20, 27] the mean which should be retained in all this to those who have charge of that matter, which was undertaken for His greater service and praise.

[162]—C. *To be completely suitable for the Society an appli-cant ought to have everything that has been mentioned. How-ever, if someone lacks one or another of those qualifications, such as bodily strength, or the age for the profession, or some-*

ages and other qualifications of candidates admitted during the years of Ignatius and his earlier successors. Thus we now know far more concretely the circumstances amid which the examinations described in the four chapters of Part I ([138-203]), or in the whole General Examen, [1-133], were carried on.

Of 1,705 members who were listed in the catalogues of the Italian Province of the Society for the years 1540-1565, 998 (58.5%) were Italians and 707 (41.5%) natives of other countries. There were 1,314 priests and scholastics. The age at the time of entrance can be ascertained for 748 of them. It is shown in this

Table I. Ages at Entrance, 1540-1565

Age at Entrance	Under Ignatius 1540-1556		Under Laynez 1558-1565	
11-15	31	10.6%	76	16.6%
16-20	110	37.6%	179	39.2%
21-25	85	29.1%	107	23.4%
26-30	37	12.6%	62	13.6%
31-40	24	8.2%	27	5.9%
41-53	5	1.6%	5	1 %

The theological training, attained either before or after entrance, has now been ascer-tained for 341 of the Society's priests who functioned between 1540 and 1565, and also for many in subsequent periods. It is shown in this

Table II. Theological Training of Jesuit Priests

Years	Did not possess training in theology		Did possess such training	
1540-1556	61	49.1%	63	50.8%
1557-1565	103	47.4%	114	52.6%
1600	120	30 %	278	70 %
1650	74	8.2%	817	91.8%
1700	31	2.7%	1,147	97.3%
1750	12	.9%	1,359	99.1%

Of the Jesuits living in Italy who entered the Society under Ignatius, 156 reached

*thing similar, and if it is judged in the Lord that this lack is
compensated for by his other qualities and that, when everything is taken into account, his admission would be a service
to God our Lord and conducive to the end of the Society,
authority to give him a dispensation will be possessed by the
superior general, or by the other superiors to the extent that he
has communicated his authority to them.*[n]   n) 178, 186, 187

Chapter 3
The impediments to admission

[**163**]—1. The charity and zeal for souls in which this Society
exerts itself according to the purpose of its Institute embrace
all kinds of persons, to serve and help them in the Lord of all
men to attain to beatitude. Nevertheless, when there is a question of incorporating persons into the same Society, that charity
and zeal should embrace only those who are judged useful for
the end it seeks (as has been said [143, 144]).

the priesthood. The cultural variety among them is shown in this

Table III. Kinds of Training Possessed by Jesuits Admitted by Ignatius
Who Became Priests

Grammar only,	8
Humane letters also	14
Cases of conscience also	29
A little philosophy also	4
A little theology also	16
The curriculum of philosophy	5
The doctorate in philosophy	1
The curriculum of theology	41
The doctorate in theology	2
The doctorate in law	4
Amount of training unknown	32

These tables show that, within a rather few decades, the system of studies which
Ignatius set up to train his young members greatly improved the intellectual training
possessed by the priests of his order—much as the establishment of seminaries did later in
the Church at large. All this was an important factor in the Counter-Reformation.

It is also evident that as the numbers of those above 25 years of age at entrance
decreased, the percentage of priests with theological training gradually increased. See
also fn. 18 on p. 71 above and the supplementary Note B in the Reference matter below,
pp. 349-356.

a) 23, 30, 176,
334

[164]—2. Because of the compelling reasons which move us in our Lord, there are among the impediments to admission some which bar admission absolutely.ᵃ

[165]—3. Such impediments are: to have separated oneself for a time from the bosom of the Holy Church, by denying the faith in the midst of infidels, or by falling into errors against the faith and having been condemned while in them by a public sentence [A], or by withdrawing as a schismatic from the unity of the Churchᵇ [B].

b) 22, 24

[166]—A. *Even though one has not been condemned by a public sentence, if his error has been public and he has been highly suspect and there is fear that proceedings may be instituted against him, he ought not to be admitted. But this decision will be left to the superior general.*

[167]—B. *With respect to schism, if someone was born in a schismatical region so that the schism was not a particular sin committed only by the person but a general sin, he would not be understood to be excluded from the Society for this cause (and the same holds true of one born in a heretical region). Rather, there is understood here an infamous person who was excommunicated after so contemning the authority and vigilance¹ of our holy mother the Church that the heresy or schism was a particular sin of the person and not a general sin of the nation or country.*

c) 25, 26

[168]—4. Another impediment is: to have been a homicide [C] or infamous [D] because of enormous sins.ᶜ

[169]—C. *In regard to a homicide no clarification is added, just as none is given about the remaining impediments. But when there is doubt as to whether he is a homicide or not, the decision will be left to the judgment of the generals, who in such doubts will not be lenient. If someone has deliberately ordered the committing of homicide and the effect followed, he too would be regarded as a homicide, even though he did not perpetrate the deed by his own hand.*

[170]—D. *Infamy because of enormous sins is understood to be an impediment in the place where the sinner was infamous.*

1 *Providencia* in its legal meaning of a court procedure.

If he should, when far from that place, give such signs of repentance that they reestablish confidence in him, he could be admitted in our Lord.[d] *Which sins of this kind are enormous and which are not will be left to the judgment of the superior general.*[2]   d) 26

[171]—5. Another impediment is: to have received the habit [E] of a religious institute, or to have been a hermit with the garments of a monk.

[172]—*E. Not only if he has made profession, but even if he has worn the habit a single day, such a one cannot be admitted, for the reasons touched on in the Examen [30]. However, this should be understood of taking the habit with the intention of becoming a religious, and not of taking it through some other accidental reason.*[e]   e) 27

[173]—6. Another impediment is: to be bound by the bond of matrimony or of legitimate slavery[f] [F].   f) 28, 40, 41, 217

[174]—*F. In case this bond should be dissolved by the consent of the master and of the wife, with observance of the other circumstances which are customarily carried out according to the sound doctrine and practice of the Holy Church, this impediment would cease to exist.*

[175]—7. Another impediment is: to be mentally ill, with the result that the judgment becomes obscured and unsound, or to have a notable disposition toward such illness,[g] as is treated more at length in the Examen [29] [G].   g) 29

[176]—*G. In regard to all these impediments it is expedient that neither the superior general nor the whole Society should be able to dispense, since generally it is good that no dispensation be granted from them.*[h] *But if one of these impediments should be discovered in some person who has such other qualifications as to give certitude that the Society could be much helped by him in the service of God our Lord; and if he should petition the supreme pontiff or his nuncio or chief penitentiary for permission, in spite of the Constitutions, to be received into the Society whose superior general is not showing opposition, that superior general could consent provided that the door would*   h) 23, 30, 164, 334

2 For the present law of the Church on this impediment, see Canon 2295.

not be opened to many, or to anyone without rare qualifications,
as has been stated.[i]

i) 32

[**177**]—8. There are other impediments which render the applicant less suitable,[j] even though each one taken singly does not bar admission to the Society [H]; and a defect could be so great that to receive one with it would not be a service to God.

j) 186

[**178**]—H. *Each of the impediments of this second category could of itself suffice to bar admission. But because the compensation of other very good qualities could be great enough to make it appear in our Lord that some one of these defects ought to be tolerated, the decision about this case is left to the discretion of the one who has the authority to admit. It will also belong to him to grant a dispensation in such cases, but with deference to the judgment of the superior, whom he ought to inform about a difficulty which occurs and whose opinion he should then follow.*[k]

k) 162, 186, 187

[**179**]—9. These impediments are of the following kind. In regard to the interior, passions which seem uncontrollable, or sinful habits of which there is no hope of much emendation.

[**180**]—10. An intention which is not as right as it ought to be for entrance into a religious institute but is mixed with human motives.

[**181**]—11. Inconstancy or notable lethargy so that the applicant seems unlikely to amount to much.

[**182**]—12. Indiscreet devotions which lead some to fall into illusions and errors of importance.

[**183**]—13. A lack of learning or of intellectual ability or of memory to acquire it, or of facility in speech to explain it, in applicants who manifest an intention or desire to progress farther than temporal coadjutors customarily do.[l]

l) 106, 154, 155, 308, 523

[**184**]—14. A lack of judgment, or a notable obstinacy[m] in one's personal opinions which is highly vexatious in all congregations.

m) 152, 216

[**185**]—15. In regard to the exterior, a lack of bodily integrity, illnesses and weakness, or notable ugliness[n] [I].
Age too tender or too advanced[o] [K].
Debts and civil obligations[p] [L].

n) 44, 107, 216
o) 34, 160
p) 42, 217

[186]—*I. It is to be noticed that persons who have notable dis-
figurements or defects such as humpbacks and other deformities,
whether they be natural or accidental such as those from wounds
and the like, are not suitable for this Society. For these defects
are obstacles to the priesthood and do not help toward the
edification of the neighbors with whom, according to our Institute, it is necessary to deal. These persons are unsuitable except
when, as was stated above [162, 178], outstanding virtues and
gifts of God are present with which such bodily defects would
be thought to increase rather than decrease the edification.*q   q) 162, 178

[187]—*K. In regard to an age of less than fourteen years for
admission to probation and of twenty-five for the profession,*r   r) 160
*if in some persons an anticipation of this age is for special
reasons judged to be conducive to the end sought, greater service
to God, the superior general will be able to dispense*s *after*   s) 162, 746
*weighing and considering the circumstances. Similarly, when the
age is too advanced, he will consider whether the bearing of
this inconvenience is expedient for the common welfare or not.*

[188]—*L. In regard to debts, much vigilance should be shown
that no occasion of scandal or disturbance is taken, and more
especially, in addition to the consideration for edification, in
the case of civil obligations where the law makes prescriptions.*

[189]—16. The more one suffers from all these defects, just
that much less suited is he to serve God our Lord in this Society
for the aid of souls.t Furthermore, the one charged with admissions   t) 177
should be vigilant that charity for an individual does not impair
the charity for all, which should always be preferred as being   u) 143
more important for the glory and honor of Christ our Lord.u

Chapter 4
The manner of dealing
with those admitted

[190]—1. We are convinced in our Lord that what follows is
of great importance in order that His Divine and Supreme
Majesty may make use of this least Society. The persons who

a) 18, 142, 193, 196

are accepted into it should be not only long tested before incorporation into it but also well-known[a] before they are admitted to the probation which is made by living in common with those in the house. Therefore it is expedient that near our common abode there should be a lodging [A] where those who are admitted may live as guests, for twelve to twenty days or

b) 18, 21

longer if it seems good to the superior,[b] that during this time they may inform themselves better about the concerns of the Society and the Society may come to know them better in our Lord.

[**191**]—A. *When the house of the first probation cannot be separate and near our house, an effort should be made to have some apartment set aside within our house itself, that those received may have less occasion to converse with the others except those whom the superior appoints.*

[**192**]—2. Those who request it may more promptly be admitted into this house, called the house of the first probation, if they clearly appear to be fit to serve God our Lord in this Society. Those who on the contrary are clearly seen to be unsuitable can be readily dismissed, after being helped by counsel and whatever other means charity may dictate, that they may serve God our

c) 31, 225

Lord better elsewhere.[c]

[**193**]—3. Sometimes the clarity necessary on the Society's side may still be lacking, even after the candidate has expressed his desire and has been tactfully questioned about the impediments

d) 22-29, 165-175

of the first category,[d] and after the substance of our Institute as well as the experiences and difficulties which it entails have been

e) 53-103

explained to him.[e] If this should happen, even though the applicant manifests his efficacious determination to enter the Society

f) 51, 53, 126, 511

to live and die in it[f] (and ordinarily no one who lacks that determination should be admitted to the first probation [B]), the reply and ultimate decision should be postponed for a while [C]. During this time the case can be considered and commended to God our Lord; and appropriate diligence can be employed

g) 18, 142, 190

to know the applicant and to test his constancy[g] [D]. But how extensive this postponement and investigation should be must be left to the prudent consideration of the one who has authority to admit;[1] and he should always keep in view the greater service of God.

---

1 For an example of a procedure which a superior could use in such prayerful investigation, consultation, and deliberation, see *Cons*MHSJ, I, 218-219.

[194]—B. *If for some good reasons a candidate not yet entirely resolved to serve God our Lord in this Society should be admitted into the house, he should be received as a guest and not for the first or the second probation. But the one in charge should not easily permit this for more than three days, nor without permission from the superior general or at least from the provincial. This permission can be granted less easily where novices are present than where there are none of them.*

[195]—C. *The postponement of the reply and ultimate decision for a time and the investigation in order to know the applicant better should ordinarily be observed. But in particular cases, for example, when some unusual qualifications are present and also a danger that such persons would be turned away or much disturbed by the postponement, the appropriate investigations could be made more summarily and the applicants could be admitted into the house of the first probation; or after being examined they could be sent to other houses of the Society.*

[196]—D. *The investigations which may be used to know the applicant include the summary examen,*[h] *in which the impedi-*   h) 2, 146
ments of the first and second categories treated in Chapter 3 are touched on, such as lack of health and of bodily integrity and civil obligations or debts.

It will be similarly helpful if, besides the examiner, some additional persons from among those designated by the superior deal and associate with the applicant. Further, when his name and those who know him have been learned, information about him can be gathered from outside the house, if no one inside it knows him sufficiently well.

Still further help will be gained from having him go to confession in our church for some time before he enters the house. When the doubt persists, to have him make spiritual exercises will aid not a little toward gaining the clarity needed in his regard for the glory of God our Lord.

[197]—4. After the decision has been made in our Lord that it is proper to admit such an applicant to probation, he may enter, dressed as he customarily was[i] or in the manner in which each   i) 18, 19, 579
one finds more devotion, unless the superior thinks otherwise. He should be placed as a guest in the aforementioned house or apartment, and on the second day he should be told how he should conduct himself in that place, and especially that (unless the superior for urgent reasons thinks otherwise) he should not deal either by word of mouth or by writing with others from

j) 60, 244, 246

outside or inside the house, except for some who will be assigned to him by the superior.ʲ The purpose is that he may with greater freedom deliberate with himself and with God our Lord about his vocation and intention to serve His Divine and Supreme Majesty in this Society.

k) 2, 146

l) 18, 20, 98

m) 109

[**198**]—5. When two or three days have passed after he entered the probation, he will begin to be examined more in detail according to the method explained in the Office of the Examiner.[2] The text of the Examen should be left with him that he may consider it more slowly in private.ᵏ Subsequently he will carefully read the bulls, Constitutions, and rulesˡ which must be observed in the Society and the house he enters [E]. Those who have studied should deliver a lecture about each branch of learning they have studied, in the presence of persons whom the superior assigns, that knowledge may be gained of their talent in what pertains to doctrine and to their manner of presenting it.ᵐ

n) 20

[**199**]—*E. For those who do not understand the bulls in Latin, an explanation of their substance would suffice, and likewise of the substance of the Constitutions and rules. This means that in regard to all of these, each candidate should be shown those which he must observe. A summary of them can be made and left (as also the Examen) with each candidate, that he may consider it more slowly in private.ⁿ*

o) 93

p) 65, 98

q) 57

[**200**]—6. During this time of the first probation the candidates will also manifest their consciences to the superior or the one he assigns,ᵒ unless this is postponed through the superior's decision. They will make a general confessionᵖ (if they have not done this previously) to the one appointed for them. In a book provided for this purpose, they write down and sign with their own hand what they have brought to the house [F], and also their agreement to observe everything that has been proposed to them.�q After being finally reconciled and receiving the most Holy Sacrament they will enter the house of common living and association where the second probation is made during a longer time.

[**201**]—*F. If they do not know how to write, someone else will write in their presence and in their name.*

---

2 A "Summary Instruction for the Examiner," corrected and perhaps written by Ignatius ca. 1546, is published in *Cons*MHSJ, II, 734-736. For a slightly later text, *Del officio del examinador*, see *Cons*MHSJ, IV, 402-415.

[202]–7. What has been said about those who enter for the first time will also be observed in great part with those who come from their studies or other places of the Society,[r] and who have not been admitted to profession or into the formed coadjutors nor examined carefully elsewhere [G], so that in proportion to the greater clarity in the procedure, each candidate may be just that much more stable in his vocation, and the Society may be better able to discern whether it is expedient for him to remain in it for greater glory and praise of God our Lord.

r) 129

[203]–G. *Except for the postponement of admission to the first probation, which has no place in the case of those who have already been in other houses of the Society, almost everything else holds true also of them. However, the better known and the more settled they are, the less necessary are the investigations which are made to know and strengthen those admitted to probation.*

Part II
The dismissal of those who were admitted
but did not prove themselves fit

Chapter 1
Who can be dismissed, and by whom

[**204**]—1. Just as it is proper, for the sake of the end sought in this Society, the service of God our Lord by helping souls who are His, to preserve and multiply the workers who are found fit and useful for carrying this work forward, so is it also expedient to dismiss those who are found unsuitable, and who as time passes make it evident that this is not their vocation or that their remaining in the Society does not advance the common good.[a]   a) 819
However, just as excessive readiness should not be had in admitting candidates,[b] so ought it to be used even less in dis-   b) 142, 308, 819
missing them; instead, one ought to proceed with much consideration and weighing in our Lord. The more fully one has been incorporated into the Society, the more serious ought the reasons to be. Nevertheless, no matter how advanced the incorporation may be, in some cases anyone can and should be separated from the Society[c] [A], as will be seen in Chapter 2.[1]   c) 774

[**205**]—A. *Although all may be dismissed, as is stated in the*

---

1 Today dismissals must conform to the new Code of Canon Law. Especially noteworthy are Canons 646 and 654, and various norms issued by the Holy See for their interpretation and application within the Society.

Constitutions, there will be less difficulty in the case of some than of others. If those admitted to the house of the first probation should show, during those days before they live in common with the others, that they are not fit for the Society, they could be

d) 31, 192, 208   *dismissed with greater facility than others.*[d]

In the second degree of difficulty are those who are in the second probation in houses or colleges and have not bound themselves by any vow, if experience leads to the judgment that their remaining in the Society is not conducive to greater service to God.

In the third degree are those who on their own side have bound themselves by vows but who have not yet been accepted among the approved scholastics or formed coadjutors of the Society, after completion of the time given them for probation.

In the fourth degree, requiring greater reflection and cause, are the approved scholastics.

In the fifth degree, entailing still greater difficulty, are the formed coadjutors whether spiritual or temporal, if it is judged necessary to dismiss them after their taking their public though

e) 119, 120, 536   *not solemn vows.*[e]

In some cases even the professed,[2] *no matter what their rank and dignity in the Society, could be dismissed, if it is judged that to retain them would be harmful to the Society and a disservice*

f) 774   *to God our Lord.*[f]

Beyond what has been stated, the more obligations there are toward some person because of his good service, or the more qualifications he has for helping the Society in the service of God our Lord, the greater should the difficulty be in dismissing him. Similarly, on the contrary, the fact that the Society has no obligation and the person is little useful for the purpose of helping the Society in the divine service will make his dismissal easier.

[**206**]—2. The authority to dismiss will be vested chiefly in the Society as a whole when it is assembled in a general congregation. The superior general will have the same authority in all

g) 736   other cases[g] except one involving himself. The other members of the Society participate, each one, in this authority to the extent that it is communicated to them by the head. But it is wise that it be communicated amply to the provincial superiors [B], and in proper proportion to those local superiors or rectors [C], to whom it seems good that it should be communicated, in order that the subordination arising from holy obedience may

---

2 Today such dismissal requires a judicial process (Canon 654).

be better preserved in the whole body of the Society, in proportion to the better understanding by the members that they depend on their immediate superiors, and that for them it is highly profitable and necessary to be subject to these superiors in all things for Christ our Lord.[h]

h) 423, 662, 663, 666, 791, 820, 821

[207]—*B. Even if the superior general communicates very ample authority in the letters patent which he sends to the individual superiors in order that the subjects may have greater respect and be the more humble and obedient toward them, this authority may nevertheless be restricted and limited by means of private letters, according to what seems expedient.*

[208]—*C. In regard to those who are in the first probation and in the second before taking their vows, whoever has the authority to admit them may also dismiss them,[i] unless special circumstances intervene. Such would be the case if they have been sent to the house or college where they are by the superior general or the provincial, or directed there by someone to whom respect is due, or if they have deserved so well of the Society that special respect is due to them. For in these and similar cases a person of this kind ought not to be sent away by any superior unless the reasons are so highly urgent and serious that beyond any doubt his dismissal would be the will of the superiors.*

i) 31, 192, 205, 219

In regard to those in the houses or colleges who are bound by vows and the scholastics already approved after the two years of probation, if it should become necessary to dismiss them, the local superior should not do this without informing the provincial. The provincial, in accordance with the authority given him by the general, will be able to dismiss them or not, without informing the general.[j]

j) 121, 205, 219

The formed coadjutors, whether spiritual or temporal, ought not to be dismissed[k] without the knowledge and consent of the general—unless in some very remote regions (such as the Indies[3]) it should be necessary to communicate this authority to the provincial, or unless by way of exception and for important reasons the general has communicated this authority to someone in whom he had as much confidence as in himself.

k) 119, 120, 205, 219, 536

In regard to the professed,[l] even less ought such authority be communicated to the lower superiors, unless the general has been informed and the matter carefully weighed so that it is

l) 205, 219, 774

---

3 In the Constitutions the Spanish word *Indias* refers both to India in Asia and to the East Indies, i.e., the Americas (See J. de la Torre, *Constitutiones* [Madrid, 1892], p. 262, fn. 8). The word occurs in [208, 517, 621, 633, 679, 682, 747, 750, 803].

seen that to dismiss such a one helps for the service of God and the common good of the Society. This is the case if he is contumacious or incorrigible and the like.

Chapter 2
The causes for dismissal

[**209**]—1. The discreet charity of the superior who has the authority to dismiss ought to ponder before God our Lord the causes which suffice for dismissal. But to speak in general, they seem to be of four kinds.

[**210**]—2. The first cause is present if it is perceived in the same Lord of ours that someone's remaining in this Society would be contrary to His honor and glory, because this person is judged to be incorrigible in some passions or vices which offend His Divine Majesty. The more serious and culpable these are, the less ought they to be tolerated, even though they do not scandalize the others because they are occult[a] [A].

a) 819

[**211**]—A. *To what extent toleration should be shown for some defects among those which are said to be contrary to the divine honor and those contrary to the good of the Society depends on many particular circumstances of persons, times, and places. Consequently it is necessary to leave it to the discreet zeal of those who have charge of the matter. The more difficulty and doubt they have, the more will they commend the matter to God our Lord and the more will they discuss it with others who in regard to it can be helpful toward perceiving the divine will.*[b]

b) 219-221

[**212**]—3. The second cause is present if it is perceived in the same Lord that to retain someone would be contrary to the good of the Society. Since this is a universal good, it ought to be preferred to the good of one individual[c] by one who is sincerely seeking the divine service. This cause would be present if in the course of the probation some impediments or notable defects should be discovered which the applicant failed to mention earlier during the examination [B], or if experience should show

c) 119, 204, 208, 215, 222

that he would be highly unprofitable and hinder rather than
aid the Society, because of his notable incompetency for any office
whatever[d] [C]. The cause is far more serious if it is judged that he   d) 123, 387
would be harmful by the bad example of his life, especially by
showing himself troublesome or scandalous in words or deeds
[D]. To tolerate this would be attributable not to charity but
to its very opposite[e] on the part of one who is obliged to   e) 217
preserve the peace and well-being of the Society which is in
his charge.

[213]—*B. If someone at the time of his entrance revealed some
illness or predisposition to it and was admitted on trial of his
health; and when he is seen not to improve and it seems that
he will be unable to carry forward the labors of the Society in
the future, it will be permissible to dismiss him, while giving
him aid after he has left the house, as true charity requires.*

*If he entered without any condition although he had mani-
fested his illness, in the hope that he would be more fit than
was found by experience to be the case, then—even though he
could be likewise dismissed in view of his lack of the health
which would be necessary for our Institute—more reflection
should be devoted to his case; and still more if he entered with
health but became ill in the service of the Society. For in that
case, if he himself is not content it would not be just to send
him out of the Society for that sole cause.*

*If someone at his entrance concealed an infirmity, when this
infirmity is discovered he can without doubt be more freely
and justly dismissed. But when he possesses other qualities
important for the divine service, whether he ought in fact to be
sent away or not will be left to the superior's discretion. This
same reasoning holds if it is discovered that in some other matter
he failed to tell the truth[f] in his examination. But if he dissimu-*   f) 217
*lated one of the five impediments, in that case it is not reasonable
that he should remain in the Society,[g] in conformity with what*   g) 31, 32, 176
was said in Part I [164, 176].

[214]—*C. If he does not bring back a good report from the
probationary experiences outside and inside the house,[h] and if*   h) 73-79
*the remedies which charity requires before dismissal do not
suffice, it is better to dismiss him than to incorporate into the
Society persons who are seen to be unsuitable for its Institute.*

[215]—*D. One who by example gives to others an occasion
of sinning is understood to be a scandal to them, and all the
more so if by persuasive words he entices them to some evil,*

especially to instability in their vocation or to discord, or if he attempts something against the superiors or the common good of the Society.[i] *For in such cases, it is not reasonable that one who falls in this manner should remain in the Society.*

i) 664, 665

If it has been necessary to send someone away not so much because of the kind or number of sins as to undo the scandal he has given to others, and if he has been a good subject except for this, prudence will consider whether it is expedient to give him permission to go to some far distant region of the Society, without leaving the Society.

[216]—4. The third cause is present if one's remaining is seen to be simultaneously contrary to the good of the Society and of the individual. For example, this could arise from the body, if during the probation such illnesses and weakness are observed in someone that it seems in our Lord that he could not carry on the labor which is required in our manner of proceeding in order to serve God our Lord by that way.[j] It could also arise from the soul, if the one who was admitted to probation is unable to bring himself to live under obedience and to adapt himself to the Society's manner of proceeding, because he is unable or does not wish to submit his own judgment,[k] or because he has other obstacles arising from nature or habits.

j) 107, 185, 213

k) 152, 184

[217]—5. The fourth cause is present if his remaining is seen to be contrary to the good of others outside the Society. This could arise from discovery of the bond of marriage, or of legitimate slavery,[l] or of debts of importance,[m] after he concealed the truth about this matter in the examination.[n]

l) 28, 173, 174
m) 42, 185, 188
n) 213

If any one whatsoever of these four causes exists, it seems that God our Lord will be better served by giving the person proper dismissal than by employing indiscreet charity in retaining him in whom the causes are found.

Chapter 3
The manner of dismissing

[218]—1. With those who must be dismissed, that manner[1] ought to be employed which before God our Lord is likely to

1 Many texts and examples pertaining to the reasons for and manner of dismissal in the

give greater satisfaction to the one who dismisses as well as
to the one dismissed and to the others within and without the
house [A]. For the satisfaction of the one who dismisses for
the causes mentioned, three things should be observed.

[219]—A. *It is to be noted that the Constitutions treat of
the manner of dismissing when this is done publicly and for
public causes. But in addition to persons dismissed in this manner, there could also be some who are dismissed occultly when
the causes have been occult (and these causes can be many,
of which some are without sin); and if the causes are not mentioned, perturbation among others is to be feared. In such a
case it is better to send those dismissed away from the house
on some pretext such as that of going through experiences,
rather than to publish their dismissal.*

*To dismiss such persons in this way it will suffice that the
superior who has authority for this, commending himself to God
our Lord and hearing the opinion of one or several others[a]
(if he judges in the Lord that he ought to discuss the matter
with them), should make his decision and put it into effect.[2]*   a) 211, 220, 221

*It is also to be noted that what has been stated about the
manner of dismissing is more applicable to those who are in
probations and less to those who have been incorporated into
the Society as approved scholastics and formed coadjutors; and
much less to the professed,[b] in whose case the charity and dis-*   b) 205, 208
*cretion of the Holy Spirit will indicate the manner which ought
to be used in the dismissal, if God our Lord should permit the
necessity of doing this.*

[220]—2. The first thing to be observed is that he should pray
and order prayers in the house for this intention (although the
person's identity remains unknown), that God our Lord may
make His holy will known in this case.[c]   c) 211

[221]—3. Another thing is that he should confer with one or
more persons in the house who seem more suitable and hear
their opinions.[d]   d) 211, 219

early Society are in Aicardo, *Comentario*, V, 517-609.

2 The procedure recommended here and in [220-222] well illustrates not only Ignatius'
habitual manner of reaching decisions through careful reasoning submitted to God in
prayer but also the use of dialogue in the early Society. For other examples of such individual and group discernment of spirits, see *Cons*MHSJ, I, 13-14, 218-219, and *Cons*,
[193, 211, 618, 809].

[222]—4. Another is that, ridding himself of all affection, and keeping before his eyes the greater divine glory and the common good, and the good of the individual as far as possible, he should weigh the reasons on both sides and make his decision to dismiss or not.

[223]—5. For the satisfaction of the one dismissed, three other things ought to be observed. One, pertaining to the exterior, is that as far as possible he should leave the house without shame or dishonor and take with him what is his [B].

e) 58

[224]—*B. In regard to what is found to be his, there is no difficulty in deciding that he should take it.^c But with respect to what he may have spent or given to the Society, or if he remained in its house or college through a fictitious statement, it will be left to the discretion of the one who dismisses him to decide, by weighing what equity and edification require, whether something more than what is his ought to be given to him or not, and if more, how much.*

[225]—6. Another thing, pertaining to the interior, is to try to send him away with as much love and charity for the house and as much consoled in our Lord as is possible.

[226]—7. Another, pertaining to the circumstances of his person, is to try to give him direction whereby he may find another good means to serve God in religious life or outside it, according to what seems more conformed to His divine will. This is done by aiding the person through counsel and prayers and through whatever in charity may appear best.

[227]—8. Likewise, for the satisfaction of the others inside and outside the house, three things ought to be observed. One is that an effort should be made, according to what is possible, that no one may remain troubled in spirit because of the dismissal, by giving a satisfying reason for it to one for whom this is necessary [C], while touching as little as possible on the defects of the dismissed person which are not public (even though he had some).

[228]—*C. To withhold or to give, in public or in private, an explanation of the causes for the dismissal will be more or less expedient, in proportion to the greater or less esteem and love in which the person was held within and without the house.*

[229]—9. Another is that they should not remain disaffected or with a bad opinion in his regard, as far as this is possible. Rather, they should have compassion for him and love him in Christ and recommend him in their prayers to the Divine Majesty, that God may deign to guide him and have mercy on him.

[230]—10. Another is to endeavor that those in the house who are not acting with as much edification as is proper may be helped by this example, and may fear the same thing if they are not willing to be helped. Likewise, efforts should be made that those outside the house who know about the matter may be edified by the fact that in the house toleration is not given to what should not be allowed, for greater glory to God our Lord.

Chapter 4
The Society's way of dealing
with those who leave of themselves
or are dismissed[1]

[231]—1. It seems to us in our Lord that those who are sent away from one region or who leave it of their own accord ought not to be received in another, unless he who dismissed them, or he who is in the place from which they left of themselves, or the superior general, or the one acting in his place has been informed and consents. The purpose here is to prevent the lack of knowledge and of information from being a cause of some error in disservice to God our Lord [A].

[232]—A. *It is said in general that one who left of his own accord or was dismissed ought not to be accepted into another house without informing the superior of the house or college where the person had been and receiving information from him. Nevertheless, it will be left to the discretion of the superior of the house where the person goes to consider whether he will accept him temporarily or not, until he receives a reply from the superior whose order he must follow.*[a]   a) 140

1 For early examples, see Aicardo, *Comentario*, V, 610-654.

[233]—2. The privileges which were granted to such persons as members of the Society are understood to cease from the time they cease to be members.

[234]—3. It should be explained to those dismissed that they remain free from the simple vows, if they took them according to the formula which the Society uses and which will be seen in Part V, and that consequently they do not need a dispensation to be freed from them.b

b) 119, 120, 121, 536, 539

[235]—4. In the case of those who leave without permission, if they were previously regarded as little suitable for the Society, there will be no need to take measures to bring them back to it, but only to direct them to another institute, where they may serve God our Lord, and to remit their vows that they may remain without scruple.

[236]—5. If these subjects are such that it seems a service to God our Lord not to let them go in this way, especially if it is clear that they left through some strong temptation or when misled by others, diligent measures can be taken to bring them back[2] and the privileges granted by the Apostolic See[3] concerning this matter can be employed, to the extent the superior thinks good in the Lord [B]. When a subject thus won back returns, it will be left to the discretion of the one in charge to consider whether he ought to make some satisfaction and how great it ought to be [C], or whether it is better to proceed completely in a spirit of gentleness, while weighing the good of the subject won back and the edification of the members of the house.

[237]—*B. If those who abandon the Society although they are judged fit for it enter another religious institute and take its habit, it seems that the Society ought not to litigate nor to try to bring them back. Before they take the religious habit, that diligence could be used which well-ordered and discreet charity may dictate, to win them back to where it is judged in our Lord that they should serve Him.*

[238]—*C. In regard to the satisfaction to be made by those who come back of their own accord and are received, or by*

2 The benevolent attitude shown throughout this chapter toward those who leave is characteristic of the tradition in religious institutes. Cf., e.g., the Rule of St. Benedict, ch. 29.
3 The reference is to *Licet debitum* of 1549, no. 6. Text in *Cons*MHSJ, I, 361.

those who return after being won back, its purpose is the edifica-
tion of the others and the aid of the person who returned.
Therefore the circumstances of the persons, times, and places
should be the means of judging whether it ought to be made or
not; and, when it should be made, how great it should be. This
entire matter must be referred to the discretion of the superior
in whose house or college the person enters.

[239]—6. If someone returns of his own accord to the house
or college which he left without permission and if he is judged
suitable in other respects to serve God our Lord in it, investigation should be made as to whether he brings a genuine
intention to persevere and to make reparations and undergo
probations of whatever sort [D]. Otherwise there would seem
to be a sign that he is not coming back with genuine repentance
and does not deserve to be accepted.

[240]—D. *When there is doubt about the constancy of those*
who return of their own will, they could be placed in a hospital
or in other experiences where, by serving Christ's poor for His
love for a time, they may show their stability and constancy. To
some extent, this would also be penance for their past fickleness.

[241]—7. If some dismissed subject returns to the same house
from which he was justly sent away and is ready to make all
satisfaction, and if the same causes for which he was dismissed
still endure, it is certain that he ought not to be admitted. If
they do not endure and the one who dismissed him judges that
God our Lord would be served through his coming back to be
received into that house or another, he should inform the general
or the provincial superior and follow the order which will be
given him.

[242]—8. Whether the one who returns left of his own will or
was dismissed, if he is readmitted he should be examined anew;
and when he reenters he should make his general confession
from the last which he made^c and go through the other pro-   c) 98, 200
bations or experiences which seem good to the superior, with
consideration always given to the universal and individual
edification for glory of God our Lord.

Part III
The preservation and progress of those who are in probation

Chapter 1
Preservation pertaining to the soul and to progress in virtues

[**243**]–1. The considerations previously expounded, dealing with the admission of those to whom God our Lord gives a call to our Institute and suitable ability for it, and with the dismissal of those who through lack of such ability reveal that they have not been called by His Divine Wisdom, are necessary. In similar manner, due consideration and prudent care[1] should be employed toward preserving in their vocation those who are being kept and tested in the houses or colleges, and toward enabling them to make progress, both in spirit and in virtues along the path of the divine service, in such a manner that there is also proper care for the health and bodily strength necessary to labor in the Lord's vineyard.[2] Therefore what pertains to the soul will be treated first and then what pertains to the body.

---

1 *Providencia:* prudent and watchful caretaking.
2 Useful background for Part III will be found in *DeGuiJes,* ch. 2, St. Ignatius' Spiritual Training of His Followers; see also the Index, p. 668, s.v. "Novitiate"; Aicardo, *Comentario,* II, 1-819 on spiritual formation and 821-999 on care of the body.

[**244**]—2. In regard to the soul, it is of great importance to keep those who are in probation away from all imperfections and from whatever can impede their greater spiritual progress. For this purpose it is highly expedient that they should cease from all communication by conversation and letters[3] with persons who may diminish their ardor for the goals they have set them-

a) 60, 197

selves[a] [A]; further, that while they advance along the path of the spirit, they should deal only with persons and about matters which help them toward what they were seeking when they entered the Society for the service of God our Lord [B].

[**245**]—*A. If in some place someone is worried or disturbed by persons who are not walking in the path of the spirit, the superior should consider whether it will be expedient to have him move to another place where he can apply himself better in the divine service. In that case the subject's future superior ought to be given as much information about the subject's case as suffices for him to give better help to the subject and to the others in his charge.*

[**246**]—*B. If it seems on some occasion that someone should be permitted to speak to relatives or friends whom he had in the world, this ought to be done in the presence of someone whom the superior designates and briefly, unless for special reasons he who holds the principal charge orders otherwise. Likewise, if someone in the house would write to some region or person, he should obtain permission and show the letter to him whom the superior appoints. If someone writes to him, the letters should likewise go first to the one who was appointed by the superior; and he will see them and give them or not to him to whom they are addressed, according to what he thinks expedient for that person's greater good unto divine glory.*

b) 80

c) 349, 350

[**247**]—3. For the same reason they should not leave the house[b] except at the time and with the companion the superior decides upon[c] [C]; and within the house they should not converse with one another according to their own choice but with those whom the superior designates, that they may edify and help one another in our Lord by their mutual example and spiritual conversation, and not the opposite [D].

---

3 On this see *DeGuiJes,* pp. 104-106. Ignatius regarded conversations and correspondence as effective means by which more advanced religious could promote fraternal union and apostolic efficacy ([648, 673]). But he also saw them as possible dangers to the recollection and interior tranquillity which beginners were only learning. See fn. 4 on [60] above.

[248]—C. *The superior will consider whether some in whom confidence is placed may be sent out alone; and also whether at one time he should grant to some a permission valid for many occasions, or whether they must request permission each time they go out.*

[249]—D. *Ordinarily it is not good for the novices to hold their conversations with one another, but rather to keep silence among themselves except for the things in which speaking is necessary,*[4] *and to deal with mature and discreet persons whom the superior will indicate for each. Likewise, if two have their beds in the same room, one of them should be a person such that with him the other will without doubt perforce become better. For the same reason, too, it is good that some who are older should be between the rooms of the younger ones who are alone.*

Ordinarily, one should not enter the room of another without permission of the superior; and if he has permission to enter, the door should always be open during the time when he is in the room with the other, that the superior may enter each time it is expedient and also the other officials appointed for the purpose.

[250]—4. All should take special care to guard with great diligence the gates of their senses (especially the eyes, ears, and tongue) from all disorder, to preserve themselves in peace and true humility of their souls, and to give an indication of it by silence when it should be kept and, when they must speak, by the discretion and edification of their words, the modesty of their countenance, the maturity of their walk, and all their movements, without giving any sign of impatience or pride. In everything they should try and desire to give the advantage to the others, esteeming them all in their hearts as better than themselves [Phil. 2:3] and showing exteriorly, in an unassuming and simple religious manner, the respect and reverence befitting each one's state, in such a manner that by observing one another they grow in devotion[5] and praise God our Lord, whom each one should endeavor to recognize in his neighbor as in His image.

4 Silence as an aid to keeping the mind on God is a traditional feature of the monastic tradition. See, e.g., St. Benedict's Rule, chs. 6, 42, 48, 49, 52; also, *Cons*MHSJ, I, 206, no. 31. For other sets of rules for novices, similar to those which were finally set down here, see *Cons*MHSJ, I, 207-209; IV, 283, 401.

5 *Devoción:* a word which Ignatius used with great frequency in all his works, especially his letters, *Spiritual Exercises, Spiritual Diary,* and *Constitutions.* It expressed his attitude of profound respect before God to whom he was totally dedicated in love and service, and he used it with multitudinous connotations, often mystical. In the *Constitutions,* as Courel (*Constitutions,* I) points out at [250], the word expresses the personal

[**251**]—5. In the refection of the body care should be taken to observe temperance, decorum, and propriety both interior and exterior in everything. A blessing should precede the meal and a thanksgiving come after it; and all ought to recite these with proper devotion and reverence. During the meal food should also be given to the soul, through the reading of some book which is devotional rather than difficult so that all can understand it and draw profit from it, or through having someone preach during *d)* 280, 281, 402, that time,[d] according to what the superiors may order, or 814 through doing something similar for the glory of God our Lord [E].

[**252**]—*E. Examples of similar things are: to read edifying let-* *e)* 673, 675 *ters*[e] *or to use some other practice if it seems proper on some occasion.*

[**253**]—6. Generally, all those who are in good health should be engaged in spiritual or exterior occupations. Furthermore, just as those who perform duties should be given alleviation if they need it, so when they have time left over they should occupy *f)* 428 themselves in other things,[f] that idleness, which is the source of all evils, may have no place in the house, as far as this is possible.

[**254**]—7. That they may begin to experience the virtue of holy *g)* 287 poverty,[g] all should be taught that they should not have the use *h)* 57, 570, 571 of anything of their own as being their own.[h] However, it is not necessary for them to dispossess themselves of their property during the probation, unless the superior should order them to do *i)* 54, 55, 59, so after the first year has elapsed,[i] because he judges that in such 287, 348, 571 property some novice has an occasion of temptation and of making less progress in spirit, insofar as disorder arises from his placing some love and confidence in it [F]. In that case the dispossession ought to be made in conformity with the counsels of Christ

or communitarian pursuit of spiritual progress; it is linked to discernment of spirits (see fn. 1 at [142]) and the avoidance of illusions [260], to respect in prayer [251], to abnegation and all virtue [263, 289, 362], to the edification and well-being of the neighbor [487]. A. de la Mora, in *La devoción en el espíritu de San Ignacio* (Rome, 1960), has extensively studied the usages of this word in the *Spiritual Diary* and the *Exercises*, where it is a factor of great importance in discernment of spirits. He concludes that for Ignatius "'devotion' was the actuation of the virtue of religion by means of an affection for God which is prompt, compliant, warmly loving, and impelled by charity. Its goal is the worship of God which is accomplished in all things and actions of oneself and one's fellow men, since it gives worship to Him by finding and serving Him in all things" (p. 82). In the Ignatian vocabulary "devotion" is intimately linked with other key phrases worthy of extensive technical investigation, such as union with God, consolation, familiarity with God, charity, discreet charity (on which see fn. 2 on [582] below), love, fervor, finding God in all things, and the like.

our Lord [G]. But it is left to the devotion of each one to apply
his property, or a part of it, to one pious work rather than to
another, according to what God our Lord will give him to perceive as being more conducive to His divine service,ʲ as was   ʲ) 53, 59
stated in the Examen [53-59].

[255]—F. *The dispossessing of oneself is understood to refer
both to one's own property which he presently holds in his own
possession or in that of others and also to his right or claim in
court to what he expects, whether it consists of secular or
ecclesiastical goods. When this dispossession ought to be carried
out will be left to the arrangement of the superior general or
the one to whom he delegates the matter.*

[256]—G. *Before he enters, each one may do what he pleases
with his property; but after his entrance he ought to dispose of
it, whether it be ecclesiastical or secular, in a manner which is
proper for a man who is leading the spiritual life. Consequently,
if he judges that he ought to dispose of it by giving it to relatives,
he ought to submit himself and act according to the judgment
of one, two, or three persons of learning and goodness,ᵏ in order*   ᵏ) 55, 56, 59
*to do what they judge to be more perfect and pleasing to God
our Lord, after consideration of all the circumstances, as is stated
at greater length in the Examen [53-59].*

[257]—8. Likewise they should understand that they may not
lend, borrow, or dispose of anything in the house unless the
superior knows it and consents.

[258]—9. If someone upon entering or after placing himself
under obedience should find devotion in disposing of his temporal goods or a part of them in favor of the Society, it is beyond
any doubt a matter of greater perfection, self-dispossession, and
abnegation of all self-love, not to single out particular places with
fond affection, or through that affection to apply his goods to one
place rather than to another [H]. Rather, he does better if, while
desiring the greater and more universal good of the Society
(which is directed to greater divine service and greater universal
good and spiritual progress of souls), he leaves to him who has
charge of the whole Society this judgment as to whether the
goods ought to be applied to one place rather than to another
of that same province. For the general can know better than
another what is expedient as well as all the urgent matters which
there are in all the regions of it. Furthermore, he can take
account of the kings, princes, and lords, seeing to it that no

l) 823, 824

cause of offense may be given to them[1] and that the matter may lead to the greater edification of all, and to greater spiritual progress of souls and glory of God our Lord.

[259]—H. *In this matter just as in all the rest, the rectors, local superiors, or provincials, and any other persons who deal with him who desires to dispose of his possessions in that manner, ought to represent to him that which is more perfect and in which he will gain greater merit before God our Lord. Nevertheless, if they should observe in him a preference for one place more than another (which is something imperfect), even though he does give up his own judgment, they could inform the superior general, or the one who holds his place, as to whether it seems that some imperfection ought to be tolerated, in the hope that it will some day cease and that God our Lord will supply what is lacking to the person for greater divine glory and his own greater perfection.*

m) 813

[260]—10. They should be taught how to guard themselves from the illusions of the devil in their devotions and how to defend themselves from all temptations. They should know the means which can be found to overcome them and to apply themselves to the pursuit of the true and solid virtues,[m] whether this be with many spiritual visitations or with fewer, by endeavoring always to go forward in the path of the divine service.

n) 342, 344
o) 80, 278, 342,
343, 584
p) 278, 584

q) 263, 278

r) 35, 91, 92,
424

[261]—11. They should practice the daily examination of their consciences[n] and confess and receive Communion at least every eight days,[o] unless the superior for some reason orders otherwise. There should be one confessor for all, assigned by him who has charge of the others.[p] Or if this is impossible [I], everyone should at least have his own regular confessor to whom he should keep his conscience completely open,[q] and who should be informed about the cases which the superior reserves to himself.[6] These cases will be those where it appears necessary or highly expedient for the superior to have knowledge, that he may the better provide remedies and protect from difficulties those whom he has in his charge.[r]

[262]—I. *To do this without inconvenience could be impossible because of the large numbers or because some individual would seem to be aided more by another confessor than by the ordinary*

---

6 In 1923 General Congregation XXVII brought details of [261] into conformity with the new Code, especially Canons 519 and 595 on confessions and Communion.

one, through reasons which could arise. The superior will take account of these and provide what he judges in our Lord to be expedient.

[263]—12. It will be beneficial to have a faithful and competent person whose function is to instruct and teach the novices in regard to their interior and exterior conduct, to encourage them toward this correct deportment, to remind them of it, and to give them kindly admonition[s] [K]; a person whom all those who are in probation may love and to whom they may have recourse in their temptations and open themselves with confidence, hoping to receive from him in our Lord counsel and aid in everything. They should be advised, too, that they ought not to keep secret any temptation which they do not tell to him or their confessor[t] or the superior,[u] being happy that their entire soul is completely open to them. Moreover, they will tell him not only their defects but also their penances or mortifications,[v] or their devotions and all their virtues,[7] with a pure desire to be directed if in anything they have gone astray, and without desiring to be guided by their own judgment unless it agrees with the opinion of him whom they have in place of Christ our Lord.

s) 431

t) 261, 278
u) 91-97, 424, 551
v) 8, 300, 582

[264]—K. *This person will be the master of novices or whomever the superior appoints as being more fit for this charge.*

[265]—13. Temptations ought to be anticipated by their opposites, for example, if someone is observed to be inclined toward pride, by exercising him in lowly matters thought fit to aid toward humbling him; and similarly of other evil inclinations.[8]

[266]—14. Furthermore, for the sake of decorum and propriety, it is expedient that women should not enter the houses or colleges but only the churches [L]; and that arms should not be kept in the house, nor instruments for vain purposes [M], but only those implements which are helpful toward the end which the Society seeks, the divine service and praise.

[267]—L. *The nonentrance of women into houses or colleges of the Society ought generally to be observed. But if they are persons of great charity or of high rank as well as of great*

---

7 See fn. 18 on [92] above.
8 For other examples of this typically Ignatian tendency to contrast opposites, see above, Introduction, pp. 23-24, [101] with fn. 24; also *SpEx*, [22, 142, 146, 157, 167].

charity, the superior in his discretion will have the power to grant a dispensation for just reasons, that if they so desire they may enter to see it.

[268]—M. *Examples are instruments for games, and those for music,[9] and profane books, and similar objects.*

[269]—15. In regard to the corrections and penances, the measure which ought to be observed will be left to the discreet charity of the superior and of those whom he has delegated in his place, that they may adjust them in accordance with the disposition of the persons and with the edification of each and every one of them for divine glory[w] [N]. Each one ought to accept them in a good spirit with a genuine desire of his emendation and spiritual profit, even when the reason for their imposition[10] is not that of some blameworthy defect.[x]

w) 727, 754

x) 8, 90, 98

[270]—N. *In corrections, the following order is to be noticed, although discretion may change it in a particular case. Those who fall into a fault should be admonished, the first time, with love and sweetness;[y] the second time, with love and also in such a way that they feel humiliating shame; the third time, with love but in such a way that they have fear. In the case of public defects, however, the penance ought to be public but with announcement only of what is conducive to the edification of all.*

y) 667

[271]—16. In the house there should be a syndic[11] whose duty is to observe all the individuals in regard to matters of decorum and exterior propriety.[z] He should go through the church and the house, note what is unbecoming, and inform the superior or, if he has received such authority, the individual himself who is at fault, that he may be more helpful in the Lord.

z) 431, 504-506

[272]—17. In their illnesses all should try to draw fruit from them not only for themselves but for the edification of others. They should not be impatient nor difficult to please. Rather, they should have and show much patience and obedience to the physician and infirmarian, and employ good and edifying words

---

9 Ignatius himself approved the use of music to comfort the sick. See *ConsMHSJ*, II, 355, no. 28; *FN*, I, 636, no. 178.

10 Other reasons for which Ignatius imposed penances were to test men or to give them an opportunity of meriting. See also *DeGuiJes*, pp. 92-95.

11 *Síndico*: a person who could be a censor, observer, inspector, corrector, or watchman (see Covarrubias, p. 940), especially in regard to domestic observance—as also in [386, 431, 504] below. In modern Jesuit houses his duties are usually exercised by the minister. The syndic or censor was one of the customary officials of medieval universities. His

which show that the sickness is accepted as a gift from the hand
of our Creator and Lord, since it is a gift not less than is health.ᵃ   *a*) 89, 304, 595

[273]—18. As far as possible, we should all think alike and
speak alike,ᵇ in conformity with the Apostle's teaching [Phil. 2:2];   *b*) 358, 464, 671,
and differing doctrines ought not to be permitted, either orally   672, 821
in sermons or public lectures, or in books [O]; (and it will not
be permissible to publish books without the approval and permission of the superior general,ᶜ who will entrust the examination   *c*) 389, 653
of them to at least three persons of sound doctrine and clear
judgment about the field in question). Even in regard to things
which are to be done, diversity, which is generally the mother
of discord and the enemy of union of wills, should be avoided as
far as possible. This union and agreement among them all ought
to be sought with great care and the opposite ought not to be
permitted [P], in order that, being united among themselves
by the bond of fraternal charity, they may be able better and
more efficaciously to apply themselves in the service of God and
the aid of their fellowmen.ᵈ   *d*) 655, 664, 821

[274]—*O. Novel doctrines ought not to be admitted; and
if there should be opinions which diverge from what is commonly
held by the Church and its teachers, those holding them ought
to submit to what is determined in the Society,ᵉ as was explained   e*) 47
in the Examen [47]. Furthermore, an effort should be made to
obtain conformity in the Society in regard to the divergent or
contrary opinions which Catholic teachers hold.*

[275]—*P. Passion or any anger of some toward others should
not be allowed among the residents of the house. If something
of the sort arises, efforts should be made to bring the parties
to prompt reconciliation and fitting satisfaction.*

[276]—19. The good example of the older members, which
encourages the others to imitate them, is a great aid toward
progress in the virtues. Therefore on some occasion within the
year the superior (if he does not for special reasons judge something else expedient), and all the other priests for whom he thinks
it wise should for a period of time perform the duty or duties
of those who serve, that the practice of such duties may be more

functions varied according to centuries and countries. See J. B. Herman, *La Pédagogie
des Jésuites* (Louvain, 1914), pp. 113-115; A. P. Farrell, *The Jesuit Code of Liberal
Education* (Milwaukee, 1938), pp. 59-61; *Oxford English Dictionary*, IX, part 2, p.
379, s.v.

satisfying to those others who are assigned to them for the greater service and glory of God our Lord.

f) 80

[277]—20. On certain days of each week instruction should be given about Christian doctrine,[f] the manner of making a good and fruitful confession [Q], receiving Communion, assisting at Mass and serving it, praying, meditating, and reading [good

g) 343-345

spiritual books], in accordance with each one's capacity.[g] Likewise, care should be taken that they learn what is proper and do not let it be forgotten, and put it into practice; that is, all of

h) 342-344

them should give time to spiritual things[h] and strive to acquire as much devotion[12] as divine grace imparts to them. Toward this purpose it will help to give some of the Spiritual Exercises,

i) 65

or all of them,[i] to those who have not made them, according to what is judged expedient for them in our Lord [R].

j) 80, 261, 342

[278]—Q. *In addition to the manner of confessing well, a time to confess will be assigned to them;[j] and if they miss it, they should not be given food for the body until they have taken their spiritual nourishment. Moreover, one who confesses to another than to his ordinary confessor ought later to open his*

k) 261, 263

whole conscience to his own confessor,[k] as far as he remembers, that he, being ignorant of nothing which pertains to it, may the better aid him in our Lord.

[279]—R. *Those who on their own part are acquainted with the Spiritual Exercises and are making progress in them and have a plan for proceeding in them, or those who have other occupations, may be dispensed by the superior in whole or in part from the rules applying to all in this matter.*

Some are capable of making the Spiritual Exercises but do not have experience in them. It is good to aid these on occasions by coming down with them to detailed considerations which incite them to the fear and love of God and to the virtues and their

l) 343

practice, as discretion will show to be expedient.[l]

If some subject is seen to be unfit for exercises of this kind (as could be the case with some temporal coadjutor), such exercises as are suitable for his capacity should be given to him, that by them he may aid himself and serve God our Lord.

m) 80, 251, 402, 814

[280]—21. It is good for all to exercise themselves in preaching inside the house[m] [S] (unless the superior has exempted some-

---

12 On *devoción*, see fn. 5 on [250] above.

one). The purpose is that, in addition to the fact that some time after eating would be well spent in this practice, they may encourage themselves and acquire a facility of voice, bearing, and the like, and show the talent which God our Lord gives them in this field; still further, that they may express their good ideas for their own edification and that of their fellowmen, by speaking often of what pertains to the abnegation of themselves as well as of the virtues and all perfection, and by exhorting one another to all of these, especially to union and fraternal charity.

[281]—S. *Those who preach in the house should not reprimand any of their brethren of the house or of the Society. The preachers in the churches should also beware of giving such a reprimand, unless the superior has been informed about the matter. However, a preacher may both encourage himself and his brethren to go forward in greater service to God. But this is more suitable in sermons within the house than in the church.*

[282]—22. It will be very specially helpful to perform with all possible devotion the tasks in which humility and charity are practiced more;[n] and, to speak in general, the more one binds himself to God our Lord and shows himself more generous toward His Divine Majesty [T], the more will he find God more generous toward himself and the more disposed will he be to receive graces and spiritual gifts which are greater each day.

n) 68, 83

[283]—T. *To bind oneself more to God our Lord and to show oneself generous toward Him is to consecrate oneself completely and irrevocably to His service,[o] [13] as those do who dedicate themselves to Him by vow. But although this is a great help toward receiving more abundant grace, no one ought to be commanded or in any way constrained to do it within the first two years.*

o) 30, 53

But if some through their own devotion are spontaneously impelled to anticipate the vow,[p] it ought not to be received into anyone's hands[14] nor should there be any solemnity; but each one should offer the vow to God our Lord in the secret of his own soul. And when any do this, it is also good for them to request

p) 17, 544

---

13 This simple, spontaneous expression of Ignatius contains the heart or essence of what religious life is: total and irrevocable self-dedication to God through love. From this flows love of the neighbor. See also [288] below, and pp. 15-16 above.

14 "Not to be received into anyone's hands": this technical sixteenth-century terminology is used to indicate that the vow is made to God and not to man. See [534, 537, 539] below, and fn. 17 on [7] above; also, *Colld*, no. 152, §2. According to the modern terminology of Canon 1308, §1, the vow of devotion mentioned in [283] is a private rather than a public vow (see p. 42 above).

the ordinary form of the simple vows and, as an aid to memory, to retain in writing what they have promised to God our Lord.

[284]—23. To make progress, it is very expedient and highly necessary that all should devote themselves to complete obedience,[15] by recognizing the superior, whoever he is, as being in the place of Christ our Lord[q] and by maintaining interior reverence and love for him. They should obey entirely and promptly, not only by exterior execution of what the superior commands, with becoming energy and humility, and without excuses and murmurings even though things are commanded which are difficult and repugnant to sensitive nature [V]; but they should try to maintain in their inmost souls genuine resignation and true abnegation of their own wills and judgments, by bringing their wills and judgments wholly into conformity with what the superior wills and judges, in all things in which no sin is seen, and by regarding the superior's will and judgment as the rule of their own, in order to conform themselves more completely to the first and supreme rule of all good will and judgment, which is the Eternal Goodness and Wisdom.[r]

[285]—V. *It will be helpful from time to time for superiors to see to it that those who are in probation feel their obedience and poverty, by testing them for their greater spiritual progress in the manner in which God tested Abraham [Gen., ch. 22], and that they may give an example of their virtue and grow in it. But in this the superiors should as far as possible observe the measure and proportion of what each one can bear, as discretion will dictate.*

[286]—24. That they may exercise themselves more in obedience, it is good and likewise highly necessary that they should obey not only the superior of the Society or house, but also the subordinate officials who hold their authority from him, in regard to everything for which that authority over them was given.[s] They should accustom themselves to consider not who the person is whom they obey, but rather who He is for whose sake they obey and whom they obey in all, who is Christ our Lord.[t]

[287]—25. All should love poverty[u] as a mother,[16] and accord-

q) 84, 85, 286, 342, 424, 547, 551, 552, 618, 619, 627, 661, 765

r) 424, 547, 549, 550

s) 84-88, 434
t) 84, 85, 284, 342, 424, 547, 551, 552, 618, 619, 627, 661, 765
u) 553, 816

15 Ignatius here gives the novices a preliminary but succinct and comprehensive sketch of his concept of obedience which is developed at greater length later, especially in Part VI, [547-552]. See the footnotes there and above on [84].
16 This similar preliminary sketch on poverty is developed below, [553-581]. See the footnotes there and above on [4, 5].

ing to the measure of holy discretion all should, when occasions arise, feel some effects of it.ᵛ Further, as is stated in the Examen [53-59], after the first year they should be ready, each one, to dispose of their temporal goods whenever the superior may command it,ʷ in the manner which was explained to them in the aforementioned Examen.

v) 254

w) 54, 55, 59, 254, 571

[288]—26. All should make diligent efforts to keep their intention right,¹⁷ not only in regard to their state of life but also in all particular details. In these they should always aim at serving and pleasing the Divine Goodness for its own sake and because of the incomparable love and benefits with which God has anticipated us, rather than for fear of punishments or hope of rewards, although they ought to draw help also from them. Further, they should often be exhorted to seek God our Lord in all things, stripping off from themselves the love of creatures to the extent that this is possible, in order to turn their love upon the Creator of them, by loving Him in all creatures and all of them in Him, in conformity with His holy and divine will.

[289]—27. The study which those who are in probation will have in the houses of the Society should, it seems, be about what will help them toward what has been said on the abnegation of themselvesˣ and toward further growth in virtue and devotion. To speak in general, literary studies will not take place in a house (unless it appears that for special reasons a dispensation ought to be given to some members) [X]. For the colleges exist for the acquisition of learning,ʸ the houses that those who have acquired it may use it in practice,¹⁸ or that those who must still acquire it may lay a foundation of humility and virtue for it.

x) 103

y) 307, 308, 333, 392, 440, 815

[290]—X. *Although in general literary studies are not pursued*

---

17 Constitution [288] contains another spontaneous and typical expression of Ignatius' desire to live totally and simply for God and to have his religious do the same (cf. [283] above and [813] below). The purity of intention recommended here is well treated in Coemans, trans. M. Germing, *Commentary on the Rules* (El Paso, 1948), esp. pp. 154-162. See also [340, 360] below, and [805] with fn. 3. In these three related passages we have a characteristic example of Ignatius' style and habits of thinking: his use of "doublets" and "triplets." He uses the terms *intención recta . . . pretendiente . . . puramente el servir* here in [288], *con pura intención* in [340], *ánima pura, y la intención . . . recta* in [360], and in text *a* of [360] *con consciencia pura y con intención recta* (see *Cons*MHSJ, II, 181, 182). All these terms overlap in meaning and each colors and clarifies the other. See also [277] above and *SpEx*, [169].

18 On the distinction between houses and colleges, see fn. 8 on [2] above. In the earlier years both houses and colleges served as houses of probation (*Cons*MHSJ, II, cxxxix). Houses of probation were often attached to colleges, that the fixed revenues of the colleges might be used to support the novices. Cf. *Exam*, [5, 6].

in the houses[19] of the Society, all those who attend to preaching and confessing may study what is helpful toward their purpose. If it is expedient for some particular individual to study other matters also, it will be left to the superior's discretion to see this and to grant a dispensation for it.

[291]—28. There should be someone who gives these reminders, or similar ones, to the novices every week or at least every fifteen days, or they should be required to read them,[z] that these precepts may not be forgotten through the condition of our frail human nature, with the result that their practice would cease. Furthermore, several times within the year all should ask the superior to order that penances should be given to them for their negligence in keeping the rules, that this concern may show their care to progress in the service of God.

z) 439, 826

19 Cf. the Formula of the Institute, *Regimini* (1540), [5], *Exposcit* (1550), [5]. The statement in [289] reflects Ignatius' early ideal, intention, and expectation: the formed or professed members were to live in houses exclusively on alms ([4-5]) and devote themselves to ministerial pursuits, the scholastics in colleges and on fixed revenues to avoid impeding studies by too much time spent in gathering alms. That simple distinction of purpose and function, however, did not work out fully according to his original expectations, as we gather from Declaration X [290] and elsewhere (see, e.g., Lukács, in *AHSJ*, XXIX [1960], 190-191; *WL*, XCI [1962], 126-127). After externs were admitted into the classes for Jesuit scholastics at Gandía in 1546, and especially after the ministry of teaching extern students was found to be so fruitful (e.g., at Messina in 1548 and at Rome in 1551), colleges (some for Jesuits and externs, and some chiefly for externs) multiplied far more rapidly than houses of the professed. Through his secretary, Polanco, in 1555 Ignatius himself expressed to Borgia his preference for colleges over professed houses: "Our Father's intention is, especially in the beginning, that colleges should be multiplied and not houses. For it is necessary to have accommodations to receive and instruct many students" (*EppIgn*, IX, 82-83). Nobles and cities were eager to endow colleges for the instruction of their young men but comparatively few persons showed willingness to support professed houses. At Ignatius' death in 1556 there were two professed houses (at Rome with 60 Jesuits and at Lisbon with 22), while the colleges had multiplied to 46. Moreover, many professed Jesuits were living in the colleges who were engaged in ministries other than teaching. Thus they seemed (at least to many after 1570) to be benefiting from the fixed revenues of the colleges, contrary to the bulls *Regimini*, [5], *Exposcit*, [5], *Exam*, [4, 5], and *Cons*, [553-555]. In reality, Ignatius' practice had evolved (with full knowledge of the popes who praised the new colleges and their successful procedures) beyond what many passages of his Constitutions and even of the papal bulls seemed to allow; and he failed to update these passages before his death in 1556. Consequently great controversies about the poverty of the colleges arose about 1570. Many Jesuits thought that the Society's practice was not faithful to the bulls and Constitutions. In 1608 settlement came from General Congregation VI, which in Decree 18 vindicated the practice inaugurated by Ignatius and authoritatively interpreted the controverted passages of the Constitutions. See L. Lukács, "De origine collegiorum externorum deque controversiis circa eorum paupertatem obortis, 1539-1608," *AHSJ*, XXIX (1960), 189-245, XXX (1961), 3-89; English digest in *WL*, XCI (1962), 123-166, in which see esp. 139-147, 164-166.

Chapter 2
The preservation of the body

[292]—1. Just as an excessive preoccupation over the needs of the body is blameworthy, so too a proper concern about the preservation of one's health and bodily strength[1] for the divine service is praiseworthy,[a] and all should exercise it. Consequently, when they perceive that something is harmful to them or that something else is necessary in regard to their diet, clothing, living quarters, office or the manner of carrying it out, and similarly of other matters, all ought to inform the superior about it or the one whom he appoints. But meanwhile they should observe two things. First, before informing him they should recollect themselves to pray, and after this, if they perceive that they ought to represent the matter to him who is in charge, they should do it. Second, after they have represented it by word of mouth or by a short note as a precaution against his forgetting it, they should leave the whole care of the matter to him and regard what he ordains as better, without arguing or insisting upon it either themselves or through another, whether he grants the request or not [A]. For the subject must persuade himself that what the superior decides after being informed is more suitable for the divine service and the subject's own greater good in our Lord.[b]

a) 243, 339, 582, 827

b) 131, 543, 627

[293]—A. *Even though the subject who represents his need ought not personally to argue or urge the matter, nevertheless if the superior has not yet understood it, and if he requests further explanation, the subject will give it. If by chance he forgets to provide after he has indicated his intention to do so, it is not out of order to recall it to his memory or to represent it with becoming modesty.*

1 Ignatius' concern to preserve the health and bodily welfare of his subjects flows as a corollary from his esteem for natural gifts, seen e.g. in [147, 156-162, 300, 339, 728-734, 814]. His experience increased this concern. Mannaerts (1523-1614) relates (*Exhortationes*, II, 613-614) that "a few years after the foundation of the Society, when . . . Ignatius observed that many, shortly after their entrance, were wasting away and dying, he called a meeting of physicians." When they learned of the austere life many were leading, they marveled that the number of those who had died was not greater. Then they urged that seven hours of sleep should be common to all each night; that mental prayer should not exceed an hour, except for the examens of conscience at their appointed times; that there should be an hour of rest after eating; that study should not be prolonged beyond two hours; that there should be time each week for a walk and other proper recreation. Many of these recommendations, which harmonize with the ordinary schedule and tempo of life in Mediterranean countries, were incorporated into the Constitutions. See *Cons*-MHSJ, II, cxcii.

c) 435

[294]—2. There should be a proper order, as far as may be possible, for the time of eating, sleeping, and rising,^c and ordinarily all should observe it [B].

[295]—*B. All ought ordinarily to observe the order of times for eating and sleeping. However, if for special reasons something else is expedient for someone, the superior will consider whether or not he should be given a dispensation.*

d) 81, 577-581

[296]—3. In regard to food, clothing [C], living quarters, and other bodily needs,^d although something should be done to test their virtue and self-abnegation, nevertheless with the divine aid care should be taken to avoid a lack of the things by which nature is sustained and preserved for God's service and praise. That consideration of persons should be exercised which is proper in our Lord.

e) 18, 19, 197, 579

[297]—*C. In regard to clothing, its purpose, which is protection from cold and indecorum, should be kept in view. Beyond this, it is good for those who are in probation to take advantage of their garments as means to the mortification and abnegation of themselves and to trample on the world and its vanities.^e This should be done to the extent that the nature, usage, office, and other circumstances of the persons permit.*

In the case of approved scholastics and those attending to study, it seems that in respect to clothing more attention could be paid to exterior propriety and convenience, in view of the labors of study and the fact that the colleges have a fixed income, although all superfluity should be ever avoided. With particular persons one could well act as is fitting for them.

f) 339, 822

[298]—4. Just as it is unwise to assign so much physical labor that the spirit should be oppressed and the body be harmed^f [D], so too some bodily exercise to help both the body and the spirit is ordinarily expedient for all, even for those who must apply themselves to mental labors. These too ought to be interrupted by exterior activities and not prolonged or undertaken beyond the measure of discretion.

g) 339

h) 280

[299]—*D. For an hour or two after taking a meal, especially during the summer, strenuous exertions of body or mind ought not to be permitted,^g as far as this is possible (with all needs being judged with all possible charity). But other light activities may be pursued during this time.^h Even outside these hours it*

*is not good to continue to work for a long time without some
relaxation or proper recreation.*

[300]—5. The chastisement of the body ought not to be immoderate or indiscreet in abstinences, vigils [E] and other external penances and labors [F] which damage and impede greater goods. Therefore it is expedient for each one to keep his confessor informed of what he does in this matter. If the confessor thinks that there is excess or has a doubt, he should refer the matter to the superior.[i] All this is done that the procedure may be attended by greater light and God our Lord may be more glorified through our souls and bodies.

i) 8, 9, 263, 582

[301]—*E. It seems that the time for sleeping ought to be, in general, between six and seven hours,[j] and that they ought not to sleep without nightclothes, unless it be because of some necessity which the superior recognizes. But since no precise rule is possible in such great diversity of persons and constitutions, the shortening or prolonging of this time will be left to the discretion of the superior, who will take care that each one receives what his constitution requires.*

j) 339, 580

[302]—*F. Each one ought to be ready to undertake whatever employment may be assigned to him. Nevertheless, in the case of those which require stronger and more vigorous men, such as those in the sacristy, porter's lodge, or infirmary, care should be taken to assign to them persons who have the physical constitution suitable for the requirements of the office, as far as will be possible.*

[303]—6. It is good to have in the house someone who superintends what pertains to the preservation of health for those who have it, especially for those who are weaker because of age or other causes, and to its restoration in the case of the sick. If these feel more than ordinarily indisposed, they are obliged to tell him, that a suitable remedy may be provided, as charity requires [G].

[304]—*G. Great care should be taken of the sick. Their illness should be reported to the infirmarian, and if he judges it to be of moment he should inform the superior and a physician should be called. Ordinarily there will be only one physician, unless the superior thinks otherwise in particular cases. Furthermore, his order should be followed, as far as possible, in regard to the*

k) 580

regimen and medicines,[k] *without the sick man intruding himself in anything other than in exercising his patience and obedience, by leaving the care of everything else to the superior and his*

l) 89, 272, 595

ministers, by means of whom Divine Providence directs him.[l]

     Moreover, although our vocation is to travel through the world and to live in any part of it whatsoever where there is hope of greater service to God and of help of souls,[m] *nevertheless, if it*

m) 82, 92, 308, 588, 603, 605, 626

becomes apparent through experience that someone cannot bear the circumstances of some region and continues in bad health there, it will be the superior's part to consider whether the sub- ject ought to be transferred to another place where he may have better bodily health and be able to employ himself more in service of God our Lord. But to request such a change or to show oneself inclined to it will not be the part of any of those sick, who should leave this concern to the superior.

     [305]—7. In what pertains to the conservation of the temporal goods, all should have the concern to which charity and reason oblige them. But beyond that, it will be good to have someone who is charged more particularly with caring for these goods as

n) 591

the estate and property of Christ our Lord.[n] Likewise in regard to other necessary things, an endeavor should be made to have

o) 148, 149, 334, 428

a sufficiency of officials,[o] especially for those things which are more appropriately done inside the house than outside it [H]. Furthermore, it is good that the temporal coadjutors should learn these tasks, if they do not know them, with all things always being directed to greater glory of God our Creator and Lord.

     [306]—H. *The officials for the things which are done more appropriately inside the house than outside it are understood to be the launderer, barber, and similar ones whom it is expedient to have in a house if it is possible.*

Part IV
The instruction of those who are retained in the Society, in learning and in other means of helping their fellowmen

[Preamble]¹

[307]—1. The aim which the Society of Jesus directly seeks is to aid its own members and their fellowmen to attain the ultimate end for which they were created.ᵃ To achieve this purpose, in addition to the example of one's life, learning and a method of

a) 3, 156, 163, 258, 446, 586, 603, 813

---

1 The word "preamble" comes, not from Ignatius' text B, but from the Latin translators of 1558.

Part IV was composed in stages. Texts *a* (drafted during the years 1547-1550) and A (of 1550) contain only the chapters now numbered 1-6 and 8-10, and envisaged almost exclusively the scholastics of the Society. But the experience and apostolic success of colleges and classes conducted for externs at Gandía (founded in 1545, opened to lay students in 1546, made a university in 1547), Messina (1548), and elsewhere led Ignatius to plan a treatise on the colleges and classes for externs and still another on the universities of the Society. Hence in 1553 and 1554 he composed, with Polanco's help, the present ch. 7 focused on colleges and classes for extern students, even those not seeking the priesthood, and chs. 11-17 on the universities, all of which are in text B of 1556. Although he added these chapters, 7 and 11-17, to the Constitutions, he did not make changes or revisions of note in the earlier chapters but changed merely a few phrases here and there. See *Cons*MHSJ, II, lxvii-lix and 170, lines 27-28; Lukács in *MonPaed* (1965), pp. 7*-8*, 14*, 25*, 210-211, 261, 270-273, and in *AHSJ*, XXIX (1960), 214-219, XXX (1961), 28-33; *WL*, XCI (1962), 129-134. The newly revised *Monumenta Paedagogica*, I (1540-1556), ed. Lukács (Rome, 1965) (abbreviated hereafter as *MonPaed* [1965]), is now the most important and scholarly source available on the Society's work in education during Ignatius' lifetime. Its scholarship is outstandingly thorough.

expounding it are also necessary.[2] Therefore, after the proper foundation of abnegation of themselves is seen to be present in those who were admitted and also the required progress in virtues, it will be necessary to provide for the edifice of their learning and the manner of employing it,[3] that these may be aids toward better knowledge and service of God, our Creator and Lord.

Toward achieving this purpose the Society takes charge of the colleges and also of some universities,[b] that in them those who prove themselves worthy in the houses but have entered the Society unequipped with the necessary learning may receive instruction in it and in the other means of helping souls [A]. Therefore with the favor of the Divine and Eternal Wisdom and for His greater glory and praise, we shall treat first of what pertains to the colleges and then of the universities.[4]

b) 289, 333, 351, 360, 440, 446, 815

[308]—*A. The aim and end of this Society is, by traveling through the various regions of the world[c] at the order of the supreme vicar of Christ our Lord or of the superior of the Society itself, to preach, hear confessions, and use all the other means it can with the grace of God to help souls. Consequently it has seemed necessary to us, or at least highly expedient, that those who will enter the Society should be persons of good life and sufficient learning for the aforementioned work.[d] But in comparison with others, those who are both good and learned are few; and even among these few, most of them already seek rest from their previous labors. As a result, the increase of the Society from such men of letters who are both good and learned is,*

c) 82, 92, 304, 588, 603, 605, 626

d) 12, 516, 518, 656-658, 819

---

2 The rest of Part IV makes clear that Ignatius desired his priests to adapt this method to their hearers. To deal with the educated, for whom the preaching was often in Latin, they were to cultivate the polished style which the tastes of the age demanded ([381, 456, 484]). For more unlearned folk, they were to learn the vernacular and speak in simple style ([402]).

3 Some influence from this passage appears in the similar statement by St. John Baptist de la Salle (1651-1719) in the Constitutions of the Brothers of the Christian Schools, P. 2, c. 10, n. 1. See *Cons*MHSJ, III, 99.

4 In [307] Ignatius clearly directs the Society's educational activities to the ultimate purpose of a man's life and to greater glory to God. This paragraph, especially when taken in conjunction with [440] and with ch. 12 [446-452] below, is a striking example of his habit of viewing everything in an ascending hierarchy of beings leading men to happiness in God. See above, pp. 18-19.

On Ignatius' place among the world's educators, an important work is Robert R. Rusk, *The Doctrines of the Great Educators*, 3rd ed. rev. (London, 1965). In this, the fifteenth printing of his widely used book which first appeared in 1918, Rusk treats thirteen men whose educational doctrines have made an outstanding impact on educational practice: Plato, Quintilian, Elyot, Ignatius, Comenius, Milton, Locke, Rousseau, Pestalozzi, Herbart, Froebel, Montessori, and Dewey. Rusk rightly states (p. 88) that Ignatius "is as worthy of a place amongst the great educators as amongst the saints."

we find, something very difficult to achieve, because of the great labors and the great abnegation of oneself which are required in the Society.

Therefore all of us, desiring to preserve and develop the Society for greater glory and service to God our Lord have thought it wise to proceed by another path.⁵ That is, our procedure will be to admit young men who because of their good habits of life and ability give hope that they will become both virtuous and learned in order to labor in the vineyard of Christ our Lord.ᵉ We shall likewise accept colleges under the conditions stated in the apostolic bull,⁶ whether these colleges are within universities or outside of them; and, if they are within universities, whether these universities are governed by the Society or not.ᶠ For we are convinced in our Lord that in this manner greater service will be given to His Divine Majesty, because those who will be employed in that service will be multiplied in number and aided to make progress in learning and virtues.

Consequently, we shall treat first of what pertains to the colleges and then of what concerns the universities.⁷ With regard

e) 183, 334, 523

f) 320, 440, 441, 762

5 Theoretically, in the first infancy of the Society two paths were open to Ignatius and his companions: (1) to admit to their new Society only men already educated or (2) to admit men already formed and also some youths still to be educated. Did they actually ever intend to try the first procedure? The evidence points to a negative reply. For already in August, 1539, they planned to educate in universities apt young men whom they hoped would later enter the Society (*Prima . . . Instituti Summa*, [5], in *Cons*MHSJ, I, 19; cf. *FN*, I, 121). For such students the bull of 1540, *Regimini*, [6] approved residences (*in universitatibus . . . collegia*) with fixed revenues. These residences, however, were not then considered domiciles of the Society but institutions superintended by it, as is shown by the statement "In the Society there are no studies or lectures" (*Cons*-MHSJ, I, 47), in the document there entitled *Constitutiones anni 1541*, but which in its first draft probably stems from 1539 (*AHSJ*, XII [1943], 93-94). Hence colleges of this first type, residences without lectures and for Jesuit scholastics attending a public university, arose very early in the Society. They were established at Paris in 1540, Coimbra, Padua, and Louvain in 1542, Cologne and Valencia in 1544, and elsewhere. However, the university lectures were often found to be unsatisfactory and without organized sequence, e.g., at Padua. Consequently lectures were gradually introduced into some of these Jesuit colleges (see *MonPaed* [1965], pp. 6*-7*). The practice of educating extern students, lay or clerical, in addition to Jesuits arose later, in 1543 in India and in 1546 at Gandía, Spain (*MonPaed* [1965], pp. 7*-8*, 499-504).

6 *Regimini* (1540), [6], *Exposcit* (1550), [5].

7 In organizing his schools and writing constitutions or statutes for them, Ignatius appropriated many features from the practices and constitutions of non-Jesuit schools of his day. He had experience of what was done in the universities of Alcalá, Salamanca, and Paris. Moreover, in 1549 when he was thinking much about the composition of the constitutions of his own colleges and universities, he tried to obtain the constitutions of the universities of Valencia, Salamanca, Alcalá, Coimbra, Paris, Louvain, Cologne, Bologna, and Padua. He clearly stated his purpose, that "after seeing what other universities employ and practice, and what is fitting to our Institute and manner of proceeding, general constitutions can be composed to be of service to the universities of the Society and to the colleges as well" (*EppIgn*, II, 550; see also *Cons*MHSJ, II, lxxii). His originality consisted not in inventing new pedagogical methods but in choosing from others the features which seemed best to him and adapting them to his far-reaching objectives. Furthermore,

to the colleges, we shall discuss first what pertains to the founders
[in Chapter 1]; second, what pertains to the colleges founded,
in regard to their material or temporal aspects [Chapter 2];
third, what pertains to the scholastics who will study in them, in
regard to their admission [Chapter 3], preservation [Chapter 4],
progress in learning [Chapters 5, 6, 7] and in other means of
helping their fellowmen [Chapter 8], and their removal from
study [Chapter 9]; fourth, what pertains to the government of
the colleges [Chapter 10].

Chapter 1
The remembrance of the
founders and benefactors
of the colleges

[309]–1. It is highly proper for us to do something on our
part in return for the devotion and generosity shown toward the
Society by those whom the Divine Goodness employs as His
ministers to found and endow its colleges.[1] First of all, therefore,
in any college let a Mass be said in perpetuity each week for
its founder and benefactors, living and dead.

[310]–2. Likewise, at the beginning of each month all the
priests in the college should be obliged, in perpetuity, to celebrate one Mass for these same persons.

Each year, too, on the anniversary of the day when the possession of the college was handed over, let a solemn Mass [A] be

---

he established a whole system of schools which aimed to carry out those same, precisely
formulated objectives. In many respects it was the first educational system in history.
1 Five types of Jesuit colleges evolved by 1556: (1) dwellings in which there were no lectures, for Jesuit scholastics attending public universities (see note 5 on [308] above),
although gradually some lectures were introduced (*MonPaed* [1965], pp. 8*, 517); (2)
dwellings in which lectures by Jesuit professors were given both to Jesuits and externs,
as occurred at Gandía in 1546 (*FN*, II, 207; *MonPaed* [1965], pp. 8*, 504, 507, 512);
(3) colleges founded chiefly for lay extern students, but with some Jesuit scholastics as
students (that these colleges might have the fixed revenues permitted by the bulls
Regimini, [5] and *Exposcit,* [6]), as at Messina in 1548-1549 and Rome in 1551; (4)
dwellings or boarding colleges for aspirants to the priesthood who went elsewhere nearby
for lectures, as in the German College founded in 1552, whose extern ecclesiastical
students went to the Roman College for lectures; (5) a boarding college (*convictus*) for
lay students, like that opened in Vienna in 1553. For further details, see *Cons*MHSJ, II,

celebrated in it for the founder and benefactors.ᵃ All the other *a*) 587
priests dwelling there are to celebrate Mass for the same intention.

[311]—A. *The solemnity is understood to be according to the
manner employed in the Society and in the place where the
Mass is celebrated.*

[312]—3. On that day a wax candle is to be presented to the
founder, or to one of his closer relatives [B], or in whatever
way the founder may stipulate. The candle should contain his
coat of arms or emblems of his devotions, as a sign of the
gratitude due him in our Lord [C].

[313]—B. *If there is, after a time, no descendant of the founder
in the region where such a college was founded, the candle can
be sent to a place where there is one of his descendants, or it
can be placed on the altar on which the divine sacrifice is offered,
in the name and place of the founder.*

[314]—C. *This candle signifies the gratitude due to the founders and not any right of patronage or any claim belonging to
them or their successors against the college or its temporal goods.
Nothing of this kind will exist.*

[315]—4. As soon as a college is handed over to the Society,
the superior general should notify the entire Society, in order
that each priest may celebrate three Masses for the living founder
and the benefactors, that God our Lord may sustain them by
His own hand and cause them to advance in His service. When
the general learns that God has taken them from this life to the
other [D], he should instruct all the priests to celebrate three
more Masses for their souls.

Whenever it is stated that Masses must be celebrated by the
priests, all the rest who dwell in the colleges and are not priests
ought to pray for the same intention for which the priests are
celebrating. For the same obligation of showing gratitude is incumbent in the Lord on them as well as on the priests.

[316]—D. *In the case of communities,² which have continuous
existence, these Masses will be celebrated for their deceased*

---

cxli-cxlv; *MonPaed* (1965), pp. 7*-8*; *AHSJ*, XXIX (1960), 192-210, 215-226; *WL*,
XCI (1962), 126-137; Leturia in *JesEdQuar*, IV (1941), 44-49; Farrell, *The Jesuit
Code*, pp. 431-433; *IdeaJesUn*, pp. 20-24.
2 E.g., the city of Messina.

members, especially for those to whom we are more indebted in our Lord.

[317]—5. The founders and benefactors of such colleges become in a special way sharers in all the good works of those colleges and of the whole Society.

[318]—6. In general, the Society should deem itself especially obligated to them [E] and to their dear ones, both during their lifetime and after their death. It is bound, by an obligation of charity and love, to show them whatever service it can according to our humble profession, for the divine glory.[3]

[319]—E. *What has been stated ought to be observed in its entirety in the case of those who found complete colleges. That part of it which the superior general will judge proper in the Lord will be carried out with those who give only an initial foundation.*

Chapter 2
The material aspects of the colleges

[320]—1. In regard to accepting colleges which are freely offered to the Society that it may administer them in all respects according to its Constitutions,[1] the superior general will have the full authority to accept them[2] in the name of the whole Society.[a]

a) 308, 762

3 In 1551 Ignatius, urging Araoz, provincial of Spain, to found colleges for externs, commissioned Polanco to write a letter detailing the procedure of finding benefactors and setting up colleges for externs. The letter is a remarkable synthesis of Ignatius' entire concept of Jesuit educational endeavor and of his procedures in establishing it. He treats the method of founding a college, the benefits accruing to the members of the Society themselves, the extern students, and then the social benefits or objectives he aimed to achieve for the inhabitants and the city or province where the college is situated. The Spanish text is in *EppIgn*, IV, 4-9 and *MonPaed* (1965), pp. 413-419; English in *Idea-JesUn*, pp. 25-29.
1 While the first ten companions were deliberating about difficulties connected with poverty if they should accept young men not yet trained into the Society, Laynez first thought of the idea of having colleges as "seed beds" (*seminaria*) for the Society, i.e., as residences possessing fixed revenues where scholastics could be supported during their studies in some public university. For centuries religious had been educating boys. But it was something new to have young men take simple vows of poverty and of entering the Society years later, and then to have them retain the ownership but not the use of their

[321]—2. When a founder desires to attach some conditions which are not fully in conformity with the order and manner of proceeding which the Society customarily uses, it will be left to the same general to consider (after hearing the opinion of the others whom he will judge to have better understanding in these matters), whether or not, when everything is taken into account, the acceptance of the college is helpful to the Society toward the end it is seeking, the service of God. But if in the course of time the Society should find itself burdened, it can bring the matter up in a general congregation and decree that the college should be abandoned, or that the burden should be lightened, or that additional means should be found to bear it, in case the general has not made provision for the matter before the congregation assembles, as is expedient in our Lord.[b]

b) 325, 441, 442, 762

[322]—3. The authority to abandon or alienate colleges or houses once accepted will belong jointly to the general and the Society [A]. Since this is like severing a member from the Society's body and is a lasting and important matter, it is better that the whole Society should be consulted about it.[c]

c) 420, 441, 680, 743, 762, 763

[323]—A. *The superior general and the Society will decide jointly whether colleges or houses once accepted ought to be abandoned or not.[3] But this can be done in a general congregation, or without it through votes sent in by those who have the right. In a case of this kind neither the Society nor its general may give away to persons outside the Society that which is thus abandoned, or any part of it. But when the Society relinquishes the charge it held, the parties who in the foundation may on their side have reserved this authority to themselves, will be able to apply what is thus abandoned to something else, according to their own devotion. If there is no reservation of this kind, the Society may proceed according to its Institute in whatever way it judges to be more conducive to the glory of God.*

[324]—4. In colleges of the Society, curacies of souls[d] should not be accepted,[4] nor obligations[e] to celebrate Masses, nor

d) 588

e) 589, 590

goods until after ordination, and that in the Society where the professed could not own. Residential colleges with fixed revenues solved the problem and received approval in *Regimini*, [6]. See Da Câmara, *Memoriale*, [138], in *FN*, I, 612; *Cons*MHSJ, II, cxlii; and [348] below.

2 Today acceptance is governed by Canon 497.

3 Today the factors of Canon 498 must be added.

4 Because the Church's discipline in regard to parishes committed to religious has changed, and because of the decree of Vatican II on the Pastoral Office of Bishops, no. 35, §1, General

similar duties which may much distract from study and obstruct the purpose which is sought in these colleges in view of the service of God. Similarly, such duties should not be undertaken in the houses or churches of the Professed Society, which as far as possible ought to be left free to accept the missions from the Apostolic See and other works for the service of God and the help of souls [B].

[325]—*B. This nonacceptance of obligations and similar duties means that it is not permitted to accept obligations of saying Masses or of similar duties which are proportioned to an assigned fixed revenue. However, when a sufficient reason is seen it is not considered to be thus unsuitable when some obligation is accepted which is small and easy (and which is not a curacy of souls), especially something which causes little or no distraction and consumption of time. But in the houses of the professed such obligations are not fitting, since these houses do not have any fixed income and since the professed themselves do not have so fixed a residence. Other obligations pertaining to lectures or lecturers are not being treated here. However, these too will be accepted in the colleges and universities only after much consideration, and not beyond the limit which the superior general will judge to be conducive to the common good and that of the Society for the glory of God our Lord.*[f]

f) 321, 441, 442, 762

[326]—5. The Society will take possession of the colleges with the temporal goods which pertain to them[g] [C]. It will appoint a rector who has more appropriate talent for that work.[h] He will take charge of maintaining and administering their temporal goods, providing for the necessities both of the material building and of the scholastics who are dwelling in the colleges or of those who are preparing themselves to go to them [D], and also of those who are carrying on the affairs of the colleges outside of them [E]. The rector should keep an account of the entire establishment so that he can give it at any time to whomsoever the general may ask him to do so.[i] Since the general cannot apply the temporal goods of the colleges to his own use or that of his relatives or of the Professed Society[j] [F], in his superintendence of these goods he will proceed all the more purely toward greater glory and service of God our Lord.

g) 419, 420, 740, 815

h) 421, 424, 490, 740, 757

i) 421, 741, 742, 759

j) 5, 419, 557, 763, 774, 776, 816

[327]—*C. As the bulls state,*[5] *for the use of its scholastics the*

Congregation XXXI declared (Decree 27, III) that to accept such curacies is not now contrary to the principles of the Society's *Constitutions*.

5 *Regimini*, [6], *Exposcit*, [5]. Because of textual difficulties and problems pertaining to

Society will carry on the administration of the fixed revenue through the superior general or the provincial or someone else to whom the general will entrust the matter, in order to guard and preserve the possessions and the fixed revenues of the colleges even in court if this should be expedient or necessary. The same general or someone to whom he entrusts the work will also have the care of receiving whatever else is given to such colleges for their maintenance and development in regard to their temporalities.

[328]—*D. Those who are preparing themselves to go to the colleges are those who are living in the houses of probation,*[k] *and those who are being sent to their studies from the houses of the Professed Society or from the houses of probation.*

k) 6

[329]—*E. Those who are carrying on the affairs of the colleges outside of them are understood to be chiefly the procurators, who take care of the affairs of the Society in the curia of the supreme pontiff or of other rulers.*[l] *But in regard to what must be contributed for these and other necessary expenditures, the general, observing due proportion, will issue the order by himself or through another.*

l) 591, 760, 806-808

[330]—*F. When it is stated that the Society or its general may not avail themselves of the fixed revenues of the colleges, this should be understood, in conformity with the statements in the bull,*[6] *as meaning that they may not divert these fixed revenues to their own private uses. However, they may make expenditures in favor of all those who advance the work of these colleges, as, for example, when some members are administrators, preachers, lecturers, confessors, visitors, and other professed or similar persons who further the spiritual or temporal welfare of those colleges.*[m] *Likewise even without such a reason some small sum may be spent upon any member whatever of the Society, in giving him food for a day or some little traveling money or something similar when he passes through the college en route to one place or another. For that which is such a small amount is regarded as nothing and scruples are removed, on the one hand about acting in an inhuman manner and on the other about acting contrary to the intention of the Apostolic See.*[n]

m) 422, 558

n) 558, 559

poverty, the present wording of [327] results from a modification of General Congregation I (see *Cons*MHSJ, II, ciii-cv and *Inst*SJ, II, 169).
6 *Exposcit*, [5].

[331]—6. In colleges which from their own fixed revenue can support twelve scholastics[7] in addition to their teachers, neither alms nor other gifts should be begged or accepted, for the greater edification of the people [G]. When the colleges were not endowed sufficiently for that, some alms could be accepted but not begged, unless the college happens to be so poor that it is also necessary to beg them, at least from some persons. For in such a case, with a view always kept on the greater service of God and the universal good, it will be permissible to beg alms, and even for a time from door to door in all the necessities which require it.[o]

o) 67, 82, 569

[332]—G. *However, if there are benefactors who wish to give some estate or fixed revenue, it could be accepted in order to maintain a proportionally larger number of scholastics and teachers for greater service to God.*

Chapter 3
The scholastics who are
to be stationed in the colleges

[333]—1. In regard to the scholastics[1] for whose instruction the colleges are accepted,[a] the point to be considered in our Lord among others is what qualifications they should have to be sent to the colleges or admitted into them.[b]

a) 289, 307, 440, 815

b) 14, 308, 523, 815

c) 23, 30, 164, 176

[334]—2. First of all, no one with any of the five impediments[c]

---

7 In 1553 Ignatius issued a new formula for accepting colleges. For ten years no new college was to be accepted unless 14 Jesuits could be supported in it. This was sanctioned by General Congregation I, Decree 72. See Lukács, *AHSJ*, XXIX (1960), 238-240; *WL*, XCL (1962), 140.

1 *Los scolares*, Latin *scholastici*. Ignatius used the term *scolares* to designate both the student members of his order (who were the ones he had chiefly in view in chs. 1-6, 8-10) and also extern students whether lay or candidates for the priesthood. The material in chs. 7, 11-17 applies to both Jesuit and extern students. In the Latin translation of 1558, *scolares* was translated occasionally by *scholares* (e.g., in [326]) but usually by *scholastici*. Consequently, in time English-speaking Jesuits became accustomed to call Jesuit seminarians "scholastics." The present translation turns *scolares* by "scholastics" when in the context it clearly means chiefly the Jesuit students, and by "students" when it refers chiefly to extern students whether clerical or lay (e.g., in [338]), or to Jesuit and extern students together (e.g., in [456]).

stated in Part I [164-176] will have a place as a scholastic in
any college of the Society [A]. Apart from the coadjutors who
are necessary[d] for the service and help of the college, the rest   d) 148, 149, 305,
ought to be such subjects that they give reasonable hope that   428
they will turn out to be fit laborers in the vineyard of Christ our
Lord through their example and learning.[e] The more capable they   e) 308, 523
are, the better their habits of conduct, and the healthier they are
to endure the labor of study, the more suitable are they and the
sooner can they be sent to the colleges and admitted into them.

[335]—A. *When someone has been declared suitable by the
vicar of Christ to live in a house of the Society,[2] he is also
understood to be suitable to live in the colleges.*

[336]—3. However, only those are admitted as approved
scholastics who have undergone their probation[3] in the houses
or in the colleges themselves[f] and who, after two years of   f) 14, 128, 523
experiences and probation[g] and their pronouncing their vows   g) 16, 71, 98,
along with the promise to enter the Society,[h] are then admitted   119, 346, 514,
that they may live and die in it for the glory of God our Lord.   537, 544
                                                  h) 14, 121, 348,
                                                  511, 537-541

[337]—4. Besides those just mentioned, others too are admitted
to study, namely, those who before the end of the two-year
period and its aforementioned probations are sent from the
houses to the colleges because this seems expedient, or those who
are received in the colleges. But these are not considered to be
approved scholastics until they have completed the two years
and pronounced their vows with the promise and are then
admitted as such [B].

[338]—B. *If a proper number of scholastics who have the
promise or intention of serving God our Lord in the Society
should not be present in its colleges, it will not be contrary to our
Institute,[i] with permission from the general and for the time   i) 416
which seems good to him, to admit other poor students who do
not have such an intention, provided that the impediments mentioned in Part I [164-176] are not found in them and they are
subjects of such fitness as to give hope that they will turn out
to be good workers in the vineyard of Christ our Lord, because
of their ability or basic knowledge of letters, good habits of
conduct, suitable age, and other qualities which appear in them
for the divine service, which alone is sought in the case of those*

---

2 E.g., by dispensation from an impediment.
3 On the age and academic attainments of those admitted to the first or second probation
and subsequently to the colleges under Ignatius, see fn. 2 on [160] above.

who are members of the Society and of those who are externs.

Students of this kind ought to conform themselves to the scholastics of the Society in the matter of confessions, studies, and manner of living. But their dress should be different and their living quarters separate within the same college, in such a way that the scholastics of the Society are apart by themselves without being mingled among the externs, although they may have dealings with the externs as far as the superior judges this suitable for greater edification and service to God our Lord.

Even though there should be a considerable number of our own scholastics, it is not contrary to our Institute to admit into the colleges someone who does not have the intention of becoming a member of the Society, if the agreement made with the founders so requires, when it is seen that to accept the college under that condition or for other rare and important reasons is useful for the end which the Society seeks. But students of this kind ought to dwell apart and, with the superior's permission, to associate only with designated members of the Society.

The poverty of these extern students will be judged by the superior general, or by someone to whom he communicates this authority. Moreover, from time to time and for good reasons, to admit the sons of the rich or of nobles when they pay their own expenses does not seem forbidden.

The suitable age seems to be from fourteen to twenty-three years, unless the students are persons who possess a basic knowledge of letters. Generally speaking, the more qualities they possess of those desired in the Society, the more suitable will they be for admission. Nevertheless, circumspection should be used to close rather than to extend the arms of welcome to students of this kind. Furthermore, careful choice should be made of those who are to be admitted, by preparing a special Examen for all such applicants.

Some, although these are infrequent, could be admitted among our own members because of special reasons which the superior judges to be cogent.

Chapter 4
The care and welfare
of the scholastics admitted

[339]—1. What was stated in Part III [292-306] will suffice about the care and welfare, in regard to the body and external matters, of those who live in the colleges. That is, special attention should be given to their abstaining from studies at times inopportune for bodily health,ᵃ to their taking sufficient sleep,ᵇ and to their observance of moderation in mental labors, that they may have greater endurance in them both during the years of study and later on in using what they have studied for the glory of God our Lord.ᶜ

a) 299
b) 301, 580

c) 298, 300, 822

[340]—2. In regard to spiritual matters,¹ the same order of procedure will be used with those who are received in the colleges, as long as they are still going through probations, as that which is observed with those who are received in the houses. But after they have been approved and while they are applying themselves to their studies, just as care must be taken that through fervor in study they do not grow cool in their love of true virtues and of religious life, so also during that time there will not be much placeᵈ for mortifications and long prayers and meditations² [A]. For their devoting themselves to learning, which they acquire with a pure intention³ of serving God and which in a certain way requires the whole man, will be not less but rather more pleasing⁴ to God our Lord during this time of study.ᵉ

d) 362, 363

e) 361

1 Other noteworthy sets of rules for the spiritual and intellectual formation of the scholastics, helpful in interpreting these directives given in the Constitutions, are in *Cons*MHSJ, IV, 213-245, 481-486, and in *MonPaed* (1901), pp. 135-140, 301-304.
2 Paragraphs [340-345] contain Ignatius' own legislation on prayer for those in formation, and [582-584] on that for the formed. See fnn. 8 on [65] and 2 on [582].
3 What Ignatius means by "a pure intention" receives additional light from [288] and [360].
4 "For their devoting themselves to learning . . . will be not less but rather more pleasing": This brief statement flows naturally as a corollary from Ignatius' far-reaching theory of apostolic spirituality. One serves or pleases God at some times by focusing attention on Him in prayer and at other times by working for Him and one's neighbor through love. This statement in [340] entails all that Ignatius meant by his oft-reiterated phrase of "finding God in all things," which led Nadal to call him "a contemplative in action" (*MonNad*, IV, 651-652). Here Ignatius' outlook is highly similar in many details to that of St. Thomas Aquinas, from whom he may have learned it. St. Thomas writes about Rom. 1:18 (*Commentary on Romans*, ch. 1, lect. 5): ". . . as long as a man is acting in his heart, speech, or work in such a manner that he is tending toward God, he is praying; and thus one who is directing his whole life toward God is praying always"; and Ignatius similarly writes (*EppIgn*, VI, 91): "In the midst of actions and studies, the mind can be lifted to God; and by means of this directing everything to the divine service, everything is prayer." Ac-

[341]—A. *If the rector because of special reasons judges some prolongation expedient in a particular case, there will always be place for discretion.*

[342]—3. Consequently, in addition to confession and Communion [B], which they will frequent every eight[5] days,[f] and Mass which they will hear every day, they will have one hour. During it, they will recite the Hours of Our Lady,[6] and examine their consciences[g] twice each day, and add other prayers according to the devotion of each one until the aforementioned hour is completed, in case it has not yet run its course.[7] They will do all this according to the arrangements and judgment of their superiors, whom they oblige themselves to obey in place of Christ our Lord.[h]

f) 80, 261, 278, 584

g) 261, 344

h) 84, 85, 284, 286, 424, 547, 551, 552, 618, 619, 627, 661, 765

[343]—B. *To go more frequently than every eight days should not be permitted, except for special reasons and more because*

cording to St. Thomas, the works of the active life sometimes hinder the act of contemplation (*ST*, II, Q. 182, a. 3); but one can remain a contemplative person, one in the unitive stage of spiritual growth whose dominant inclination is toward contemplation of God, even while engaged in apostolic activities. And such a man may "merit more by the works of the active life than another by the works of the contemplative life; e.g., if through . . . divine love . . . he consents to be withdrawn from the sweetness of divine contemplation for a time" to aid his neighbor (*ibid.*, a. 2). In a similar vein Ignatius writes (*EppIgn*, IV, 127): ". . . the distracting occupations undertaken for His greater service, in conformity with His divine will . . . can be, not only the equivalent of the union and recollection of uninterrupted contemplation, but even more acceptable, proceeding as they do from a more active and vigorous charity." Similar texts are cited in Giuliani, trans. W. J. Young, *Finding God in All Things* (Chicago, 1958), pp. 3-24; J. Stierli, trans. M. J. Hill, S.J., in *WL*, XC (1961), 135-166; Ganss, in *WL*, XCIV (1964), 161-164; "'Active Life' or 'Contemplative Life'?" *RevRel*, XXII (1963), 53-66; Proceedings of the Conference at Santa Clara, IV: *Background Papers on the Total Development of the Jesuit Priest* (St. Louis, 1967), pp. 48-58.

Ignatius' concept of apostolic spirituality entails both the "formal" prayer of personal contact with God and the prayer (in a wider sense of the term) which finds God in the fellowmen for whom one works. In other words, the "vertical" and the "horizontal" prayer are both necessary in a flexible proportion for each person; and to choose either the one or the other exclusively is not apostolic prayer or apostolic spirituality as he conceived them in [340-342] and [582-583].

5 See [80] with fn. 13, and [584].

6 *Las Horas de nuestra Señora*, also called by St. Ignatius "officio de nuestra Señora" (*Cons*-MHSJ, I, 175), meant the *Officium Parvum B. Mariae Virginis* still printed in the *Breviarium Romanum* (see ConsMHSJ, IV, 221, fn. 10). Also in widespread use in the 1500's were prayerbooks which had the title *Libro de Horas* and were often called the "Breviary of the Laity." Most copies contained both the *Horas de nuestra Señora* or other offices and also a collection of vocal prayers to the Trinity, Christ, Mary, or the saints, such as the *Anima Christi*. On them and their use by Ignatius see Leturia in *Estudios Ignacianos*, II, 102-133, and Fiorito in *Stromata*, XXIII (1967), 37-44; *WL*, XCVII (1968), 180-187.

7 In his *Scholia in Constitutiones* (Prato, 1883), p. 79, Nadal comments: "From these words it can be gathered that the two quarters of an hour need not be devoted only to the examens, but a part of them can be given to prayer." See also M. Fiorito, "St. Ignatius' Own Legislation on Prayer in the Society of Jesus," *Stromata*, XXIII (1967), 46-47, and *WL*, XCVII (1968), 188-190.

of necessity than of devotion. But neither shall the reception be deferred beyond eight days without special reasons. For such reasons Mass too could be omitted on some day, and with some the period of prayer could be lengthened or shortened. All this will remain within the discretionary power of the superior.[8]

Although the determined hour, or a little more or less, is taken for the recitation of the Hours of Our Lady, nevertheless in the case of the scholastics who are not obliged to recite the Divine Office, that hour can more easily be changed at times to meditations and other spiritual exercises by which the hour is filled out, especially with some who do not advance spiritually by one method, that with the grace of God they may be helped more by another. This is to be done with the permission or through the order of their superiors, whose duty it will always be to consider whether, for certain reasons with particular persons, something different is more expedient, in order to carry it out while keeping in view the genuine devotion of the subjects or of the founder, and also the circumstances of persons, times, and places.

For those who do not have experience in spiritual things and desire to be helped in them, some points for meditation and prayer could be proposed to them in the way that seems best for persons of this kind.[i] *The elders*[9] *or superiors will have the right to decide whether or not the scholastics may recite a part of the Hours, for which they have the assigned hour, during that time of the Mass when the priest is not speaking aloud in order that the people may understand him. These superiors should provide for this according to the subjects, places, conditions, and times, in the way which seems best to them for greater divine glory.*   i) 277, 279

[344]—4. Others (for example, some of the temporal coadjutors who do not know how to read[10]) will have in addition to the Mass their hour, during which they will recite the rosary or crown of our Lady [C], and they will likewise examine their consciences twice a day,[j] or engage in some other prayers according to their devotion, as was said about the scholastics.   j) 261, 342

---

8 The translator owes the punctuation used here to a suggestion of A. de Aldama. Both the history of the text (see esp. text A in *Cons*MHSJ, II, 410) and the manuscript of text B (see p. 115r of the photographic edition) support this punctuation better than that used in *Cons*MHSJ, II, 411.

9 *Mayores:* in Ignatius' usage in the Constitutions, the noun *mayores* always has the meaning of "superiors" (see [63, 342, 343, 353, 425]), and does not indicate age.

10 See fn. 3 on [43].

[345]—C. *In regard to the recitation of the rosary, they should be instructed how to think or meditate about the mysteries which it contains, that they may take part in this exercise with greater attention and devotion.*[k] *Moreover, if those who know how to read should find more progress in it than in the recitation of the Hours, they could be changed for what will be more helpful, as was already stated.*

k) 277

[346]—5. For greater devotion, and to refresh the memory of the obligation they are under, and to confirm themselves more solidly in their vocation, it will be good for the scholastics twice each year, at the paschal feast of the Resurrection and at Christmas [D], to renew their simple vows[l] [E], which will be treated in Part V, [Chapter 4]. Anyone who has not taken these vows will pronounce them when the two years of probation have passed,[m] as the Examen states.

l) 544, 546

m) 16, 71, 98, 119, 336, 514, 537, 544

[347]—D. *If the rector, with authorization from the superior, should think that it would be more convenient to hold this renewal on some other principal feasts in some particular cases, this too could be done. Likewise, by the feasts of the Resurrection and Christmas is meant either the time until and including their octave-days, or that within eight days before the feasts.*

[348]—E. *What the scholastic promises in the Society is to incorporate himself into it, to begin immediately his actual observance of chastity, poverty, and obedience according to the usages of the Society, whether he is admitted to become after his studies a professed or a formed coadjutor. Consequently, the superior can admit him immediately as a scholastic, and as one being tested only as to whether in the course of time he is to become a professed member or a coadjutor. This stated arrangement brings it about that although a vow of poverty is in force, the temporal goods may be possessed within the period of probation up to a certain time*[11] *which will seem good to the superior.*[n]

n) 54, 55, 59, 254, 287, 571

[349]—6. When they must go to schools open to the public (for they will not go to other places without requesting permission), they should go and return in pairs[o] [F], and with the interior and exterior decorum which is proper for the edification of themselves and of others. Their conversation with students from outside the Society should be only about matters pertaining

o) 247, 248

11 See fn. 1 on [320].

to learning or spirituality, that thereby they may find help in everything toward greater divine glory.

[350]—*F. The rector will designate those who are to accompany each other, and these will be those who can be mutually helpful to each other.*

Chapter 5
The subjects which the scholastics
of the Society should study

[351]—1. Since the end of the learning which is acquired in this Society is with God's favor to help the souls of its own members and those of their fellowmen,[a][1] it is by this norm that *a*) 307, 360, 440 the decision will be made, both in general and in the case of individual persons, as to what branches[2] ours ought to learn, and how far they ought to advance in them. And since, generally

1 From this and many similar statements (e.g., in [307, 361, 400, 440, 446, 622] and *EppIgn*, IV, 5-9), we come to know Ignatius' concept of education and his reasons for undertaking educational work. His concept of education is an application of his outlook on life to the work of training the students in the schools he founded for secondary and higher education. He desired to stimulate those students, through self-activity, to a well-balanced perfection of their faculties or powers: the aesthetic abilities according to the culture of their day, and their intellectual and volitional powers on both the natural and the supernatural levels of action. Through this he aimed to form them into cultivated persons who would be able and eager to take a capable part in the social, cultural, and religious life of their era and leaven their environment with the principles of Christ. As means to this objective, he appropriated the best elements he could find in the educational organization, curricula, and procedures of his day and organized them into an instrument truly fit to achieve his purposes, particularly in his contemporary era. Many instances of such appropriation appear in ch. 5 and the rest of Part IV, which contains many perennial principles of Christian education, although they are there mingled with measures which were timely or suited to that particular era, the Renaissance. Social purposes are very prominent in Ignatius' concept of education. On this concept, see *IdeaJesUn*, esp. chs. 3, 9, 10; Ganss, "St. Ignatius the Educator," *AHSJ*, XXV (1956), 598-612, esp. 599-600; *JesEdQuar*, XXIII (1961), 129-150, esp. 137-140; *The Jesuit Educational Tradition and St. Louis University* (St. Louis, 1969), pp. 7-24; J. W. Donohue, *Jesuit Education* (New York, 1963), esp. pp. 3-28, 130-131, 186-188.
2 *Facultades:* in Ignatius' usage, this word sometimes means a group of professors (e.g., in [498, 501, 502]). But more often, as especially here in ch. 5, it means a branch of learning, or even an entire curriculum in a faculty of arts, philosophy, or theology (see [453, title]). The Latin translators of 1558 perceived these different meanings of Ignatius' term; e.g., in [357] they translated *a una facultad* by *alicui ex his scientiis;* in [380], by *studia illa.* On these meanings, see De la Torre, *Constitutiones*, p. 150, fn. 3.

b) 336, 446-451

c) 740, 741

d) 448

speaking, help is derived from the humane letters[3] of different languages [A], logic, natural and moral philosophy, metaphysics,[4] scholastic and positive theology[5] [B], and Sacred Scripture, these are the branches which those who are sent to the colleges should study[b] [C]. They will devote themselves with greater diligence to the parts which are more helpful for the end mentioned above, with circumstances of times, places, persons, and other such factors taken into account, according to what seems expedient in our Lord to him who holds the principal charge.[c]

[352]—A. *In addition to grammar, rhetoric is understood to be under the classification of humane letters.*[d]

[353]—B. *If there should not be enough time in the colleges to read the councils, decrees, holy doctors, and other moral subjects, each one could, with the approval of his superiors, read these privately after his departure from studies, especially if he is well grounded in the scholastic doctrine.*

---

3 Ignatius' proximate reason for prescribing the study of humane letters and philosophy, the aid they give for study of theology, is expounded more fully below in [447, 450]. His general attitude on the study and use of Latin and Greek in his era of the Renaissance appears clearly in two letters, his of 1555 to a scholastic, Gerard (*EppIgn*, VII, 618, English in *IdeaJesUn*, p. 157), and Polanco's of 1547 (*EppIgn*, I, 519-526, English in *LettersIgn*, pp. 132-137, and summarized in *IdeaJesUn*, pp. 155-156). On Ignatius' attitude toward Ciceronianism, elegance of style, and on his lack of interest in form for form's sake, see *IdeaJesUn*, pp. 153-157, 177 and *DeGuiJes*, pp. 70, 164.

4 In the sixteenth-century treatment of these branches (called "the arts or natural sciences" in [450, 451; cf. also 470]), most attention was generally given to Aristotelian physics and ethics. An example of a typical textbook of philosophy used at the University of Paris during Ignatius' stay there, and which he may have employed in an earlier edition, is: Pierre Tartaret, *In Aristotelis philosophiam, naturalem, divinam, & moralem exactissima commentaria* (Venetiis, 1592). There is a copy of this rare book in the Pius XII Library of St. Louis University. The titles of the sections and the number of pages allotted to each no doubt reflects the importance attributed in that era to each branch, as follows: Quaestio praeambula, pages 1-5; Physicorum Libri, 6-145; De Coelo et Mundo, 145-181; De Generatione et Corruptione, 181-210; De Meteorologicis libris Aristotelis, 210-241; In libros Aristotelis De Anima, 241-280; In Parva Naturalia, 280-300; In Metaphysicae, 301-321; In sex priores Aristotelis Moralium (= Ethicorum libros), 321-389. Students today would find such a textbook excessively abstract, subtle, and dry, as did many students in the 1500's (see fn. 1 on [516] below). On Tartaret, see W. Ong, *Ramus: Method, and the Decay of Dialogue* (Cambridge, Mass., 1958), index, s.v. "Tartaret."

5 Theology is science, derived from God's revelation, about Him and His creatures. The terms positive and scholastic refer to different emphases in the methodology. By positive theology the student seeks to possess the data of revelation more accurately, through study, e.g., of biblical history, the Fathers, definitions and decrees of councils, canon law, archeology, and other organs of tradition. By scholastic or speculative theology, he seeks deeper insight into the revelation itself, especially through the methods used by the medieval schoolmen. For Ignatius, outstanding examples of scholastic theology were Peter Lombard and St. Thomas Aquinas ([464, 466]).

[354]—*C. According to the age, ability, inclination, and basic knowledge which a particular person has, or in accordance with the common good which is hoped for, he could be applied to all these branches or to one or several of them. For one who cannot distinguish himself in all of them ought to try to do so in the case of some one of them.*

[355]—2. In detail, what some or other scholastics ought to study will likewise be left to the discretion of the superiors[e] [D]. But when someone has aptitude, the better the foundation he lays in the aforementioned branches, the better will it be.[f]

e) 124, 460, 461, 739

f) 460, 461, 814

[356]—*D. Some could be sent to the colleges, not in the hope that they will come forth from them as learned men according to the manner previously described, but rather that they may lighten the burden of others; for example, a priest to hear confessions and do similar work.[g] For these and others, who because of age or other reasons cannot be expected to come forth with an extensive foundation in all the branches mentioned, it would be good, under the direction of the superior, to study what they can and endeavor to make progress in the languages and cases of conscience and, finally, in whatever can be of greatest use to them for the common good of souls.[h]*

g) 365, 558

h) 461

[357]—3. The rector will consider and decide by means of a suitable examination how much time should be given to one branch, and when the scholastics should pass on to another.[i]

i) 124, 460, 471

[358]—4. The doctrine which they ought to follow in each branch should be that which is safer and more approved, as also the authors who teach it.[j] The rectors will take care of this, by conforming themselves to what is decided in the Society as a whole for the greater glory of God [E].

j) **274, 464-470,** 671, 672

[359]—*E. In the books of humane letters by pagan authors, nothing immoral should be lectured on;[6] and what remains can be used by the Society like the spoils of Egypt. In the case of Christian authors, even though a work may be good it should not be lectured on when the author is bad, lest attachment to him be acquired.[7] Furthermore, it is good to determine in detail*

---

6 It should be remembered that the students in the colleges (called *niños, pueri* in [483] and *EppIgn,* IV, 6) were often 10 to 14 years of age. See the fnn. on [360, 451, 483] below, fn. 2 on [160] above, and, for a schematic presentation, *IdeaJesUn,* p. 45.
7 See fn. 2 on [465] below.

*the books which should be lectured on and those which should
not, both in the humanities and in the other faculties.*

Chapter 6
Means by which the scholastics
will progress toward learning
the aforementioned branches well

[360]—1. In order to make great progress in these branches,[1] the scholastics should strive first of all to keep their souls pure and their intention in studying right,[2] by seeking in their studies nothing except the glory of God and the good of souls.[a] Moreover, they should frequently beg in prayer for grace to make progress in learning for the sake of this end.

a) 307, 351, 440, 486

[361]—2. Furthermore, they should keep their resolution firm to be thoroughly genuine and earnest students, by persuading themselves that while they are in the colleges they cannot do anything more pleasing[3] to God our Lord than to study with the intention mentioned above;[b] likewise, that even if they never have occasion to employ the matter studied, their very labor in studying, taken up as it ought to be because of charity and obedience, is itself work highly meritorious in the sight of the Divine and Supreme Majesty.[4]

b) 340, 360

[362]—3. The impediments which distract from study should also be removed, both those arising from devotions and mortifications which are too numerous or without proper order[c] [A] and also those springing from their cares and exterior occupations whether in duties inside the house [B] or outside it in conversations, confessions, and other activities with one's fellowmen, as

c) 340, 341

---

1 This chapter reveals Ignatius as an interested counselor trying to help the students devise efficient methods of study for their day. Although the chapter is one of those composed chiefly for Jesuit scholastics, most of it was equally applicable to externs whether religious or lay. On the ages and academic qualities of the students in Ignatius' day, see fn. 2 on [160], and, for a schematic presentation, *IdeaJesUn*, p. 45.

2 See [288, 340], with the fnn., above. *El ánima pura* here is a slight alteration from *con conscientia pura . . . y con intención recta* as found in text *a* (*Cons*MHSJ, II, 181-182).

3 See [340] above, with fn. 4.

4 See the similar ideas in Ignatius' letter of 1547 to the scholastics of Coimbra (*EppIgn*, I, 508; *LettersIgn*, pp. 128-129). In [360] and [361] is noticeable a parallel esteem for both supernatural and natural gifts which is similar to what Ignatius shows in [813] and [814] below. See also above, pp. 22-23.

far as it is possible in our Lord to excuse oneself from them^d [C]. *d*) 437
For in order that the scholastics may be able to help their fellow-
men better later on by what they have learned, it is wise to
postpone exercises such as these, pious though they are, until
after the years of study,^e since there will be others to attend to *e*) 400
them in the meantime. All this should be done with a greater
intention of service and divine glory.

[363]—*A. This is the general practice. But if some individual
finds it necessary to apply himself to devotion and mortification,
it will be left to the discretion of the one who holds the principal
charge to consider how far he should go in these matters.*

[364]—*B. To give aid at some hour to those who hold these
burdensome duties is not improper;^f but to assume them per-* *f*) 433
*manently is more properly the work of the coadjutors, and
they could be provided to lighten this burden for those who* *g*) 114, 148, 149,
are studying.^g   433

[365]—*C. For this reason, in the case of those who have not
yet been ordained, it is wise to defer their Sacred Orders, in
order to keep them from being impeded in this way before they
come to the end of their studies. However, because of arising
needs it is necessary from time to time to grant a dispensation
or the like.*

*Moreover, this work of helping one's fellowmen could be sup-
plied by some of those who have finished their studies, or by
some of those who could be sent to the colleges chiefly for this
purpose.*^h *In regard to those domestic offices which are more* *h*) 356, 558
*time-consuming in the college, it will also be good to have some
persons who do not have study as their chief purpose, such as* *i*) 114, 148, 149,
*the temporal coadjutors,*ⁱ *or some members of the Society who*   364, 433
are in their probation and not present for the purpose of study.^j *j*) 68, 83

[366]—4. An order should be observed in pursuing the
branches of knowledge. The scholastics should acquire a good
foundation in Latin before they attend lectures on the arts;[5]
and in the arts before they pass on to scholastic theology; and
in it before they study positive theology.[6] Scripture may be
studied either concomitantly or later on.

---

5 "The arts" is Ignatius' term to designate the branches taught in his higher faculty of
  philosophy: logic, physics, metaphysics, moral philosophy, and some mathematics. See,
  e.g., [351, 450, 498, 501]; *IdeaJesUn*, pp. 45, 57-58, 332, no. 4, and index, s.v. "Arts."
6 This constitution [366], especially if taken with [378-381, 390, 456, and 484] below, well
  illustrates Ignatius' esteem for "the method of Paris." Through experience he knew the

[367]—5. The languages too in which Scripture was written or into which it was translated may be studied either previously or later on, according to what seems best to the superior in accordance with the various cases and the diversity of the persons.ᵏ This too will remain within his discretion [D]. But if the languages are learned, among the ends which are pursued one should be to defend⁷ the version which the Church holds as approved.

k) 351, 447, 449, 460

[368]—*D. It would be good for them to have their degrees in theology or at least to be fairly well versed in it, so that they know the interpretations of the Holy Doctors and the decisions of the Church, in order that this study of languages may be profitable rather than harmful. However, if some are seen to be so humble and firm in their faith that in their cases nothing harmful is to be feared from the study of languages, the superior may grant a dispensation to them that they may devote themselves to these languages when this would be conducive to the common good or that of the individual.*

[369]—6. All those who are studying should attend the lectures of the public professors whom the rector will designate for them [E]. It is desirable that these professors should be learned, diligent, and assiduous; and that, whether they be members of the Society [F] or from outside it,¹ they should be eager to further the progress of the students, both during the lectures and in the academic exercises.ᵐ ⁸

l) 452, 457
m) 446, 447, 450, 456

educational organization and practices of Spain, France, the Low Countries, and Italy. In them there was great lack of order, especially in Italy, where the students, not arranged in classes according to age or ability, often studied higher branches before acquiring a foundation in the lower ones. Often, too, there were no exercises or repetitions to supplement the lectures (*MonPaed* [1965], pp. 7*, 358). But in the colleges of the University of Paris there was an orderly sequence and much self-activity of the students. Hence Ignatius constantly esteemed, imitated, and urged his men to conform "al modo de Paris, con mucho exercitio." For example, while urging Araoz, provincial of Spain, to found colleges, Ignatius wrote in 1551: ". . . When there is a good number of students already grounded in humane letters, someone is appointed to inaugurate the course in arts. When there is a number . . . well grounded in the arts too, someone is appointed to give the lectures of the course in theology, according to the method of Paris, with much exercise . . ." (*EppIgn*, IV, 7; *IdeaJesUn*, p. 26). For more on the method of Paris, see the indices in the books by Donohue, Farrell, Ganss, Herman, and Lukács; also the recent book published too late for extensive use here: G. C. Mir, *Aux sources de la pédagogie des Jésuites: le "modus Parisiensis"* (Rome, 1968).

7 Ignatius' text had here "to the extent possible." General Congregation I suppressed these words (see *Cons*MHSJ, II, 427, and Courel's note on [367]).

8 Distinction should be made between (1) Ignatius' large and perennial guiding principles or objectives in education (on which see fn. 1 on [446] below), and (2) the pedagogical methods by which he strove to achieve those objectives in his own era. The present ch. 6 deals largely with those pedagogical methods; and to understand his directives for efficient

[370]—E. *If another procedure is expedient for someone, the superior will consider the matter with prudence and he may grant a dispensation. What has been said about public lectures does not exclude private lectures within the college or outside it when these may be necessary or profitable.*

[371]—F. *No member of the Society will give lectures publicly without the approbation and permission of the provincial superior, except in the lower classes or for a time because of some necessity. But those who have the talent, especially those who have finished their studies, could be employed in lecturing if matters of greater importance do not require something else.*[n]   n) 391, 417

[372]—7. There should be a general library[9] in the colleges, if possible, and those who in the judgment of the rector ought to have a key should have one. Furthermore, the individuals should have the books which are necessary for them [G].

[373]—G. *However, they ought not to write annotations in these books; and he who has charge of the books should keep an account of them.*

[374]—8. The scholastics should be regular in going to the lectures, diligent in preparing for them beforehand, in repeating them afterwards [H], in asking about points they do not understand, and in noting down what may be useful to assist the memory later on[o] [I].   o) 385, 388, 389

study here, one must consider their appropriateness to the chief classroom procedures of the Middle Ages and the Renaissance—before or shortly after the invention of printing, when libraries rarely had 1,000 volumes and textbooks were very rare.

The general practice was that the professor (*doctor* or *magister*) gave a lecture (*lectio* or *praelectio*) in Latin. It was the imparting of information, and its essential purpose was to expound a text, for example, Aristotle's *Ethics,* which the student usually did not possess. The activity of the professors was commonly expressed by the verbs *legere* or *praelegere,* to lecture in front of the students, and that of the students in the lecture rooms (*scholae*) by the words *lectiones* or *praelectiones audire,* to listen to the lectures.

Outside of class hours, the professors (or at least the better ones) also conducted repetitions or reviewings (*repetitiones*). These were detailed discussions by a group of students on some point pertaining to a recent lecture. These repetitions were frequently in the form of circles or disputations. In an ordinary disputation, a defendant expounded his thesis, and objectors raised difficulties. Often the professor summed up the entire discussion in what was called *determinatio.* Another type of disputation was that called *disputatio de quolibet.* It was a public discussion on solemn feasts or other occasions of importance. In medieval and even Renaissance times, educated persons took a widespread interest in disputations. All these procedures and exercises were still the common practice in Ignatius' century and long after, even into the twentieth century in many places. See *IdeaJesUn,* Appendix 2, pp. 257-270.

9 In comparison with modern times, such libraries were small. That of Queens College, Oxford, contained 199 volumes in 1472. See also the illustration in *IdealJesUn,* p. 260.

p) 456, 459

[375]—H. *The rector should take care that these repetitions take place at a fixed time in the schools or in the house.*p *One student should repeat the matter and the others should listen. They should propose to one another the difficulties which occur and have recourse to the professor in matters which they cannot solve satisfactorily among themselves. The rector will also take care of the disputations and the other scholastic exercises which will be judged expedient in accordance with the branches which*

q) 378, 455, 456   *are being treated.*q

[376]—I. *The superiors should consider whether it will be helpful for those just beginning their studies in the lower classes to have paper notebooks in order to write down the lectures, and note above[10] and in the margin whatever seems useful. Those who are more advanced in the humanities and the other faculties should carry with them paper to jot down what they hear or anything which strikes them as noteworthy. Later on they should rewrite in the paper notebooks, with better arrangement and order, what they desire to keep for the future.*

[377]—9. The rector of the college should also take care to see how all, the teachers as well as the students, are fulfilling their duty in our Lord.

[378]—10. Because of the utility there is in the practice of disputation,[11] especially for those who are studying arts and scholastic theology, the scholastics should participate in the disputations or ordinary circles of the schools which they attend, even though these schools are not those of the Society itself; and they should endeavor to distinguish themselves both by their learning and by their modesty. Within the college too, after dinner on Sunday or some other day of the week (unless a special reason impedes the exercise), it is good to have someone from each class of the students of arts and theology,

10 The Latin translators interpreted "above" (*encima*) to mean "between the lines" (*inter lineas*).

11 In the 1500's, disputations in the schools had a utility at least threefold. First, they provided a discussion session for the students to assimilate the material of the lectures, and on occasions they provided an academic display or specimen. Second, they prepared the students to participate in the disputations of real life among Catholics in the serious work of research to discover the truth, such as the disputations at the Council of Trent. The early Jesuits were much occupied in such disputations. Third, the disputations prepared the students to participate in the public disputations with the Protestants. Such public theological disputations were very frequent and were often attended by large crowds. In 1625 they were forbidden as useless by the Sacred Congregation *De Propaganda Fide* (*IdeaJesUn*, pp. 268-270; *CathEnc*, V, 34-37).

whom the rector will designate, defend some theses. During the preceding afternoon these theses will be posted in writing on the door of the schools, that those who wish may come to dispute or to listen. After these defendants have briefly proved their theses, those from within and without the house who wish to object may do so. Someone will preside to direct the disputants, to sum up the doctrine about the subject under discussion and to make it clear for the benefit of those listening,[r] and to give the   r) 379, 380, 456
signal to stop to those who are disputing, meanwhile distributing the time in such a way that there will be room for the disputations of all of them.[12]

[379]—11. In addition to the two kinds of disputations mentioned, an hour ought also to be designated each day for holding disputation within the college, with someone presiding[s] in the   s) 378, 380, 456
manner already stated. The purpose is that the intellectual powers[13] may be exercised more and that difficult matters occurring in these branches may be clarified, for the glory of God our Lord.

[380]—12. Those who are studying humanities should also have their fixed times to discuss and debate about the matters of their branch in the presence of someone who directs them.[t] After   t) 378, 379, 456
dinner on one Sunday or other designated day they too will defend theses; and on another they will exercise themselves in writing compositions in prose or in verse, whether that is done impromptu to show their facility, or whether they bring a composition previously written and read it publicly there. In the first case the subject to write about is given at the place of the exercise, and in the latter case it is given earlier.

[381]—13. All, and especially the students of the humanities, should ordinarily speak Latin[u][14] [K], and commit to memory   u) 456

---

12 "Of all," i.e., the defendants and objectors from each class of philosophy and theology.
13 *Los ingenios. El ingenio* is the faculty of discoursing, reflecting, or inventing with alacrity and facility. Ignatius expected mastery of the subject matter and acquisition of the related skills to be the student's immediate objective in studying any given branch. He did not hold a "disciplinary theory of education"; that is, he nowhere sets up mental discipline as the chief reason or objective for studying or choosing a branch. But like almost all the great educators from Plato onward, he was aware that by means of mastering that subject matter and related skills, the student concomitantly though accidentally acquired much training of mind, i.e., methods of study and ideals of mastery which he would probably transfer to other fields in later life. See *IdeaJesUn*, pp. 75-79, 219.
14 The fact that Latin was still the language in which virtually all the lectures, discussions, and writing in the universities were carried on is the obvious reason for this statute. Similar prescriptions were in the statutes of virtually all contemporary schools, e.g., at Paris or Guyenne. Samples are in *IdeaJesUn*, p. 314.

what was indicated by their teachers, and bestow much practice
v) 456, 484   upon the style[15] in their compositions[v] [L], and have someone
to correct them. Moreover, some with the approval of the rector
may read privately some authors besides those on whom they
w) 384, 385, 388   have lectures.[w] After dinner on some day of each week, one of
the more advanced students should deliver a Latin or Greek
oration[16] about some subject likely to edify those within and
without the college and to encourage them to greater perfection
x) 484   in our Lord.[x]

[382]—K. *In regard to the exercises of the repetitions, the disputations, and the speaking of Latin, if something ought to be
changed because of the circumstances of places, times, and
persons, this decision will be left to the discretion of the rector
with authorization, at least in general, from his superior.*

[383]—L. *That the students may be helped more, it would be
wise to place together some of equal ability who with holy
rivalry may spur one another on. From time to time it will also
be helpful to send to the place where the provincial superior or
the superior general is some specimen of their work, now from
one student, now from another, for example, some compositions
from the students of the humanities, or theses from those studying
arts or theology. It will also aid them if they are reminded that
upon their arrival at the houses after their studies they will have*
y) 518   *to be examined in all the branches which they have learned.*[y]

[384]—14. Moreover, especially those studying the arts and
theology, but also the rest, ought to have their own private and
undisturbed study, that they may better and more profoundly
understand the matters treated [M].

[385]—M. *In this private study (if the rector thinks it good),*
z) 381, 388   *they could read some commentary.*[z] *While they are still attending lectures in a group, there should be one, and that carefully*

---

15 Ignatius saw Ciceronian style, and even elegance in Latin when possible, as an important
means of reaching some people, "especially in these times" [447] of the Renaissance. On
his attitudes here, see *IdeaJesUn*, pp. 153-157. Cf. [307, 351] above.

16 Preaching in Latin was very common in the 1500's. Occasionally, like much of the preaching in Greek, it was a matter of display, as at the papal court in Rome during the pontificate of Leo X, where what the preacher said mattered little as long as he filled his sermons
with resounding Ciceronic periods and mythological allusions (see Pastor, *History*, XII,
241-242). But most of it was serious preaching meant to profit the hearers, as when
Ribadeneyra won widespread fame by his Latin sermons to the students of the University
of Louvain (see Dudon, *St. Ignatius*, p. 326).

chosen. The students could also write down what seems likely
to be more useful to them.[a]

a) 374, 376, 388, 389

[386]—15. Just as it is necessary to restrain those who are run-
ning too rapidly, so is it proper to stimulate, urge on, and
encourage those for whom this is necessary. For this purpose the
rector ought to keep himself informed through his own activity
and through someone to whom he will give the charge of
syndic[17] or visitor of the students.[b]

b) 504-506

If it is seen that someone is wasting his time in the college
because either he does not care to advance or cannot, it is better
to remove him from it[c] and to let someone else enter in his place
who will make better progress for the end sought, the service
of God [N].

c) 123, 739

[387]—*N. If someone should be unfit to study but fit for other*
ministries, he could be employed within the colleges or houses
of the Society in something judged proper. But if he entered to
become a scholastic and should be unfit for both study and the
other ministries, he may be dismissed.[d] *However, it will be good*

d) 212

for the rector, after considering the case, to inform the provincial
or general and to follow his order.[e]

e) 206-208

[388]—16. When the subject matter of one faculty has been
completed, it will be good to review it, by reading, with the
rector's approval, one or more authors than the one used the
first time,[f] and by making, also with his approval, a compendium[18] of what pertains to that branch. This compendium
can be briefer and more accurately digested than the first notes
which the scholastic composed while he did not yet have the
understanding of the matter which he has after his courses have
been completed[g] [O].

f) 381, 384, 385

g) 374, 376, 385

[389]—*O. It is good to have these compendia made only by*
persons who have greater knowledge, clarity of mind, and judg-
ment, from whose work the others could profit. It would also be
good to have these compendia approved by the professor. The
rest of the students will be able to draw help from the pro-
fessor's annotations and from the matters worthy of noting
which they themselves have gathered. It will make these com-

---

17 Syndic: see fn. 11 on [271].
18 When textbooks and other books were scarce, it was natural for students to pool their
notes, have one of their more capable members make a digest, then have the professor
touch it up, and pass it around as a set of notes for study.

pendia more useful if they have their indicating marks in the margin and a table of the contents treated, to make it easier to find what is sought. Although these books of excerpts and personal ideas or other writings of any sort have been made, it is understood that no one should publish any book without the examination and special approval of the superior general, as

h) 273, 653

has been said[h] *[273].*

[390]—17. At the times designated for them they should pre-

i) 473, 476

pare themselves for the public acts of examinations and replies.[i] Those who after careful examination are found to deserve their degrees may receive them. But to avoid every appearance of ambition or inordinate desires, they should not take special places. Rather, they should place themselves in a group inde-pendently of rank, even though indications of rank are customarily

j) 478, 817

given in the university where they are studying.[j] More-over, they should not make expenditures inappropriate for poor men when they take their degrees, which should be received, without detriment to humility, for the sole purpose of being better able to help one's fellowmen for glory to God.

[391]—18. The superior should consider whether it is advisable for those who have finished their studies to lecture in private or in public for their own progress or for that of others. He should make provision according to what seems more expedient

k) 371, 417

in our Lord.[k]

Chapter 7
The schools maintained
in colleges of the Society

[392]—1. To take care that in our colleges not only our own

a) 289, 307, 308,
333, 815

scholastics[a] may be helped in learning, but also those from out-

b) 395, 440, 481

side[b] [1] in both learning and good habits of conduct, where schools [open to the public][2] can be conveniently had, they

1 This ch. 7 was composed especially because of the colleges for externs established after 1546 and envisages them chiefly but not exclusively (see above, [307-309], 318], with the fnn. there).
2 This clarifying phrase is the interpretation of the Latin translators of 1558.

should be established at least in humane letters [A], and in more advanced subjects in accordance with the possibility³ which obtains in the regions where such colleges are situated [B]. The greater service of God our Lord is always to be kept in view.

[393]—A. *It will belong to the general to decide where it will be opportune to have such schools.*

[394]—B. *The resources of the Society should also be taken into account. However, our intention would be that ordinarily there should be taught in the colleges humane letters, languages, and Christian doctrine;⁴ and if it should be necessary instruction should be given about cases of conscience. If personnel is available for preaching and hearing confessions, this should be done. But all this should be done without extending the undertaking into the higher branches of knowledge. To learn them, those students who have studied humane letters should be sent from these colleges to the universities of the Society.⁵*

[395]—2. In these schools the procedure should be such that the extern students are well instructed in what pertains to Christian doctrine.ᶜ Care should be taken that they confess every month if possible, that they frequent the sermons,ᵈ and finally, that they acquire along with their letters the habits of conduct worthy of a Christian.ᵉ Since there must be great variety in particular cases in accordance with the circumstances of place and persons, this present treatment will not descend further to what is particular, except to state that there should be rules which come down to everything necessary in each collegeᶠ [C]. Only this recommendation will be made here, that fitting correction should not be lacking [D] in the case of those externs for whom it is necessary, and that it should not be given by the hand of any member of the Society.ᵍ

c) 437, 438

d) 481, 482

e) 392, 403

f) 136, 428, 455, 495-497

g) 488, 500

[396]—C. *From the "Rules of the Roman College,"⁶ the part which is suitable to the other colleges can be adapted to them.*

3 Cf. the procedure sketched in the letter to Araoz (*EppIgn*, IV, 6, English in *IdeaJesUn*, pp. 26-27). See also fn. 3 on [318] and fn. 6 on [366] above.
4 How this plan of studies was carried out at Messina is seen in a letter of 1551 composed by Hannibal du Coudret, to which Polanco added a title, *De ratione studiorum. Messanae.* It was the first of a long series of Jesuit documents to bear this title. The text is in *Litt-Quad*, I, 349-358; *MonPaed* (1965), pp. 94-106; English digest in *IdeaJesUn*, pp. 107-109.
5 Chs. 11-17 below treat the universities.
6 These rules, dating from 1551, are in *ConsMHSJ*, IV, 250-275 and *MonPaed* (1965), pp. 64-93.

[397]—D. *For this purpose there should be a corrector where this is possible. Where this is not possible, there should be some method of administering punishment, either through one of the students or in some suitable way.*

[398]—3. Since it is so proper to our profession not to accept any temporal remuneration[7] for the spiritual ministries in which we employ ourselves according to our Institute to aid our fellow-men,[h] it is not fitting for us to accept for a college any endowment with an attached obligation of supplying a preacher or a confessor or some lecturer on theology [E]. For, although the reason of equity and gratitude moves us to give more careful service in those ministrations proper to our Institute in those colleges which have been founded with greater liberality and devotion, there ought nevertheless to be no entering into obligations or agreements which impair the sincerity of our manner of proceeding, which is to give freely what we have freely received [Matt. 10:8]. However, for the sustenance of those who serve the common good of the colleges or who study for the sake of it, the endowment which the charity of the founders is wont to assign for divine glory is accepted.[8]

h) 4, 82, 478, 495, 499, 565, 566, 640, 816

[399]—E. *When the superior general or the Society accepts the charge of some university, the fact that an obligation arises to give the ordinary lectures of the university will not be against the intention of this constitution, even if some lectures on theology are included in them.*

Chapter 8
The instruction of the scholastics
in the means
of helping their fellowmen

a) 289, 307, 308, 351, 360, 446, 815

[400]—1. In view of the objective which the Society seeks by means of its studies,[a] toward the end of them it is good for the scholastics to begin to accustom themselves to the spiritual arms

---

7 On gratuity of instruction, see [478] and [495], with the footnotes.
8 Paragraphs [398-399], written by Ignatius but found outside text B after his death, were inserted here by General Congregation I, Decrees 74, 75 (*InstSJ*, II, 171-172).

which they must employ in aiding their fellowmen;[b] and this
work can be begun in the colleges, even though it is more
properly and extensively done in the houses.[c]

b) 362, 365, 437

c) 289, 636-649

[**401**]—2. First of all, those who in the judgment of the
superior should be ordained are to be taught how to say Mass
not only with interior understanding and devotion but also with
an exterior manner good for the edification of those who hear
the Mass. All the members of the Society should as far as possible
use the same uniform ceremonies,[d] by conforming themselves in
them, as far as the diversity of regions permits, to the Roman
usage as the one which is more universal and embraced in a
special way by the Apostolic See.[1]

d) 110, 671

[**402**]—3. Similarly, they will exercise themselves in preaching
and in delivering [sacred[2]] lectures in a manner suitable for
the edification of the people,[e] which is different from the scholastic manner [A], by endeavoring to learn the [vernacular[3]]
language well, to have, as matters previously studied and ready
at hand, the means which are more useful for this ministry [B],
and to avail themselves of all appropriate means to perform it
better and with greater fruit for souls [C].

e) 80, 251, 280,
814

[**403**]—*A. While lecturing, in addition to giving the interpretation, they ought to keep alert to touch upon matters helpful
for habits of conduct and for Christian living. They should do
the same when teaching in their classes[f] in the schools, too, but
much more so when lecturing to the people.[g]*

f) 486

g) 645

[**404**]—*B. It will be helpful if they have studied, in a manner
that is special and directed toward preaching, the gospel passages
which occur throughout the year; and to have studied some part*

---

1 See fn. 2 on [110] above.
2 "Sacred" is the interpretation of the Latin translation of 1558. Nadal distinguishes (1)
lectures (*lectiones*) held in the classrooms, which present speculative investigation of the
truth and aim at intellectual formation, (2) sacred lectures, usually held in the churches,
which aim to communicate truth and instruction but also in a sedate manner to move the
hearers to virtue and Christian devotion, and (3) sermons (*conciones*), given in the
churches in an oratorical manner. See *MonNad*, V, 830-831; cf. 195, 341; and *Scholia in
Constitutiones* (Prato, 1883), p. 89: "In the classroom truth, even that which pertains to
practice, is investigated and treated in a speculative manner"; but later all truths, practical
and speculative, "are brought to bear on practice, . . . anointed with the grace of our
vocation, imbued with devotion, . . . applied . . . in a spiritual manner and ought to
excite devotional and genuinely Christian affections."
3 The translators of 1558 turned Ignatius' *la lengua* by *linguam . . . vernaculam*, which
the context amply justifies. In 1555 and 1556 Ignatius himself urged the learning of the
vernacular languages (see *ConsMHSJ*, III, 131, fn. 3 for many references).

*of Scripture for purposes of lecturing; likewise, to have con-
sidered in advance what pertains to the vices and leads to
abhorrence of them and to their correction; and, on the contrary,
what pertains to the commandments, virtues, good works, and
motives for esteeming them and means of acquiring them. It
will be better, if possible, to have this material in excerpts, to
avoid so great a need of books.*

[405]—C. *Some means are these: to have studied the precepts
about the manner of preaching given by those who have performed this ministry well and to listen to good preachers; to
practice oneself in preaching either in the house or in monasteries; to have a good corrector who points out defects either
in the matter preached or in the voice, tones, gestures, and
movements. Finally, the scholastic himself, by reflecting on what
he has done, can help himself more in every respect.*

[406]—4. They should also practice themselves in the administration of the sacraments of confession and Communion[h] [D],
by keeping fresh in mind and endeavoring to put into practice
not merely what pertains to themselves, but also what pertains
to the penitents and communicants, that they may receive and
frequent these sacraments well and fruitfully for divine glory.

h) 356, 437, 642, 643

[407]—D. *In regard to the confessions, beyond the classroom
study and the cases of conscience, especially in the matter of
restitution, it is good to have a compendium containing the
reserved cases and censures, that one may know how far his
jurisdiction extends, and the extraordinary formulas of abso-
lutions which occur. Moreover, it is good to have a brief list of
questions about the sins and their remedies, and an instruction
helping toward the good and prudent exercise of this ministry
in the Lord without harm to oneself and with profit to one's
fellowmen.[4] Especially at the beginning of the confessor's
ministry, when someone has heard a confession he should
accustom himself to reflect to see whether he has been deficient
in any regard and to improve himself for the future.*

[408]—5. After they have had experience of the Spiritual
Exercises in their ownselves, they should acquire experience in

---

4 In compliance with these directives Polanco published in 1554 a directory for confessors:
Breve directorium ad confessarii ac confitentis munus rite obeundum; and Cristobal de
Madrid published his *Libellus de frequenti usu sacramenti Eucharistiae* (Naples, 1556).
See *DeGuiJes*, pp. 376-377; also pp. 211, 244.

giving them to others.ⁱ Each one should know how to give an   i) 437, 648
explanation of them and how to employ this spiritual weapon,
since it is obvious that God our Lord has made it so effective
for His service [E].

[**409**]—*E. They could begin by giving the Exercises to some
in whose cases less is risked, and by conferring about their
method of procedure with someone more experienced, noting
well what he finds more useful and what less so. Their explanation of the Exercises should be given in such a manner that
it does not merely give satisfaction to the others but also moves
them to desire to be helped by the Exercises. Generally, only
the exercises of the first week⁵ should be given. When they are
given in their entirety, this should be done with outstanding
persons⁶ or with those who desire to decide upon their state
of life.ʲ*   j) 649

[**410**]—6. They should likewise bestow appropriate study upon
the method of teaching Christian doctrine⁷ and of adapting
themselves to the capacities of children or simple persilnsᵏ [F].   k) 437, 528, 645

[**411**]—*F. It will be helpful to have a written compendiary
explanation of the matters necessary for the faith and Christian
life.*

[**412**]—7. Just as one's fellowmen are helped to live well by
what has been stated above, so an effort should be made to know
what helps them to die well and what procedure should be used

---

5 I.e., the Exercises of *SpEx*, [24-90], which deal chiefly with purification from sin.
6 The chief reason why Ignatius advised against giving the more advanced Exercises of
   SpEx [91-312] indiscriminately to all persons was seemingly his principle for selecting ministries which is given in Part VII below, esp. [622-624]. The time of priests was to be
   reserved for far-reaching and long-lasting works. One priest usually directed a single
   exercitant and, except for a few rare instances, group retreats had not yet arisen. See
   DeGuiJes, p. 125; cf. pp. 111, 123-124, 131-132, 237, 301-304, 532-534. See also *EppIgn*,
   XII, 677, and *Directoria Ignatiana dictata*, in *SpExMHSJ*, pp. 785-794.
7 Few things better illustrate Ignatius' sensitivity to the needs of his times than the importance he attached to the instruction of children and simple persons in the rudiments of
   Christian doctrine. The early Jesuits' esteem for this work already in 1539 can be seen
   in *ConsMHSJ*, I, 10-11, 43-45, and in the bulls *Regimini* and *Exposcit*, [3]. See also
   MonNad, V, 343, 385, 788, 847-849, 877; and *Cons*, [528] below. On the appalling
   religious ignorance of his times, see above, pp. 11-12; fn. 2 on [160]; and the supplementary Note B in the Reference matter below. The Reformation brought numerous new
   catechisms both Protestant and Catholic, e.g., Luther's *Kleiner Katechismus* (1520);
   Canisius' *Summa Doctrinae Christianae* (1554), and his smaller catechisms in German
   in 1555, 1556, 1558; and copious others by various authors in many languages. See, e.g.,
   NCathEnc, III, 233, 277; *OxDCCh*, p. 246; Koch, *Jesuiten-Lexikon*, cols. 964-969.

at a moment so important for gaining or losing the ultimate end, eternal happiness [G].

[413]—*G. It is good to have a compendium on the method of helping someone to die well, to refresh the memory when this holy ministry must be exercised.*

[414]—8. In general, they ought to be instructed about the manner of acting proper to a member of the Society, who has to associate with so great a diversity of persons throughout such varied regions. Hence they should foresee the inconveniences which may arise and the opportunities which can be grasped for the greater service of God, by using some means at one time and others at another. Although all this can be taught only by the unction of the Holy Spirit [1 John 2:20, 27] and by the prudence which God our Lord communicates to those who trust in His Divine Majesty, nevertheless the way can at least be opened by some suggestions which aid and dispose one for the effect which must be produced by divine grace.

Chapter 9
The removal from studies

[415]—1. Some are removed from the colleges for the reasons stated in Part II and in the manner explained there [209-230], that others in their place may make better progress in the service of God our Lord, since the same reason holds true for removing from the colleges as from the houses [A].

a) 338

[416]—*A. Others are removed after seven years, namely, those who were admitted to the colleges for that length of time without a fixed resolution to enter the Society,*[a] *as has been said [338]. But a dispensation could be given in regard to this period of seven years, by prolonging it when such students give much good example in such a way that much service of God is expected from them, or when they are useful to the college.*

[417]—2. Sometimes, too, they will be removed because some other place is useful for their better progress in spirit or in learning; or because it is useful for the universal good of the

Society, as is the case when someone is removed from one college where he has studied arts to lecture[1] on them in another before he studies theology,[b] and similarly in regard to other purposes for the greater service of God our Lord.

b) 371, 391

[418]—3. The ordinary method of removal from a college where all the branches are studied will be that after one has finished his studies, namely, after he has completed the course in arts and studied theology for four years.[c] Near the end of this period the rector ought to inform the general or provincial by reporting about his competence, and then to follow the order given him for the glory of God our Lord.[d]

c) 473, 474, 476

d) 424

Chapter 10
The government of the colleges

[419]—1. In accordance with the bulls[1] of the Apostolic See, the Professed Society will hold the superintendency over the colleges.[a] For since it may not seek any gain from the fixed revenues nor employ them for itself,[b] in all probability it will in the long run proceed with greater disinterestedness and a more spiritual attitude in regard to what ought to be provided in the colleges for the greater service of God our Lord and for the good government of the colleges.

a) 326, 327, 420, 740, 815
b) 5, 326, 557, 763, 774, 816

[420]—2. Except for what pertains to the Constitutions and the suppression or alienation of such colleges,[c] all the authority, the administration, and in general the execution of this super-intendency will be vested in the superior general.[d] He, keeping his mind fixed on the end of the colleges and of the entire Society, will see better what is expedient in them.

c) 322, 441, 680, 743, 762, 763
d) 326, 327, 419, 740

[421]—3. Therefore the general, by himself or through another to whom he delegates his authority in this matter, will appoint one of the coadjutors[2] in the Society as the rector who is to have

---

1 In the early Society there was great variety in the manner and duration of the period of "regency." For examples, see *IdeaJesUn*, pp. 71-72.
1 See *Regimini*, [6], *Exposcit*, [5].
2 Since the colleges possessed fixed revenues which had to be administered, and since the professed were forbidden to have or profit from them, it was thought better to have

e) 326, 490, 557,
740, 757, 759
f) 326, 741, 742,
759

the principal charge[e] [A]. This rector will give account of his charge to the provincial or to whomever the general designates.[f] The general will likewise have power to remove the rector, or to change him from this charge, as seems better to him in our Lord.

[422]—A. *This does not prevent a professed member who has been sent to visit or reform the affairs of some college from dwelling there, or presiding over all those who live there, for a time or in some other manner, as may seem more expedient for the welfare of the college or for the universal good.[g]*

g) 330, 558

h) 434, 659

[423]—4. Care should be taken that the rector[3] be a man of great example, edification, and mortification of all his evil inclinations, and one especially approved in regard to his obedience and humility.[h] He ought likewise to be discreet, fit for governing, experienced both in matters of business and of the spiritual life. He should know how to mingle severity with kindness at the proper times. He should be solicitous, stalwart under work, a man of learning, and finally, one in whom the higher superiors can confide and to whom they can with security delegate their authority. For the greater this delegated authority will be, the better will the colleges be governed for greater divine glory.[i]

i) 206, 207, 791,
820

j) 723, 790, 812
k) 547, 602, 746,
790, 826

[424]—5. The function of the rector will be first of all to sustain the whole college by his prayer and holy desires,[j] and then to bring it about that the Constitutions are observed[k] [B]. He should watch over all his subjects with great care, and guard them against difficulties from within or without the house by anticipating the difficulties and remedying them if they have occurred, in the way that seems conducive to the good of the individuals and to that of all. He should strive to promote their progress in virtues and learning,[l] and care for their health and for the temporal goods both stable and movable[m] [C]. He should appoint officials discreetly, observe how they proceed, and retain them in office or change them as he judges appropriate in the Lord. In general he ought to see to it that what has been stated about the colleges in the preceding chapters is carried out.

l) 91, 92, 261
m) 326

ordinarily a spiritual coadjutor as the rector (see Nadal, *Scholia*, p. 92). But the practice was not rigid. Already in 1552 Andrés de Oviedo, a professed, was rector of the college at Naples. See also [557, 558], and fn. 1 on [490] below.

3 Ignatius' ideal of a superior as sketched here [423-427] is rightly compared with that of the superior general which he gives below in Part IX, ch. 2 [723-735]. Both passages (which have often been taken as Ignatius' self-portrait) are given concrete illustration in Ribadeneyra's treatise (in *FN*, III, 608-634) on "Ignatius' Manner of Governing." See [551] and [723-727] below, with the notes.

He should observe in its entirety the submission he ought to maintain not merely toward the superior general but also to the provincial superior, by keeping him informed and having recourse to him in the matters of greater moment, and by following the order given him,[n] since the provincial is his superior, in the same way as those of his own college should act toward him. His subjects ought to hold him in great respect and reverence as one who holds the place of Christ our Lord,[o] while leaving to him with true obedience the free disposal of themselves and their affairs,[p] not keeping anything closed to him [D], not even their own conscience.[q] Rather, as has been stated in the Examen [93-97], they should manifest their conscience to him at fixed times, and more frequently when there is reason, without showing any repugnance or any manifestations of contrary opinion,[r] that by the union of their opinion and will with his and by proper submission they may be better preserved and make greater progress in the divine service.[s]

n) 206, 662, 663, 666, 820, 821

o) 84, 85, 284, 286, 342, 547, 551, 552, 618, 619, 627, 661, 765

p) 292, 618, 627

q) 91-97, 263, 551

r) 284, 547, 550

s) 655, 821

[425]—B. *Thus, just as it will pertain to the rector to endeavor to have the Constitutions observed in their entirety, so it will be his to grant dispensations from them with authority from his own superiors, when he judges that such would be the intention of the one who composed them, in a particular case according to occurrences and necessities and while keeping his attention fixed on the greater common good.*[t]

t) 747

[426]—C. *This statement includes appropriate care to retain friendships and to render adversaries benevolent.*[u]

u) 823, 824

[427]—D. *Something closed means a door, cabinet, and the like.*

[428]—6. For the good government of the house, the rector ought to appoint not merely as many officials as are necessary,[v] but also, as far as possible, those who are fit for their office [E]. He should give each one the rules of what he ought to do[w] [F] and take care that no one interferes in the business of another. Furthermore, just as he ought to have help given to them when they need it, so when time is left over he ought to see to it that they employ it fruitfully in the service of God our Lord.[x]

v) 148, 149, 305, 306, 334, 431, 433

w) 136, 395, 396, 455, 654, 811

x) 253

[429]—E. *Fit, I mean, in respect both to the sufficiency of persons and to their occupations. For it would not be proper to give offices which demand much work to subjects much occupied with other things. Furthermore, since some occupations require*

experience to be done well, their personnel ought not easily to be changed.

[430]—*F. Among the rules, each one ought to read those which concern him once each week.*

[431]—7. The officials whom the rector must have seem to be, first of all, a good minister, to be vice rector or manager of the house, who should make provision for all the things necessary for the common good; a syndic to observe what is exterior[y] and another person to superintend the spiritual matters;[z] and two or more persons in whose discretion and goodness the rector has much confidence, so that he can confer with them about the matters which entail difficulty and which he thinks it proper to discuss with them for greater divine glory[a] [G]; and others too who are necessary for more particular offices[b] [H].

[432]—*G. If that many persons should not be available, one could hold more offices. For example, the minister and the aforementioned superintendent could have the charge of matters which pertain to the rector or to the novices, and so on.*

[433]—*H. Thus, there could be one who is to do the secretarial work, a porter, a sacristan, a cook, and a launderer.[c] Other less burdensome offices could be divided among those who are studying,[d] when there are not others who can do the work.*

[434]—8. The rector should endeavor that all those in the college practice an integral obedience to each official in his own office, and these officials to the minister[e] and to the rector himself, in accordance with the order which he prescribes to them. Ordinarily those who have charge of others who must obey them ought to give them an example by the obedience which they themselves observe to their own superiors as persons holding the place of Christ our Lord.[f]

[435]—9. A suitable order of time for study, prayer, Masses, lectures, eating and sleeping, and so on, will be helpful for everything.[g] Thus a signal will be given at designated times [I]. When it is heard, all should go immediately, leaving even a letter[4] they have begun.[h] When these hours ought to be changed

y) 271, 504-506
z) 263

a) 490, 502, 810, 811
b) 148, 305, 334, 428

c) 149, 306

d) 364

e) 87, 88, 286

f) 423, 659

g) 294, 295

h) 284, 547

---

4 *La letra* here means a letter of the alphabet, e.g., an A or a B (see *EppIgn*, III, 156). The example is found in the *Apophthegmata Patrum* of the fourth or fifth century, in PG 65:296. The idea of prompt obedience is part of the monastic tradition. See, e.g., St. Benedict's Rule, ch. 5.

because of the seasons or other unusual reasons, the rector or the one in charge should consider the matter and what he orders should be observed.

[436]—*I. The signal will be given by a bell which will be sounded for retiring for sleep, for taking meals, and so forth.*

[437]—10. The rector ought himself to explain or teach[5] Christian doctrine for forty days [K]. He should also consider which of his subjects should deal with their neighbors inside the house or outside of it, and for what length of time they should do this, in spiritual conversations, conducting exercises, hearing confessions, and also in preaching or lecturing[6] or in teaching Christian doctrine. They should do this work partly to gain practice themselves, especially when they are near the end of their studies, and partly for the fruit which will be reaped by the others within and without the house.[i] After pondering all the factors, the rector should in everything provide what he thinks to be more pleasing to the Divine and Supreme Goodness and for His greater service and glory [L].

i) 362, 365, 400-414

[438]—*K. If for reasons of edification or for some other sufficient reason it does not seem proper for the rector to do this teaching himself, he may inform the provincial. If the provincial has the same opinion, the rector may have someone else do it for him.*

[439]—*L. The Constitutions which pertain to the colleges could be kept apart and read publicly two or three times a year.*

---

5 *Leer o enseñar:* these words are synonyms here, and were so understood by General Congregation II, d. 65 (*InstSJ*, II, 208). Covarrubias defines *leer* as "enseñar alguna disciplina públicamente."

6 *En predicar o leer o en enseñar:* the position of *leer* between "preaching" and "teaching Christian doctrine" shows that the lecturing refers to "sacred lectures," on which see [402] above with fn. 2, and [565] below with fn. 13.

The universities of the Society[1]

Chapter 11
The acceptance of universities

[440]—1. Through a motive of charity colleges are accepted and schools open to the public are maintained in them for the improvement in learning and in living not only of our own members[a] but even more especially[2] of those from outside the Society.[b] Through this same motive the Society can extend itself to undertaking the work of universities,[3] that through them this

a) 289, 307, 308, 333, 815
b) 392

---

1 Chs. 11-17 on the Universities of the Society were once a separate fascicle, written probably in 1553 or 1554, and were referred to by Da Câmara as "the Second Part" of Part IV. They were inserted into the text of the Constitutions before the death of Ignatius (see *MonPaed* [1965], pp. 25*, 272-273, which well treats the subtle difficulties entailed; and also *Cons*MHSJ, II, lxx-lxxiii). Like ch. 7, they refer to both Jesuit scholastics and externs (see the notes on [307] and [392] above).

2 Ignatius' words "not only" and "but even more especially" were deleted from text B and again restored in Polanco's handwriting (see *Cons*MHSJ, II, 464). In General Congregation II in 1565, Polanco proposed that these words should be corrected but the Congregation took no action. On the possible implication of these measures, see Lukács in *AHSJ*, XXIX (1960), 219-224, XXX (1961), 66-76, and *WL*, XC (1962), 134-137, 147-150.

3 Here in [440] Ignatius once more points out how the Society's ministry of education fits into his world view, as he also does in [307, 351, 361, 369, 400, 440, 446, 622]. Among his perennial principles and objectives in educational work which he expressed in his Constitutions (see the notes on [307, 351, and 369] above), some eleven can be singled out here as being especially important for understanding Part IV, particularly chs. 11-17: (1) The educator has the ultimate objective of stimulating the student to relate his activity to his final end: knowledge and love of God and the salvation of his

fruit sought in the colleges may be spread more universally through the branches taught, the number of persons attending, and the degrees which are conferred in order that the recipients may be able to teach with authority elsewhere what they have learned well in these universities of the Society for the glory to God our Lord.

[**441**]—2. However, to decide under what conditions and obligations [A] and in what places universities should be accepted will be left to the judgment of the one who has the universal care of the Society. After he has heard the opinion of his assistants and of the others of whose counsel he may wish to avail himself, he will himself have the power to decide upon the acceptance.ᶜ But once such universities have been accepted, he cannot suppress them without the general congregation.ᵈ

c) 321, 325, 762

d) 322, 420, 680, 743, 762, 763

[**442**]—A. *When the founder desires that the Society should be obliged to provide a certain number of lecturers, or to undertake some other obligations, it should be remarked that if these obligations are accepted, namely because it still seems likely that this will aid the Society toward achieving its ends in the service of God our Lord, there ought to be no failure to fulfill them. But neither should one easily do more in this regard than*

soul ([307, 351, 369, 440, 446]). (2) The immediate objective of professor and student is the student's mastery of his fields of study, both sacred and secular ([460]; cf. [341, 355, 356, 361]). (3) The Society hopes by means of its educational work to pour capable and zealous leaders into the social order, in numbers large enough to leaven it effectively for good ([622]; cf. [440] and *EppIgn*, IV, 9, English in *IdeaJesUn*, pp. 28-29). (4) The branches of study should be so integrated that each makes its proper contribution toward the goal of the curriculum as a whole: a scientifically reasoned Christian outlook on life, enabling the student to live well and meaningfully for this world and the next ([446-452]; see also *IdeaJesUn*, pp. 54, 175, 185, 272, 321, 322). (5) Theology is the most important branch, since the light it offers is the chief means of gaining the Christian outlook, and of tying matters treated elsewhere into a unity by showing how all creation can be consecrated to God's greater glory ([446-452]; cf. Vatican Council II, "The Church in the Modern World," nos. 4-6, 12, 34-39, 53-62; "The Apostolate of the Laity," nos. 4-7, 13, 14). (6) In a Jesuit university, any faculty can function as long as it contributes to the Society's general purpose (see [446-452], where Ignatius lists all the higher faculties of his era). (7) The formation offered should be both intellectual and moral, insofar as it provides scientifically reasoned motives for moral living ([481; cf. 392, 395, 403]). (8) As far as possible, the professors should be personally interested in the students and their progress ([481]). (9) Jesuit schools should transmit the cultural heritage of the past and also provide facilities for men engaged in research or creative activity ([446]; cf. [653] and see *IdeaJesUn*, pp. 52, 53, 195, 264, 268). (10) Jesuit schools should be alert to appropriate and adapt the best procedures emerging in other schools of the day—as Ignatius showed by his example and letters (see *ConsMHSJ*, II, lxxi and *IdeaJesUn*, pp. 29-31, 38). (11) Jesuit schools should continually adapt their procedures and pedagogical methods to circumstances of times, places, and persons ([455]; cf. [395, 466]). Further references on these matters are in fn. 1 on [351], above.

e) 325

what is obligatory (especially if this could be interpreted as inducing a new obligation) without the general's consent. Neither ought the general to be lenient in such a matter;[e] *rather, consulting his assistants he should take care that he does not burden the Society. If he makes a concession on some point, it should be made clear that no obligation is assumed but that what is added is something voluntary.*

[443]–3. However, the religious tranquility and spiritual occupations of the Society do not permit it to have the distraction and other inconveniences which would be entailed by holding the office of judge in civil or criminal affairs. Therefore there should be no acceptance of jurisdiction of this kind which the Society would have to exercise by itself or through others who depend upon it. However, for that which properly pertains to the well-being of the university, it is desirable that in regard to the students the ordinary civil or ecclesiastical ministry of justice should carry out the will of the rector of the university when he has expressed it in regard to punishing the students [B]; and that this ministry should in general give its support in matters pertaining to the studies, especially when such matters have been recommended to it by the rector [C].

f) 488, 489

[444]–*B. If some student has been rebellious or scandalous so that it would be proper to expel him not only from the schools but also from the city or to put him into prison, it would be a matter properly pertaining to the well-being of the university.*[f] *Therefore the ordinary ministers of justice ought to be informed and soon after to execute the punishment by deed. For this and similar matters it would be wise to have the authorization in writing from the ruler or supreme power. Similarly, the recommendation from the rector in favor of some student ought to carry weight with the ministers of justice toward preventing the students from being oppressed.*

[445]–*C. Since there cannot be exemption from the ordinary judges as a means to attract a large number of students, an effort should be made to compensate for this by other concessions and privileges.*

Chapter 12
The branches to be taught
in the universities of the Society[1]

[446]—1. Since the end of the Society and of its studies is to aid our fellowmen to the knowledge and love of God and to the salvation of their souls;[a] and since the branch of theology is the means most suitable to this end, in the universities of the Society the principal emphasis ought to be put upon it.[2] Thus diligent treatment by highly capable professors[b] should be given to what pertains to scholastic doctrine and Sacred Scripture, and also to the part of positive theology[c] which is conducive to the aforementioned end, without entering into the part of the canons which is directed toward trials in court.

a) 3, 156, 163, 258, 307, 351, 360, 603, 813

b) 369, 456

c) 351, 353, 464, 467

[447]—2. Moreover, since both the learning of theology and the use of it require (especially in these times) knowledge of

---

1 Ch. 12 is a remarkable synthesis which in brief compass reflects Ignatius' concept both of (1) educational work in general, with its major objectives fitted into his hierarchical world view (see above, [307, 351, 361, 369, 400, 440, 446, 622] and the notes there), and of (2) the organizational structure of his schools. Since approximately 1190, universities had been composed of four faculties. First was the lower faculty which taught the branches of learning named the liberal arts (the trivium of grammar, rhetoric, and dialectic, and the quadrivium of arithmetic, geometry, musical theory, and astronomical theory). Next came the higher faculties teaching the professional branches of law, medicine, and theology. This structure, slightly modified by Renaissance practices, is what Ignatius inherited and used. In his concept of a Jesuit university, there was the lower faculty with which it usually began in the form of a college (see [318, 366, 392, 394] above and notes there). The chief instructional objective in the college was to teach boys the art of speaking, reading, and writing Latin with facility and with elegance as far as possible, according to the Renaissance ideal of *eloquentia*. A college became a university by addition of the higher faculties of (1) arts or philosophy (largely Aristotelian, divided into the branches named in [451]), and (2) theology, with instruction in scholastic and positive theology, canon law, and Scripture. For a diagrammatic outline of a university as conceived by Ignatius, see *IdeaJesUn*, p. 45. His ideal was best realized in his cherished Roman College, which opened in 1551 and became a university in fact though not in name in 1553, when classes in philosophy and theology were begun with papal approval.
2 See objectives 4 and 5 in fn. 3 on [440]. Theology is the chief source of the scientifically reasoned Christian philosophy of life and the source of integration for the other branches, as their arrangement in ch. 12 indicates. But this importance given to theology in [446] is a matter of emphasis and outlook or attitude rather than of the hours of instruction or number of courses prescribed; of an atmosphere in which professors and students alike think that all the particular truths learned in other faculties should be viewed also in the light of God's revelation whenever this throws light upon them—as it sometimes though not always does. In early Jesuit colleges or universities, formal instruction in theology was usually confined to students for the priesthood. But the light of theology filtered down to all the students in various ways because of the environment. Virtually all the professors had at least some theological training.

humane letters [A] and of the Latin, Greek, and Hebrew[3]
d) 351, 352, 367, languages,[d] there should be capable professors of these lan-
460
e) 369, 456
guages, and that in sufficient number.[e] Furthermore, there may
also be teachers of other languages such as Chaldaic, Arabic,
and Indian, where these are necessary or useful for the end
stated, with attention given to the diversities of place and reasons
which may move us to teach them [B].

[**448**]—*A. Under the heading of humane letters is understood,
in addition to grammar, what pertains to rhetoric, poetry, and*
f) 352   *history.*[f]

[**449**]—*B. When a plan is being worked out in some college
or university to prepare persons to go among the Moors or
Turks, Arabic or Chaldaic would be expedient; and Indian
would be proper for those about to go among the Indians; and
the same holds true for similar reasons in regard to other languages which could have greater utility in other regions.*

[**450**]—3. Likewise, since the arts or natural sciences dispose
the intellectual powers for theology, and are useful for the perfect understanding and use of it,[4] and also by their own nature
g) 351   help toward the same ends,[g] they should be treated with fitting
h) 369, 456   diligence and by learned professors.[h] In all this the honor and
glory of God our Lord should be sincerely sought [C].

[**451**]—*C. Logic, physics, metaphysics, and moral philosophy
should be treated, and also mathematics in the measure appropriate to secure the end which is being sought.*
*To teach how to read and write would also be a work of
charity if the Society had enough members to be able to attend
to everything.*[5] *But because of the lack of members these elementary branches are not ordinarily taught.*

3 In Ignatius' text B, the word "Hebrew" was below in [449]. It was transferred here by
  General Congregation I in 1558 (*InstSJ*, II, 164).
4 As in the medieval universities, the arts or branches learned from natural reason are conceived here both as worthy of penetrating study in themselves [361, 450] and also as
  handmaids to theology [447-451]. They are fitted into Ignatius' hierarchy of ends, mentioned above on pp. 18-19.
5 Ignatius' principle for selecting ministries [622-624] is his manifest reason for ordinarily
  omitting elementary education, which was occasionally accepted because of special circumstances (see, e.g., *MonPaed* [1901], p. 852 and *IdeaJesUn*, pp. 68-69). In a typical
  case, a boy might receive his elementary education from tutors at the ages of 5 through 9,
  then enter a Jesuit university and study languages from 10 through 13, arts from 14
  through 16, and theology from 17 through 21, as is illustrated (with variations characteristic of the era) by the concrete cases of Canisius, Bellarmine, Lessius, Corneille, and
  Calderón (*IdeaJesUn*, pp. 44-51, 68-73).

[452]—4. The study of medicine and laws, being more remote from our Institute, will not be treated in the universities of the Society, or at least the Society will not undertake this teaching through its own members.[6]

Chapter 13
The method and order of treating
the aforementioned branches

[453]—1. To give such treatment of both the lower branches and also of theology, there should be a suitable arrangement and order both for the morning and the afternoon.

[454]—2. And although the order and hours which are spent in these studies[1] may vary according to the regions and seasons, there should be such conformity[2] that in every region that is done which is there judged to be most conducive to greater progress in learning [A].

[455]—A. *Concerning the hours of the lectures, their order, and their method,[a] and concerning the exercises both in com-*   a) 375
positions, which ought to be corrected by the teachers, and in disputations within all the faculties, and in delivering orations and reading verses in public—all this will be treated in detail in a separate treatise,[b] [approved by the general].[3] This present   b) 395, 396
constitution refers the reader to it, with the remark that it ought

---

6 Faculties of law and medicine actually functioned only rarely in early Jesuit universities. The chief instance is the University of Pont-à-Mousson in Lorraine, opened in 1574. A course in law was given by a layman in 1577; and gradually a faculty of law formed under a lay dean. A similar faculty of medicine arose in 1592. Cf. P. Delattre, *Les établissements des Jésuites en France* . . . (Paris, 1910), I, 604-615; and Ganss, *The Jesuit Educational Tradition* . . . , pp. 29-31.

1 In this context *studios* means "in the exercises within the classroom" in these faculties. There is not question here of the hours spent in private study (De la Torre, *Constitutiones,* p. 152, fn. 3).

2 Nadal's comment on this (*Scholia,* p. 101) is interesting as reflecting his attitude, one which was found also in the writers of the successive drafts of the *Ratio studiorum:* "As far as possible, all our universities should use the same set (*communibus*) of rules and the same plan of studies (*ratione studiorum*)."

3 "Approved by the general" was added by General Congregation I (*InstSJ,* II, 164).

> *to be adapted to places, times, and persons, even though it
> would be desirable to reach that order as far as this is possible.*[4]

[456]—3. Furthermore, there should be not only lectures which
are delivered in public but also different masters according to
the capacity and number of the students[c] [B]. These masters
should take an interest in the progress of each one of their
students,[d][5] require them to give an account of their lessons
[C], and make them hold repetitions[e] [D]. They should also
make those who are studying humane letters gain practice by
ordinarily speaking Latin, and by composing in a good style[6]
and delivering well what they have composed.[f] They should
make them, and much more those studying the higher branches,
engage in disputations often.[g] Days and hours should be designated for this; and in these disputations the students should
debate not only with the members of their own class, but those
who are somewhat lower down should dispute about matters
they understand with students who are more advanced, and
conversely those who are more advanced should debate with
those lower down by coming down to subjects which these
latter are studying. The professors too ought to hold disputations
with one another, always preserving the proper modesty and

*c) 369, 446, 447,
450*

d) 369

e) 374, 375

f) 381, 484

g) 375, 378

---

4 This paragraph of Ignatius gave rise to successive drafts of a plan of studies (*Ratio
studiorum*): Nadal's (1565?), Borgia's (1565-1569; see *AHSJ*, XXVII [1958], 209-232),
Ledesma's (ca. 1575), and the more concerted versions published by committees in 1586,
1591, and 1592 which culminated in the text promulgated by Aquaviva in 1599, the
definitive *Ratio studiorum* which governed practice in Jesuit schools until the suppression
of the Society in 1773. Through these drafts Ignatius and the Jesuits set up the first extensive school system in history, i.e., an organization of individual schools in close contact with one another, deliberately reviewing and evaluating classroom and administrative
experience, and sharing and exchanging teachers on a large scale according to needs
(Ganss, *The Jesuit Educational Tradition* . . . , pp. 3-5). Numerous *Rationes studiorum*
were produced by Renaissance educators, but the Jesuit *Ratio* of 1599 is perhaps the most
influential in practice and the most famous of them all. In its complete form, like Part IV
of Ignatius' Constitutions, it gives directives for an entire Jesuit university, i.e., for both
the lower and higher faculties. The *Ratio* is, however, more a treatment of curricular
organization and pedagogical procedure than of educational theory. In the main, it presupposes rather than repeats or expounds the inspiring guiding principles or objectives expressed by Ignatius in his Constitutions, Part IV (on which see fnn. 8 on [369] and 3 on
[440] above). One great merit of the *Ratio* of 1599 is that it produced a unity of procedure throughout the far-flung hundreds of Jesuit schools in Europe and the Americas.
That procedural unity was greater than would be desirable or possible today; but it was
a significant advantage and achievement amid the educational disorganization of the
1500's and 1600's. The setting up of such a widespread system is what made the Jesuits'
educational work the success which is described in histories of education. See *IdeaJesUn*,
ch. 10, pp. 202-217.

5 See objective 8 in fn. 3 on [440] above.

6 The words "in a good style" are not explicitly in Ignatius' Spanish text but give the
interpretation of the Latin translators of 1558, who used "stilum . . . expoliant." Taken
literally, the Spanish can mean "by composing well and delivering well."

having someone preside to stop the debate and give the doctrinal solution.[h]   *h*) 378-380

[457]—*B. Ordinarily, there will be three teachers in three different classes of grammar, another who is to lecture on humanities, and another on rhetoric. In the class of these last two groups there will be lectures on the Greek and Hebrew languages, and on any other if it is to be learned.[i] In consequence of this arrangement there will always be five classes. If there should be so much to do in some of them that one teacher alone does not suffice, a helper should be given to him. If the number of students makes it impossible for one teacher to attend to them even though he has helpers, the class can be divided into two sections so that there are two fifth classes or two fourth classes; and all the teachers, if possible, should be members of the Society,[j] although there may be others according to necessity. If the small number or the arrangement of the students is such that so many classes or teachers are not required, discretion will be used in everything to adjust the number by assigning those who suffice and no more.*   *i*) 367, 368, 447, 449, 460

j) 369, 452

[458]—*C. Whether in addition to the ordinary masters who have special care of the students there ought to be some one or several who in the capacity of public lecturers are to give lectures on philosophy or mathematics or some other branch, with greater solemnity than the ordinary lecturers,[7] prudence will decide, in accordance with the places and persons involved. But the greater edification and service of God our Lord will always be kept in view.*

[459]—*D. There will be repetitions not merely of the last lesson, but also of those of the week and of a longer time when it is judged that this ought to be the case.[k]*   *k*) 374, 375

[460]—4. Likewise, it will always be the function of the rector to see to it himself or through the chancellor[l] that the newcomers are examined and placed in those classes and with those teachers that are suitable for them. Furthermore, it is left to his discretion   *l*) 471, 493, 494

---

7 The esteem of Ignatius and the early Jesuits for the "method of Paris" is very evident throughout this ch. 13. It appears, e.g., in Nadal's comment on this passage (*Scholia*, p. 350): "In the Academies of Italy, the public professors are accustomed to employ great display of learning in explaining rhetoric, Aristotle, and canon and civil law. Such a lecture would indeed be useful for the public, but care should be taken . . . that the Plan of Studies of Paris (*Ratio studiorum Parisiensis*), which our schools have made their very own, should not be dropped."

m) 357, 471, 472

n) 367, 368, 447, 449

o) 354-357, 471, 472

p) 355

q) 356

(after he has heard the counsel of those deputed for this purpose) to decide whether they ought to be retained longer in the same class or to advance into another.^m So too in regard to the study of the languages other than Latin, he is to determine whether it should precede the arts and theology or follow them, and how long each should study these languages.^n The same holds true for the other higher branches. According to the difference of abilities, ages, and other circumstances that must be considered, it will be the rector's function to investigate how far each student should progress into these branches and how long he should apply himself to them,^o although it is better for those who have the age and ability to advance and distinguish themselves in all these areas⁸ for the glory of God our Lord^p [E].

[**461**]—E. *There may be someone of such an age or ability that he needs only the Latin language and as much of the other faculties as is necessary to hear confessions and deal with his neighbors. Of this type, perhaps, will be some of those who have a curacy of souls and are not capable of great learning.^q On the other hand, there may be others who will progress farther in the sciences, although to judge to what extent it is expedient to drop some branches and take up others will belong to the superior. After he has explained this to the students from outside the Society and if they still desire to proceed differently, they should not be coerced.*

[**462**]—5. Just as steady application is necessary in the work of studying, so also is some relaxation. The proper amount and the times of this relaxation will be left to the prudent consideration of the rector to determine, according to the circumstances of persons and places [F].

[**463**]—F. *At least one day during the week should be given to rest from dinner on. On other points the rector should consult with the provincial about the order to be observed in regard to the vacations or ordinary interruptions of the studies.*

---

8 Ignatius shows this same attitude on earnest application to study in *EppIgn*, III, 502, cited in *MonPaed* (1965), p. 217. See also *Cons*, [340, 361, 450].

Chapter 14
The books which should be expounded

[464]–1. In general, as was stated in the treatise on the colleges [358], in each faculty those books will be lectured on which are found to contain more solid and safe doctrine; and those which are suspect, or whose authors are suspect, will not be taken up[a] [A]. But in each university these should be individually designated.

a) 274, 358

In theology there should be lectures on the Old and New Testaments and on the scholastic doctrine of St. Thomas[1] [B]; and in positive theology[b] those authors should be selected who are more suitable for our end [C].

b) 351, 446

[465]–*A. Even though the book is without suspicion of bad doctrine, when its author is suspect it is not expedient that it be lectured on. For through the book affection is acquired for the author; and some part of the credence given to him in what he says well could be given to him later in what he says unsoundly. Furthermore, it rarely occurs that some poison is not mixed into what comes forth from a heart full of it.[c] [2]*

c) 359

[466]–*B. The Master of the Sentences will also be lectured on. But if in time it seems that the students will draw more help from another author,[3] as would be the case through the writing of some compendium or book of scholastic theology that seems better adapted to these times of ours, it will be permitted to make this book the subject of the lectures, after much weighing of counsel and examination of the matter by the persons deemed*

---

1 Until well into the 1500's, Peter Lombard's *Sentences* was the most widely used textbook on theology. But in the first half of the sixteenth century the use of St. Thomas' *Summa theologiae* was much furthered by the Dominicans Cajetan in Italy, Vitoria and others in Spain, and Crockaert, Vitoria, and Peter of Nijmegen at Paris from about 1504 to 1526 (see *NCathEnc*, XIV, 132-134). Ignatius was within this influence during his study of theology under the Dominicans at Paris in 1534 (*MonBobad*, p. 614; Dudon, *St. Ignatius*, pp. 143-145, 424-425). Ever afterwards he and the early Jesuits, especially Nadal, had the esteem of St. Thomas manifested in the legislation contained in [464, 466], though they were not slavishly bound to his opinions (*MonPaed* (1965), pp. 34, 296; *MonSalm*, II, 709-717).

2 Erasmus is one example. Ignatius read his *Enchiridion militis Christiani* at Barcelona in about 1525 and ever after held Erasmus in suspicion (*FN*, IV, 172-173). For references to other authors, see *ConsMHSJ*, II, 476, fn. 2. On Ignatius' attitude toward Erasmus, see R. García-Villoslada, "San Ignacio . . . y Erasmo . . ." in *EstEcl*, XVI (1942), 235-264, 399-426; XVII (1943), 75-103.

3 General Congregation I substituted "author" for Ignatius' phrase "theology not contrary to this" (*InstSJ*, II, 170, d. 65).

fit in the whole Society and with the superior general's approval. In regard to the other branches and humane letters too, if some books written in the Society are adopted as being more useful than those commonly used, this adoption will be made after much consideration, with our objective of greater universal good always kept in view.

[467]—C. *For example, in connection with some section of canon law, the councils, and so on.*

[468]—2. In regard to the books of humane letters in Latin or Greek, in the universities as well as in the colleges,[4] lecturing to the adolescents on any book which contains matters harmful to good habits of conduct should be avoided, as far as possible, unless the books are previously expurgated of the objectionable matters and words[d] [D].

d) 359

[469]—D. *If some books, such as Terence, cannot be expurgated[5] at all, it is better that they should not be lectured on, in order that the nature of the contents may not injure the purity of the minds.*

[470]—3. In logic, natural and moral philosophy, and metaphysics, the doctrine of Aristotle should be followed, as also in the other liberal arts. In regard to the commentaries, both on these authors and on those treating humanities, a selection should be made. Those which the students ought to see should be designated, and also those which the masters ought to follow by preference in the doctrine they teach. In everything which the rector ordains, he should proceed in conformity with what is judged throughout the whole Society to be more suitable to the glory of God our Lord.[e]

e) 358

4 It should be remembered that the students were often very young. See fn. 6 on [359] and fn. 5 on [451].
5 For further references, see *FN*, III, 229, fn. 36. Such expurgation of classical texts, especially for boys 6 to 12, was a common practice among Renaissance educators such as Vegio, Aeneas Silvius, and Vives (see Farrell, *The Jesuit Code*, pp. 55-57).

Chapter 15
The terms and degrees

[471]—1. In the study of humane letters and the languages a definite period of time[1] for their completion cannot be established, because of the difference in abilities and knowledge of those who attend the lectures, and because of many other reasons which permit no other prescription of time save that which the prudent consideration of the rector or chancellor[a] will dictate for each student [A].   *a*) 355, 460, 493

[472]—*A. In the case of beginners of good ability, an effort should be made to discern whether a semester in each of the four lower classes would be enough, and two semesters in the highest class spent in studying rhetoric and the languages. But a definite rule cannot be given.*

[473]—2. In the arts, it will be necessary to arrange the terms in which the natural sciences are to be lectured upon. It seems that less than three years would be insufficient for them [B]. Another half year will remain for the student to review, perform his academic acts, and take the degree of master[2] in the case of those who are to receive degrees.[b] In this way the whole curriculum enabling a student to become a master of arts will last   *b*) 388, 390 three years and a half. Each year with the help of God one such cycle of treatises will begin and another will come to its end [C].

[474]—*B. If someone has attended the lectures on some part of the arts elsewhere, this can be taken into account. But ordinarily, in order to be graduated one must have studied for the three years mentioned. This holds true also for the four years of theology, in regard to being admitted to the acts[3] and receiving a degree in it.*

[475]—*C. If because of insufficient personnel or for other reasons facilities for that arrangement are lacking, the best that will be possible should be done, with the approval of the general or at least of the provincial.*

---

1 In ch. 15, *curso* means a term or period of time, rather than a series of lectures on one branch of studies (see Covarrubias, p. 388: "*Curso* signifies a space of time").
2 The lower degrees of baccalaureate and licentiate are here presupposed as previously received (cf. Nadal, *Scholia,* p. 104).
3 I.e., the academic exercises and public acts such as disputations and public examinations required for the degree. See also [390, 478, 493].

[**476**]–3. The curriculum in theology will be one of six years. In the first four years all the matter which must be lectured on

c) 418, 518, 519

will be expounded.ᶜ In the remaining two, in addition to the reviewing, the acts customary for a doctorate will be performed

d) 388, 390

by those who are to receive it.ᵈ

Ordinarily, the cycle of the curriculum will be begun every fourth year and the books which are to be lectured on will be arranged in such a sequence that a student can enter the curriculum at the beginning of any one of the four years [D]. By hearing the lectures on what remains of the four-year curriculum, and then on the matter immediately following until he reaches the point where he began, he will hear the lectures of the entire curriculum within four years.

[**477**]–D. *If in some college or university of the Society the situation is such that it appears better to begin the cycle of subjects every two years, or somewhat later than every four, with the consent of the general or of the provincial that which is found to be more suitable may be done.*

[**478**]–4. In the matter of the degrees, both of master of arts and of doctor of theology, three things should be observed. First, no one, whether a member of the Society or an extern, should be promoted to a degree unless he has been carefully and publicly examined [E] by persons deputed for this office, which they should perform well, and unless he has been found fit to lecture in that faculty. Second, the door to ambition should be closed by giving no fixed places to those who receive degrees; rather, they should "anticipate one another with honor" [Rom. 12:10], with-

e) 390, 817

out observing any distinction which arises from places.ᵉ ⁴ Third, just as the Society teaches altogether gratis,⁵ so should it confer

f) 4, 82, 398, 495, 499, 565, 566, 640, 816

the degrees completely free,ᶠ and only a very small expenditure, even though it is voluntary, should be allowed to the extern students, that the custom may not come to have the force of law and that excess in this matter may not creep in with time [F]. The rector should also take care not to permit any of the teachers or other members of the Society to accept money or gifts, either for themselves or for the college, from any person for anything he has done to help him. For according to our

---

4 This present reading is a change made by General Congregation I (*InstSJ*, II, 164) from Ignatius' phrase: "and the more learned should take the lowest places."
5 On the gratuity of instruction, see [398] and [495], with the notes.

Institute, our reward should be only Christ our Lord,ᵍ who is   g) 82
"our reward exceeding great" [Gen. 15:1].

[479]—E. *If it appears, for sufficiently weighty reasons, that
someone ought not to be examined publicly, with the permission
of the general or provincial that may be done which the rector
judges will be for the greater glory of God our Lord.*

[480]—F. *Thus, banquets should not be permitted, nor other
celebrations which are costly and not useful for our end. Neither
should there be any conferring of college caps or gloves or any
other object.*

Chapter 16
What pertains to good moral habits

[481]—1. Very special care should be taken that those who
come to the universities of the Society to obtain knowledge
should acquire along with it good and Christian moral habits.ᵃ ¹   a) 392, 440
It will help much toward this if all go to confession at least once
every month, hear Mass every day and a sermon every feast day
when one is given.ᵇ The teachers will take care of this, each one   b) 395
with his own students [A].

[482]—A. *Those who can be easily constrained should be
obliged to what has been said about confession, Mass, the sermon,
Christian doctrine, and declamation. The others should be persuaded gently and not be forced to it nor expelled from the
schools for not complying, provided that dissoluteness or scandal
to others is not observed in them.*

[483]—2. Furthermore, on some day of the week Christian
doctrine should be taught in the college.ᶜ Care should be taken   c) 394, 395
to make the young boys² learn and recite it; also, that all, even
the older ones, should know it, if possible.

1 See objective 7 in fn. 3 on [440]; also [392, 395, 403]; also *EppIgn,* IV, 100, nos. 3-7;
  V, 374-375; XI, 537-539, nos. 6, 14-17.
2 *Los niños,* boys of any age up to adolescence (cf. [338, 359, 360, 451] with the fnn.
  there). Amid the appalling religious ignorance of Ignatius' day, the method of imparting
  Christian doctrine to these younger boys was largely memorization of the catechism (see

[484]—3. Likewise each week, as was said about the colleges, one of the students will deliver a declamation about matters which edify the hearers and lead them to desire to grow in all purity and virtue.[d] The purpose is not only practice in literary style[e] but also the encouraging of moral habits [B]. All those who understand Latin ought to be present.

d) 381
e) 381, 456

[485]—*B. Ordinarily the one who must deliver this declamation should be a member of the highest class, whether he is one of the scholastics of the Society or one of the externs. However, at times someone else could give it or deliver what another has composed, according to the rector's judgment. But no matter who delivers the declamation, since the performance is public, it ought to be such that it will not be judged unworthy of being given in that place.*

[486]—4. In the schools no curses, nor injurious words or deeds, nor anything immoral, nor dissoluteness on the part of the externs who come to the school from without should be allowed. The masters should make it their special aim, both in their lectures when occasion is offered and outside of them too, to inspire the students to the love and service of God our Lord, and to a love of the virtues by which they will please Him.[f] They should urge the students to direct all their studies to this end.[g] To recall this to their minds, before the lesson begins, someone should recite some short prayer which is ordered for this purpose, while the master and students are attentive and have their heads uncovered [C].

f) 403
g) 360

[487]—*C. The prayer should be recited in a manner which furthers edification and devotion, or else it should not be said, but the teacher should uncover his head, make the sign of the cross, and begin.*

[488]—5. For those who in some regard fail to attain to the proper diligence either in their studies or in what pertains to good moral habits, and for whom kind words and admonitions alone are not sufficient, there should be a corrector from outside

---

fn. 7 on [410] above). On [483] Nadal states that all the boys in the lower classes and in philosophy should "hold it [Christian doctrine] in memory, for thus the rudiments of the faith will mature with the boys in our schools. But there is no reason for a separate explanation of Christian doctrine to the students of theology, since they are by their very occupation completely devoted to the consummation of Christian doctrine" (cited, with other references, in *MonPaed* [1965], p. 309).

the Society.[h] He should keep in fear and should punish those   h) 395, 397, 500
who need chastisement and are fit for it. When neither words nor
the corrector avail and some student is seen to be incorrigible
and a scandal to others, it is better to dismiss him from the
schools[i] rather than to keep him where he himself is not progress-   i) 444
ing and others are receiving harm [D]. This decision will be
left to the rector of the university, that everything may proceed
in a manner conducive to glory and service to God our Lord.

[489]—*D. If a case should arise in which dismissal from the
schools is not enough to remedy the scandal, the rector will take
care to provide what is more suitable. However, as far as
possible he ought to proceed in a spirit of leniency and to maintain peace and charity with all.*[j]   j) 823

Chapter 17
The officials or ministers
of the university

[490]—1. The complete charge, that is, the supervision and
government of the university, will belong to the rector[1] [A]. He
may be the same person who governs the principal college of
the Society and should have the same qualities that have been
stated about him [423], that he may be able to perform satisfactorily the office entrusted to him of directing the whole university
in learning and habits of conduct. The task of selecting him will
be vested in the general or in someone else to whom he entrusts
it, such as the provincial or a visitor;[a] but the confirmation of   a) 326, 421, 740,
the appointment will always belong to the general. The rector   757, 759
will have four consultors or assistants who in general can aid
him in matters pertaining to his office and with whom he dis-
cusses the matters of importance[b] [B].   b) 431, 502, 810,
                                                811

[491]—*A. However, the rector will not change the principal
lecturers, nor the officials such as the chancellor, without in-*

---

1 According to Nadal, the rector of a university ought to be a professed, and outstanding
  in learning as well as in virtue (*Scholia*, p. 107). This is in contrast with [421] above but
  also shows that procedures were accommodated to circumstances and experience of needs.

forming the provincial, or the general if he is nearer (unless the higher superior has entrusted the matter to the rector). The rector ought to keep the higher superior informed about all things.

c) 659

[492]—*B. One of these consultors can be a collateral associate*[c] [2] *if this seems necessary to the superior general. If the personnel is not sufficient to have so many officials, the best that will be possible should be done.*

[493]—2. There will also be a chancellor[3] [C], a person distinguished for learning and great zeal who is able to judge wisely in the matters which will be entrusted to him. It is his duty to act as general representative of the rector in carefully organizing the studies, in directing the disputations in the public acts, and in judging the competence of those to be admitted to

d) 460, 471, 502   the acts and degrees. He himself will confer the degrees.[d]

[494]—*C. If the rector can perform the office of chancellor in addition to his own, these two functions can be vested in one person.*

[495]—3. There should be a secretary who is a member of the Society. He should keep a list containing the names of all the students who continue to attend the schools [D] and should receive their promise to obey the rector and to observe the Con-

e) 395, 396   stitutions, which he ought to propose to them[e] [E]. He should keep the seal of the rector and of the university. But all this

f) 398, 478   should be done without cost[4] to the students.[f]

2 On the collateral associate, see [659] with fn. 3. He was a counselor and charitable admonitor of the superior, and an intermediary between the superior and subjects [661]. See also [504, 505, 507]. This office did not work out well in practice and, though not abolished juridically, ceased to exist.

3 The chancellor, according to Nadal (*Scholia*, p. 108, cited in *MonPaed* [1965], p. 316), was to be a prefect of studies over all the faculties, each of which had its own particular dean. On the evolution of the office of chancellor, see H. Rashdall, *The Universities of Europe in the Middle Ages* (Oxford, 1936), I, 279-282.

4 Cf. [398, 478] above. Ignatius clearly regarded educational work as a ministry of the Society [398] and hence insisted that it be given gratis to the students, although he sought endowments to support the colleges and universities. In most instances cities supplied these endowments; and hence many of the early Jesuit schools can be called "public schools" in the modern sense of this term. The Society long adhered to this policy of imparting instruction free, thereby occasionally incurring anger from other teachers who did, rightfully enough, charge for their services. But in time it became impossible to conduct schools free. Hence papal dispensations permitting acceptance of tuition were granted in 1833 and 1853 (*InstSJ*, II, 494, 519), and General Congregation XXXI ratified this now necessary acceptance. On the history of gratuity of instruction, see Farrell, *The Jesuit Code*, pp. 436-440.

[496]—*D. When they attend steadily for a week or longer, it is wise to invite them to have their names written on the list. The Constitutions should be read to them, not in their entirety, but those which each student ought to observe. A promise, but not an oath, should be exacted from them to obey and observe the constitutions proposed. If some should be unwilling either to bind themselves with a promise or to enter their names on the list, the door of the schools should not for that reason be closed to them, provided that they behave peacefully and give no scandal in the schools. They should be told this, but also informed that more particular care is taken of the students named on the list.*

[497]—*E. Later on, however, the constitutions which all ought to observe should be posted where they can be read publicly, and those pertaining to each class should be posted there.*

[498]—4. There will also be a notary to give public certification to the degrees and other matters which will occur [F]; and two or three beadles,[5] one in the faculty of languages, another in that of arts, and another in that of theology [G].

[499]—*F. This notary can receive a fee from the extern students who desire to have their degrees certified. But this fee should be moderate and never redound to the gain of the Society. The letters patent of the rector will suffice for the members of the Society.*

[500]—*G. These beadles will not be members of the Society. However, since they will have much to do they should receive a good salary; and one of them can be the corrector.*[g]   g) 395, 397, 488

[501]—5. The university will be divided into these three faculties.[h] In each one of them there will be a dean[6] and two   h) 446, 447, 450
other representatives, chosen from among those who better understand the affairs of that faculty. When they are summoned by the rector they can tell him what they think would be advantageous for the welfare of their faculty. When they perceive

---

5 The *bidellus* is one of the most ancient university officials. Beadles performed various offices, such as sweeping and caring for the doctor's classroom and carrying his books to it. See Rashdall, *The Universities*, I, 191-192, and Index, s.v. "bedel."

6 *Decano:* the dean, originally a chief of ten persons such as soldiers, monks, or others, was in the medieval universities an administrative officer, under the rector, of a faculty such as theology, law, or arts. The office was at first elective. See Rashdall, *The Universities*, I, 252, 326, 327.

something of this kind while conferring among themselves, they should inform the rector even though they have not been summoned.

[502]—6. In regard to the matters pertaining to one faculty alone the rector will summon, in addition to the chancellor[i] and his assistants,[j] the dean and the representatives of the faculty involved. In what pertains to all the faculties, the deans and representatives of all of them should be summoned [H]. If it seems wise to the rector, he may also summon others from within and without the Society to the meeting, in order that by learning the opinions of all he may the better decide upon what is expedient.

i) 460, 471, 493

j) 490

[503]—*H. Although the decision will not depend upon their votes, it is proper that they be summoned and heard.[k] The rector should take fitting account of the opinion of those who are more cognizant. However, if all have an opinion contrary to his, he should not go against them all without consulting the provincial about the matter.*

k) 431, 805, 810

[504]—7. There will also be a general syndic[7] who is to give information to the rector, the provincial, and the general about both the persons and the things which he will deem noteworthy[l] [I]. He should be a person of great fidelity and judgment.

l) 271, 431

In addition to this general syndic the rector will have his own particular syndics to refer to him what happens in each class and requires his intervention [K]. The rector will write about the teachers and other persons of the Society. The collateral associate, the syndic, and the board of consultors will write about the rector and about the others once each year to the superior general and twice to the provincial[m] [L], who will inform the general about whatever seems appropriate, in order to proceed in everything with greater circumspection and care to do what each one should.

m) 673

[505]—*I. This office of syndic could be combined with that of collateral associate or consultor if this should seem fitting because no one better suited than one of them is to be found in the university.*

[506]—*K. Even if the syndics have no business of moment,*

---

7 On the syndic, see fn. 11 on [271] and cf. [386].

*they should report this fact to the superior, at least every Satur-
day.*

[507]—L. *Letters of this kind should be sent sealed in such a
manner that one does not know what the other writes. When
the superior general or the provincial desires more complete
information, not only should the collateral associate, syndic, and
board of consultors write about the rector and all the others, but
each of the teachers and approved scholastics as well as of the
formed coadjutors should write his opinion about all of them,
the rector included. That this may not seem to be something
new, this report should be written as something ordinary at least
every three years.*

[508]—8. Whether the rector, chancellor, and beadles and also
the doctors and masters ought to have some insignia in order to
be recognized in the university or at least during the public
acts and, if they do have these insignia, of what sort they ought
to be, will be left to the consideration of him who is general at
the time when some university is accepted [M]. After considering
the circumstances he will order, either by himself or through
someone else, what he judges to be for the greater glory and
service of God our Lord and for the universal good, which is
the only end sought in this matter and in all others.

[509]—M. *However, what seems best for each place in regard
to these insignia will be clearly stated in the rules of each
university.*

Part V
Admission or incorporation into the Society

Chapter 1
Admission, who should admit, and when

[**510**]—1. Those who have been tested in the Society sufficiently and for a time long enough that both parties may know
whether their remaining in it is conducive to greater service
and glory to God our Lord, ought to be admitted, not to
probation as was the case in the beginning, but in a more
intrinsic manner as members of one same body of the Society
[A]. This is the case chiefly with those who are admitted to
profession or into the ranks of the formed coadjutors. But since
the approved scholastics too are admitted in a different and
more intrinsic manner than those received into the probation,[1]
in this Fifth Part we shall also state what we think in our Lord
ought to be observed about the admission of these scholastics.

[**511**]—A. *The Society, when we speak in the most comprehensive sense of the term, includes all those who live under
obedience to its superior general. Thus it comprises even the
novices and the persons who, desiring to live and die in the*

---

1 "The probation" is the interpretation of General Congregation I, which judged that the
statement of Ignatius, who had written "first probation," applied equally to the entire
biennium (*InstSJ*, II, 170).

a) 51, 126, 193
b) 10

Society,[a] *are in probation to be admitted into it under one of the other categories of membership*[2] *about to be described.*[b]

In the second and less universal sense, the Society includes not only the professed and the formed coadjutors but also approved scholastics. For the body of the Society is composed of these three kinds of parts or members.

In the third and more precise sense, the Society is comprised of the professed and the formed coadjutors. This is the sense which is understood in regard to that entrance into the Society

c) 14, 121, 348, 541

which the scholastics promise; that is, they promise to become either professed or formed coadjutors in the Society.[c]

The fourth and most precise meaning of this name, the Society, comprehends only the professed. The reason is, not that the body of the Society contains no other members, but that the professed are the principal members, some of whom, as will be explained later, have active and passive voice in the election of

d) 682, 683, 699

the superior general[d] *and in other such matters.*

No matter in which one of these four categories one finds himself in the Society, he is capable of sharing in the spiritual favors which, according to the grant of the Apostolic See, the superior

e) 666, 753

general may dispense in the Society for greater glory to God.[e] *However, when the Society is understood in the first sense, admission is the same as reception into probation of the novitiate and has been treated above in Part I. In the present Part V, therefore, our treatment deals with the remaining three kinds of admission which follow that into the novitiate.*

[512]—2. First of all, the authority to admit into the body of the Society those who ought to be admitted will be vested in

f) 516, 519, 522, 523, 736

him who is its head,[f] as reason requires. But since the superior general cannot be present in all places, he may communicate to other members of the Society that part of his authority which seems good to him for the welfare of the entire body of the

g) 517, 519, 521- 523, 737

Society[g] [B].

[513]—*B. The others to whom he will more ordinarily and completely communicate this authority will be the provincial*

---

2 On the classes of members, see fnn. 20 on [10], 25 on [14], and 27 on [15] above. By the time of Ignatius' death in 1556, the Society probably contained between 1,000 and 1,500 members, of whom most were not yet definitively incorporated (*FN*, I, 63°). *FN*, I, 64°-66° lists those who, in addition to Ignatius and his five companions on April 22, 1541, were incorporated by 1556: 43 professed of four solemn vows, 11 professed of three solemn vows, 5 formed spiritual coadjutors, and 13 temporal coadjutors. According to Lukács, "De graduum diversitate," *AHSJ*, XXXVII (1968), 296, the professed of four vows under Ignatius numbered 46 and the spiritual coadjutors 4. See supplementary Note B in the Reference matter, below.

*superiors. But the general may communicate it to some local
superiors or rectors and to other visitors or important persons;
and even, occasionally, to one who is not a member of the
Society, such as some bishop[3] or other person established in an
ecclesiastical dignity, when no professed member of the Society
itself is in the place where someone ought to be so admitted.*

[514]—3. The period of time required for admission in the
manner mentioned should always be more than two years[h] [C].   h) 16, 71, 98,
But if one who was tested for a long time before being sent to   119, 336, 346,
his studies or during them; and if he is to be admitted to   537, 544
profession, he will have another year after the completion of
these studies[i] to become still better known before pronouncing   i) 16, 71, 119,
it.[4] As was stated in the Examen [100], this period can be   516
prolonged when the Society, or he who in our Lord has this
charge from it, desires more complete satisfaction.[j]   j) 16, 100

[515]—C. *However, just as this period may be prolonged, so
too, according to the judgment of the superior general (who
will have the power of dispensing), it may be shortened in some
cases and for important reasons. But this power should be
used rarely.*

3 According to Polanco, Benedetto Palmio made his profession "into the hands" of a bishop
of Padua. This occurred August 15, 1559.
4 On this year of the third and final probation or testing, and simultaneously of training,
before final incorporation into the Society, see also [16, 71, 119, 516]; on the designa-
tion "third" probation or year, see fn. 9 on [2] and fn. 11 on [71]. In Ignatius' concept,
this year (later often called "the tertianship") was to be (1) a test and also (2), like the
novitiate, an apprenticeship or training in the manner of apostolic living and ministering
(see fnn. 9 on [2], 7 on [64], 11 on [71]) which were expected to be the young member's
ordinary later life.
    The gradual growth of Ignatius' ideas on this important year, which was original
with him, can be traced in many documents previous to the Constitutions. Primary sources
especially noteworthy are: *Autobiog*, nos. 92-96, esp. 95, on his stay at Venice and Vicenza,
giving the Exercises, living on alms with his companions, serving the sick in hospitals,
and his spiritual consolations contrasting with the dryness he had experienced during studies; *Cons*MHSJ, I, 53-56, nos. 6-10, and 10 in the column dated 1544, on experiences and tests; *ibid.*, I, 59-60, nos. 17-18, on apprenticeship to the Society's manner of
living and working; *EppIgn*, I, 467-468, on Polanco, who was in the "school of letters"
at Padua (1542-1546) and then in the "school of the heart" (1546-1547) exercising
priestly ministries in Bologna, Pistoia, and Florence, and is thus perhaps our clearest
example of how tertianship was made under Ignatius' supervision; *PolCompl*, II, 744-
748, Polanco's "5a Industria," esp. 1°, 2°, 3°, 11°, 12°, surely reflecting Ignatius'
thought, on the "scuela del affecto" which should follow the "scuela de letras" as a preparation for final incorporation into the Society; and the Constitutions themselves, where
ch. 8 of P. 4 [400-414] describes ministerial training of the theological students which is
equally applicable to the tertian fathers, as the case of Polanco illustrates (*EppIgn*, I,
467-468). See also Aicardo, *Comentario*, V, 667-668, 670-674; *DeGuiJes*, pp. 37, 235,
236; and the articles by A. Ruhan in *WL*, XCIV (1965), 407-419 and Ganss, *WL*, XCV
(1966), 462-466.

Chapter 2
The qualities of those to be admitted

a) 12, 308, 657, 819

[516]—1. Since no one should be admitted into any of the aforementioned categories unless he has been judged fit in our Lord, for admission to profession those persons will be judged worthy whose life is well-known through long and thorough probations and is approved by the superior general, to whom a report will be sent by the other superiors or others from whom the general desires information[a] [A].

b) 16, 71, 119, 514

For this purpose, after those who were sent to studies have achieved the diligent and careful formation of the intellect by learning, they will find it helpful during the period of the last probation to apply themselves in the school of the heart, by exercising themselves in spiritual and corporal pursuits which can engender in them greater humility, abnegation of all sensual love and will and judgment of their own, and also greater knowledge and love of God our Lord;[b] that when they themselves have made progress they can better help others to progress for glory to God our Lord.[1]

1 *Affecto* is here contrasted with the intellect and means the affective faculty or will and the acts proceeding from it, the emotions included. This is clear from the original phrasing in text *a*, "acabada la scuela del entendimiento, insistir en la del affecto" (*Cons*MHSJ, II, 199), which in text B was abbreviated to the present elliptical expression. See also [724] (with fn. 2), where Ignatius similarly uses *affecto* in contrast to *entendimiento*. Hence "heart" is used in the translation as meaning the will or affective faculty with its attendant emotions, the emotional or moral nature as distinguished from the intellectual. The expression *schola affectus* (*scuela del affecto*) apparently derives from John Gerson (d. 1492), who wrote: "Mystica vero theologia . . . non habet necessariam talem scholam, quae schola intellectus dici potest, sed acquiritur per scholam affectus et per exercitium vehemens moralium virtutum . . . et in theologicis [virtutibus] . . ." (*De mystica theologia*, Pars VI, consid. xxx).
    In [514-516] Ignatius clearly envisages two periods of training, with the stress on intellectual formation in the first and on affective or spiritual formation in the second. These stresses are overlapping rather than mutually exclusive (see, e.g., [400, 481]). In [514-516] too he gives his compressed and legislative expression of his ideas on the third probation or tertianship. This final concept of his is one which was distilled from many of his earlier personal spiritual experiences. He saw any young priest of his order as one still proving himself worthy and also preparing himself for a life spent in bringing glory to God through lowly but effective apostolic works, such as preaching or serving in hospitals. Such labors required much long-continued self-abnegation and humility as indispensable means—means which all too many ecclesiastics of the day were neglecting through the then prevalent tendency to use their priesthood as a stepping-stone to wealth, pleasure, and places of preferment. In Ignatius' day the philosophical and theological studies, directed too much to the intellect alone, were often both dry and desiccating (see fn. 4 on [351] above). He found himself spiritually dry during his years of study at Paris. But after them, when he engaged in lowly but effective spiritual ministrations and prayer in and near Venice in 1536-1537, he found his affections again warmed and he experienced anew his former consolations and even mystic visitations. Involvement with

[517]—A. *In some very remote regions, such as the Indies, the general may leave it to the judgment of the provincial to decide whether or not certain subjects should be admitted to profession without awaiting the approval from here [in Rome], since it would arrive only after many years. But in the regions where better communications exist he ought not easily to allow himself to entrust the admission to profession to any provincial. Rather, he should himself be previously informed and give consent for each case in regard to those whom he thinks in our Lord should be admitted to profession.*c

c) 512, 513, 737

[518]—2. Similarly, such persons ought to possess sufficient[2] learning in humane letters and the liberal arts and, beyond that, in scholastic theology and Sacred Scripture.d Some will be able,   d) 12, 308

the people he was helping through his ministries brought him and his companions a more vivid perception of their need of prayer and union with God, which in turn motivated them anew to apostolic works, thus setting up the cycle of work to prayer to work described by Favre (*MonFab*, pp. 554-555, as edited in *DeGuiJes*, p. 584).

In the hope that his young priests would have roughly similar experiences and through them prove themselves worthy of definitive incorporation, in [516] Ignatius clearly expressed two purposes of the third year of probation: (1) testing (*probación*) through which the young priest would prove his willingness to do the Society's hard and humble work to bring men to God, and (2) training of the heart (*scuela del affecto*) through the exercise of virtues such as zeal, willing service, humility, and love of God and neighbor. The structure or means he used to attain these ends consisted of involvement with people through apostolic ministries which would bring an increased perception of the need of prayer, such as those the ministries listed in *Cons*, [400-414], as Polanco's third probation at Bologna and Florence shows (*EppIgn*, I, 468). The young priest could not succeed in these ministries and tests without willingness to undertake the means indicated in [516], hard physical and spiritual work which often entailed humiliations, humility, self-abnegation, and obedience. Ignatius did not prescribe a separate and secluded house or fixed lectures for this year; the young priest lived in ordinary communities like other Jesuits.

After Ignatius' death, however, the structure of the tertianship gradually changed, as was natural. After Decree 14 of General Congregation II (*InstSJ*, II, 197), separate novitiates with a determined order of the day were established, beginning with San Andrea in Quirinale in 1566. Mercurian prescribed, in the rules of the provincial, that the third probation should be made in novitiates. In more and more instances the tertian fathers lived in them and had the master of novices as their director. In 1587 Aquaviva requested the masters of novices to express their opinions about the manner of carrying on the tertianship more effectively, and received many replies (ArchRSJ, Inst. 186 c pp. 919-1011). Adjusting thus to the needs of his times, Aquaviva crystallized the new evolution in three ordinations and instructions (1583, 1592, 1601) and in letters to the provincials in 1602. In 1616 these earlier ordinations and instructions were contracted (*InstSJ*, III, 153) into the ordination on the tertianship now found *ibid.*, 262-267. According to this document of 1616, the third probation should be made in a separate house, which could be a novitiate (*ibid.*, 262); and the training of the heart, *schola affectus*, was sought largely by seclusion, prayer, spiritual reading, and lectures (*ibid.*, 164-267). This structure remained until recently. In 1966 General Congregation XXXI, seeking adaptation and renewal of the tertianship, stressed anew Ignatius' ends as expressed in the Constitutions; and toward achieving them, it authorized experimentation in the structure of the tertianship.

2 *Doctrina . . . suficiente*: This is the criterion of Ignatius for the profession of solemn vows and his explanation of the word *conspicuos* found in *Exposcit*, [6], which that

indeed, to make as much progress in a shorter time as others would in a longer period; yet nevertheless, to obtain a common duration some termination will have to be set, and this will be *e) 418, 476* the study of theology for four complete years^e after the arts [B]. Thus, to be admitted to profession one should have exercised himself in theology for that four-year period and made good progress to the glory of God our Lord. As evidence of his progress each one should before his profession defend theses in logic, philosophy, and scholastic theology. Four persons will be designated to object and to judge his sufficiency according to what they think in all truth and sincerity. When the subjects are found not to have enough learning, it is better that they wait until they have it. Similarly, those also ought to wait who do not have testimony entirely suitable in regard to the *f) 819* abnegation of themselves and religious virtues.^f

[519]—B. *This standard period of four years of theology (beyond the study of humanities and the arts) should ordinarily be observed, as also the aforementioned examination to make the progress in it manifest. Nevertheless one who has sufficient learning in canon law, or other outstanding qualities which can make up for his lack of proficiency in the study of theology, could without that proficiency be admitted to the profession of three vows. Furthermore, some outstanding persons could be admitted also to the profession of four vows, although this practice ought not to be extended.*

The judgment about these qualities will be left entirely to the superior general, or to another to whom he entrusts it by a special commission, in order to do what is for greater glory to God our Lord.

[520]—3. In addition to these, some can be admitted to the *g) 11, 531, 532* profession of only three solemn vows.^g But this will be done rarely and for special and important reasons. These members should have been known in the Society for seven years during which they have given in it great satisfaction by their talent and virtues, for glory to God our Lord [C].

[521]—C. *Those who are admitted to the profession of three solemn vows should ordinarily possess sufficient³ learning, at*

bull empowered him as general to make. On this criterion, see above, fn. 18 on p. 71, fn. 20 on [10], and below, [521, 819], and the supplementary Note B in the Reference matter.
3 *Suficiencia en letras:* a variant expression of Ignatius' criterion. See fn. 24 on [13], and fn. 2 on [518] above, with the cross-references there.

*least that which suffices for them to be good confessors, or some
rare qualities which are its equivalent, in such a manner that the
superior general, or one to whom he entrusts the matter by a
special commission, judges that their admission to profession is
expedient for the greater service of God and the good of the
Society.*[h] *These will ordinarily be persons who, it seems in our
Lord, ought to be admitted because of their meritorious achievements and great devotion, even though they do not possess such
great learning and ability in preaching as our Institute requires
in the professed.*

h) 512, 513, 736, 737

[522]—4. To be admitted among the formed coadjutors, a subject should likewise have given satisfaction in regard to his life
and good example and his ability to aid the Society, either in
spiritual matters by his learning or in exterior matters without
the learning, each one according to what God has communicated
to him.[i] By his discretion the superior general will have to
appraise this matter too, unless it seems good to him to entrust
it to the particular persons in whom he has much confidence in
our Lord.[j]

i) 112, 657, 819

j) 512, 513

[523]—5. That subjects may be admitted among the approved
scholastics, proportionately the same set of requirements remains.
Especially in regard to their ability, there should be hope that
they will succeed in their studies,[k] in the judgment of the
general or of the one whom he designates[l] while confiding in
the discretion and goodness which God our Lord has given
to him.

k) 14, 308, 333-336

l) 512, 513

Chapter 3
The procedure in admission to profession

[524]—1. When certain members should be admitted to the
profession after they have completed the experiences and other
prescriptions contained in the Examen and after the Society or
its superior is entirely satisfied in our Lord,[a] the profession will
be made in the following manner.

a) 516, 518

[525]—2. First of all the superior general or the one who with
his authority admits the subject to profession will celebrate Mass

in the church publicly before the members of the house and the externs who happen to be present. Then with the most Holy Sacrament he will turn toward the one who is making the profession [A] who, after reciting the confiteor and the words which precede Holy Communion, will in a loud voice read his written vow (which he will have pondered for some days in advance). The text is this [in 527, below]:

[526]—A. *These details and those which follow below are becoming and should be observed when possible, but they are not necessary. For it could happen that the one who through the superior general's order is admitting to profession is not a priest or is unable to celebrate Mass. What is essential is that the vow is read publicly in the presence of the Society's members and the externs who happen to be there, and that it is made and received as a solemn vow.*

[527]—3. I, N, make profession, and I promise to Almighty God, in the presence of His Virgin Mother, the whole heavenly court, and all those here present, and to you, Reverend Father [N], superior general of the Society of Jesus and the one holding the place of God, and to your successors (or, to you, Reverend Father [N], representing the superior general of the Society of Jesus and his successors and holding the place of God), per-

b) 4, 547-581

c) 532, 535

petual poverty, chastity, and obedience;[b] and, in conformity with it, special care for the instruction of children[c] [B], according to the manner of living contained in the apostolic letters of the Society of Jesus and in its Constitutions.[1]

I further promise a special obedience to the sovereign pontiff

d) 7, 602, 603, 605

in regard to the missions[d] [C], according to the same apostolic letters and the Constitutions. Rome, or elsewhere, on such a day, month, and year, and in such a church.

[528]—B. *The promise to instruct the children and uneducated persons in conformity with the apostolic letters and the Constitutions does not induce a greater obligation than the other spiritual exercises by which the neighbor is aided, such as confessions, preaching, and the like. Each one ought to employ himself obediently in these according to the assignment received from his superiors. But the promise about the children is placed in the vow that this holy practice may be held as something*

---

1 This formula is highly similar to those which Ignatius and his companions respectively pronounced in the basilica of St. Paul-outside-the-Walls on April 22, 1541. The texts are in *Cons*MHSJ, I, 67-68; cf. lxiv.

more especially recommended and may be exercised with greater devotion, because of the outstanding service which is given through it to God our Lord by aiding the souls which belong to Him, and because it is in greater danger of being allowed to fall into oblivion and dropped than other more conspicuous services such as preaching and the like.[2]

[529]—C. *The entire meaning of this fourth vow of obedience to the pope*[3] *was and is in regard to the missions. In this manner too should be understood the bulls*[4] *in which this obedience is treated: in everything which the sovereign pontiff commands and wheresoever he sends one, and the like.*

[530]—4. Thereupon the professed will receive the most Holy Sacrament of the Eucharist. When this has been done, the name of the professed should be written in the book of the Society which will exist for this purpose, and also the name of the person into whose hands he made the profession, with the day, month, and year in which it was made.[e] His written vow should   e) 545
be preserved that it may always be evidence of all this, unto glory to God our Lord.

[531]—5. Those who are admitted to the profession of only three solemn vows[f] will read their written vow in the church   f) 11, 520, 521
before receiving the most Holy Sacrament, in the presence of the residents of the house and the other externs who happen to be there. The formula is the following:

[532]—6. I, N, make profession, and I promise to Almighty God, in the presence of His Virgin Mother, the whole heavenly court, and all those here present, and to you, Reverend Father [N], superior general of the Society of Jesus and the one holding the place of God, and to your successors (or, to you, Reverend Father [N], representing the superior general of the Society of Jesus and his successors and holding the place of God), perpetual poverty, chastity, and obedience;[g] and, in conformity   g) 4, 547-581
with it, special care for the instruction of children,[h] according   h) 527, 528, 535
to the manner of living contained in the apostolic letters of the Society of Jesus and in its Constitutions. Rome, or elsewhere, on such a day, month, and year, and in such a church.
    Thereupon Holy Communion will follow and all the rest, as was stated above.

2 See fn. 7 on [410] above.
3 See fnn. 17 and 18 on [7].
4 *Regimini*, [4], and *Exposcit*, [5]; see also fn. 17 on [7] above.

Chapter 4
The admission of the formed
coadjutors and scholastics

a) 13

[**533**]—1. Those who are admitted into the formed spiritual coadjutors, with simple but not solemn vows,ᵃ will make their vow into the hands of the one who admits them, in the church or the chapel of the house or in another fitting place, in the presence of the residents of the house and all the other externs who happen to be present [A]. They too will read the vow in this formula [in 535, below]:

[**534**]—A. *The vows are said to be made into the hands¹ when they are made in the presence of the recipient who has authority for this. And even if many persons happen to be present when these vows are taken, they do not for this reason cease to be simple vows. For, in accordance with the authority of the Apostolic See granted to the Society,² the intention of the one who makes them and of the one who receives them is this, that they are neither made nor received as solemn. But it will be left to the discretion of the one who receives them to take thought for the edification which can follow. Accordingly he will give an order that others are to be present in greater or lesser number; for in other respects, both the temporal coadjutors and the spiritual coadjutors will have the same formula; and the formula of the one group and of the other group will be exteriorly very similar to that of the professed.*

[**535**]—2. I, N, promise to Almighty God, in the presence of His Virgin Mother and the whole heavenly court, and to you, Reverend Father [N], superior general of the Society of Jesus and the one holding the place of God, and to your successors (or, to you, Reverend Father [N], representing the superior general of the Society of Jesus and his successors and holding the place of God), perpetual poverty, chastity, and obedience;ᵇ and, in conformity with it, special care for the instruction of children,ᶜ according to the manner indicated in the apostolic letters and Constitutions of the aforementioned Society [B]. Rome, or elsewhere, in such a place, day, month, year, and so forth.

b) 13, 119, 547-581

c) 527, 528, 532

1 See fn. 14 on [283] above and [539] below.
2 In *Exponi nobis* (1546), in *Cons*MHSJ, I, 171, and in *Exposcit*, [6] above.

Thereupon he will receive Holy Communion and all that was stated in regard to the professed [530] will be done.

[536]—*B. The reference to the bulls and the Constitutions makes clear that the coadjutors take these vows with a tacit condition in regard to the perpetuity. This condition is: if the Society will desire to retain them. For although they on their own side bind themselves perpetually for their devotion and stability, the Society remains free to dismiss them,*^d *as is explained in Part II [204, 205]; and in that case they are entirely freed from their vows.*^e

d) 119, 120, 204, 205

e) 119, 120, 234

[537]—3. The formula for the temporal coadjutors will be the same [C], with the statement about the instruction of children omitted.

Those who, after finishing their first probation and experiences through two years^f are received as approved scholastics, will make their vow in the presence of some residents of the house, although not into the hands of anyone [D], according to the following formula [in 540, below]:

f) 16, 71, 98, 119, 336, 346, 515, 544

[538]—*C. If they are persons who do not know Latin, as some temporal coadjutors could be, the vow should be expressed in the vernacular; and they should read it, or someone else should read it for them while they follow him.*

[539]—*D. Just as this vow is made to God alone and not to a man, so no man whatsoever receives it. This is the reason why it is not said to be made into the hands of anyone. And the tacit condition about the perpetuity which the vow of the coadjutors contains, as was stated [in 536], is present in this one too; that is to say, it is: if the Society will desire to retain them.*^g

g) 121, 122, 536

[540]—4. Almighty and eternal God I, N, though altogether most unworthy in Your divine sight, yet relying on Your infinite goodness and mercy and moved with a desire of serving You, in the presence of the most Holy Virgin Mary and Your whole heavenly court, vow to Your Divine Majesty perpetual poverty, chastity, and obedience^h in the Society of Jesus; and I promise that I shall enter that same Society³ [E] in order to lead my entire life in it, understanding all things according to its Consti-

h) 4, 14, 121, 336

---

3 "I shall enter that same Society," i.e., through the definitive incorporation of the final vows if the Society will then grant its approval (see Nadal, *Scholia*, p. 117).

tutions. Therefore I suppliantly beg Your Immense Goodness and Clemency, through the blood of Jesus Christ, to deign to receive this holocaust in an odor of sweetness; and that just as You gave me the grace to desire and offer this, so You will also bestow abundant grace to fulfill it. Rome, or elsewhere, in such a place, day, month, year, and so forth.

After this the one vowing will likewise receive Holy Communion and all the rest will be done as is stated above [530].

[541]—*E. The promise to enter the Society, as was stated in the beginning [511], means: to become one of its professed or its formed coadjutors, according to what its general judges to be for greater service to God.*[i]

i) 14, 121, 348, 511

[542]—5. After anyone has been incorporated into the Society in one grade he should not seek to pass to another [F], but should strive to perfect himself in the first one and to serve and glorify God our Lord in it, leaving the care of everything else to the superior whom he has in place of Christ our Lord.[j]

j) 116, 117

[543]—*F. To represent his thoughts and what occurs to him is permissible. Nevertheless, as is stated in the Examen [130-132], he should be ready in everything to hold as better that which appears to be so to his superior.*[k]

k) 131, 292, 627

[544]—6. Thus, as the scholastics ought to take their vows at the end of two years[l] and bind themselves to Christ our Lord, so also those who are in the houses, even though there is no intention of their studying, and even though also it does not seem expedient to admit them so soon among the formed coadjutors or the professed, ought to take their vows in the same manner as the scholastics. If someone because of his personal devotion takes the vows before the end of the two years,[m] he may use the same formula. Handing in one copy [G], he may retain the other copy of his vow that he may know what he has offered to God our Lord. For the same purpose too and for an increase of devotion, it is good that at certain times which will appear fitting these persons should renew their vows [H]. To do this is not to take on a new obligation but to remind themselves of the one they already have in our Lord and to confirm it.[n]

l) 16, 71, 98, 119, 336, 346, 514, 537

m) 17, 283

n) 346

[545]—*G. The record of such vows as these ought also to be kept in a book, in the same way as the others, for good reasons.*[o]

o) 530

[**546**]—*H. In regard to the scholastics, the times at which they ought to renew their vows have already been stated in Part IV.*ᴾ   p) 346, 347 *The same holds true of those in the houses who will have them. That is, they should renew them on two principal feasts of the year, and on some other feast if this seems wise to the superior. They will not make them into the hands of anyone, but each one will read his own before the most Blessed Sacrament, with the other members of the Society, or some of them, present, that they may stir themselves up more to devotion in observing what they have promised to God our Lord and may hold more clearly before their eyes what they are obliged to do in Him.*

Part VI
The personal life of those already admitted or incorporated into the Society

Chapter 1
What pertains to obedience

[**547**]—1. In order that those already admitted to profession or to membership among the formed coadjutors may be able to apply themselves more fruitfully according to our Institute in the service of God and the aid of their fellowmen, they themselves ought to observe certain things. Although the most important of these are reduced to their vows which they offer to God our Creator and Lord in conformity with the apostolic letters,[a] nevertheless, in order that these points may be further explained and commended, they will be treated in this present Part VI. a) 527, 535

What pertains to the vow of chastity does not require explanation,[1] since it is evident how perfectly it should be preserved

---

1 Christ (Matt. 19:10-12) and St. Paul (1 Cor. 7:32-35) clearly state the value of virginity embraced to give one greater freedom to devote himself completely to the things of God. This value of virginity as an ideal was accepted almost universally and without questioning in the Catholic countries of the 1500's, in spite of the many and well-known lapses in its practice. Moreover, even though some humanists and Protestants had attacked celibacy and Ignatius had opposed them in his Rules for Thinking Rightly within the Church (*SpEx*, [356]), the twentieth-century interest in psychological studies and in problems pertaining to celibacy so widely discussed today obviously had not yet arisen. Hence it was natural for Ignatius, as for other spiritual writers of his age, to dismiss the vow of chastity with the brief remark in [547]. He was not faced with complicated questions

through the endeavor in this matter to imitate the angelic purity[2] by the purity of the body and mind. Therefore, with this presupposed, we shall now treat of holy obedience.[3]

All should keep their resolution firm to observe obedience and to distinguish themselves in it, not only in the matters of obligation but also in the others, even though nothing else is perceived *b*) 84, 284, 286, except the indication of the superior's will without an expressed
342, 424, 551, 552, 618, 619, command. They should keep in view God our Creator and Lord, 627, 661, 765 for whom such obedience is practiced,[b] and they should endeavor to proceed in a spirit of love and not as men troubled by fear.

about chastity such as he had to meet on obedience and poverty, and no one in his century seems to have expressed surprise at his brevity on chastity. This appears from Nadal's comment, "There is no perfection of chastity which Ignatius did not encompass within these few words" (*Scholia*, p. 119). One can safely conjecture that if Ignatius were alive today, he would be impelled to a fuller treatment by his sensitivity to contemporary needs and by his loyalty to the pope, the Church, Vatican Council II, and the members of his order.

2 The allusion is to Christ's eschatological doctrine found in Matt. 22:29-30 and 1 Cor. 7:32-35. Ignatius is urging a purity like that of the blessed in heaven. He is not implying that on earth the purity of men who have bodies can be identical with that of angels who do not have them (cf. Nadal, *Scholia*, p. 119). The expression "angelic purity" was very ancient in the monastic tradition and it was natural for Ignatius to repeat it.

3 In [547-552] Ignatius gives his final (1556) and most complete, though highly compressed, doctrinal and legislative expression of his concept of religious obedience. It is a concept distilled from many earlier thoughts, experiences, and sketches. Some knowledge of these earlier ideas is virtually necessary for accurate interpretation of his succinct legislative expression and for perception of the rich doctrinal and spiritual connotations which its single phrases bear. The genesis of his notions on obedience can be traced in important primary sources such as these: his attitude of ready obedience to the pope, already in 1523, in *Autobiog*, nos. 46-47, in *FN*, I, 425-427; the controlling eagerness of Ignatius and his first companions to discover and carry out "the will of God within the scope of our vocation," and their "Deliberation" whether to vow obedience to one of their number, as a means to this discovery of the divine good pleasure, in *Cons*MHSJ, I, esp. 2, 4, 5-7, English in *WL*, XCV (1966), 327, 329, 331-333; the result of their decision, in the bull *Regimini* (1540), [3-5], in *Cons*MHSJ, I, 26-29; Ignatius' letter to Viola, 1542, in *EppIgn*, I, 228, *LettersIgn*, p. 60; the "Annotations" of 1544-1549, in *Cons*MHSJ, I, 216-217; his statements on obedience in text *a* of the Constitutions (1547-1550), in *Cons*MHSJ, II, 207-209; Ignatius' letters on obedience of July, 1547, January, 1548, and March, 1548, respectively, in *EppIgn*, I, 551-562, 687-693, II, 54-65, English in Espinosa Pólit, *Perfect Obedience*, pp. 269-275, 276-279, 279-288; the bull *Exposcit*, [3, 4]; and *Cons*, [547-552] (substantially completed by 1550), where the very core of the matter is in [550]. One is then in position to understand better Ignatius' well-known Letter on Obedience, sent to Portugal in March, 1553 (in *EppIgn*, IV, 669-681, English in Espinosa Pólit, pp. 20-30 and *LettersIgn*, pp. 287-295). Important, too, are the points dictated by Ignatius to Giovanni Filippo Vito, a secretary from 1554 onward, found in *FN*, IV, 788-792, English in Espinosa Pólit, pp. 289-290.

Espinosa Pólit's *Perfect Obedience* is a thorough commentary on the letter of 1553 and contains numerous illuminating primary sources. But it is chiefly an analysis of the text and does not give adequate exposition of the historical circumstances for which the letter was written. On them, see *PolChron*, II, 694-717; A. Astráin, *Historia* (Madrid, 1902), I, 586-637; F. Rodrigues, *História* (Pôrto, 1931), I, pt. 2, 9-281. The cultural, historical, and linguistic background from which the above mentioned sixteenth-century documents sprang is given, perhaps the best in English, in the not yet published dissertation of J. C. Futrell mentioned in fn. 15 on [84] above.

Hence all of us should exert ourselves not to miss any point of perfection which we can with God's grace attain in the observance of all the Constitutions[c] [A] and in our manner of proceeding in our Lord, by applying all our energies with very special care to the virtue of obedience shown first to the sovereign pontiff[4] and then to the superiors of the Society.   c) 424, 602, 746, 790, 826

Consequently, in all the things into which obedience can with charity be extended [B], we should be ready to receive its command just as if it were coming from Christ our Savior,[d] since   d) 85 we are practicing the obedience to one in His place and because

---

4 This brief statement springs from Ignatius' world view as it was crystallized through his visions at the Cardoner and at La Storta (see above, pp. 3-4, 16-17, 20, 22), epitomizes it, and applies it to religious obedience. (See also fn. 15 on [84], p. 102 above.)

From that world view sprang his desire to cooperate with Christ in the gradual accomplishment of God's redemptive plan as it unfolds in the history of salvation; to cooperate, that is, with Christ as prolonged and living in His mystical body, and in His vicar as its head on earth, and in all who derive jurisdiction from him, including the superiors of the Society (see *EppIgn*, I, 553-554 [where Ignatius cites John 21:17 and Heb. 12:17], and 561; English in Espinosa Pólit, pp. 270, 275, 277). This profound intuition inspired and controlled the foundation and organization of the Society and the development of Ignatius' concept of obedience. He desired to have a company or cohort of devoted men ready for any task needed by the pope, the vicar of Christ as King; and he hoped that many fit persons would volunteer for service in that company. All this required obedience as a principle of unity, cooperation, and coordination. In Ignatius' concept, the foundation of obedience is authority derived from God through Christ to the pope, who in turn delegates it to subordinate officials such as bishops and religious superiors. What descends from God, at least in ordinary cases, is not new divine light on the problem under consideration, but the right to decide and command. This right is usually exercised after consultation, reflection, and prayer. These superiors, therefore, command "in the place of Christ" (*en lugar de Cristo*), but should do so according to "the pattern set by Peter and Paul" (*Exposcit*, [4], on p. 69 above). Obedience is the act by which the subject freely makes a legitimate command of the superior his own will and carries it out. He thereby cooperates with the company of his fellow members toward upbuilding the Church. On all this, see: B. Schneider, "Nuestro principio y principal fundamento. Zum historischen Verständnis des Papstgehorsamsgelübdes," *AHSJ*, XXV (1956), 488-513; P. Blet, "Les fondements de l'obéissance ignatienne," *ibid.*, XXV (1956), 513-538; Blet in *Gregor*, XXXV (1954), 99-111; Granero, "San Ignacio . . . al servicio de la Iglesia," *La ciencia tomista*, LXXXIII (1956), 529-572; Iparraguirre, "Perspectivas ignacianas de la obediencia," *Revista de espiritualidad*, XXI (1962), 71-93. Further references are in Iparraguirre, *Orientaciones bibliográficas*, pp. 169-172. On the foundations of obedience and the history of the vow in the Church, see *NCathEnc*, X, 602-606. Ignatius' idea of authority is, to some extent, an early example of what John Courtney Murray aptly termed the "classical" concept, seen, e.g., in *Satis cognitum* of Leo XIII. Ignatius, however, expressly provided for representation and democratic procedures whereby subjects participated in preparing the decision, far more than did Leo. An excellent discussion on supplementation of the classical concept by new emphases from Vatican Council II is Walter J. Burghardt, "The Authority-Freedom Issue: Destructive or Creative?" *Spiritual Life*, XV (1969), 228-240.

Pues en su lugar . . . la hacemos, "since we are practicing the obedience *to one* in His [Christ's] place." Ignatius' Spanish phrase here in [547] is vexingly elliptical and must be interpreted to harmonize with his constant doctrine (see, e.g., [84] with fn. 15, [85, 284, 551, 627]) that the superior commands in the place of Christ—not that we obey in His place. Hence the words *to one* were necessary in the translation. For a similar Ignatian ellipsis, see [17] with fn. 17.

e) 435

f) 284, 424

g) 284, 549

of love and reverence for Him. Therefore we should be ready to leave unfinished any letter[5] or anything else of ours which has been begun[e] and to apply our whole mind and all the energy we have in the Lord of all that our obedience may be perfect[6] in every detail [C], in regard to the execution, the willing, and the understanding.[f] We should perform with great alacrity, spiritual joy, and perseverance whatever has been commanded to us, persuading ourselves that everything is just and renouncing with blind obedience[7] any contrary opinion and judgment of our own in all things which the superior commands and in which (as it was stated [284]) some species of sin cannot be judged to be present.[g] We ought to be firmly convinced that everyone of those who live under obedience ought to allow himself to be

5 See fn. 4 on [435] above.
6 This brief statement, to the effect that to be "perfect," obedience should comprise execution as reinforced by the will and even the judgment, expresses the essence or core of Ignatius' concept, and is explained just below in Declaration C [550]. But instead of giving further explanation here in the text itself, he illustrates this essence by means of figures or metaphors which were traditional in the literature of monasticism, and which were perhaps gathered by Polanco and approved by Ignatius. They were familiar and esteemed in the 1500's but are often found to be less attractive today. All comparisons limp. What truly matters in the interpretation of any classic is to distinguish the figures from the substance they illustrate and to grasp accurately the authentic thought which the author expressed by means of his similes or metaphors.
7 The idea of "blind obedience" is at least as old as the *Constitutiones monachorum* long attributed to St. Basil (see PG 13, 1409). Its meaning here in [547], its only occurrence in the Constitutions, has been much debated (see the references in Espinosa Pólit, pp. 148-161). Blind obedience surely entails a willingness to obey cheerfully and a propensity to presume that the superior's order is right and prudent until some cogent reason to the contrary has become manifest (see the Letter on Obedience of March, 1553, nos. 17, 18, in *EppIgn*, IV, 679; Espinosa Pólit, p. 28). If Ignatius' metaphor should be pressed too far, he could be taken to mean that the subject should abdicate his judgment, responsibility, and initiative—something which no man may do and which is incompatible with the dignity of the human person. But such an interpretation falsifies Ignatius. His own texts and example reveal that the "blindness" was not total. The subject was expected to keep his eyes sufficiently open to see that there was no sin [549], and whether there were factors which should be represented to the superior (see [92, 131, 543, 627]; Letter of 1553, no. 19, in *EppIgn*, IV, 680, and Espinosa Pólit, p. 9; Letter to Viola, in *EppIgn*, IX, 90-92, *LettersIgn*, pp. 390-392). Ignatius' example can be gathered, for instance, from the measures he took, after learning that the pope remained firm in his decision to make Jay a bishop, to convince him that there were sound reasons to the contrary, for God's greater glory (see *EppIgn*, I, 450-453 and 460-466, English in *LettersIgn*, pp. 111-113 and 460-466). See also *Manresa*, XXXV (1962), 263-280.
    What Ignatius truly desired to find in the subject was this complex: (1) the fundamental desire to learn and carry out God's will; (2) genuine religious indifference or impartiality in regard to what is commanded; (3) a willingness, as a guard against self-deception, to give the superior the benefit of possible doubts about the prudence of the command, at least until cogent reasons against it were examined, usually in dialogue; (4) recognition of the superior's right to make the final decision (see [810]); and finally (5) cheerful, wholehearted execution. Much the same procedure has been commended anew by Vatican Council II, Decree on the Renewal of Religious Life, no. 14, and by General Congregation XXXI, Decree on Obedience, nos. 6-8.

carried and directed by Divine Providence through the agency of the superior as if he were a lifeless body which allows itself to be carried to any place and to be treated in any manner desired, or as if he were an old man's staff[8] which serves in any place and in any manner whatsoever in which the holder wishes to use it. For in this way the obedient man ought joyfully to devote himself to any task whatsoever in which the superior desires to employ him to aid the whole body of the religious Institute; and he ought to hold it as certain that by this procedure he is conforming himself with the divine will more than by anything else he could do while following his own will and different judgment.

[548]—A. *These first Declarations which are published along with the Constitutions bind with the same authority as the Constitutions.*[h] *Therefore in the observance, equal care should be bestowed upon the Declarations and the Constitutions.*   h) 136

[549]—B. *Such things are all those in which some sin is not manifest.*[i]   i) 284, 547

[550]—C. *The command of obedience is fulfilled in regard to the execution when the thing commanded is done; in regard to the willing when the one who obeys wills the same thing as the one who commands; in regard to the understanding when he forms the same judgment as the one commanding and regards what he is commanded as good. And that obedience is imperfect in which there does not exist, in addition to the execution, also that agreement in willing and judging between him who commands and him who obeys.*[9]

8 The simile of an artisan's tool was used to illustrate blind obedience in the *Constitutiones monachorum* (ch. 22, no. 5, in PG 31, 1409). A staff is not far different. The figure of the corpse appears in the Life of St. Francis of Assisi by St. Bonaventure (*Opera,* VIII, 52).

9 The very core of Ignatius' concept of an act of obedience with its three degrees of perfection is succinctly expressed in [550]. Execution of the command is the basic essential, the matter comprised by the vow. But if a subject's act of obedience is to be raised to higher degrees of value and become perfect, he must make it more effective and valuable by a lively concurrence of his own desire, which he conforms to that of the superior; and he will be aided toward this by inclining himself to see the prudence of the superior's command and to give him the benefit of possible doubts, at least until reflection or dialogue, in a genuine and prayerful spirit of indifference, reveals something which he ought to represent to the superior ([543, 610, 627]). The subject ought also to recognize the superior's right to the final decision ([810]). In his Letter on Obedience of 1553, Ignatius explains obedience of execution in no. 5; of the will, in 6-8; of the judgment, in 14; means to achieve it, in 15-18; representation, in 19 (*EppIgn,* IV, 669-681; English in Espinosa Pólit, pp. 20-30).

i) 84, 85, 284,
286, 342, 424,
547, 552, 618,
619, 627, 661,
765

k) 91-97, 263,
424

l) 97

[**551**]—2. Likewise, it should be strongly recommended to all that they should have and show great reverence, especially interior reverence, to their superiors, by considering^j and reverencing Jesus Christ in them; and from their hearts they should warmly love their superiors as fathers¹⁰ in Him. Thus in everything they should proceed in a spirit of charity, keeping nothing exterior or interior hidden from the superiors^k and desiring them to be informed about everything, in order that the superiors may be the better able to direct them in everything along the path of salvation and perfection. For that reason, once a year and as many times more as their superior thinks good, all the professed and formed coadjutors should be ready to manifest their consciences to him, in confession, or secret, or in another manner, for the sake of the great profit this practice contains,¹ as was stated in the Examen [91, 92, 97]. Thus too they should be ready to make a general confession, from the last one they made, to the one whom the superior thinks it wise to designate in his place.

m) 84, 85, 284,
286, 342, 424,
547, 551, 618,
619, 627, 661,
765

[**552**]—3. All should have recourse to the superior for the things which they happen to desire; and without his permission and approval no individual should directly or indirectly request, or cause to be requested, any favor from the sovereign pontiff or from another person outside the Society, either for himself or for someone else. He should be convinced that if he does not get that which he desires from the hands of the superior or with his approval, it is not useful to him for the divine service; and that if it is useful for that service, that he will get it with the consent of the superior, as from the one who holds the place of Christ our Lord for him.^m

---

10 Ignatius wanted superiors to rule much as kindly fathers and as taking the place of Christ, so that as far as possible the relations between subjects and superiors would be firm but characterized by love [551, 727, 810], mutual esteem [423, 551, 667], and cordial and open communication [91-93]. According to Ignatius' ideal, therefore, government by superiors should be paternal in the sense of their being kindly and inspiring the "filial confidence" praised today in Canon 530, §2; but not in the sense that a superior should either exercise his authority in an authoritarian manner or bear himself toward his subjects as if they were still immature minors. For concrete examples of how obedience was practiced under Ignatius' personal superiorship, see Ribadeneyra, *De ratione quam in gubernando tenebat Ignatius*, in *FN*, III, 613, 618-619; Canisius' letter of 1548, cited in Espinosa Pólit, pp. 173-174. See also the fnn. on [91, 723]; Ignatius' ideal of the superior general [723-735]; *DeGuiJes*, pp. 71, 82, 92-93, 98-102, 220; *Epistolae Praepositorum Generalium* (Rolarii, 1909), I, 76-81; and *InstSJ*, III, 397.

Chapter 2
What pertains to poverty
and its consequences

[553]—1. Poverty, as the strong wall[1] of the religious life, should be loved and preserved in its integrity as far as this is possible with God's grace.[a] The enemy of the human race gen- *a)* 287, 816 erally tries to weaken this defense and rampart which God our Lord inspired religious institutes to raise against him and the other adversaries of their perfection. Into what was well ordered

---

1 Ignatius' esteem of the virtue of poverty had an intensity and tenderness which remind one of St. Francis of Assisi's love of "Lady Poverty." This appears from the figures by which he describes it: a mother [287], a strong wall [553], and a bulwark [816]. Among many reasons for this esteem of Ignatius, two stand out: (1) his enthusiastic embracing, already in his first conversion, of the mendicant spirit of St. Francis and St. Dominic which he found in Ludolph's *Life of Christ* and in Jacobus' *Flos sanctorum,* and (2) his antipathy to the prevalent avarice of so many of his contemporary ecclesiastics which was scandalizing and damaging the Church so much (see fn. 23 on [101] above and, in ch. 1, pp. 11-14). Through the Gospel and Ludolph's meditations on it, Ignatius conceived a love for the poor Christ (Luke 9:58) and also for the devout poor (Matt. 5:3) who have learned to place their trust in Providence rather than in wealth. (Compare, e.g., Ludolph, *Vita Jesu Christi* [Paris, 1877], I, ch. 9, no. 9, p. 70, and ch. 15, no. 15, p. 134, with *SpEx,* [116, 146, 147], and also with [98, 157, 272].) Imitating St. Francis and St. Dominic, Ignatius practiced poverty first as a solitary mendicant, going sometimes to extremes. But guided by God's grace, both at Manresa and later, to apostolic life, he continually adjusted his poverty to its needs. He inspired companions with his ideal of being "voluntarily poor priests of Christ" (*sponte pauperes Christi sacerdotes, Cons*MHSJ, I, 15) and of desiring to "preach in poverty" (*predicar en pobreza, Epp*Ign, I, 96; *Letters*Ign, p. 16).

Their decision of 1539 to form a new religious institute made it necessary for them to embrace one of the juridical forms of religious poverty which the Holy See would approve in their day. Two chief forms were at hand through which Ignatius could give to his spirit or tenor of thought on poverty precise legislative expression, the poverty of the ancient monasteries and the newer type of the mendicant orders, that which had been so inspiringly practiced by St. Francis and so skillfully structured and codified by St. Dominic. Already in August, 1539, Ignatius and his companions chose the poverty of the mendicants, whereby neither the professed members nor their houses could have either endowments or fixed revenues but had to live on voluntary alms. But they also devised the colleges with endowments and fixed revenues to support the scholastics during their training, lest the need of continual begging interfere with their studies. These scholastics were to have the simple but perpetual vow of poverty whereby they could retain ownership but not independent use of any possessions or inheritance they happened to have. Thus Ignatius also took something from the ancient monastic poverty and adapted it to his apostolic purpose. These measures were incorporated in August, 1539, into the First Sketch of the Society, [5], whence it passed into the bulls *Regimini,* [6], of 1540 and *Exposcit,* [5], of 1550 (in *Cons*MHSJ, I, 19, 29, 379; see esp. fn. 3 on 35). From this spirit of poverty sprang Ignatius' great trust in Providence and his insistence on gratuity of ministries ([4, 5, 398, 478, 495, 498, 499, 565-567, 640, 816]). He desired them to be exercised solely for the service of God and men and not for the sake of gain. On the genesis of Ignatius' concept of poverty, see A. Delchard, "La genèse de la pauvreté ignatienne," *Christus,* VI (1959), 464-486. Throughout history, changing economic and

by their first founders[2] he induces alterations by means of interpretations and innovations not in conformity with those founders' spirit. Therefore, that provision may be made in this matter as far as lies in our power, all those who make profession in this Society should promise not to take part in altering what pertains to poverty in the Constitutions [A], unless it be in some manner to make it more strict, according to the circumstances in the Lord.

b) 5

[554]—A. *To alter what touches upon poverty would be to relax one's hand in order to have some fixed revenue[3] or possession for personal use, or for the sacristy, or for the building, or for some other purpose, apart from what pertains to the colleges and the houses of probation.*[b] *To prevent the Constitutions from being changed in so important a matter, each one after making his profession will make this promise[4] in the presence of the superior general and those who happen to be present with him, by pledging in the sight of our Creator and Lord that he will take no part in altering what pertains to poverty in the Constitutions, either in a congregation assembled from the entire Society or by attempting this himself in any manner.*

social circumstances have stimulated and required new forms and legislative expressions to achieve the ideal of evangelical poverty, such as the decrees on poverty of General Congregation XXXI in 1965. See fn. 15 on [4] above.

2 By "first founders" Ignatius probably meant, in the concrete, St. Francis of Assisi and St. Dominic, and also himself and his first nine companions whose spirit, from the vows of 1534 at Montmartre onward, was one of complete poverty (see, e.g., *Cons*MHSJ, I, 71-81). The "interpretations and innovations" he mentions here in [553] were probably some changes, still canonically licit in the 1540's, which had been introduced into the "mitigated mendicant poverty" by the "privileges" granted by Popes John XXII (1322), Martin V (1430), and Leo X (1517), as H. Rahner (referring to Heimbucher, *Die Orden und Kongregationen*, I, 703-719, *Cons*MHSJ, I, 35, fn. 3, and Villasanta in *Manresa*, XXVIII [1956], 424-427) has pointed out in a still unpublished study. Among other mitigations, these popes permitted the churches or sacristies of the mendicant orders to have fixed revenues. In 1541 Ignatius and his companions knew the difficulties of the Franciscans and the mitigations of poverty discussed in the canonical commentaries of Tabiena (1517), Silvestrina (40 editions after 1518), and others (see *Cons*MHSJ, I, 35, fn. 3; fn. 14 on [4] above; and *EppIgn*, I, 265).

3 *Renta*, Latin *reditus*. On the meaning, fixed or regularly recurring revenues, see fn. 13 on [4] above.

4 Precisely what did Ignatius intend to be the matter covered by this promise or vow? This problem has given rise to many controversies and difficulties from at least the time of A. Sanchez (1550-1610) and Suarez (1548-1617) onward (see Fine, *Iuris Regularis . . .* S.I., p. 468). Through consideration in the concrete of the matters discussed by Ignatius and his companions from 1539 to 1556 during the genesis of the text of [554], a strong case can be made to show that the "alteration" which Ignatius meant to forestall was completely epitomized in the first sentence of [554]. Important primary sources for this case are: *Cons*MHSJ, I, 15, 35 with fn. 3, 89-90 (lines 65-71), 125 (line 70), and statements from text *a* of the Constitutions, in *Cons*MHSJ, II, 203-204. Constitutions [5, 816] also throw light on the first sentence of [554]. To some, however, this case does not seem

[**555**]—2. In the houses or churches which the Society accepts to aid souls, it should not be licit to have any fixed revenue, even for the sacristy or building or anything else,[5] in such a manner that any administration of this revenue is in the control of the Society[c] [B]. But the Society, relying on God our Lord whom it serves with the aid of His divine grace, should trust that without its having fixed revenue He will cause everything to be provided which can be expedient for His greater praise and glory.

c) 4, 5, 561-564, 816

[**556**]—*B. If a founder of houses or churches should desire to leave some amount of regular revenue for the maintenance of the building*[6] *or for other similar matters, this would not be at variance with the Society's poverty,*[7] *provided that this revenue is not at the disposition of the Society and that the Society is not in charge of this revenue. (However, the Society should take care that the one who has that charge does his duty.)*

[**557**]—3. The professed should live on alms in the houses (when they have not been sent away on missions), and they should not hold the ordinary office of rectors of the colleges or universities of the Society[d] [C], (unless this is necessary or

d) 421

decisive, because of the words in the second sentence of [554], to "take no part in altering" ff., which are possibly but not necessarily more general. By these words Ignatius may have meant precisely that alteration described in the preceding sentence, or possibly something beyond it. His words here contain an obscurity which can scarcely be removed by analyzing them; otherwise the controversies would not have lasted so long. But be all that as it may, the matter covered by the promise is determined juridically not by what Ignatius meant but by the authority of a general congregation. To forestall any further doubts about what the promise entails, in 1965 General Congregation XXXI decreed that the obligation of the promise does not extend beyond what is contained in the first sentence of [554].

5 This clause is the result of Ignatius' deliberation on poverty of 1544 (text in *Cons*MHSJ, I, 78-81) and it was the topic of his discernment of spirits and election recorded in his *Spiritual Diary* of February 2, 1544, to March 27, 1545 (text *ibid.*, I, 86-158; for his decision, see lines 65-71 on pp. 89-90 and line 70 on p. 125). In March, 1541, before Ignatius was general, he and his companions decided by a majority vote to accept the mitigated mendicant poverty then prevalent which permitted the mendicant orders to have fixed revenues for their churches or sacristies (*Cons*MHSJ, I, 35). How Ignatius voted then is unknown. But later he was manifestly fearful that that alteration was an injury to the purity of poverty. Hence arose his deliberation and election of 1544-1545.

6 The Spanish is *para la fábrica*. Covarrubias defines *fábrica* as "the regular revenue which churches . . . have for their repairs." On the acceptance, in the mitigated mendicant poverty of the 1500's, of fixed revenues without a civil title to them, see *Cons*MHSJ, I, 35, fn 3.

7 In 1555, when the professed house at Rome was in great penury, the pope and some cardinals offered it a steady gift of 50 scudi a month. In a gracious manner Ignatius refused it for the house but said that it could be given to the Roman College (Da Câmara, *Memoriale*, no. 252, in *FN*, I, 662).

e) 5, 326, 419, 763, 774, 816   notably useful for these institutions); and they should not avail themselves of the fixed revenues of these colleges[e] [D].

f) 330, 559

g) 330, 422

[**558**]—C. *The statement that the professed should not live in the colleges is understood to mean a prolonged stay.*[8] *But they may remain there in passing for a day or some fitting time.*[f] *They could also live there for a longer time when this is necessary or expedient for the good of the same college or university, for example, if they are necessary for the administration of the studies, or if they lecture or devote themselves to the spiritual exercises of confessions and preaching in order to relieve the scholastics who would have to do this, or in order to supply what the scholastics cannot do, or if they are sent to make a visitation of these colleges or universities and to set things right[g] in them; and also when it is necessary or fitting for the universal good, for example, if someone with an explicit commission from the superior general retires there for a time for the purpose of writing.*[9]

h) 330, 558

[**559**]—D. *Very small things are counted for nothing. Thus, in order to guard against scrupulosity, this explanation is made. When the rector by means of some provisions for a journey helps someone who is passing through a college and who lacks those provisions, thus giving him an alms, it may be accepted.*[h] *Also, the fact that the colleges supply certain expenditures which the houses would otherwise make if they could, for example, expenditures for clothing and the giving of provisions for traveling to those who are sent from the houses to the colleges, even though it is or seems to be an aid to the house, is not against the intention of this constitution which states that these members should not avail themselves of the fixed revenues of the colleges for their food or clothing or other expenses which are proper to the house. Likewise, the fact that the sick or the well from the houses take some recreation in a garden of the college is not understood to be against the constitution, provided that these persons are not supported at the expense of the college during the time when they are members of the houses. The same judgment can be made in regard to similar matters.*

[**560**]—4. The coadjutors dwelling in the houses will live on alms according to the manner of living in these houses. When

---

8 See fn. 2 on [421] above.

9 The papal brief of 1552, *Sacrae Religionis,* [6] (text in *ConsMHSJ,* I, 402) also gave a dispensation permitting the aged and sick, even though professed, to live in the colleges and thus benefit from their fixed revenues.

they are dwelling in the colleges, being rectors or lecturers or helping in things necessary or highly useful to these same colleges, they will live on the fixed revenues of the colleges just as the other persons, as long as the necessity of their being there lasts. When the necessity ceases, they should not reside in the colleges but in the houses of the Society, as has been said about the professed.

[561]–5. Not only fixed revenue,[i] but also stable goods[j] [10] of any kind, should not be possessed by the houses or churches of the Society, either in particular or in common,[11] except for what is necessary or highly expedient for the members' habitation and use [E]. An example of this latter case would arise if some place apart from the common habitation should be accepted for those who are convalescing and those who withdraw there to devote themselves to spiritual matters, because of the better air or other advantages which it has. In such a case it should be something which is not rented to others and does not bring profits equivalent to fixed revenue [F].

i) 4, 555, 816
j) 816

[562]–E. For, as the bull states,[12] the Society will not have the civil right to retain any stable possession beyond what is opportune for its habitation and use. The Society should be obliged to dispossess itself as soon as possible of any stable possession which is given to it, by selling it to relieve the penury of the poor of the Society or outside it.

But nevertheless the opportune time to sell is not thus excluded; and this should be understood to mean: when that stable possession is not necessary for the use of the house, such as some thing among those mentioned above. In regard to other goods which are movable, such as money or books or what is connected with food and clothing, the Society may in common have property for its use.

---

10 The Spanish is *possessiones,* which refers to stable goods. This term was added in *Exposcit,* [5], where it clarifies "ad bona stabilia" of *Regimini,* [6]. See the texts in *Cons*MHSJ, I, 29 and 379 with fn. 18.
11 The meaning of the technical phrase "in particular or in common" is "either by the individual religious or by all of them as a community." The thought contained in the rather involved first sentence of [561] is more clearly expressed in *Exposcit debitum,* [5]: ". . . neither the professed, either as individuals or in common, nor any house or church of theirs can acquire any civil right . . ." Among the monks, the individual religious were forbidden to own property, but the community could possess it; among the mendicants, such as the Franciscans, the community itself was forbidden to own.
12 *Exposcit,* [5], where there is a change from what was prescribed in *Regimini,* [6]. See the respective texts in *Cons*MHSJ, I, 379 and 29.

[563]—F. *There would be such profits if the aforementioned possessions yielded wine or oil or wheat, or if the fruits or vegetables of the garden were being sold. But none of this will be licit, although the residents should be able to enjoy the fruit or a part of it for the use of the house. Likewise, if the Society should have some gardener or lay person who has charge of the garden or lands which the above houses possess, he ought not to be prohibited from doing what seems proper for his own profit, provided that in such cases no profit comes to the houses or individual members of the Society.*

[564]—6. Although it is praiseworthy to induce others to do good and holy works, especially those which endure perpetually, nevertheless, with a view to greater edification, no one of the Society ought to or may induce any person to establish perpetual alms for the houses or churches of the Society itself. Moreover, if some persons do of their own accord establish such alms, no civil right should be acquired which makes it possible to claim these alms through a court of justice; but rather, let the persons give these alms when charity moves them for a service to God our Lord.

[565]—7. All who are under the obedience of the Society should remember that they ought to give gratuitously what they have gratuitously received [Matt. 10:9], without demanding or accepting any stipend or alms in recompense for Masses or confessions or preaching or lecturing[13] or visiting or any other ministry among those which the Society may exercise according to our Institute[k] [G], that thus it may proceed in the divine service with greater liberty and greater edification of the neighbor.[14]

k) 4, 82, 398, 478, 499, 640, 816

[566]—G. *Although all those who desire may give an alms to the house or the church, whether or not it be on the occasion of their receiving spiritual help there, nothing ought to be accepted as a stipend or alms for that which is given to them solely for the sake of service to Christ our Lord, in such a manner that the one item is given or taken in exchange for the other.*

[567]—8. To avoid all appearance of avarice, especially in the spiritual ministries which the Society exercises in order to aid

13 There is question here of "sacred lectures," on which see fn. 2 on [402] and fn. 6 on [437].
14 On gratuity of ministries and on the fruit or proceeds of labor, see fn. 15 on [4] above; also fn. 1 on [553].

souls, in the church there should not be a box in which those who come to the sermons, Masses, confessions, or the like, customarily place their alms.

[568]—9. For the same reason, the members should not give small objects to important persons as presents which are customarily given to draw greater gifts from them. Neither shall they make it a practice to visit important persons of this kind, unless it is for spiritual purposes of doing good works or when the persons were so intimately benevolent in our Lord that such a service seems due to them at times.

[569]—10. The members should be ready to beg from door to door when obedience or necessity requires it.[1] Some person or persons should be designated to request alms by which the members of the Society may be supported. These persons should ask for them simply for the love of God our Lord.

l) 67, 82, 331, 574, 610, 625

[570]—11. Just as no personal possession may be held in the house, so neither may one be held outside the house in the hands of another [H]. Each one should be content with what is given to him from the common supply for his necessary or proper use, without any superfluity.[m]

m) 297

[571]—*H. This is understood absolutely about the professed and the formed coadjutors.[n] But in the case of the scholastics and others who are in the time of their probation, it should be understood to refer to things which are at present within their disposition, so that they do not have anything unless the superior knows it and agrees to it.[o] It does not refer to the goods which they may happen to have far away in houses or other properties. But even with respect to these houses or properties, they ought to be ready to dispossess themselves of them whenever the superior thinks this wise,[p] as was said in the Examen [54, 59].*

n) 4

o) 57, 254

p) 54, 55, 59, 254, 255, 287, 348

[572]—12. That poverty may be the better preserved in all its integrity, and also the tranquility which it brings with it, the individual professed or formed coadjutors will be incapable of receiving an inheritance; and more than this, not even the houses or churches or colleges will be able to do so through those individual members. In this way all lawsuits and controversies will be more effectively eliminated and charity with all will be preserved to the glory of God our Lord.[15]

15 Text B, the Autograph, contains a declaration on [572], but there is doubt as to whether

[573]—13. When the sovereign pontiff or the superior sends such professed and coadjutors to labor in the vineyard of the Lord,q they may not demand any provision for the journey;r but they should generously present themselves that these superiors may send them in the manner which they think will be for the greater glory of God [I].

q) 7, 527, 529, 603, 605
r) 7, 609, 610

[574]—I. That is to say, on foot or on horseback, with money or without it; and they should be ready to carry out in deed what the sender judges to be more fitting and for greater universal edification.s

s) 82, 569, 609, 610, 625

[575]—14. To proceed here too in a manner in harmony with the requirements of poverty, in the houses of the Society ordinarily no mount will be kept for any member of the Society itself, either superior or subject [K].

[576]—K. Unless it should be because of constant infirmities or of urgent necessities in regard to public business, especially in large and populous places. For then more account should be taken of the universal good and the health of the individuals than of the time as temporary or permanent, or of the fact of going on foot or by other means. The purpose sought should always be necessity and decorum, and in no way ostentation.

[577]—15. The clothing too should have three characteristics: first, it should be proper; second, conformed to the usage of the region where one is living [L]; and third, not contradictory to the poverty we profess,t as would happen through the wearing of silk or expensive cloths [M]. These ought not to be used, in order that in everything humility and proper lowliness may be preserved, unto greater glory to God.u

t) 81, 296, 297

u) 580

[578]—L. Or at least, it should not be altogether different.

[579]—M. This refers to those to whom the house gives clothing anew. But if those entering the house are wearing some expensive cloth or similar item, it does not forbid them.v Further, if someone in some circumstance or necessity wears better but decent garments, it does not forbid him either; but these ought not to be used for ordinary wear. Nevertheless it should be observed that all do not have the same bodily strength, nor does

v) 18, 19, 297

Ignatius is truly its author. Out of concern for poverty, General Congregation I suppressed it (InstSJ, II, 165; cf. ConsMHSJ, II, 541, fn. 17). Text in ConsMHSJ, II, 540.

health of body belong to all nor an age which favors it. There-
fore care should be taken both for the particular good of such
persons and for the universal good of many others, and what
provision is possible should be made, for greater glory to God.

[580]—16. What pertains to food, sleep,[w] and the use of the   w) 301, 339
other things necessary or proper for living, will be ordinary[x]   x) 8
and not different from that which appears good to the physician
of the region where one lives[y] [N], in such a manner that what   y) 304
each one subtracts from this will be withdrawn through his own
devotion and not through obligation. Nevertheless there should
be concern for the humility, poverty,[z] and spiritual edification   z) 81, 577
which we ought to keep always in view in our Lord.[a]   a) 637

[581]—*N. Whether something more or less will be necessary*
for individual persons according to their circumstances will be
left to those in charge of them to judge, as also to provide as
is fitting.

Chapter 3
The occupations which those
in the Society should undertake
and those which they should avoid

[582]—1. In view of the time and approval of their life through
which those wait before being admitted among the professed
and even among the formed coadjutors, it is presupposed that
they will be men who are spiritual and sufficiently advanced to
run in the path of Christ our Lord to the extent that their bodily
strength and the exterior occupations undertaken through charity
and obedience allow. Therefore, in what pertains to prayer,
meditation,[1] and study and also in regard to the bodily practices

---

1 *Oración, meditación:* In general, in Ignatius' usage *oración* is a general term for any form
of prayer or communication with God (see, e.g., *SpEx,* [1, 238, 249, 258]; *Exam,*
[46, 65]; and Covarrubias, p. 838), while *meditación* is prayer in which reasoning has
a large part (see, e.g., *SpEx,* [45, 55]; *Exam,* [65]). Ignatius was not attending to other
constantly varying technical meanings which these terms had in different eras of the
history of Christian spirituality. On Ignatius' own distinctions between *meditación* and
contemplación, see fn. 8 on [65] above.

a) 134

b) 8, 9, 263, 300

c) 292, 300

d) 340

of fasts, vigils, and other austerities or penances, it does not seem expedient to give them any other rule[2] than that which discreet charity dictates to them[a] [A], provided that the confessor should always be informed and also, when a doubt about expediency arises, the superior.[b] The following statement is the only one which will be made in general. On the one hand, the members should keep themselves alert that the excessive use of these practices may not weaken the bodily energies[c] and consume time to such an extent that these energies are insufficient for the spiritual help of one's fellowmen according to our Institute; and on the other hand, they should be vigilant that these practices may not be relaxed to such an extent that the spirit grows cold and the human and lower passions grow warm.[d]

[583]—A. *If the superior thinks it expedient to give some subjects a determined time to keep them from being either excessive or deficient in their spiritual exercises, he will have the authority to do this. So too in regard to the use of the other means, if he judges in some case that one of these means ought to be employed without leaving this matter to the discretion of the individual, he will proceed in accordance with what God our Lord leads him to think proper. And the part of the subject will be to accept with complete devotion the order which is given to him.*

2 *Regla:* Just as constitutions [340-345] give Ignatius' legislation on prayer for those still in formation (see the footnotes there), so [582-584] give it for the members already formed. He reached the formulation of these constitutions after much experience and experimentation in directing others in prayer. For exercitants making the Spiritual Exercises, he prescribed mental prayer of a full hour (*SpEx*, [12]), in accordance with the purpose of the Exercises. But in regard to the prayer of daily living, he did not establish either a method (such as mental rather than vocal prayer) or a length which was to be obligatory on all alike (see [340] and the fnn. there). Instead, in point of method he expected each member, whether formed or still in formation, to experiment under the impulse of the rule of "discreet charity" in search, with counsel from his superior or spiritual advisor ([340-342, 582]), for that method or manner of praying by which he found that God most effectively communicated Himself to him with his own personality and temperament (*EppIgn*, II, 236; *LettersIgn*, p. 181). With respect to the length, Ignatius assigned for the scholastics still in formation one hour of prayer daily, which could be divided into different periods ([342]). But he steadily refused to prescribe one universal rule obliging all the formed members to one specified duration of daily prayer ([582-583]). One reason for his refusal came from his disagreeable experiences with some members, such as Oviedo or Onfroy, who followed a tendency, then present especially in Spain and Portugal, to go to excess. But there were other reasons too which sprang from his experience in guiding others whose temperaments and psychological needs greatly varied. He expected the formed members to continue their search for effective prayer, under the impulse of "discreet charity" and the guidance of the superior or confessor ([582, 583]).

After the death of Laynez in 1565, the tendency toward lengthy prayer of a prescribed length gradually won the ascendancy and in 1581 General Congregation IV decreed one hour of prayer each day for all, whether formed or still in formation. In time,

[584]—2. The frequentation of the sacraments³ should be highly recommended; and Holy Communion or the celebration of Mass should not be postponed beyond eight days without reasons legitimate in the opinion of the superior.ᵉ All should confess to the confessor who is assigned to them, or according to the order which each one has from the superior.ᶠ

e) 80, 261, 342, 343

f) 261, 278

[585]—3. In regard to the particular rules which are employed in the houses where they happen to be, it is proper that they should endeavor to observe the part which is expedient either for their own progress and edification or for that of the rest among whom they find themselves, and which is proposed to them according to the judgment of the superior.

[586]—4. Because the occupations which are undertaken for the aid of souls are of great importance, proper to our Institute,ᵍ and very frequent; and because, on the other hand, our residence in one place or another is so highly uncertain, our members will not regularly hold choir for the canonical hours or sing Masses and offices [B]. For one who experiences devotion in listening to those chanted services will suffer no lack of places where he can find his satisfaction; and it is expedient that our members should apply their efforts to the pursuits that are more proper to our vocation, for glory to God our Lord.⁴

g) 3, 307

---

further legislation prescribed that this prayer should be mental and continuous. In 1966 General Congregation XXXI sought to combine the best features taken from both the Ignatian and post-Ignatian legislation. Especially noteworthy and scholarly treatments of this much discussed subject are the following: P. Leturia, "La hora matutina de meditación en la Compañía naciente," *AHSJ*, III (1934), 47-108, reprinted in his *Estudios Ignacianos* (Rome, 1957), II, 189-268. His material is compressed in English in *DeGuiJes*, pp. 86-90, 169, 192-196, 205, 222, 227-229, 237, 552-554. New aspects of the entire problem are bought out in Fiorito, "La ley Ignaciana de la oración en la Compañía de Jesús," *Stromata*, XXIII (1967), 3-89, translated into English by A. Jacobsmeyer in "St. Ignatius' Own Legislation on Prayer in the Society of Jesus," *WL*, XCVII (1968), 149-224.

"Discreet charity" (*discreta caridad*), translated in 1558 by *prudens caritas* or *discreta caritas*, and sometimes today by "discerning love," is a phrase characteristic of Ignatius, a figure of speech by which he means the charity exercised by a discreet person, one who exercises natural and supernatural prudence or judgment in his actions. This discreet charity impels him to choose the objectively better course after all the circumstances have been considered. Ignatius presents discreet charity as a norm of acting in [209, 237, 269, 582]. In his usage the phrase also connotes discernment of spirits (*discreción de espíritus*, SpEx, [176, 328]), in which he exercised his natural and supernatural prudence with special care. See also fnn. 18 on [92] and 2 on [134] above.

3 See fn. 13 on [80] and fn. 17 on [261].

4 In the 1500's many religious were singing the Office in choir and celebrating conventual Masses (chiefly inside their own monasteries and churches), as was proper according to their vocation which Ignatius always esteemed (see, e.g., *SpEx*, [355]). He himself always loved the liturgy as practiced in his day and derived great devotion from it (see *FN*, I,

[587]—B. *If it is judged expedient in some houses or colleges, at the time of the afternoon when a sermon or lecture is about to be given, Vespers alone could be recited, to please the people immediately before these sermons or lectures. This could also be done ordinarily on Sundays and feast days, without organ music or plain chant but in a devout, smooth, and plain tone. This is done for the purpose of attracting the people to more frequent attendance at the confessions, sermons, and lectures and to the extent that it is judged useful for this, and in no other manner. In Holy Week tenebrae with its ceremonies could be recited in the same tone.*

In the more solemn Masses which are celebrated (although not sung), there could be, with attention to devotion and propriety, two assistants vested in surplices, or one, with everything h) 311 *done according to what is possible in the Lord.*[h]

[588]—5. Likewise, because the members of this Society ought to be ready at any hour to go to some or other parts of the i) 82, 92, 304, world where they may be sent by the sovereign pontiff or their 308, 603, 605, 626 own superiors,[i] they ought not to take a curacy of souls,[j] and j) 324, 325 still less ought they to take charge of religious women or any

---

391, 636; II, 337; also G. Ellard, "St. Ignatius Loyola and Public Worship," *Thought*, XIX [1944], 649-670). But in many places the Church's pastoral care of the people had almost collapsed, so that there were innumerable persons whom the liturgy was not reaching, or at least not reaching effectively. Seeing this great and unmet need of pastoral care, he strove to organize a religious order whose proper office would be pastoral care of the people at large. This apostolic end was his motive for excluding, with papal approval, the obligation of choral recitation of the Office, lest it interfere with the freedom and mobility of his men to work with the people outside the religious house when and where their needs arose ([586]). But he permitted lengthier or more elaborate ceremonies when they were truly furthering such pastoral care in the circumstances of his day ([587]). Important primary sources on this topic are: the document of 1539, *Prima . . . Instituti Summa*, [6], the papal bulls of 1540 and 1550, *Regimini*, [7] and *Exposcit*, [6], in *Cons*MHSJ, I, 19, 30, 380; other statements *ibid.*, I, 214, 309-310, 329; *FN*, I, 609.

In an age when the Church found it expedient to keep the liturgy in Latin even though it remained unintelligible to many people and resulted in strong protest (see, e.g., the instances in T. Campbell, *The Jesuits* [New York, 1925], I, 119-125), Ignatius and his followers labored strenuously to bring the people at large to attend Mass, receive the sacraments, and practice their faith. Like other zealous priests of the day, they devised para-liturgical devotions to help toward this goal. Also, in an age when even annual reception of Communion was often neglected, they were pioneers in promoting weekly confession and Communion (*SpEx*, [344]) and frequent sermons, often based on the liturgy and liturgical year. They did not call those activities "liturgy" then, since only in 1558 was that word introduced in Renaissance humanism to designate the Church's official worship, and this new term spread very slowly (H. Schmidt, *Introductio in liturgiam Occidentalem* [Rome, 1960], p. 45). But those activities do fall within the scope of what is called liturgy today: the exercise of Christ's priesthood performed by His mystical body, Head and members (*Mediator Dei*, nos. 2, 3, 20, 22, 27; Vatican Council II, "On the Liturgy," no. 7; see also Schmidt, *Introductio*, pp. 60-61).

263

Ch. 3   Occupations to be undertaken

other women whatever to be their confessors regularly or to
direct them.[5] However, nothing prohibits them in passing from
hearing the confessions of a whole monastery for special reasons.

[589]—6. Neither should the members take on obligations of
Masses which are to be celebrated perpetually in their churches,
or similar burdens which are not compatible with the liberty that
is necessary for our manner of proceeding in the Lord[k] [C].   k) 324, 325

[590]—C. *In regard to the colleges, what can be tolerated in
this matter is treated in Part IV [324, 325]. In regard to the
houses, not to undertake such burdens is altogether proper.*

[591]—7. That the Society may be able to devote itself more
entirely to the spiritual pursuits pertaining to its profession, it
should abstain as far as possible from all secular employments,
such as those of being executors of testaments or of mandates
or of being procurators of civil affairs or of any such business,[l]   l) 793, 794
through not accepting such burdens and not employing itself
in them because of any requests [D]. If such business affairs
occur in connection with the colleges, they should have a procurator to take care of them and defend their rights. If such
affairs arise in connection with the houses of the Society or its
whole body, to enable the Society itself to preserve its peace,
the same procurator, or another coadjutor, or some person from
outside the Society, or some family which undertakes the pro-

---

5 Ignatius' voluminous correspondence with women right up to the time of his death reveals him as a zealous, interested, prudent, and understanding spiritual director of women
whom they highly esteemed. He inaugurated many works in their behalf, received much
help from them, and ever remained grateful to them. From 1539 to 1544 he, Rodrigues,
Broët, Laynez, and other Jesuits labored strenuously to help convents of nuns in their
efforts at reform, to such an extent that Ignatius began to fear that these efforts, fruitful
as they were, would keep his men too much occupied and endanger other works of
great moment, including the missions for the Holy See. In 1545 Isabel Roser and two
companions, Francisca Cruyllas and Lucretia de Biadene, successfully petitioned Paul III
to pronounce religious vows and to place themselves under obedience to Ignatius (*Cons-*
MHSJ, I, cxxxviii). After a time, however, distressing experiences ensued, as a result of
which Ignatius addressed a petition to the pope (text *ibid.*, I, 183-185, English in H.
Rahner, *St. Ignatius Loyola: Letters to Women* [New York, 1960], p. 255), asking to be
freed from obligation of being the regular or steady directors of convents of religious
women and of receiving them under obedience to the Society. The pope approved this
in 1547 and confirmed it anew in the bull *Licet debitum*, [13], of 1549 (*Cons*MHSJ, I,
363). Then Ignatius incorporated his experience and decisions into the compressed
legislation of this constitution [588]. In this whole matter, just as in the choral recitation
of the Office, his chief motive was avoidance of impediment to the mobility of his men.
The outstanding book which enables one to keep proper perspective in viewing Ignatius'
dealings with women is that of H. Rahner, mentioned just above. See esp. pp. 252-260,
on the spiritual direction of women, and the index, p. 553, s.v. "Jesuitesses."

tection of the house could defend the Society's rights for greater glory to God.

[592]—*D. This should be observed as far as possible. But the authority to dispense for a time, in a case of necessity and importance for the end of the divine service which is sought, should be left to the superior. This superior will be the general or the one to whom he delegates his authority in this matter.*

m) 823, 824

[593]—8. For the same reason, and to avoid occasions of unrest foreign to our profession, and also the better to preserve the peace and benevolent relations with all unto greater glory to God,[m] no professed or coadjutor or scholastic of the Society will consent to be cross-examined in criminal trials or even in civil trials (unless he is compelled to do so by someone who can oblige him under sin), without permission of the superior [E]. The superior will not give the permission except in the trials which touch upon the Catholic religion, or in other pious cases which are favorable to one party in such a way that they do not do damage to another. For it is proper to our Institute to serve all in our Lord without offense to anyone, as far as this is possible.

[594]—*E. If the superior gives permission to someone in regard to a civil trial out of respect for some person whom he seems unable to refuse, in that situation there is need of a restriction prohibiting him, in case some criminal or defamatory question occurs, from being questioned about it. For no superior ought to give permission for this.*

Chapter 4
The help given to the dying members
and the suffrages after death

[595]—1. Both during his whole life and also and even more at the time of his death, each member of the Society ought to strive earnestly that through him God our Lord may be glorified and served and his fellowmen may be edified, at least by the

example of his patience and fortitude along with his living faith, hope, and love of the eternal goods which Christ our Lord merited and acquired for us by those altogether incomparable sufferings of His temporal life and death.ᵃ But sickness is often *a*) 89, 272, 304 such that it greatly impairs the use of the mental faculties; and through the vehement attacks of the devil and the great importance of not succumbing to him, the passing away is itself such that the sick man needs help from fraternal charity. Therefore with great vigilance the superior should see to it that the one who in the physician's opinion is in danger should, before being deprived of his judgment, receive all the holy sacraments and fortify himself for the passage from this temporal life to that which is eternal, by means of the arms which the divine liberality of Christ our Lord offers.

[596]—2. He ought likewise to be aided by the very special prayers of all the residents of the house, until he has given up his soul to his Creator. Besides others who may enter to see the sick man die, in greater or less numbers according to the superior's judgment [A], some ought to be especially assigned to keep him company. They should encourage him and recall to his mind the helpful thoughts which are appropriate at that moment. When in time he can no longer be helped, they should commend him to God our Lord, until his soul now freed from the body is received by Him who redeemed it by that price so high, His blood and life.

[597]—A. *When some sick persons fall into delirium in which, with the use of reason lost, there is neither blame nor merit for what they say, or when it happens that someone does not give as much edification as he ought to in his infirmity, those assisting could be few and chosen from among those in whom more confidence is placed.*

[598]—3. From the hour when one has expired until his interment, his body should be kept decently **for the** proper time [B] and then, after the office has been recited in the usual manner before the residents of the house [C], it should be buried. On the first morning after his death all the priests of the house should celebrate a Mass for his soul and the rest should offer some special prayer for him. They should continue this subsequently, according to the judgment of the superior, the devotion of each one, and the obligations which exist in our Lord.

[599]—B. *On occasion the time up to the ordinary day could be shortened by some hours, especially in periods of heat, when*

the superior *judges this anticipation expedient because of the bad odor. But ordinarily what was stated will be done.*

[**600**]—C. *The practice should be that of reciting the office in a moderately loud voice and with the residents of the house present in the church with their candles lit, and so on.*

[**601**]—4. Likewise, a notice should be sent to the other places of the Society which the superior thinks proper, that the same thing may be done, so that charity may be shown in our Lord toward the departed no less than toward the living.

Chapter 5
The Constitutions do not oblige
under pain of sin

a) 424, 547, 746, 790, 826

b) 7, 527, 603, 605

c) 765

[**602**]—The Society desires that all the Constitutions and Declarations and its regime of living should be observed in every regard according to our Institute, without deviation in anything;[a] and on the other hand it also desires that its individual members may be free from anxiety or aided against falling into any snare of sin which could arise through the obligation of these Constitutions or ordinations. For that reason our considered opinion in our Lord is that, apart from the express vow which the Society has with respect to the currently reigning sovereign pontiff,[b] and apart from the other three essential vows of poverty, chastity, and obedience, no constitutions, declarations, or regime of living can oblige under mortal or venial sin, unless the superior orders the subjects in the name of our Lord Jesus Christ or in virtue of obedience,[c] which may be done in regard to things and persons where it is judged to be highly expedient for the particular good of each one or for the universal good. Thus in place of the fear of giving offense there should arise a love and desire of all perfection, and a desire that greater glory and praise of Christ our Creator and Lord may follow.[1]

---

1 This constitution is almost the same as a paragraph in the "Constituta et annotata" of 1544-1549 (text in *Cons*MHSJ, I, 216-217). The idea contained in the first sentence of [602] is also in the prologue of the Constitutions of the Dominicans.

Part VII
The distribution of the incorporated members
in Christ's vineyard and
their relations there with their fellowmen

Chapter 1
Missions¹ from the Holy Father

[603]—1. Just as Part VI treats of the duties which each member of the Society has in regard to himself, so Part VII deals with the members' duties toward their fellowmen (which is an end² eminently characteristic of our Instituteᵃ) when these members are dispersed to any part of Christ's vineyard, to labor in that part of it and in that work which have been entrusted to them. They may be sent to some places or others by the supreme vicar of Christ our Lord, or by the superiors of the Society, who for them are similarly in the place of His Divine Majesty;ᵇ or they themselves may choose where and in what work they will labor, when they have been commissioned to travel to any place where they judge that greater service of God and the

a) 3, 156, 163, 258, 307, 308, 446, 586, 813

b) 7, 527, 529, 573, 618, 749-752

---

1 In Ignatius' usage, the word "mission" sometimes has its radical meaning, the act of sending someone, and sometimes a derived meaning, the errand on which one is sent. See fn. 18 on [7] above.
2 "An end," i.e., an intermediate or subordinate end by means of which the principal end, greater glory to God, is sought. In the Constitutions Ignatius mentions many such subordinate ends, e.g., in [446], "the end of the Society and of its studies." See fn. 11 on [3] above.

c) 616, 633

good of souls will follow;ᶜ or they may carry on their labor, not by traveling but by residing steadily and continually in certain places where much fruit of glory and service to God is expectedᵈ [A].

d) 636

Since one's being sent on a mission of His Holiness will be treated first, as being most important, it should be observed that the vow³ which the Society made to obey him as the supreme vicar of Christ without any excuse, meant that the members were to go to any place whatsoever where he judges it expedient to send them for the greater glory of God and the good of souls,

e) 7, 529

whether among the faithful or the infidelsᵉ [B]. The Society did not mean any particular place, but rather that it was to be distributed into diverse regions and places throughout the

f) 82, 92, 304, 308, 626

world,ᶠ and it desired to proceed more correctly in this matter by leaving the distribution of its members to the sovereign pontiff.

[604]—*A. These are the four more general ways of distribution into the vineyard of Christ our Lord. Each of them is treated in its own chapter in this Part VII.*

[605]—*B. The intention of the fourth vow pertaining to the pope was not to designate a particular place but to have the members distributed throughout the various parts of the world. For those who first united to form the Society were from different provinces and realms and did not know into which regions they were to go, whether among the faithful or the unbelievers; and therefore, to avoid erring in the path of the Lord, they made that promise or vow in order that His Holiness might distribute them for greater glory to God. They did this in conformity with their intention to travel throughout the world and, when they could not find the desired spiritual fruit in one region, to pass on to another and another, ever intent on seeking the greater glory of God our Lord and the greater aid of souls.*

[606]—2. In this matter, the Society has placed its own judgment and desire under that of Christ our Lord and His vicar; and neither the superior for himself nor any individual member of the Society will be able for himself or for another to arrange or to try to arrange, directly or indirectly, with the pope or his ministers to reside in or to be sent rather to one place than another. The individual members will leave this entire concern to

g) 621, 627, 633

the supreme vicar of Christ and to their own superiorᵍ [C]; and

3 See fn. 17 on [7] and fn. 4 on [547] above.

in regard to his own person the superior will in our Lord leave this concern to His Holiness and to the Society [D].

[607]–C. *When one of the subjects has been designated for some place or undertaking and it is judged that the supreme vicar of Christ, if well-informed, would not send him to it, the superior general may give him better information, while finally leaving the entire matter to the decision of His Holiness.*

[608]–D. *"The Society" should be understood to mean those members of it who happen to be in the place where the general is. These could give good information to the sovereign pontiff when, because of different reports from others, he seemed to be about to send the general to some place which is not conducive to the common good of the Society and greater service to God.*

[609]–3. Moreover, he who has been designated by His Holiness to go to some region should offer his person generously, without requesting provisions for the journey or causing a request for anything temporal to be made,[h] except that His Holiness   h) 7, 573, 574 should order the member to be sent in the manner that His Holiness judges to be a greater service of God and of the Apostolic See, without taking thought about anything else [E].

[610]–E. *Representation may well be made, and even should be, through the agency of the prelate or person through whom His Holiness issues the command to go somewhere, by asking how he desires him to accomplish the journey and to remain in the destination, namely, by living on alms and by begging for the love of God our Lord, or in some other manner. This is asked that what seems better to His Holiness may be done with greater devotion and security in our Lord.*

[611]–4. If His Holiness does not designate the person but orders that one or more should go to one region or another, and if he thus leaves it to the superior to judge who would be most fit for such a mission, the superior, while pondering the greater universal good and also the minimum damage possible to the other employments which are undertaken in the service of God our Lord, will designate in conformity with His Holiness' command those who are capable or more suitable for the mission.

[612]–5. It is highly expedient that the mission should be entirely explained to the one who is thus sent, as well as the intention of His Holiness and the result in hope of which he is

sent. This should be given to him in writing,[4] if possible [F], that he may be better able to accomplish what is entrusted to him. The superior too will try to help him by what further counsels he can [G], that in everything God our Lord and the Apostolic *i*) 629, 630   See may be better served.[i]

[**613**]—*F. If this help is not given, at least an effort should be made to procure by word of mouth the meaning which His Holiness intended, whether His Holiness explains it directly to the one who is to go or through the agency of the superior, or some prelate, or other person.*

[**614**]—*G. The superior can also be helpful by some instruction, not only in his own missions but also in those of His Holiness, in order to attain better the end which is sought in the service of Christ our Lord.*

[**615**]—6. When they are sent to particular places without determination of the time by His Holiness, it is understood that the residence should last three months, and longer or shorter in proportion to the greater or less spiritual fruit which is seen to be reaped there or is expected elsewhere, or in accordance with *j*) 626, 751   what seems most expedient for some universal good.[j] All this will be done according to the judgment of the superior, who will consider the holy intention of the pontiff and the service of Christ our Lord.

[**616**]—7. When the residence in determined places must be prolonged and when it is possible without prejudice to the principal mission and intention of the sovereign pontiff, it will not be improper for the one on the mission to make some excursions to aid the souls in the neighboring regions and afterwards to return to his residence, if such excursions are possible and it appears to him that they could be fruitful in service to *k*) 603, 633   God our Lord.[k] Likewise in the territory where he resides, he ought to attend with special care to the charge which was especially given to him and not to neglect it for other opportunities in the divine service, even good ones. Yet in addition to that charge he can and he ought to consider, but without prejudice to his mission, as has been said, in what other things he can employ himself for the glory of God and the good of souls.

---

4 For examples of such explanations composed by Ignatius see *LettersIgn*, pp. 51, 93, 212, 267, 365.

Thus he does not lose the opportunity for this which God sends him, to the extent that he will judge expedient in the Lord.

[617]—8. In order to achieve better the end of our profession and promise, he who happens to be the superior general when a new vicar of Christ takes office should be obliged, either himself or through another and within the year after the pontiff's election and coronation, to manifest to His Holiness the profession and express promise which the Society has to be obedient to him, especially in regard to the missions, to the glory of God our Lord.[1]   *l*) 7, 527, 603

Chapter 2
The missions received from
the superior of the Society

[618]—1. To be able to meet the spiritual needs of souls in many regions with greater facility and with greater security for those who go among them for this purpose [A], the superiors of the Society, according to the faculty granted by the sovereign pontiff, will have authority to send any of the Society's members whomsoever [B] to whatsoever place these superiors think it more expedient to send them[a] [C], although these members,   *a*) 749-752 wherever they are, will always be at the disposition of His Holiness.

However, there are many who request help while considering more their own spiritual obligations to their flocks, or other advantages not so immediately their own,[1] rather than the common or universal benefits. Therefore the superior general, or whoever holds this authority from him, ought to bestow much careful thought on missions of this kind in order that, when he sends subjects to one region rather than to another [D], or for one purpose rather than for another [E], or one particular person rather than another or several of them [F], in this manner or in that [G], for a greater or lesser time [H], that procedure may

---

1 That is, not so immediately their own as is the welfare of their flocks. The Spanish phrase *no tanto inmediatos que los communes o universales* is obscure and has been variously interpreted.

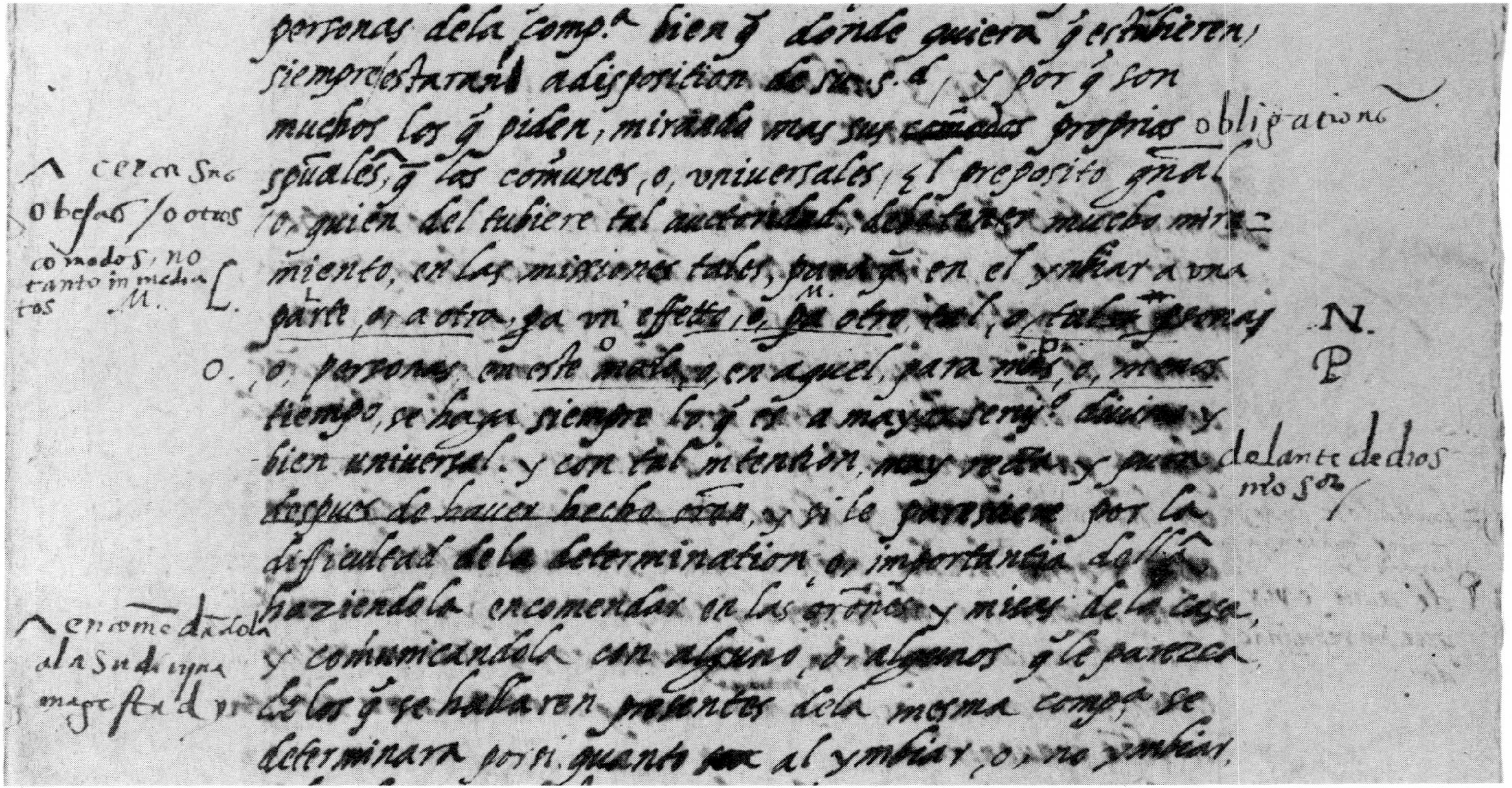

Figure 4. Facsimile from text B, the Autograph

Lines, in actual size, from *Constituciones*, [618]. The marginal additions are in St. Ignatius' handwriting. They read: "obligatione"; "cerca sus obejas, o otros cómodos no tanto immediatos"; "delante de dios nro Sõr"; and "encomendándola a su divina magestad y."

always be used which is conducive to the greater service of God and the universal good.

If the superior thinks, while holding fast to this thoroughly right and pure intention² in the presence of God our Lord, that it is wise because of the difficulty or importance of the decision, he will commend the matter to His Divine Majesty and cause it to be commended in the prayers and Masses of the house. He will also discuss it with one or more members of the Society who happen to be present and whom he thinks suitable. Then he himself will decide about sending or not sending, and about the other circumstances, as he will judge to be expedient for greater glory to God.

The part of him who is sent will be, without interposing himself in favor of going or remaining in one place rather than another, to leave the disposition of himself completely and freely to the superiorᵇ who in the place of Christ our Lord directs himᶜ in the path of His greater service and praise [I]. In similar manner, too, no one ought to try by any means to bring it about that others will remain in one place or go to another, unless he does so with the approval of his superior, by whom he should be governed in our Lord [K].

b) 606, 633
c) 84, 85, 284, 286, 342, 424, 547, 551, 552, 661, **765**

[**619**]—*A. The superior of the Society can more easily and more expeditiously make provision for many places (especially those remote from the Apostolic See), than would be the case if those who need members of the Society must always approach the sovereign pontiff. For the individual members, too, there is greater security if they go from obedience to their superiors rather than through their own decision (even if they were capable of making it), and not as men sent by him whom they have in place of Christ to direct them as the interpreter of His divine will.*ᵈ

d) 618

[**620**]—*B. Just as the general can perform the other functions by himself and through persons under him, so too can he perform this one of sending his subjects on missions, by reserving to himself the missions which he thinks should be thus reserved.*

[**621**]—*C. The sending of subjects "to whatsoever place these superiors think it expedient" means either among the faithful, even though it be in the Indies, or among the unbelievers, especially where there is a colony of believers, as in Greece and elsewhere.*ᵉ *Where the inhabitants are more exclusively unbelievers,*

e) 749, 750

2 See fn. 1 on [193] above.

the superior should ponder seriously in the sight of God our Lord whether he ought to send subjects or not, and where, and whom. The part of the subject will always be to accept his appointment joyfully as something from God our Lord.[f]

f) 606, 633

[**622, a**]—D. *To proceed more successfully in this sending of subjects to one place or another, one should keep the greater service of God and the more universal good before his eyes as the norm to hold oneself on the right course.*[g] [3] *It appears that in the vineyard of the Lord, which is so extensive, the following procedure of selection ought to be used. When other considerations are equal (and this should be understood in everything that follows), that part of the vineyard ought to be chosen which has greater need, because of the lack of other workers or because of the misery and weakness of one's fellowmen in it and the danger of their eternal*[4] *condemnation.*

g) 603, 623, 633

[**b**]. *Consideration should also be given to where the greater fruit will probably be reaped through the means which the Society uses. This case would arise, for example, where one sees the door more widely open and a better disposition among the people along with compliancy favorable to their progress. This disposition consists in the people's greater devotion and desire (which can be judged in part by the insistence they show), or in the condition and quality of the persons who are more capable of making progress and of preserving the fruit produced, to the glory of God our Savior.*

[**c**]. *In places where our indebtedness is greater, for example, where there is a house or college of the Society or where there are members of it who study and are the recipients of charitable deeds from those people, and when it is granted that the other considerations pertaining to spiritual progress are equal, it would be more fitting to have some laborers there, and*

---

3 This statement, so typical of Ignatius and of his world view (see p. 8 in ch. 1 above, and fn. 1 on [693] below), is his simple and fundamental criterion for choosing ministries, and all that follows is an application of it to details—as we readily see if we recall that greater service to God also brings greater glory to Him ([603, 609]).

While supplying the bracketed numbers in *Societatis Iesu Constitutiones et Epitomes* (Rome, 1949), the editor, A. de Aldama, numbered only those paragraphs designated by a number or a letter in the manuscript of text B. This makes it somewhat difficult to refer with precision to the many criteria and paragraphs (generally indicated in the manuscript but left undesignated) within [622-624]. Hence, with Father de Aldama's encouragement, the translator has here added the subdivisions designated by small letters within square brackets, e.g., [c].

4 *Eterna,* "eternal," is a reading taken from text *a,* in place of *entera,* "entire," which is found in texts A, B, and D but is manifestly a copyist's error (*Cons*MHSJ, II, 217, fn. 8 and 577, fn. 7).

*for that reason to prefer these places to others, in conformity
with perfect charity.*

[**d**]. *The more universal the good is, the more is it divine.*[h]   h) 623
*Therefore preference ought to be given to those persons and
places which, through their own improvement, become a cause
which can spread the good accomplished to many others who
are under their influence or take guidance from them.*

[**e**]. *For that reason, the spiritual aid which is given to
important and public persons ought to be regarded as more
important, since it is a more universal good. This is true whether
these persons are laymen such as princes, lords, magistrates, or
ministers of justice, or whether they are clerics such as prelates.
The same also holds true of the spiritual aid which is given to
persons distinguished for learning and authority, because of
that reason of its being the more universal good. For that same
reason, too, preference ought to be shown to the aid which is
given to the great nations such as the Indies, or to important
cities, or to universities, which are generally attended by
numerous persons who by being aided themselves can become
laborers for the help of others.*

[**f**]. *Similarly, the Society ought to labor more intensely
in those places where the enemy of Christ our Lord has sown
cockle [Matt. 13:24-30], and especially where he has spread bad
opinion about the Society or stirred up ill will against it so as to
impede the fruit which the Society could produce. This is
especially to be observed if the place is an important one of
which account should be taken, by sending there, if possible,
persons such that by their life and learning they may undo the
evil opinion founded on false reports.*

[**623, a**]—*E. For better success in the choice of undertakings
for which the superior sends his subjects, the same norm should
be kept in view, namely, that of considering the greater divine
honor and the greater universal good.*[i] *This consideration can*   i) 622
*supply completely just reasons for sending a subject to one place
rather than to another. To touch upon some motives which can
exist in favor of one place or another, we mention these.*

[**b**]. *First of all, the members of the Society may occupy
themselves in undertakings directed toward benefits for the soul,
and also in those directed toward benefits for the body through
the practice of mercy and charity. Similarly, they may help
some persons in matters pertaining to their greater perfection,
or to their lesser perfection; and finally, in regard to things
which are of themselves of more good, or of less good. In all these*

cases, if both things cannot be done simultaneously and the other considerations are equal, the spiritual goods ought to be preferred to the bodily, the matters of greater perfection to those of less, and the things more good to those less good.ʲ

j) 650

[c]. *Likewise, when there are some things in the service of God our Lord which are more urgent, and others which are less pressing and can better suffer postponement of the remedy, even though they are of equal importance, the first ought to be preferred to the second.*

[d]. *Similarly too, when there are some things which are especially incumbent upon the Society or it is seen that there are no others to attend to them, and other things in regard to which others do have care and a method of providing for them, in choosing missions there is reason to prefer the first to the second.*

[e]. *Likewise also, among the pious works of equal importance, urgency, and need, when some are safer for the one who cares for them and others are more dangerous; and when some are easier and more quickly dispatched and others are more difficult and finished only in a longer time, the first should be similarly preferred over the second.*

k) 622

[f]. *When everything mentioned above is equal and when there are some occupations which are of more universal good and extend to the aid of more of our fellowmen,ᵏ such as preaching or lecturing,⁵ and others which are concerned more with individuals, such as hearing confessions or giving Exercises; and when further it is impossible to accomplish both sets of occupations simultaneously, preference should be given to the first set, unless there should be some circumstances through which it would be judged that to take up the second set would be more expedient.*

[g]. *Similarly too, when there are some spiritual works which continue longer and are of more lasting value, such as certain pious foundations for the aid of our fellowmen, and other works less durable which give help on a few occasions and only for a short while, then it is certain that the first ought to be preferred to the second. Hence it is also certain that the superior of the Society ought to employ his subjects more in the first type rather than in the second, since that is a greater service to God and a greater good for our fellowmen.*

[624, a]—*F. Although it is the supreme providence and direction of the Holy Spirit that must efficaciously guide us to bring deliberations to a right conclusionˡ in everything, and in*

l) 134, 161, 414, 582

---

5 *Leer:* again, there is question of giving "sacred lectures," as in [402, 437, 565, 634].

sending to each place those who are more suitable and who will fit in better with the men and work to which they are sent, still this can be said in general. First, that for a matter of greater importance and one in which more depends on avoidance of error, as far as this depends on the part of the one who with God's grace must provide, subjects ought to be sent who are more select and in whom greater confidence is had.

[**b**]. *In matters which involve greater bodily labors, persons more strong and healthy.*

[**c**]. *In matters which contain greater spiritual dangers, persons more approved in virtue and more reliable.*

[**d**]. *To go to discreet persons who hold posts of spiritual or temporal government, those members seem most suitable who excel in discretion and grace of conversation and (while not lacking interior qualities), have a pleasing appearance which increases their prestige.*ᵐ *For their counsel can be highly im-*   m) 157, 158
portant.

[**e**]. *To treat with cultivated persons of talent and learning, those are more suitable who likewise have a special gift of skill and learning. For these persons can be more successful in lectures and conversations.*

[**f**]. *For the ordinary people, those will generally be most apt who have talent for preaching, hearing confessions, and the like.*

[**g**]. *The number and combination of such laborers who are to be sent should also receive consideration. First of all, it would be wise when possible that one member should not be sent alone. At least two should be sent, that thus they may be more helpful to one another in spiritual and bodily matters and also, by distributing among themselves the labors in the service of their neighbor, be more profitable to those to whom they are sent.*

[**h**]. *And if two set out, it seems that with a preacher or lecturer there could well go another who in confessions and spiritual exercises could gather in the harvest which the speaker prepares for him, and who could aid the speaker by conversations and the other means used in dealing with our fellowmen.*

[**i**]. *Likewise, when one less experienced in the Society's manner of proceeding and of dealing with the neighbor is sent, it seems that he ought to be accompanied by another who has more experience in that procedure, whom he can imitate, with whom he can confer, and from whom he can take counsel in the perplexing matters which he encounters.*

[**j**]. *With one very ardent and daring it seems that there could well go another more circumspect and cautious. Procedure*

similar to this, too, could be used in regard to other combinations, in such wise that the diversity may, when united by the bond of charity, be helpful to both of them and may not engender contradiction or discord, either among them or with their

n) 659, 660   *fellowmen.*[n]

[k]. *To send more than two when the importance of the work intended in the service of God our Lord is greater and requires a larger number, and when the Society can provide more laborers without prejudice to other things conducive to greater divine glory and universal good, is something which the superior will have authority to do, accordingly as the unction of the Holy Spirit inspires him [1 John 2:20, 27] or as he judges in the sight of His Divine Majesty to be better and more expedient.*

[625]—G. *In regard to the manner in which he is to send them*

o) 612-614, 629-632   *(after the proper instruction),*[o] *the superior should deliberate whether he will send them in the manner of the poor, so that they would go on foot and without money, or with better facil-*

p) 574, 610   *ities;*[p] *whether with letters to be helpful toward winning acceptance and benevolence at their destination; and whether these*

q) 631   *letters should be addressed to individuals, or the city, or its head.*[q] *In regard to all the details, the superior will consider the greater edification of the neighbor and the service of God our Lord and then decide what should be done.*

[626]—H. *When no limitation has been set by the sovereign pontiff as regards the time for which some laborers are sent to one place and others to another, it seems that the length of their stay ought to be regulated by the following considerations. Thought should be given to the nature of the spiritual affairs being dealt with, to the greater or less importance the men themselves have as viewed against the need and the fruit which*

r) 615, 751   *is being reaped or expected.*[r] *Then, too, attention must be given to the opportunities available in other places, to the obligation there is to take up these works, and to the resources which the Society possesses to provide for these other undertakings. One should also weigh the accidents which can intervene to shorten or prolong the time. Finally, one should attend to the first characteristic of our Institute. Since this is to travel through some regions and others, remaining for a shorter or longer time*

s) 82, 92, 304, 308, 588, 603, 605   *in proportion to the fruit which is seen,*[s] *it will be necessary to judge whether it is expedient to give more time or less to certain missions or to others. That this may be perceived, it is*

*important that those who are sent should keep the superior
informed by frequent reports about the fruit which is reaped.*ᵗ   t) 629, 673, 674
    *When it is necessary to change someone, the superior should
remember that in recalling him he should, as far as possible,
use such means that those from among whom he is taken will
retain all their benevolence rather than suffer a certain dis-
edification,*ᵘ *being persuaded that in everything the honor and*   u) 823, 824
glory of God and the universal good are being sought.

    [627]*—I. For someone to propose the motions*⁶ *or thoughts
which occur to him contrary to an order received, meanwhile
submitting his entire judgment and will to the judgment and
will of his superior who is in the place of Christ, is not against
this prescription.*ᵛ   v) 92, 131, 543

    [628]*—K. By this it is clearly forbidden that any member
should influence some prince, or community, or person of
authority to write a request to the superior for some member of
the Society or to ask this of him by word of mouth, unless the
member has first communicated the matter to the superior and
understood this procedure to be his will.*

    [629]—2. No matter where the superior sends anyone, he will
give him complete instructions,⁷ ordinarily in writing [L], about
the manner of proceeding, and the means which he desires to
be used for the end sought.ʷ Moreover, by maintaining frequent   w) 612-614
communication through lettersˣ and by being informed, as far   x) 626, 673, 674
as possible, about the entire outcome, from the place where he
resides he will provide (accordingly as persons and affairs require) advice and all other aids he can [M] that God our Lord
may be better served and the common good promoted by the
members of the Society. All this should be done with a care
proportionately greater according to the nature of the work,
whether important or difficult, and of the character of the persons sent, and insofar as they do or do not need advice and
instruction [N].

    [630]*—L. The word "ordinarily" is used because sometimes
the person sent is so instructed and sagacious that this writing
is not necessary. But in a word, whenever these instructions
are necessary, they should be given.*

---

6 *Mociones* is here a technical term. It can mean either inclinations arising on the natural
   level or spiritual experiences produced by good or evil spirits. See fn. 18 on [92] above.
7 See fn. 4 on [612] above.

[631]—M. *Such aids would be prayer and Masses applied especially in the beginnings of the undertakings or when greater need of such succor is observed because the matters are important or the occurring difficulties great. Thus in this matter, as in other helps such as letters patent or bulls, and the like which may be necessary, the superior will provide what reason and charity require.*

[632]—N. *This counsel and instruction can be useful not only in regard to the business but also in regard to the persons, in accordance with what is necessary to encourage or restrain each one. This should also be applied to everything else.*

Chapter 3
A member's free movement
from one place to another

[633]—1. It is the part of those who live under obedience to the Society not to scheme, directly or indirectly, to be sent here or there, either by His Holiness or by their own superior in the name of Christ our Lord.ᵃ Nevertheless one who is sent to an extensive region such as the Indies[1] or other provinces and for whom no particular district is marked out, may remain in one place for a longer or shorter period. Or, after considering the reasons on one side and the other, while praying and keeping his will indifferent, he may travel about wherever he judges this to be more expedient for the glory of God our Lord.ᵇ

a) 606, 618, 627

b) 603, 616

From this it is clear that, without swerving from that foremost and supreme order of His Holiness, in missions of this type the superior will have much greater power to direct a member to one place rather than another, as he judges in the Lord to be expedient.

[634]—2. Wherever anyone is stationed, if he is not limited to the use of some means such as lecturing[2] or preaching, he may use the means which he judges more suitable among those which the Society employs.ᶜ They have been mentioned in

c) 622, 623

---

1 I.e., either Asia or the Americas. See fn. 3 on [208] above.
2 *Leer:* there is question here of sacred lectures.

Part IV³ [402-414] and will be mentioned again in the following chapter [A]. Similarly, he will avoid what those passages disapprove, for greater service to God.

[635]—A. *However, it will always be safer for him to confer with his nearest superior about the means to be used.*

Chapter 4
Ways in which the houses and colleges can help their fellowmen

[636]—1. Since the Society endeavors to aid its fellowmen not merely by traveling through diverse regions but also by residing continually in some places, for example, in the houses and colleges, it is important to have learned the ways in which souls can be helped in those places, in order to use that selection of these ways which is possible for the glory of God our Lord.

[637]—2. The first way that comes to mind is the good example of a thoroughly upright life and of Christian virtue, through the effort to edify by good deeds no less but rather more than by words those with whom one deals.[a]

a) 89, 272, 580, 595, 825

[638]—3. Likewise, the neighbor is aided by desires in the presence of God our Lord and by prayers for all the Church, especially for those persons in it who are of greater importance for the common good [A]. They should also pray for friends and benefactors, living and dead, whether they request these prayers or not. Similarly, let them pray for those for whose special benefit they and the other members of the Society are working in diverse places among believers or unbelievers, that God may dispose them all to receive His grace through the feeble instruments of this least Society.

[639]—A. *Examples of such persons are the ecclesiastical princes, the secular princes, and other persons who have great*

---

3 The original reading in text B, "la 4ᵗᵃ parte," was crossed out and in some later texts was changed to "Part VI," meaning [586-594]. But this latter reference deals with occupations to be avoided and it seems less appropriate. On this textual problem, see *Cons*MHSJ, II, 595, fn. 2.

power to promote or impede the good of souls and the divine service.

[640]—4. Furthermore, aid can be given by Masses and other divine services which, whether they are said at the request of individuals or merely for the devotion of the celebrant, are to be celebrated without accepting any alms[b] [B]. In regard to the Masses, beyond those said for the founders,[c] one or two or more Masses (according to the number of priests and their convenience) should be ordered each week for the benefactors living and dead. Thus God is begged to accept this Holy Sacrifice for them and through His infinite and sovereign liberality to requite with eternal recompense that liberality which they have shown to the Society because of their love and reverence for Him.

b) 4, 565, 566, 816
c) 309-315

[641]—*B. As was explained in Part VI [565, 566].*

[642]—5. Further still, the neighbor can be aided through the administration of the sacraments,[d] especially the hearing of confessions (with some priests being assigned by the superior for this service [C]) and through administering Holy Communion, apart from the Communion of Easter time received in the communicant's parish church[1] [D].

d) 113, 406, 407

[643]—*C. As spiritual needs occur the superior will have the duty of considering whether others too, in addition to those who were assigned as ordinary confessors, ought to attend to the administration of these sacraments, and of ordering what is proper.*

[644]—*D. Easter time is understood to mean the eight days before and after the feast. However, during this time it is permissible to admit to Communion those who have permission, or pilgrims and the others whom the law excepts, and also those who have fulfilled their duty in their own parish and desire to communicate one or more times in our churches during these fifteen days.*

[645]—6. In the church the word of God should be proposed to the people unremittingly by means of sermons, lectures,[e] [2]

e) 402-405

1 In Ignatius' day, the faithful could not fulfill their Easter duty in the churches of religious. The present practice is governed by Canon 859, §3.
2 On the difference between sermons and sacred lectures, see fn. 2 on [402]; *MonNad*, IV, 659; and Coemans, *Introductio*, no. 57, b.

and the teaching of Christian doctrine,[f] by those whom the
superior approves and designates for this work, and at the
times and in the manner which he judges to be most conducive
to greater divine glory and edification of souls [E].

f) 113, 410, 437, 528

[646]—*E. Since it could happen in some places that on some
occasion it is not expedient to employ these means or some part
of them, this constitution does not oblige except when the
superior thinks that these means should be used. However, it
shows the Society's intention in the places where it will have
a domicile, namely, that use should be made of all three of these
means of proposing God's word, or two of them, or that one
which seems more suitable.*

[647]—7. The same procedure described above may also be
followed outside the Society's church, in other churches, squares,
or places of the region, when the one in charge judges it
expedient for God's greater glory.

[648]—8. Likewise, they will endeavor to be profitable to individuals by spiritual conversations,[g] by counseling and exhorting
to good works, and by conducting Spiritual Exercises[h][3] [F].

g) 115, 349

h) 408, 437

[649]—*F. The Spiritual Exercises should not be given in their
entirety except to a few persons, namely, those of such a character that from their progress notable fruit is expected for the
glory of God. But the exercises of the first week can be made
available to large numbers; and some examinations of conscience
and methods of prayer (especially the first of those which are
touched on in the Exercises) can also be given far more widely;
for anyone who has good will seems to be capable of these
exercises.*[i]

i) 409

[650]—9. The members will also occupy themselves in corporal
works of mercy to the extent that the more important spiritual
activities permit and their own energies allow.[j] For example,
they can help the sick, especially those in hospitals, by visiting
them and by sending others to serve them. They can reconcile
the disaffected and do what they can for the poor and for
prisoners in the jails, both by their personal work and by getting
others to do it [G]. How much of all this it is expedient to do
will be regulated by the discretion of the superior, who will

j) 623

3 *Cons*MHSJ, III, 214, fn. 5 gives references to primary sources for numerous illustrations
of [648].

keep always in view the greater service of God and the universal good.

[651]—G. *However, it is not expedient that the Society, or its houses or colleges, should become mingled with some other congregation,*[4] *or that such a group should hold its meetings within the Society for some purpose other than that which is proper for these same houses or colleges in the service of God our Lord.*

k) 289, 400

[652]—10. That part of what was stated about the houses which can also be done in the colleges and their churches should be carried out,[k] according to the opportunity which exists and the superior's decision, as has been mentioned.

l) 558

[653]—11. One who has talent to write books useful for the common good and who has written them[l] ought not to publish any writing unless the superior general sees it first, and has it read and examined.[5] The purpose is that if it is judged to be something which will edify, it may be published, and otherwise not.[m]

m) 273, 389

n) 136, 428, 585, 811

[654]—12. What pertains to the offices of a house and other things more particular will be seen in the rules of the house,[n] without our stating more here about the missions or distribution of the Society's members in the vineyard of Christ our Lord.

---

4 There is question here not so much of religious institutes as of a variety of companies, confraternities, or congregations (see fn. 3 on [1] above, and the supplementary Note A in the Reference matter, below). Ignatius thought it inadvisable for the Society or its houses or colleges to become involved in the affairs of such confraternities which did not depend on it. See *ConsMHSJ*, III, 215, fn. 6.

5 See also [273, 358, 389] above. During Ignatius' activity in Rome, 1537-1556, censorship of books was far more common and stringent in both civil and ecclesiastical society than it had been previously or is today. In 1542 Paul III reorganized the General Inquisition, in 1546 the Council of Trent stressed the need of censorship anew, and in 1559 the first *Index librorum prohibitorum* was published under Paul IV. See *CathEnc*, III, esp. 520-523; *NCathEnc*, esp. III, 391-392 and VII, 434.

Part VIII
Helps toward uniting the distant members with their head and among themselves

Chapter 1
Aids toward the union of hearts

[655]—1. The more difficult it is for the members of this congregation to be united with their head[1] and among themselves, since they are so scattered among the faithful and among the unbelievers in diverse regions of the world [A], the more ought means to be sought for that union. For the Society cannot be preserved, or governed, or, consequently, attain the end it seeks for the greater glory of God unless its members are united among themselves and with their head. Therefore the present treatise will deal first with what can aid the union of hearts[2]

1 See fn. 10 on [137] above, and the supplementary Note A in the Reference matter below.
2 Ignatius' usage of *de los ánimos* in [655], union "of hearts," should be carefully distinguished from his *de las ánimas* in [3], the salvation of the members' "souls" as meaning the persons or selves (see fn. 10 on [3]). In 1558 Polanco discerningly translated *ánimos* of [655] by the Latin *animus*, the soul as the seat of feeling, the heart, and *ánimas* of [3] by the Latin *anima*, the soul taken for the person or self—a meaning common in Scripture and in classical Latin. In the sixteenth century the English word heart had among its meanings, like Ignatius' *ánimo*, the seat of love or affection; hence, affection, love, devotion—a meaning which it had already in medieval times and still retains today. Ignatius' hope and ideal expressed here in [655] is a union of persons through their minds and hearts.

and later with helps toward the union of persons in congregations or chapters. With respect to the union of hearts, some of the helpful means lie on the side of the subjects, others on the side of the superiors, and others on both sides.

[656]—*A. There are also other reasons, for example, the fact that ordinarily they will be learned men, that they will have the favor of princes or important persons, or of peoples, and so forth.*

[657]—2. On the side of the subjects, it will be helpful neither to admit a large crowd of persons to profession[a] nor to retain any other than select persons even as formed coadjutors or scholastics [B]. For a large number of persons whose vices are not well mortified is an obstruction to order and that union which is in Christ our Lord so necessary for the preservation of this Society's good condition and manner of proceeding.

a) 12, 308, 516-523, 819

[658]—*B. This does not exclude the number, even though it is very large, of persons who are suitable for profession or for the formed coadjutors or the approved scholastics. But it recommends avoidance of leniency in regarding as fit those who are not, especially for admission among the professed. When that which was stated in Part I and Part V is well observed, enough will be done. For a group of members of that quality, even if it is numerous, is not to be regarded as a crowd, but as an elite race.*

[659]—3. Since this union is produced in great part by the bond of obedience, this virtue should always be maintained in its vigor;[b] and those who are sent out from the houses to labor in the Lord's field should as far as possible be persons practiced in this virtue [C]. Those who are more important in the Society should give a good example of obedience to the others, by being closely united to their own superior and by obeying him promptly, humbly, and devoutly.[c] Thus too one who has not given a good example of this virtue ought at least to go in the company of someone who has given it;[d] because in general a companion more advanced in obedience will help one who is less so, with the divine favor. And even when this purpose does not exist, a collateral associate[3] can be given to one who is sent

b) 284, 547, 551, 821

c) 423, 434

d) 624

3 The office of collateral (see fn. 2 on [492] above) was devised, apparently later than 1551 since this passage first appears in text B, in the hope of alleviating some overburdened superiors, of moderating the action of some superiors in whom less confidence

with some charge[e] [D], if the superior thinks that thus the one   *e*) 492
entrusted with this charge will carry out better what has been
entrusted to him. The collateral will conduct himself in such a
manner with him who has the charge, and he in turn with the
collateral, that neither the obedience nor the reverence of the
others is weakened; and also in such a manner that the one in
authority has in his collateral a true and faithful aid as well as
an alleviation for himself and for the others who are in his
charge.

[660]—C. *When experience reveals that some of those sent
are not proceeding correctly in regard to obedience, either they
ought to be recalled or a companion advanced in it ought to
be sent to them, even though one was not sent in the beginning.*

[661]—D. *Although the collateral associate is not under
obedience to the superior or person to whom he is given, he
ought to have interior and exterior reverence for him and thus
to give an example to the others who are under his obedience.
Similarly he should with all possible diligence help him who
has the charge, in all the matters pertaining to his office in which
his aid is requested.*

*Even though nothing has been asked of him, when he per-
ceives that it is fitting for him to tell the superior something
about the latter's person or about matters pertaining to his
office, he ought to inform him faithfully and to express his
opinion with freedom and Christian modesty. But once he has
expounded his reasons and motives, if the one put in charge
holds an opposite opinion, the collateral ought to submit his*

was felt, and of strengthening the bond of union in the Society (see *EppIgn*, V, 164-165,
182, 198). The collateral had no authority over either the superior or the subjects but was
expected to be an intermediary between them. He was also to be a counselor and
charitable admonitor to the superior, from whose jurisdiction he was exempt. Ignatius
assigned Francesco Palmio as collateral to the rector at Ferrara (*EppIgn*, III, 487) and
Andrés de Oviedo as collateral to Bobadilla (*ibid.*, III, 99). But the office did not work
out well in practice. Polanco, narrating the case of Adrianus Candidus, collateral of
Caesar Aversanus at Mutina in 1552, states that "experience showed that an office of this
kind tended more to enervate the practice of obedience than to give any great help to
the rector or the subjects" (*PolChron*, II, 457). The office soon ceased to exist. On it, see
*Cons*MHSJ, I, 387-388; Aicardo, *Comentario*, V, 831-835.
    Especially since 1689, the collateral associate has sometimes been taken, erroneously,
as identical with a "superintendent" who occasionally functioned in some colleges, as
Nadal did in the Roman College in about 1563. Coemans has shown that the two
offices were distinct, in "Collatéral et surintendant," *AHSJ*, I (1936), 293-295. In the
name of the Society and the general, the superintendent of 1563 supervised all the affairs
of the college and had authority over the rector. This office of superintendent, which
was also distinct from that of the superintendent or prefect of spiritual matters of [431,
432], was suppressed in Decree 86 of General Congregation II.

*personal judgment and conform himself to the one in charge,
unless the collateral sees with great clarity that he is erring.
In that case the collateral ought to inform their superior.*

*The collateral should also endeavor to bring the subjects to
agree among themselves and with their immediate superior as
far as this is possible, by moving among them as an angel of
peace and getting them to hold the proper esteem and love
toward their superior, whom they have in the place of Christ
our Lord.*[f]

*f) 84, 85, 286,
342, 424, 547,
551, 552, 618,
619, 627, 765*

*The collateral ought also to inform his own superior, whether
superior general or provincial superior, about the matters which
this superior of his own will entrust to him, and also about those
things entrusted to him by the person to whom he is assigned
as collateral.*[g] *Furthermore, of his own initiative he even ought
to serve as a substitute for the one in charge, by sending the
information when he fails because of illness, or occupations, or
some other reason.*

g) 504, 673, 674

*On the other hand, the one in charge ought to observe certain
things in regard to his collateral. First, seeing that the collateral
is assigned to him not as a subject but as one to assist him and
lighten his burden, he ought to have and show special love and
respect for his collateral, by conversing familiarly with him that
he in turn may have more courage and ease in expressing his
opinion and may see more clearly the matters in which he can
help. The one in charge should also try to bring those under
his authority to esteem and love the collateral, for in this way
he will have the collateral as a more useful instrument in dealing with them.*

*The one in charge will do well to discuss the matters which
he thinks difficult with the collateral, by asking for his opinion,
and also by encouraging him to express it even when it has not
been requested and to bring to his attention any suitable observations about his person or office. After hearing his collateral's
opinion, the one in charge will himself make the decision better
later on.*

*In what pertains to his carrying out his duty of governing
those in his charge, the superior should use the collateral as a
faithful instrument in the matters of greater importance,
whether they concern the general interests of the house or the
particular interests of each of the brethren.*

*The superior should likewise use the collateral's help in what
pertains to the superior general and is due to him; and in
everything except his authority he should regard the collateral
as another self, in a unity of spirit in our Lord.*

It should be noticed that there are two chief cases in which a collateral ought to be assigned. The first occurs when far greater help is desired for the one who is sent with the principal charge, because he is not yet much practiced or experienced in such government, or because there are other reasons, although his ideals and life are worthy of high approval for greater glory to God. The second case occurs when the superior in charge will have in his company someone of such a character that he is thought less likely to be profitable as a subject than he would be as a companion, provided that he has the qualities to be helpful to the superior.

[662]—4. To this same virtue of obedience is related the properly observed subordination of the superiors, one to another, and of the subjects to the superiors,[h] in such wise that the individuals dwelling in some house or college have recourse to their local superior or rector and are governed by him in every respect. Those who are distributed throughout the province refer to the provincial or some other local superior who is closer,[i] according to the orders they received; and all the local superiors or rectors should communicate often with the provincial and thus too be directed by him in everything;[j] and the provincials in their turn will deal in the same way with the general. For this subordination, when well observed in this manner [E], will preserve the union[4] which is attained chiefly through it, with the help of the grace of God our Lord.[k]

h) 206, 424, 666, 821

i) 635

j) 791

k) 666, 821

[663]—E. *When in particular cases the provincial superior thinks it more expedient for the divine service that someone of those dwelling in the houses or colleges should be under direct obedience to himself, he may exempt him from obedience to the rector or local superior. Similarly the general may make some individuals and local superiors or rectors directly dependent on himself. But ordinarily, the more entirely the aforementioned subordination is observed, the better it is.*

[664]—5. One who is seen to be a cause of division among those who live together, estranging them either among themselves or from their head, ought with great diligence to be separated from that community, as a pestilence which can infect it seriously if a remedy is not quickly applied[l] [F].

l) 215

4 Ignatius' hierarchically arranged series of superiors through which authority to govern descends and the function of this series in furthering unity appear very clearly in this constitution [662]. See fnn. 3 and 4 on [547] above.

[665]—*F. To separate can mean either to expel the person from the Society completely or to transfer him to another place, if this seems sufficient and more expedient for the divine service and the common good, in the judgment of him who has charge of the matter.*

[666]—6. On the side of the superior general, that which will aid toward this union of hearts consists in the qualities of his person [G]. They will be treated in Part IX [723-725]. With them he will carry on his office, which is to be for all the members a head from whom descends to all of them the impulse necessary for the end which the Society seeks. Thus it is that from the general as the head flows all the authority of the provincials, and from the provincials that of the local superiors, and from that of these local superiors that of the individual members.[m] Thus too from that same head come the assignments to missions; or at least they come by his mandate and approval.[n] The same should be understood about the communication of the graces of the Society;[o] for the more the subjects are dependent upon their superiors, the better will the love, obedience, and union among them be preserved.[p]

m) 736, 740, 757, 759, 820
n) 618, 620, 749, 751
o) 511, 753
p) 206, 662, 821

[667]—*G. Among other qualities, his good reputation and prestige among his subjects[q] will be very specially helpful; and so will his having and manifesting love and concern for them, in such a way that the subjects hold the opinion that their superior has the knowledge, desire, and ability to rule them well in our Lord. For this and many other matters he will find it profitable to have with him persons able to give good counsel, as will be stated in Part IX [803, 804], whose help he can use in what he must order for the Society's good manner of proceeding in diverse regions, unto divine glory.[r]*

q) 725, 733, 790

r) 779, 803-805

Further help will be found in his having his method of commanding well thought out and organized, through his endeavoring to maintain obedience in the subjects in such a manner that the superior on his part uses all the love and modesty and charity possible in our Lord,[s] so that the subjects can dispose themselves to have always toward their superiors greater love than fear,[5] even though both are useful at times. He can also do this by referring some matters to them when it appears probable that they will be helped by this; and at other times, by going along with them to some extent and sympathizing with them when this, it seems, could be more expedient.

s) 270

5 On superiors' manner of government, see fn. 10 on [551] above.

[668]—7. That the location may be favorable for communication between the head and his members, it can be a great help for the general to reside for the most part in Rome[t] [H], where communications with all regions can more easily be maintained. Similarly, for the greater part of the time the provincials should be in places where they can communicate with their subjects and the superior general [I], as far as they find this possible in our Lord.

t) 690

[669]—*H. He may visit his subjects in other places, according to the circumstances and necessities which arise. Likewise, he may at times live near Rome, in accordance with what is judged to be for the greater glory of God.*

[670]—*I. What was said about the general will hold true of the provincial superior's visits, namely, that he may do such visiting when he thinks that by it greater service will be given to God our Lord; and it is something very proper to his office. But when he must reside in some place for a longer time, he should if possible choose a location where communication with his subjects and the general is possible.*

[671]—8. The chief bond to cement the union of the members among themselves and with their head is, on both sides, the love of God our Lord. For when the superior and the subjects are closely united to His Divine and Supreme Goodness, they will very easily be united among themselves, through that same love which will descend from the Divine Goodness and spread to all other men, and particularly into the body of the Society. Thus from both sides charity will come to further this union between superiors and subjects, and in general all goodness and virtues through which one proceeds in conformity with the spirit.[u] Consequently there will also come total contempt of temporal things, in regard to which self-love, the chief enemy of this union and universal good, frequently induces disorder.

u) 821

Still another great help can be found in uniformity, both interior uniformity of doctrine, judgments, and wills,[v] as far as this is possible [K], and exterior uniformity in respect to clothing, ceremonies of the Mass, and other such matters,[w] to the extent that the different qualities of persons, places, and the like, permit.

v) 30, 47, 273, 274, 821

w) 110, 136, 401

[672]—*K. In the case of those who have not studied it is good to try to bring it about that all will ordinarily follow one doctrine, that which was selected in the Society as being the*

better and more expedient for its members. One who has already completed his studies should be alert to prevent any diversity from damaging the union of charity and to accommodate himself in what is possible to the doctrine which is more common in the Society.

x) 504, 507, 618, 626, 661, 679, 821

[673]—9. Still another very special help will be found in the exchange of letters between the subjects and the superiors[x] [L], through which they learn about one another frequently and hear the news [M] and reports [N] which come from the various regions. The superiors, especially the general and the provincials, will take charge of this, by providing an arrangement through which each region can learn from the others whatever promotes mutual consolation and edification in our Lord.[6]

[674]—*L. The local superiors or rectors who are in one province and those who are sent to produce fruit in the Lord's field ought to write to their provincial superior every week, if facilities for this exist. The provincial and the others should likewise write to the general every week if he is near. If they are in a distant realm where such facility for communication does not exist, the local superiors and rectors, like the provincials, and likewise the individuals who have been sent to produce fruit as was mentioned, will similarly write once a month to the*

y) 790

general.[y] The general too will see to it that a letter is written to them ordinarily once a month, at least to the provincials; and the provincials in turn will take care that a letter is sent to the local superiors, rectors, and individuals in whose cases there is need, likewise once a month, and more frequently from one side and the other according to the occurrences in our Lord.

[675]—*M. That the news about the Society may be communicated to all, the following procedure should be followed. At the beginning of every four-month period, those who in diverse houses or colleges are under one provincial should write a letter which contains only the edifying reports, in the vernacular*

---

6 The prescriptions in [673-676] have given rise to an immense amount of correspondence, of which the most important has been preserved in the archives of the Society in Rome and has been a mine of information for historians of the Society from Orlandini (1614) to the present (see Coemans, *Breves notitiae*, nos. 187-222). The project of publishing the most significant of these manuscripts and documents in the series "Monumenta Historica Societatis Iesu," the Historical Records or Sources of the Society of Jesus, was begun in Madrid in 1894 and transferred to Rome in 1929. See E. J. Burrus, "Monumenta Historica Societatis Iesu (1894-1954)," WL, LXXXIII (1954), 158-168. For a list of the titles to date, see, in the Reference matter below, Abbreviations, s.v. "MHSJ."

language of the province and another in Latin with the same content. They should send two copies of each of these letters to the provincial, that he may send one Latin and one vernacular copy to the general with another of his own in which he should state anything noteworthy or pertaining to edification which the individuals omit. Then he should have the remaining letters reproduced in enough copies to suffice to supply the information to the others of his own province. If the sending of these letters to the provincial should entail much loss of time, the local superiors and rectors may address their Latin and vernacular letters directly to the general and the copy to the provincial. Also, when the provincial thinks it advisable he may tell some of the local superiors to inform the rest in his province by sending them copies of what these superiors write to the provincial.

However, that what pertains to one province may be known in another, the general will order that sufficient copies of the letters sent to him from the provinces should be made to provide for all the other provincials; and these provincials will likewise have copies made for the members of their own province.

When there is much interchange between one province and another, like that between Portugal and Castile or between Sicily and Naples, the provincial of the one province may send to the provincial of the other the copy of those letters which he sends to the general.

[676]—N. That more complete information may be had about all the persons, every four months there should be sent from each house and college to the provincial a brief list in duplicate of all who are in that house, and of those who are now missing because of death or some other cause, from the time of the last list sent until the date of the present one, with a brief account of the qualities of these persons. In the same manner, every four months the provincial will send to the general the copies of the lists from each house and college.[z] For in this way it will be possible to have better information about the persons and to govern the whole body of the Society better, for the glory of God our Lord.

z) 792

Chapter 2
The occasions for holding a general congregation

[677]—1. In the treatment of the union of persons which takes place in congregations of the Society, various points must be considered: the occasions when the persons should assemble, who should meet, and by whom they should be summoned; also where, when, and in what manner they ought to come together; and the determination of the material to be treated in the congregation.

To begin with the explanation of the first point, the occasions on which the congregation and general chapter[1] should take place: It is presupposed that for the present it does not seem good in our Lord that such a congregation should be held at definite intervals [A] or very often;[a] for the superior general, through the communication which he has with the whole Society [B] and through the help he gets from those near him,[b] can spare the Society as a whole from that work and distraction as far as possible. Yet on some occasions a general congregation will be necessary, for example, for the election of a general, whether it be because of the death of the preceding general or because of any of the reasons for which a general may relinquish that office and which will be treated further on [774, 782].

a) 689, 722

b) 798-808

[678]—A. *An example would be: every three or six years, more or less.*

c) 673, 674, 790

[679]—B. *This communication is maintained through letters*[c] *and through the persons, at least one from each province, who should come every three years, but every four from the Indies, after being elected by the votes of the professed and rectors of the provinces, to inform the general about many things. When necessary, this communication can also be understood to mean the opinion of those from the whole Society whom the general considers to have better judgment. Thus, in company with those whom he has nearby for purposes of consultation, he will be able to decide upon many things without assembling the whole Society. For to a great extent the congregation is an aid toward*

---

1 The general congregation or chapter is the highest legislative body in the Society beneath the pope. Even the superior general is bound by its decrees; and his ordinary government consists largely in administering them. In practice, the congregations usually give extensive prudential powers to the general.

settling something wisely, either through the greater information which it possesses or through some more distinguished persons who express their opinion. In many cases all this can be accomplished without a general congregation, as has been stated.

[680]–2. The second occasion arises when it is necessary to deal with long-lasting[2] and important matters [C], as would be the suppression or transference of houses or colleges;[d] or with other very difficult matters pertaining to the whole body of the Society or its manner of proceeding, for greater service to God our Lord.

d) 322, 420, 441, 743, 762, 763

[681]–*C. Long-lasting matters of any sort do not suffice to require a general congregation if they are not also important. But some matters of importance, even if not long-lasting, could suffice. The decision about the importance will be left to the superior general.[e] But when matters arise which are urgent and of great importance, so that the assistants to the general, the provincials, and the local superiors judge by a majority of votes that a general chapter should be held, as is treated in Part IX [773, 786], it should be convoked. Moreover, the general should acquiesce and order that chapter to be held with great diligence.*

e) 689, 755

Chapter 3
Those who should come

[682]–1. Those who should assemble in a general congregation are not all the subjects under obedience to the Society, nor even the approved scholastics, but the professed [A], and some coadjutors if it seems opportune in our Lord to summon them; and even from among all these, those who can come conveniently.[a] Thus it is clear that those who are physically ill are not included, nor those who are in places very distant, for example, in the Indies, nor those who have in their hands some undertakings of grave importance which cannot be omitted without great inconvenience. This matter will be left to the

a) 692

---

2 The Spanish is *perpetuo*, "perpetual" in the meaning which is common in legal documents, "permanent" or "lasting indefinitely."

judgment of the superior general if he calls the congregation, or of those who attend the congregation in a province[1] to elect those who are to go.

To give some method[2] of procedure, if the congregation is taking place for the election of a general or to treat matters pertaining to him, three will come from each province: the provincial [B] and two others chosen by the other participants in the provincial congregation, which will be held for this purpose before the general congregation. In the provincial congregation the following will assemble and have a right to vote: all the professed who can come, the superiors of the houses, the rectors *b) 692* of colleges, and the procurators,[b] or those whom they send in their place.

When the congregation is held to deal with other matters, with the general's consent the provincial may select the two members of his province without convoking a chapter. It will be the general's part to determine according to the circumstances whether such a provincial chapter is to be held for the election of the two, or whether the provincial is to select them without a chapter as appears good to him in the Lord.

Those who remain behind will rely on these three and on the general chapter [C]. If in addition to the aforementioned three some individuals are named by the general, or if the provincial thinks that they ought to come, their standing will be the same as that of the others. But if the provincial names some in addition to the three, he should not name more than two, so that altogether they are five at the most.

c) 699 [683]—*A. When he who holds the principal charge of the Society summons the congregation, he will judge whether some of the professed of three vows or some coadjutors ought to come, that he may hold discussions with them about the matters which are to be treated in the congregation.[c] For it seems that at times this could be expedient, especially if the rectors of the colleges come, and the procurators of the colleges, and other officials, all of whom will have much information about what pertains to their offices. Moreover, these officials could hold active and*

---

1 When a general congregation is convoked, in each province a provincial congregation is held to prepare for it.
2 As ordinarily happens in all deliberative bodies, general congregations have often found it expedient to decree changes in regard to the personnel and the manner of conducting business in both the general and provincial congregations. Such decrees have been gathered into two treatises entitled "Formula Congregationis Generalis" and "Formula Congregationis Provincialis," which have been often revised. See Coemans, *Introductio*, nos. 122-124.

likewise passive voice, but not the capacity to preside over the professed of four vows. If the congregation is held for the election of a general, no one who is not professed of four vows will have active or passive voice in that election.[d]   d) 511, 699

[684]—*B. The statement means that the provincial will come if he is able. If he is unable, he will send in his place another whom he judges the most fit among three whom the participants in the chapter elect.*

[685]—*C. Although those who remain behind may not send their vote in writing, if the subject matter was communicated to them they may express their opinion in writing; and those who go will state that opinion in the general congregation.*

[686]—2. Of the professed who take part in the chapter, each one will have only one vote and the general two; but if the number of votes is equal, the provincial's will be preferred over the others. If there is a tie among the provincials, the side which is favored by the general (or if he is no longer alive, by his vicar) will prevail. For, just as the divine aid is more necessary to them because of the charge they hold, so it is to be hoped that God our Lord will give that grace to them more copiously that they may perceive and state what is conducive to His service.

Chapter 4
Who should convoke a general congregation

[687]—1. When the Society must convene to elect a superior general after God our Lord has summoned to Himself him who had held that charge, the duty of informing the other members will fall upon one of the professed whom the general before his death will have designated as his vicar in that respect [A]. Ordinarily this professed will be one of those who assist the general and dwell in or very near his residence. His office will be to summon the Society for a specified place and date.

[688]—*A. If no one of the professed is present with the general and he designates one of those nearby, the same arrangement*

holds for him. But if the general is forestalled from that act by death or equivalent illness and does not name a vicar, the professed who are near him (even though they do not live in the same place as he but in its environs) will elect a vicar by a majority of votes. Whether the general has named someone absent but nearby or whether he has named no one, in either case he who holds the principal charge in the house where the general dies or, in case he dies outside a house of the Society, he who holds it in the nearest house, will immediately send word informing the neighboring professed that they should come, either to appoint a vicar, as was stated, or to recognize him who clearly was named. This vicar should hold the place of the general until a new one is elected.

[689]—2. When the congregation is not held for the election of a general, the general himself is the one who should convoke it in the other cases[a] except those which will be described in Part IX [782]. As has been stated [677], he will not summon the Society many times, but when necessity compels.[b] However, when the chapter convenes for the election of a general, after choosing him it could take up the other matters which require more consideration than that of the general and those who accompany him.

a) 681, 755

b) 677, 681, 722

Chapter 5
The place, time, and manner of assembling

[690]—1. The place to which the Society will be summoned for the election of a general should ordinarily be, it seems, the curia of the sovereign pontiff, where the general more commonly resides,[a] unless the members agree to meet in another place more convenient for all of them. Such a place could be some central location amid the diverse regions where the Society is, or another which they think more suitable. If he who convokes the congregation is the general and he summons it for the other cases,[b] it will be his part to select and designate the place which he thinks in our Lord to be more expedient.

a) 668

b) 681, 689, 755

[691]—2. When the business is the election of a general, the period which will be allowed for assembling will be five or six

months from the date of the letters of notification; and this period may be prolonged according to necessity. When the members must convene for the other cases,^c the superior general will designate the time which seems good to him.

    c) 681, 689, 755

[**692**]—3. The manner of assembling will be this. He who has the task should by various means immediately inform the provincials and other individual professed if some should be called, while stating, to the extent he thinks sufficient, the cause, the place, and the time of the congregation; and that in all regions Masses and prayers should be offered for a happy election.^d Then the provincials, if they alone do not have to do the choosing, will have the task of informing the professed who are in their province and the rectors and local superiors who will be able to come.^e When those able to do so conveniently have assembled in a provincial chapter, they will choose by a majority of votes, with the provincial having two votes, those who will have to go to the general congregation. These delegates will be the persons who are most fit to participate in the congregation and who will cause less harm through their absence.^f As soon as they can they will depart for the designated place, while leaving behind a vicar and the necessary arrangements in their own provinces.

    d) 693, 711

    e) 682

    f) 682

[**693**]—4. The superiors should also order that all those under obedience to the Society should offer prayers daily, be mindful in their Masses to commend earnestly to God our Lord those who are going to the congregation, and beg that, whatever matters will be treated in it, all may turn out as is expedient for His greater service, praise, and glory.^{g 1}

    g) 692, 711

Chapter 6
The manner of reaching a decision
in the election of a general

[**694**]—1. When the congregation summoned to elect a new general after the death of the predecessor has convened, he who has been given the function of vicar should address all its mem-

---

1 "Greater service, praise, and glory": This is a typical Ignatian "triplet" in which each word illuminates and colors the other two. In this instance the triplet gives Ignatius' highest criterion of choice, which manifestly springs from his world view and epitomizes it (see fn. 3 on [622] above, and also p. 8 in ch. 1).

bers, four days before the election of the new general. He should exhort them to do what is conducive to the greater service of God and the good government of the Society. In addition to this day, they will have another period of three days to commend themselves to God and make better investigations as to who from the whole Society could be most suitable for that office. They will seek enlightenment from those able to give good information but will not make their decision until they have entered the place of the election and been locked within it.

[**695**]—2. During this period each one will be obliged under pain of excommunication *latae sententiae* to manifest to the vicar, or to one of those professed the longest who will inform the vicar, if he knows that someone has sought this office or is directly or indirectly seeking it, either by trying to get it or by giving indications in that direction. One who is convicted of this charge should be deprived of active and passive voice and thus disqualified to elect and to be elected; and he should not be admitted to a congregation either on this occasion or any other[a] [A].

a) 817

[**696**]—*A. For one charged with such ambition to be deprived of his right to vote and to be disqualified, it would be necessary for him to have been clearly convicted through attestations, or that the truth of the alleged offense has become sufficiently evident by any way that was possible. However, when the indications beget highly probable suspicion but not certain proof, the person will not be fit for the election; and through the seeking of some occasion he is to be removed from it, but he will not be deprived of the right to vote as being a disqualified person, nor ought the suspicion to be made public; and much less ought it to be made public if it is not found probable. For in such a case damage ought in no wise to be done to one who was unjustly charged; and he will not cease to be in the congregation and to have voice like the rest.*

The one who must judge this case will be the vicar, after he has sought aid from three others of those professed the longest. The condemnation requires a vote of at least three. Those who vote inconsistently with their opinion will by that very fact incur excommunication.

If the charge is brought against the vicar himself or one of those professed the longest, there will be four judges, always drawn from those who made the profession earliest, and with the one charged excluded. Any one of these to whose ears such a disgrace has come should call the others to investigate it.

[697]–3. On the day of the election, which will be that following these three, someone should celebrate the Mass of the Holy Spirit. All will attend it and receive Communion during it.

[698]–4. Later at the sound of the bell those who have the right of voting should be summoned [B] to the place where they are to assemble. One of them should deliver a sermon in which he exhorts them, in a general manner without designating any individual, to choose as superior one likely to bring about greater service to God. After all together have recited the hymn *Veni Creator Spiritus,* they should be locked within the place of the congregation by one of the superiors or rectors or some other member of the Society to whom this charge is given in the house where the congregation is held. They are enclosed in such a manner that they may not leave nor have any other food except bread and water given to them until they have elected a general.[1]

[699]–B. *Those who have the right to vote will be only the professed of four vows, as has been said [511, 683], since there is question of the election of the general. However, to obtain more information others may be required to come, if it is necessary, and to discuss other matters after the general has been chosen. In these matters the rectors and local superiors who are summoned, whether professed of three vows or formed coadjutors, will have the right to vote, as was stated above [683].*

[700]–5. If all by a common inspiration should choose someone without waiting for the methodical voting, let that one be the superior general. For the Holy Spirit, who has moved them to such an election, supplies for all methods and arrangements.

[701]–6. When the election does not take place in that manner, the following procedure should be followed. First, each one should pray privately and, without speaking with anyone else [C], by means of the information he has he will come to his decision in the presence of his Creator and Lord. Then he will write on a paper the name of the person whom he chooses for superior general, and he should sign the paper with his name. For this there should be given a period of one hour at most.

---

1 Many details in this ch. 6 seem to be influenced by the Constitutions of the Dominicans, which also prescribed before the election of the master general a Mass of the Holy Spirit, an exhortation, fasting by the electors, and their enclosure in one room. See the texts in *Cons*MHSJ, II, ccix-ccxiii.

Thereupon all resume their places and are seated. The vicar, accompanied by a secretary who should be chosen for this purpose from among the professed and by another who is to lend assistance [D], arises and affirms that he does not desire to admit or to exclude anyone unjustly. He should give to all general absolution from all censures, to ensure the result of the canonical election [E]. After the grace of the Holy Spirit has been invoked, he should go with his companions to a table placed in the center. The three request their votes from one another; and each one, before handing it over, pronounces an oath that he is naming the man whom he judges in our Lord most fit for the office [F]. They should keep all the votes in the hands of the secretary. Then they should request each one of the members of the congregation to hand in his vote by himself and in the sight of all, likewise written and preceded by the same oath.

Afterwards in the presence of all the secretary should read the votes aloud, naming only the one picked up. The one number should be compared with the other, and the person who is found to have more than half of all the votes should be the superior general. And thus he who first named him, or the vicar, should ask the others if they consent to him whom the greater part elected; and no matter how they may reply,[2] he will formulate the decree of election by saying:

"In the name of the Father and of the Son and of the Holy Spirit. I, N, in my own name and the name of all those who have the same opinion, choose N as superior general of the Society of Jesus." This done, all should immediately step forward to pay a reverence to him. While kneeling on both knees they should kiss his hand [G]. The one elected should not have the right to refuse either the election or the reverence, being mindful in whose name he ought to accept it. Afterwards, all together should recite the *Te Deum Laudamus.*

[702]—C. *In the locked room all will keep silence until the general is elected, in such a manner that one does not speak with another about anything pertaining to the election, unless it is something which he thinks necessary and he speaks in the presence of all.*

[703]—D. *During the period of four days and before beginning their stay in the locked room, all the professed who are in the*

2 This prescription is recommended by many ancient canonists and Polanco could have

place of the congregation will meet and choose a secretary and
an assistant. Each professed gives in writing the name of the
one he chooses. The vicar with the two who have been professed the longest time will publicly examine who has received
more votes. When there is a tie, the three will be able to vote;
and he who receives the vote of two of them will be the secretary
and the assistant.

[704]—E. He absolves from all censures except those incurred
through defects concerning this election.

[705]—F. The formula of the oath may be this: "With all
reverence, I call upon Jesus Christ, who is the Eternal Wisdom,
to witness that I, N, choose and name as superior general of
the Society of Jesus him whom I think to be most fit to bear
this burden." In this way his oath covers two matters: first, the
fact that he is placing his name as the person making the choice;
and second, the fact that he places as the person chosen the
name of him whom he thinks most fit. After this he will hand
in his written vote. Each one should have this formula of oath
written on the outside of the same paper which contains his
vote; and when he hands the vote to the three designated persons, he should recite the formula in a loud voice. The place
where each one will deposit his vote, singly and in the presence
of the others, will be the table in the center where the vicar
and his assistants are.

[706]—G. The vicar and his assistants will begin, or, if one of
them was elected, the other two; and the rest will follow.

[707]—7. If no one receives more than half of the votes,
another way should be taken, that of arbitration. From among all
those present three or five should be chosen as electors by a
majority vote [H]; and whoever receives the majority of votes
from these three or five should be the superior general. His
election should be proclaimed, the reverence should be paid to
him, and thanks should be given to God our Lord, as is stated
above [701].

[708]—H. The method of choosing these electors will be this.
Each one should write the names of those whom he thinks best;

read it in the *Summa Sylvestrina*, s.v. "electio," III, q. 12. The text of a similar statement
in the *Constitutions* of the Carmelites is in *Cons*MHSJ, II, 234, fn. 4.

and those who receive the most votes will be the electors. When each one is writing the name of those whom he chooses as electors and has completed this writing, all will take an oath, likewise in writing, according to this formula: "I call upon Jesus Christ, who is the Eternal Wisdom, to witness that I, N, choose and name as superior general of the Society of Jesus him whom the electors appointed for this function will have chosen and named."

[709]—8. After the proclamation no one may change his vote or, once the election has been completed, attempt to have a new one. What has been stated should be observed by everyone who does not desire to be held as a schismatic and destroyer of the Society, and to incur the penalty of excommunication *latae sententiae* and other grave censures at the discretion of the Society [I], whose interests require complete unity and conformity to the glory of God our Lord.[b]

b) 273, 664

[710]—*I. The vicar after getting the opinion of the majority, or he who is elected superior general, will have the power to decree the censures which will seem expedient in our Lord.*

Chapter 7
The manner of reaching a decision
about matters other than
the election of the general

[711]—1. When the agenda of the congregation pertain not to the election of a general but to other important matters concerning the state of the Society, the locked enclosure will not be necessary, although an effort should be made to finish as soon as possible everything requiring discussion. But first of all, since the light to perceive what can best be decided upon must come down from the First and Supreme Wisdom, Masses and prayer will be offered in the place where the congregation is held as well as in the other regions of the Society. This should be done throughout the time the congregation lasts and the matters which should be settled within that time are being

discussed, to obtain grace to conclude them in a manner conducive to greater glory to God our Lord.ᵃ

a) 692, 693

[712]—2. Later they will meet and in one or several sessions the superior general first, and after him the provincials, rectors, and other persons summoned to the congregation, will in the presence of all propose the matters which they think should be discussed, giving brief explanations of their opinions. After each one has seriously pondered his opinion and commended it to God our Lord, he ought to put it in writing [A]. And after he has spoken it he may place the written paper in the center [B] that those who desire to see it may state what they think in the following session.

[713]—A. *Those who take the place of an absent provincial will speak in the same order as he would. However, the order to be followed will be that the first to speak will be the one longest professed, from whatever province, who is a provincial or comes in the place of a provincial. After him all the rest from his province will speak in the order of seniority from profession or of vows as a spiritual coadjutor. Then the one among the other provincials who is the longest professed will speak, and with him those from his province. After them, if there are others who are not under any provincial or who were called extraordinarily, they too will speak in the order of seniority.*[1]

[714]—B. *He will place his written copy upon the table which will be placed in the center. The secretary will have the task of seeing to it that copies are made, if this is necessary, or that each one brings previously made copies of his explanations, that they may be read by those who will express their opinion about them.*

[715]—3. When the questions have been discussed from one side and the other during one or more sessions, if a solution in favor of one view does not become manifest and win agreement from all or nearly all, by means of a majority vote four definitors ought to be chosen from among those who are present and have the right of voting in the congregation. These (to whose arbitration the rest should submit) will meet as many times as

1 Here text B had these words: "To facilitate the speaking, it would be good for them to be seated in the same order which was mentioned; and the secretary of the superior or the vicar general will take care of this, following the book of the professed and coadjutors." General Congregation I suppressed these words because it had changed the order of seating. See *ConsMHSJ*, II, 652, and *InstSJ*, II, 166.

necessary with the superior general and settle all the matters which require handling. If they fail to come to a common opinion, the side to which the majority inclines will prevail and the whole congregation will accept it as from the hand of God our Lord.

[716]—4. If the superior general should not find himself disposed to preside over all these matters, he could put someone else in his place. In this way the matters will be settled point by point according to the opinion of the majority, and the decision will be written and read in the whole congregation. If anyone still thinks it wise to express his opinion, he may do so; but in the end he should defer to what the general and definitors decide.

[717]—5. After the problem which caused the difficulty has been reconsidered and resolved in the aforementioned manner, the secretary will write the final decision in the book provided for this purpose and afterwards it will be promulgated [C].

[718]—C. *The promulgation will take place before the whole house and later throughout the houses and colleges. This refers to the ordinations or statutes which were enacted to be observed in all regions. For what pertains to one sole college or house or person need not be promulgated in other regions, even if the matters are not secret. But if they are secret, much more ought the divulgation to be forbidden, under penalty of grave censures according to the discretion of the superior general.*

The decrees passed in the congregation remain in force unless they are revoked in another general congregation, even if God our Lord relieves of office the superior general under whom they were enacted.

Part IX
The Society's head,
and the government
descending from him

Chapter 1
The need of a superior general
and his lifelong term of office

[719]—In all well-organized communities or congregations there must be, besides the persons who take care of the particular goals, one or several whose proper duty is to attend to the universal good. So too in this Society, in addition to those who have charge of its single houses or colleges and of its single provinces where it has those houses or colleges, there must be someone who holds that charge of the entire body of the Society, one whose duty is the good government, preservation, and development of the whole body of the Society;[a] and   a) 789
this person is the superior general. There is a possibility of electing him in either of two ways, namely, for a determined period or for his whole life. But since his experience and practice of government, his knowledge of the individual members [A], and the prestige he has with them [B] are a great aid in performing

this office well, his election will be for life[1] and not for a determined period. Thus too the Society, being universally occupied with important matters in the divine service, will be less disturbed and distracted by general congregations[b] [C].

b) 677, 689

c) 817

[720]—*A. Besides the reasons mentioned in this constitution, there are still others for having one general who is elected for life. One is that thoughts and occasions of ambition, which is the pestilence of such offices,[c] will be banished farther than would be the case if elections had to be held at fixed times.*

Another reason is that it is easier to find one capable person for this charge than many.

Still another reason is the example of the common practice among the most important governmental offices, which are held for life. So it is with the pope and bishops among churchmen and with princes and lords among laymen. Furthermore, the remedy for certain disadvantages which could follow the holding of such a charge for life will be treated below, in Chapter 4 [773-777].

[721]—*B. The superior's prestige will be greater if he is unchangeable than if he is elected for some one or several years: greater with the externs because he will be better known by all, and greater with the members of the Society for the same reason. On the contrary, the knowledge that he must relinquish his office and be equal or inferior to the others, as also his being new in the office, can diminish his prestige.*

[722]—*C. It is certain that congregations of the whole Society will occur less frequently if the superior general holds office for life. For the majority of congregations will be convoked to elect him, and other occasions will be few.*

1 Already in 1539 the early companions unanimously determined that the superior general whom they would elect was to hold office for life (cf. *Cons*MHSJ, I, 13, no. 14; 39, no. 14). General Congregation XXXI in 1965-1966 reaffirmed this prescription of [719]. However, it added clearer provisions for the general's honorable resignation in case he should become seriously and permanently incapacitated.

On Ignatius' terminology of body, head, and members, see fnn. 3 and 4 on [1], **10** on [137], [655, 820, 821], and Note A in the Reference matter below, esp. p. 347.

Chapter 2
The kind of person the superior general should be[1]

[723]—1. In regard to the qualities which are desirable in the superior general [A], the first is that he should be closely united with God our Lord and intimate with Him in prayer and all his actions, that from God, the fountain of all good, the general may so much the better obtain for the whole body of the Society a large share of His gifts and graces, and also great power and efficacy for all the means which will be used for the help of souls.[a]

a) 790, 812, 813

[724]—A. *The six qualities treated in this chapter are the most important, and all the rest are reduced to them. For they include the general's perfection in relation to God; further, what perfects his heart,[2] understanding, and execution; and further still, those qualities of body and those extrinsic goods which help him. Moreover, the importance of these six qualities is indicated by the order in which they are placed.*

[725]—2. The second quality is that he should be a person whose example in the practice of all virtues is a help to the other members of the Society.[b] Charity should be especially resplendent in him, toward all his fellowmen and above all

b) 667, 790

---

1 In this justly famous ch. 2 in which Ignatius sketches [723-735] his ideal of the superior general, he has also left an ideal which all the members of his order can well seek to approach (cf. [726]). Furthermore, he sketched here a "spirituality for superiors." The ideal has long been regarded as a self-portrait made subconsciously by Ignatius himself. This observation occurs already in a passage composed on Feb. 26, 1555, by Gonçalves da Câmara (*FN*, I, 656) which is worthy of citation here: ". . . how often I observed that in his whole manner of proceeding, the Father [i.e., Ignatius] observes with exactitude all the rules of the Exercises. Thus he appears to have planted these rules in his own soul and then to have drawn them from his own interior acts. The same thing can be said of Gerson [i.e., of the *Imitation of Christ*], to such an extent that to converse with the Father seems to be nothing else than to read John Gerson put into practice. I must remember to write down many instances from which this universal statement can be drawn. The same thing is true of the Constitutions, especially of the chapter in which he portrays the general, in whose case he seems to have portrayed his own self" (*Memoriale*, no. 226, in *FN*, I, 659). In the drawing of the portrait, possibly some of the touches arose from Polanco observing Ignatius before the latter approved them. See Codina's conjecture (in *Cons*MHSJ, III, 244, fn. 1) because of the statement in *Cons*MHSJ, I, 294, no. 140. In ch. 64 of the *Regula monachorum* there is a sketch of the ideal of an abbot which is often taken to be St. Benedict's self-portrait. See also the fnn. on [423, 551] above.
2 *Affecto*: the affective faculty and its acts, contrasted with the understanding or intellect (*entendimiento*) as above (see [516] with fn. 1). What perfects the heart is indicated in [725-728].

toward the members of the Society; and genuine humility too should shine forth, that these characteristics may make him highly lovable to God our Lord and to men.

[726]—3. He ought also to be independent of all passions, by his keeping them controlled and mortified, so that in his interior they may not disturb the judgment of his intellect and in his exterior he may be so composed, particularly so self-controlled when speaking, that no one, whether a member of the Society who should regard him as a mirror and model, or an extern, may observe in him any thing or word which does not edify him.

[727]—4. However, he should know how to mingle rectitude and necessary severity with kindness and gentleness to such an extent that he neither allows himself to swerve from what he judges to be more pleasing to God our Lord nor ceases to have proper sympathy for his sons. Thus although they are being *c*) 269, 270, 754   reprimanded or punished,c they will recognize that in what he 791   does he is proceeding rightly in our Lord and with charity, even though it is against their liking according to the lower man.

[728]—5. Magnanimity and fortitude of soul are likewise highly necessary for him to bear the weaknesses of many, to initiate great undertakings in the service of God our Lord, and to persevere in them with constancy when it is called for, without losing courage in the face of the contradictions (even though they come from persons of high rank and power) and without allowing himself to be moved by their entreaties or threats from what reason and the divine service require. He should be superior to all eventualities, without letting himself be exalted by those which succeed or depressed by those which go poorly, being *d*) 134, 414, 582,   altogether ready to receive death, if necessary, for the good of 624   the Society in the service of Jesus Christ, God and our Lord.d

[729]—6. The third quality is that he ought to be endowed with great understanding and judgment, in order that this talent may not fail him either in the speculative or the practical matters which may arise. And although learning is highly necessary for one who will have so many learned men in his charge, still more necessary is prudence along with experience in spiritual and interior matters, that he may be able to discern the various spirits and to give counsel and remedies to so many who will have spiritual necessities.

He also needs discretion in exterior matters and a manner of handling such diverse affairs as well as of conversing with such various persons from within and without the Society.ᵉ   *e)* 414, 735

[730]—7. The fourth quality, one highly necessary for the execution of business, is that he should be vigilant and solicitous to undertake enterprises as well as energetic in carrying them through to their completion and perfection, rather than careless and remiss in such a way that he leaves them begun but not finished.

[731]—8. The fifth quality has reference to the body. In regard to health, appearance, and age, on the one hand account should be taken of propriety and prestige, and on the other hand of the physical energies which his charge requires [B], that in it he may be able to fulfill his office to the glory of God our Lord.

[732]—*B. Thus it seems that he ought to be neither very old, since such a one is generally not fit for the labors and cares of such a charge, nor very young, since a young man generally lacks the proper prestige and experience.*

[733]—9. The sixth quality pertains to extrinsic endowments [C]. Among these, preference ought to be given to those which help more toward edification and the service of God in such a charge. Examples are generally found in reputation, high esteem, and whatever else aids toward prestige with those within and without.ᶠ   *f)* 161, 667

[734]—*C. Nobility, wealth which was possessed in the world, reputation, and the like, are extrinsic endowments. Other things being equal, these are worthy of some consideration; but even if they are lacking, there are other things more important which could suffice for election.*

[735]—10. Finally, he ought to be one of those who are most outstanding in every virtue, most deserving in the Society, and known as such for a considerable time. If any of the aforementioned qualities should be wanting, there should at least be no lack of great probity and of love for the Society, nor of good judgment accompanied by sound learning. For in regard to other things, the aids which he will have (and which will be treated below [789-808]) could through God's help and favor supply to a great extent for many deficiencies.

Chapter 3
The superior general's authority
over the Society and his functions

a) 666, 820

[736]—1. It is judged altogether proper for the good government of the Society that the superior general should have complete authority over it, in order to build it up.[a] [1] This authority (from which the general's functions also become manifest) is that described below.

First of all, the superior general will have the power to admit, personally and through others, those whom he thinks suitable for the Institute of the Society into the houses and colleges or anywhere else. He may admit them thus to probation[b] as well as to profession [A] and to membership as formed coadjutors and approved scholastics.[c] Similarly, he will have power to permit them to depart and to dismiss them[d] [B].

b) 138

c) 512, 516, 522, 523

d) 206

[737]—A. *When he admits one or several to profession through a third party, he should first receive information about them individually and be satisfied about their qualifications; or he should give a special commission to someone in whom he has confidence as in himself to admit those judged fit,[e] in accordance with what was said in Part V [513, 517].*

e) 512, 513, 517, 522, 523

[738]—B. *This is in conformity with what was stated about dismissing, in Part II [206].*

[739]—2. He will also have authority to send those whom he decides upon to studies, at the place which he thinks proper; and likewise to recall them before or after they have finished their studies, and to change them from one place to another, as he judges to be more expedient in our Lord for their personal good and for the universal good of the Society.[f]

f) 124, 417

1 Text *a* of 1547-1550 had here the Latin words "ad aedificationem et non ad destructionem," an implicit citation from 1 Cor. 10:8 and 13:10. It was abbreviated in text B but the sense remains the same. In text *a* the citation was followed by a clause about the Society's authority over the general—a topic treated in chs. 4 and 5 below [766-788]. This indicates that by "edification" here Ignatius intends not merely the ordinary spiritual meaning of the word but also administration, upbuilding. He desired the general to have all possible power for constructive purposes and yet to have that power balanced by the higher authority and provident care which the whole Society has over him and exercises ordinarily through the four general assistants ([766, 767, 779]). See also *Cons-MHSJ*, II, 240, fn. 2, and 669, fn. 1.

[740]–3. He will have the entire superintendence and government of the colleges in regard to the students, teachers, and officials.[g] Among these the principal person is the rector, whom the general may appoint and remove, while giving him the authority which he thinks is expedient in our Lord.[h] Through these rectors he will exercise the administration with respect to the material and temporal affairs of the colleges for the benefit of the students, as is stated in the bull[i] [*Exposcit debitum*, (8)].

g) 326, 327, 419, 420

h) 326, 421, 490, 757, 759

i) 326, 327, 424

[741]–4. He will require them to give an account of their office in the manner which seems best to him[j] [C]. What holds true of the colleges is also valid for the universities which are in the Society's charge, namely, that the direction of the matters which concern life and doctrine will be vested in the superior general; and he will exercise it through the ministers whom he appoints, in conformity with the Constitutions and the like.

j) 326, 421, 759

[742]–C. *Sometimes they will have to give this account to him, sometimes to the provincial superior, sometimes to someone else who has an authoritative commission to receive it.*

[743]–5. In the superior general is vested all the authority to make contracts[2] for the purchase or sale of any movable temporal goods whatsoever of the colleges and houses of the Society, and to demand or repay any annual taxes whatsoever on their immovable goods, for the utility and benefit of the same colleges, with the right of being able to free himself from the debt by restoring the money which was given. However, without a general congregation of the Society he may not alienate or completely suppress the Society's colleges or houses which are already established.[k]

k) 322, 420, 441, 680, 762, 763

[744]–6. The general will also have the power to dispose of anything which has been left in undetermined fashion to the disposition of the Society, whether it consists of immovable goods such as some house or property which the one who left it did not apply to or incorporate into some determined house or college, or of movable goods such as money or crops or anything else. The general may sell, or retain, or apply what he thinks wise to one place or another, as he perceives to be conducive to greater glory to God our Lord.

---

2 The material in [743-745] was added by General Congregation I. It had been approved by Ignatius but not yet inserted in text B (*Cons*MHSJ, II, 672, fn. 5).

[745]–7. The provincial superiors, the local superiors, the rectors, and the general's other commissioners will have the part of this authority which the general communicates to them. They will not be obliged to assemble their associates to perform acts of this nature collectively.

[746]–8. Just as it pertains to the general to see to it that the Constitutions of the Society are observed in all places,[l] so too he will have power to grant dispensations in particular cases which require such dispensation, while he takes account of the persons, places, times, and other circumstances [D]. He will use this power with the discretion which the Eternal Light gives him, meanwhile keeping his attention fixed on the purpose of the Constitutions,[m] which is the greater divine service and the good of those who live in this Institute. He may use this power in what pertains to the experiences of those who are in probation [E], as also in other matters where such dispensation is judged to be the intention of those who enacted the Constitutions, for the glory of God our Lord.

[747]–D. *The general ought to exercise this authority personally. He will also be able to exercise it through someone else in urgent cases in which delay is impossible without notable inconvenience, or in which he has given a special commission to someone in whom he has confidence as in himself, especially in far distant places such as the Indies.[n] It should be understood, too, that he may dispense where, in view of the particular circumstances, he judges in our Lord that such dispensation is within the purpose of the Constitutions, and not in any other manner.*

[748]–E. *It will be within the general's power to have all the experiences undergone, and even more than the six mentioned in the Examen [64-71], or to have one or several of them omitted or replaced by others, when in some particular case that which is generally fitting is now inexpedient, for example, the hospital, or pilgrimage, or lecturing, or one of the other experiences.[o]*

[749]–9. The same general will also have complete authority over the missions,[p] but in no case may he obstruct missions of the Apostolic See, as is stated in Part VII [618]. From among those who are under his obedience he may send all, professed or not professed, to any regions of the world [F], for the time

l) 424, 547, 602, 790, 826

m) 136

n) 425

o) 64, 71

p) 618-621, 666

which seems good to him, whether it is definite or indefinite, in order to exercise any of the means which the Society uses to aid its fellowmen. Similarly, he may recall those sent [G], acting in everything as he judges to be conducive to the greater glory to God our Lord.

Knowing the talent of those who are under his obedience, he should distribute the offices of preachers, lecturers, confessors [H], and the like, by assigning each subject to the office which he judges in our Lord to be more expedient for the divine service and the good of souls.

[750]—F. *Thus he may send them, for example, among the faithful in the Indies and among the unbelievers where there are Christian inhabitants. In some cases or urgent necessities he may even send them where there are no Christians; but he should do this only after much previous deliberation.*q   q) 621

[751]—G. *He may recall not only those sent by his predecessor or himself but also those whom the sovereign pontiff sent without determining the length of their stay.*r *This is granted in the bull   r) 615, 626 of favors which was issued by our Holy Father Paul III in 1549.*[3]

[752]—H. *The general may make this distribution through his ministers, whether they are local superiors or not, as will be the case also with many things mentioned or still to be mentioned.*

[753]—10. The general will also have the task of using the privileges granted by the Apostolic See, and to communicate to each subject under his obedience the part of those privileges which he judges will be well placed in him for the divine service, the end which is sought. The general's part will also be to recall and restrict these privileges, while keeping in view the same norm of greater service to God.s   s) 666

[754]—11. He will also have the task of giving correction and imposing the penances which he judges suitable for any faults whatsoever, with attention given to the persons and other circumstances. The consideration of these is entrusted to his prudent   t) 269, 270, 727, charity, which he will use for the glory of God our Lord.t   791

[755]—12. It is his task to summon the Society to a general congregation when one must be convoked for other matters

---

3 *Licet debitum,* in ConsMHSJ, I, 358.

u) 681, 689, 690, 691

v) 716

than the election of the general; and to order the convocation of a provincial congregation^u when he judges one expedient; and to direct those who attend^v and to dismiss them at his time when the agenda have been concluded.

w) 771, 772, 786, 817, 818

[756]—13. Without his permission and approval, no one may accept any dignity outside the Society; nor will he give permission or approval if the command of the Apostolic See does not compel him.^w

x) 326, 421, 490, 740

y) 778

z) 740

[757]—14. Furthermore, he himself (as has been said [740, 741]), should appoint those whom he judges best fitted for the purpose as the rectors of colleges and universities, and similarly as the local superiors of the houses.^x He will also appoint the provincials,^y commonly for three years, although he may shorten or lengthen this period when he thinks that this will be conducive to greater glory of God our Lord [I]. He will give to them the power which he judges wise.^z

[758]—*I. With those who perform their office well and are able to satisfy him in it, nothing is lost by the limitation of three years, since the period can be shortened or lengthened. With those who do not show themselves apt, something is gained by relieving them without humiliation after their term has run its course, unless the general should think it expedient for the sake of the universal good to relieve such a one before that time.*

a) 326, 421, 741

b) 490
c) 421, 490, 740

[759]—15. Likewise, he may revoke their authority, and extend it or restrict it, and require from them an account of their administration.^a Furthermore, if he communicates his own authority to the provincial for the appointment of local superiors and rectors,^b it will remain his part to confirm or remove them.^c

d) 329, 806-808
e) 800, 801

[760]—16. He should appoint the other officials necessary for the government of the Society, such as the procurator general^d and the secretary of the Society^e [K]. He should give them the power which he judges in our Lord to be expedient according to the nature of the business and the persons.

[761]—*K. Although in regard to these choices and other important and doubtful matters he may take counsel from others whose opinion he esteems in the Lord, ultimately the power to decide will belong to him.*

[762]—17. He may, without waiting for a general congregation, accept houses, colleges, and universities for the Society;[f] and admit to the rank of founders with the privileges mentioned in Part IV [309-319] those who, he judges in our Lord, should be so admitted; and provide for lecturers, priests, and other such needs which arise. He should endeavor to have all this done with such conditions that the Society perceives it to be an advantage for the end of the divine service which it pursues, and not a detriment.[g] But if experience should reveal that the Society is burdened rather than helped **and** the general does not find a remedy, in the next congregation of the Society there could be a discussion as to whether such a house, college, or university with those burdens should be given up or retained.[h]

f) 308, 320

g) 321, 325, 441, 442

h) 321

[763]—18. To transfer or suppress houses or colleges already founded,[i] or to convert the fixed revenue from those institutions to the use of the professed Society,[j] will not be within the general's power, as was stated in Part IV [322, 419].

i) 322, 420, 441, 680

j) 5, 326, 419, 557, 774, 816

[764]—19. He should know the consciences, as far as possible, of those whom he has in his charge,[k] especially of the provincial superiors and others to whom he entrusts charges of importance.

k) 93-97, 551

[765]—20. To speak in general, he may command in virtue of obedience all the members in regard to everything conducive to the end which the Society seeks, the perfection and aid of its fellowmen unto glory[4] to God.[l] And although he communicates his authority to other superiors or visitors or commissioners, he may approve or revoke what they did and regulate everything according to what seems good to him. At all times he should be obeyed and reverenced as the one who holds the place of Christ our Lord.[m]

l) 602

m) 84, 85, 284, 286, 342, 424, 547, 551, 552, 618, 619, 627, 661

---

4 As a study of the functioning of Ignatius' mind, notice the singular "end," and see fnn. 11 on [3], 2 on [603], and 1 on [693] above.

Chapter 4
The authority or provident care
which the Society should exercise
in regard to the superior general

[766]—1. The authority or provident care[1] which the Society will have in regard to the general, always for the sake of the universal good and greater edification, will lie in six concerns which can help toward glory to God our Lord [A].

[767]—A. *The Society will exercise this authority through the assistants, who will be described later [779].*

[768]—2. The first concern has reference to external things such as clothes, food, and any expenditures touching upon the general's person. In this area the Society will be able to make extensions or restrictions in accordance with what it judges to be fitting for the general and the Society and to be conducive to greater service to God.[a] The general in turn ought to be content with what is provided.

a) 779

[769]—3. The second concern pertains to the care of his body, that he may not go beyond measure in labors or excessive severity.[b] The superior in turn will consent to be controlled and will be satisfied with what the Society orders.

b) 779

[770]—4. The third concern pertains to his soul in relation to his person and office, since even in perfect men there could be some need of this concern. The Society should have with the superior general (and the same practice can be employed with subjects) some person who has the following obligation. After he has had recourse to God in prayer and has asked light from His Divine Goodness, if he judges it right he should, with proper modesty and humility, admonish the general about anything in him which he thinks will be more conducive to greater service and glory to God.[c] This person could be the

c) 779

---

1 *Providencia:* in Ignatius' usage this word sometimes indicates the Church's guidance or provident care of her members ([22, 167]) and sometimes, as here in [766], the similar care of the Society for its general. For Ignatius' reasons for treating this topic, see his text in *Cons*MHSJ, I, 385.

general's confessor or someone else appointed by the Society who seems suitable for this purpose.

[771]—5. The fourth concern is this. If pressure should be exerted upon the general, although it is not obliging him under sin, to accept some dignity which will require him to relinquish his office [B], he may not accept the dignity without the consent of the Society. The Society, however, keeping in view what is expedient for greater service and glory to God our Lord, will never consent unless the command of the Apostolic See compels it.[d]

d) 756, 786, 788, 817, 818

[772]—*B. This case would occur if some secular ruler should try to bring about the acceptance of some dignity and the pope should order it, but not absolutely in such a manner that he manifests his intention to oblige acceptance of the charge. For in such cases, where the obligation ceases, the general should not and may not accept the dignity without the approval of the Society; and the Society should not and may not approve if the pope does not compel it by a precept obliging under sin.*

[773]—6. The fifth concern pertains to this case. If the general through illness or advanced age should be highly careless or remiss in the important matters of his office, without hope of his improvement in this situation and with the result that the common good suffers notably, a coadjutor or vicar should be chosen who is to perform the office of the general. This vicar may be chosen by the general himself and approved by the provincial superiors; or these provincials, after each of them has learned through letters the opinion of two local superiors or rectors of his province, may by a majority of votes choose the vicar, that he may govern the Society with the authority which the general thinks it proper to give him, or which the Society thinks proper if it chooses him.[e]

e) 786, 787

[774]—7. The sixth concern refers to some cases (and there is confidence in the Divine Goodness that through His grace they will never occur) in which actual mortal sins are present, namely: sexual intercourse, infliction of a wound [C], application of the fixed revenues of the colleges to his own expenses or to making donations to someone outside the Society [D], or alienation of some immovable goods of the houses or colleges, or his holding false doctrine. In such a case, when the evidence is altogether sufficient [E], the Society can and should depose him

from his office and, if it is necessary, dismiss him from the Society,[2] doing in everything what is judged to be conducive to greater glory to God and the universal good of the Society.[f]

f) 782

[775]—C. *An example would be his wounding by means of some kind of arms, or by a knife or instrument with which a notable lesion can be inflicted.*

[776]—D. *It is especially intended to prevent him from making gifts to relatives or those who are intimately connected with him according to the world; and the door is not closed to his taking care that alms should be given,[3] or what is fitting, to one to whom the general thinks that such a gift ought to be made for the glory of God our Lord.*

[777]—E. *Since those who hold a responsibility, especially so universal a responsibility, can be calumniated by many persons for various reasons, much attention should be bestowed that the proofs of the defects mentioned may be as efficacious as is morally possible.*

Chapter 5
The Society's manner of proceeding in what pertains to the general

a) 757

[778]—1. First of all, the provincial superiors whom the general appoints with his own hand[a] should be obliged in the sight of God our Lord to consider and to do what they ought to do for the universal good of the Society in regard to what has been said which refers to the general, according to what they think in our Lord.

b) 768

[779]—2. Secondly, in regard to what pertains to his expenses, the care of his person, and other matters of small importance,[b]

---

2 Such possible offenses were foreseen already in the "Constitutions of 1541" (*Cons*MHSJ, I, 40, nos. 20, 21) and mentioned in the bull *Licet debitum,* [2], of 1549 (*ibid.,* I, 358).
3 This prescription is especially noteworthy amid the nepotism so characteristic of the

there is no need of a congregation. But the Society should depute four assistants, persons of discretion and zeal for the good of the Society, who should remain close to the general[c] [A]. They should be under obligation in the sight of their Creator and Lord to say and to do everything that they think to be for greater glory to God in regard to the first three concerns mentioned in the preceding chapter [768-771].   c) 767, 805

[780]—A. *They should be professed fathers, if this is conveniently possible. If at some time these assistants or some one of them should go away from the general, after being sent to one region or another to return soon, it will not be necessary to put others in their places. If they must be detained long, replacements should be appointed. But the superior general ought not to send them far from himself without serious reason or necessity.*

[781]—3. The election of these four persons will be vested in the same persons who elect the superior general when they are in the congregation held for that purpose. If one of the assistants dies or for important reasons must be away from the general for a long time, in the absence of opposition from the provincials of the Society the general will choose another who, with the approbation of all the provincials or the majority of them, will remain in the place of him who is missing.

[782]—4. Thirdly, if one of the sins which suffice to depose the general from office is committed (and may God never permit this),[d] and when the case becomes evident through adequate testimony or the general's own admission,[e] the four assistants should be obliged to give notice of the matter with an oath to which are attached their signatures, or the signatures of three of them, and to summon the Society to a congregation. That is to say, they must summon the provincials and two persons with each of them, and these will be obliged to convene [B]. When the offense is public and commonly known, the provincials ought to come without waiting for the summons of the four assistants, but with some provincials summoning the others. On the first day when they are locked within the place of the congregation and in which the four assistants who convoked the congregation are, and all the rest who came at their summons, the best informed person begins the speaking and   d) 774-776
e) 774, 777

1500's in the Church, and sprang from Ignatius' antipathy to avarice in the Church. See fn. 1 on [553], and also Introduction above, p. 11 in ch. 1.

explains the accusation. After the general has been heard he should leave the room. Then the oldest provincial, with the secretary and another assistant, should conduct the investigation of the case, first, as to whether the sin is established as true and then, if it is, whether it is such that because of it the general ought to be deposed. Thereupon the same provincial should announce the votes; and they will be more than two thirds if they are to be sufficient. If that sufficiency occurs, the election of another general should be taken up immediately; and if it is possible, they should not leave the room before the Society has a superior general. But if the matter cannot be resolved on that day, it should be concluded on the following or first day possible, in the manner stated in Part VIII [694-710].

[783]—B. However, they should keep the matter in its entirety as secret as possible, even in regard to the other members of the Society, until the truth has become apparent. For if what the four assistants were convinced of is not found to be certain, the name of the general should not remain tarnished without reason.

[784]—5. If the defects are found to be such that they require not his deposition but his correction [C], the task of considering what correction is fitting should be given to four persons. When they do not agree but cast equal votes, either a fifth person or three more should be added in order to determine what is expedient in our Lord.

[785]—C. When the defects are not found sufficient for his deposition, other things should be taken up to give the appearance that the congregation was called to discuss them, while the matter pertaining to the general is kept secret. Indeed, as far as possible, it ought never to be divulged. Thus too when the persons are called they ought to be forewarned not to manifest the matter to anyone; and after the case has been clarified this same warning should be seriously repeated to those who know anything about the matter, especially to the provincials. Furthermore, if the decision is to depose the superior general, even then there should be secret discussion with him about his resigning his office, that this can be published and by it his sin and deposition can be concealed.

[786]—6. If the case arises that the superior general becomes unable to govern the Society [D], the matter should be dis-

cussed partly in his presence and partly in his absence, to discern whether a vicar ought to be chosen to hold the entire authority of the superior general, though not the title, for the rest of the former general's life;[f] and if this decision seems good to more than half, it must be carried out. But if this does not seem necessary, there should be an investigation as to whether the Society would do well to provide other ministers in addition to those whom the general already has, that through his being alleviated and aided in this way no deficiency in the government of the Society may be experienced. In this matter too that should be followed which more than half of the participants in the congregation ordain should be followed.

f) 773

If the question happens to be about some dignity ordinarily incompatible with the general's office and if there is not such a command from the sovereign pontiff that its obligation could be under pain of sin, the question should not be brought up for discussion. For it should be held as certain that the general should not and may not consent to accept it[g] [E].

g) 756, 771, 772, 817, 818

[787]—D. *A general would be totally unable if he has lost the use of reason or is so gravely ill with an incurable infirmity that he cannot attend to the affairs of his office and there is no hope that he will be able later. If the infirmity should not be such as to preclude hope of his recovery, a vicar could be appointed by the same general without a general congregation, that this vicar could perform all the general's functions until he recovers. Thereupon the authority previously given will cease.*

[788]—E. *From this it is evident that a congregation need not be summoned to decide this, unless there is a manifest command from the Apostolic See obliging the general or the Society under sin if it is not carried out, as has been stated.*

Chapter 6
Aids to the superior general
for the good performance of his office

[789]—1. The proper function of the general is not to preach, hear confessions, and perform other similar ministries (though as a private person he will see what he can do in these ministries when the occupations proper to his office leave him opportunity, but under no other circumstances). Instead, his office is to govern the whole body of the Society in such a manner that through the divine grace it may be preserved and developed in its well-being and manner of proceeding for glory to God our Lord[a] [A], by employing his authority as is expedient for that end.

a) 719

[790]—A. *He will achieve this kind of government primarily by the influence and example of his life,[b] by his charity and love of the Society in Christ our Lord,[c] by his prayer which is assiduous and full of desires and by his sacrifices, to obtain the grace of the aforementioned preservation and development.[d] On his own part he should hold these means in high esteem and have great confidence in our Lord, since these are the most efficacious means of gaining grace from His Divine Majesty, the Source of what is longed for. Especially should the general do this as necessities occur.*

b) 667, 725, 735
c) 735

d) 424, 723, 812

Next, he will achieve this kind of government by his solicitude to maintain the observance of the Constitutions,[e] by keeping himself frequently informed by the provincials of what is occurring in all the provinces and by writing to the provincials his opinion about the matters which they communicate to him,[f] and by so acting that provision is made where it is proper, either through himself or through the ministers who will be described later.

e) 424, 547, 602, 746, 826

f) 673, 674, 679, 759

[791]—2. When those qualities of his intense spiritual life and great virtues which are treated above in Chapter 2 [725-728] are presupposed, he still has need of good ministers for the more detailed affairs.[g] For although he himself sometimes treats of them directly, he cannot escape the need of lower superiors, who ought to be selected men, to whom he can give much authority and ordinarily refer those particular matters.[h] More generally, his own dealing among these lower superiors

g) 820

h) 206, 207, 423, 795, 796, 820

will be with the provincials, just as the provincials' dealing will
be with the rectors and local superiors, that the proper subordination may be the better preserved.ⁱ But sometimes, in
order to have more information about all things and because of
other cases which commonly occur, the general will deal with
the rectors or local superiors and also with individual persons.
He will endeavor to help them with counsel, reprimand, and
correction, if necessary.ʲ For it pertains to him to supply for
the defects of the lower superiors and, with the divine favor and
aid, to bring toward perfection what has been imperfect in them.

i) 662, 663, 666, 821

j) 269, 270, 727, 754

[792]–3. It will also be helpful in everything for the general
to have near himself the bulls, briefs, and all the concessions
which pertain to the founding and the favors or privileges of
the Society, and a summary of all of them; and likewise a list
of all the houses and colleges of the Society with their revenues;
and another of all the persons who are in each province. This
list should contain not only the professed, the formed coadjutors,
and the approved scholastics, but also those who are in probation; and on it their names and qualities should be stated.ᵏ
He should have this list renewed each year, if this seems expedient. Finally, he should be informed about everything that
he may the better be able to make provision in all things for
the glory of God.

k) 673, 676

[793]–4. What was stated about all the members of the
Society in Part VI [591], to the effect that they should not
occupy themselves in secular affairs even though they are pious,ˡ
applies to the general more than to anyone. He should not
occupy himself in such affairs nor in other affairs not pertaining
to the Society, even though they are pious, in such a way [B]
that time and energies fail him for what is proper to his office,
which requires more than the whole man.ᵐ

l) 591, 592

m) 798

[794]–B. *This means insofar as he will be able to excuse
himself. Ultimately, however, discretion will have to reveal
whether personally or through other members of the Society on
some occasion he ought to undertake the management of some
pious works which do not pertain to the Society, because of the
importance of those works in the service of God our Lord or
because of the persons who urge the undertaking.*

[795]–5. Furthermore, he ought not to occupy himself much
in the execution of the particular ministries pertaining to the

Society which others can do [C]. An example would be the particular care of one house in regard to its temporal support and government. On the contrary, as is stated above [791], he should have his officials in each place, even where he resides; and through them he should at least alleviate and free himself from that burden, even if he does not abandon all concern.

[796]—C. *To organize the procedure which ought to be used, if it has not been what it should, is more properly the general's task, where he resides and also in the other places. But he ought to delegate the execution, as is stated.*

[797]—6. Likewise in each province he should have as provincials men worthy of great confidence, for he knows that the good government of the Society depends in great part upon them and the local superiors.[n] When they are men of this type and he shares his labor with them in the things he can and meanwhile takes care to be kept informed of everything more important, he will have more time left to himself to comprehend the matters of universal import which he alone can handle. He will also have more light to see what is expedient in connection with them, since his mind does not lose a portion of the light it has (as so easily happens) through being much absorbed with particular matters and details in which it becomes oppressed and less fit for matters of universal importance.

n) 791, 820

[798]—7. The superior general needs ministers not only for the more detailed affairs, as was stated [791, 795, 797], but also for those of universal import which are proper to his office, that he may complete them smoothly and well [D].

Therefore he must have someone to aid him by reminders connected with his solicitude to attend to the numerous affairs of his office; and another to help with counsel for organizing those affairs, and still another to carry them out with diligence and effort. For, surely, one man's memory could not suffice to remember so many things; and if it did suffice, his sole understanding would not be enough to think them out and organize them well; and even if it should be sufficient, one man's energies would not be enough to execute them.

[799]—D. *Since he must carry on business with so many persons and deal with matters which are so various and of such great importance, he would carry an unbearable burden if he did not have ministers. Even with great distraction of mind and*

shortening of his life he could not carry that burden well. Thus it becomes evident that all those who occupy important posts of government and give a good account of them have many aids for their task. Thus too the general needs them to perform his office well, promptly, and smoothly.

[800]—8. In regard to the first point, his solicitude to attend to all affairs, the general obviously ought to have one person who ordinarily accompanies him and should be his memory and hands for everything which he must write and handle, and finally for all the affairs of his office [E]. This person should take on the general's own person and imagine that he carries on his own shoulders the general's whole burden (except for his authority).°

o) 760

[801]—E. *The function of this person will be to gather from all the letters and reports the substance and the points which must be referred to the superior and which require that a reply should be given or something should be done. Further, according to the extent of the commission which the general gives him, he can reply to the letters, whether the general must sign them or the secretary himself at the general's mandate. He will show the letters to the general himself or, at his order, to the assistants or to one of them, or to no one, according to what the material treated and the circumstances of the secretary's person require.*

[802]—9. This person ought to be a man of great solicitude and judgment and, if possible, learning; one too who has a pleasant personality and a good manner of dealing with all kinds of persons by word of mouth and by letters. Above all he should be one in whom confidence can be placed and one who loves the Society in our Lord, that the general may be better aided and served by him for the glory of God.

[803]—10. The second aid mentioned was counsel for organizing the affairs of moment which occur. How necessary this aid is to the general can be understood from the multitude of those affairs and from the nature of the human intellect, which is unable to turn toward so many directions with proper attention or to make proper provision for them.

Consequently, it seems that there ought to be, in the place where the superior resides, some persons of prominence in learning and all good qualities, that they may assist him and with special care take charge of attending to the universal affairs of

p) 667, 677   the Society which the general entrusts to them.ᴾ These charges could be divided among them to enable them to penetrate all things better. One, for example, could observe the affairs of the Indies, another those of Spain and Portugal, another those of Germany and France, another those of Italy and Sicily, and so on successively as the Society spreads into more regions.

Each one would offer special prayer and be mindful in his Masses of the region especially entrusted to himself, and he would consider what could there be more helpful toward achieving the objective which the Society is seeking. Furthermore, when something seems highly apropos he could discuss it with the others and after further examination they could represent it to the superior.

Likewise, the aforementioned persons would deal with the matters which the general or the secretary of the Society proposes to them, in order that these affairs may be more thoroughly analyzed and then proposed to the superior [F]. In general, these assistants ought to alleviate and aid him in considering and settling the problems of doctrine and action which require greater thought. And in addition to this and to their being able to make better provision for many things, they could attend to preaching, lecturing, hearing confessions, and other good and pious works which contribute to divine glory and the aid of souls.

[804]—*F. Moreover, the more important matters which must be written, and the instructions for those members who are sent to one region and another, could be discussed with these persons before they are written, and the secretary could show what they think good to the superior. The same procedure could be used in matters of doctrine. This procedure, besides alleviating the general, would give greater authority to what he ordains.*

[805]—11. The number of these assistants will be four for the present, and they will be those mentioned above [779]. Although the matters of importance should be discussed with them, the decision will always belong to the general, after he has heard them.

[806]—12. In regard to the third point, that of the diligent work in carrying out or executing what was ordered in regard to the business necessary to the Society, for example, the official letters or communications about the houses and colleges, the defense of what belongs to them, and generally in regard to all business, the aid of a procurator general of the Society will be

very helpful, or rather, necessary. He should reside in Rome and be a man of prudence, fidelity, a good manner of dealing with others, and all good qualities.q However, he should not be a professed father nor one who dwells in the house of the professed Society[1] [G], but in another house of which mention was made in Part IV.[2] He too ought to have his ministers and necessary aids for the business which he could not do by himself alone [H].

q) 329, 760

[807]—G. *Ordinarily the procurators ought not to dwell in the houses of the professed Society but in the house assigned to them. Nevertheless, when they are not handling lawsuits or when there is some reason of urgent necessity or convenience, they could live in those professed houses for a time. This matter should be referred to those who have charge of the others in those houses of the professed Society, according to the order or commission they have from the general or to what is evident to them about his intentions.*

[808]—H. *An alternative is that there should be more procurators, according to the circumstances and urgent necessities in diverse and various regions.*

[809]—13. It seems, therefore, that the general, provided with those aids, ought to employ the time which his health and energies allow him, partly with God, partly with the aforementioned officials and ministers in conferring now with the former and now with the latter, and partly with himself in reflecting privately and thinking out and deciding what should be done with the help and favor of God our Lord.

[810]—14. The provincial superiors and the rectors of colleges or the local superiors of houses also ought to have their aids, more in number or fewer according to the necessity and importance of the affairs entrusted to them. In particular they should have persons designated to give counsel, with whom they

1 In Ignatius' view, a spiritual coadjutor could with greater propriety than a professed administer the temporalities and the fixed revenues permitted to colleges (see fn. 2 on [421], and [557, 591]; also Nadal, *Scholia*, pp. 259-261).
2 This was originally a reference to P. IV, ch. 2, no. 8 of text *a* (1547-1550), a paragraph which is there placed immediately after the present [326] and which provided for such houses for procurators. However, the paragraph was dropped in subsequent texts, while removal of this reference in [806] was overlooked (*Cons*MHSJ, II, 174 and 711, fn. 17).

should consult on the matters of importance which arise.[3] But
r) 431, 432, 490-   after these consultors have been heard, the decision should
492, 820   remain with the superiors[r] [4] [I].

[811]—*I. From what has been said about the general it will
be possible to infer what is applicable to the provincial superiors,
local superiors, and rectors of colleges, with respect to their
qualities, authority, function, and the aids which each one ought
to have. It will be possible to state all this expressly in the rules*
s) 136, 585, 654   *which pertain to each of these superiors.*[s]

---

3 In March, 1556, Ignatius ordered such a group of consultors, modeled on that of the
   Roman College, to be established in the College of Loretto (*EppIgn*, XI, 178).
4 See fn. 7 on [547]. A similar conclusion is given to the discussion on obedience in Vatican
   Council II, Decree on the Renewal of Religious Life, no. 14.

Part X
How the whole body of the Society can be preserved and developed in its well-being[1]

[812]—1. The Society was not instituted by human means; and neither is it through them that it can be preserved and developed, but through the omnipotent hand of Christ, God and our Lord. Therefore in Him alone must be placed the hope that He will preserve and carry forward what He deigned to begin for His service and praise and for the aid of souls.[a] In conformity with this hope, the first and best proportioned means will be the prayers and Masses[b] which ought to be offered for this holy intention through their being ordered for it every week, month, and year in all the regions where the Society resides.

a) 134, 825

b) 424, 790

---

1 Part X sums up all that has preceded it in the Constitutions—as is readily suggested by the unusually numerous marginal cross-references. It presents the finished product or fully constituted Society toward which everything treated earlier has been pointing, since Ignatius in developing his thought has been following a practical order of execution ([134]), rather than a logical order which in more theoretical fashion describes the end and then the means to attain it. Here he sketches the fully organized Society and its spirit by brief touches or bold strokes intended to recall early treatments. See pp. 37-38 above, in ch. 2. For that reason, this Part X is perhaps the richest in spiritual doctrine (see *DeGuiJes*, pp. 139-151, esp. p. 146). It should be remembered, however, that Ignatius intended the Constitutions to be, not a comprehensive treatise on the spiritual life, but rather the application of relevant elements of his world view to the government of an apostolic religious order.

[813]—2. For the preservation and development not only of the body or exterior of the Society but also of its spirit, and for the attainment of the objective it seeks, which is to aid souls to

c) 3, 156, 163, 258, 307, 308, 446, 586, 603

reach their ultimate and supernatural end,[c] the means which unite the human instrument[2] with God and so dispose it that it may be wielded dexterously by His divine hand are more effective than those which equip it in relation to men. Such means are, for example, goodness and virtue, and especially

d) 671

charity,[d] and a pure intention of the divine service, and famili-

e) 723, 790

arity with God our Lord in spiritual exercises of devotion,[e][3] and sincere zeal for souls for the sake of glory to Him who created and redeemed them and not for any other benefit.[4] Thus it appears that care should be taken in general that all the members of the Society may devote themselves to the solid and

f) 260

perfect virtues and to spiritual pursuits,[f] and attach greater importance to them than to learning and other natural and human gifts.[5] For they are the interior gifts which make those exterior means effective toward the end which is sought.

[814]—3. When based upon this foundation, the natural means[6] which equip the human instrument of God our Lord to

---

2 To be a closely united instrument in the hands of God from whom the true efficacy comes is a prominent and characteristic aspect in Ignatius' concept of an apostolic worker ([30, 638, 814], and p. 22 in ch. 1). This concept flows naturally from his desire to be closely associated with Christ in cooperating toward achieving God's redemptive plan as it unfolds in the history of salvation. See, in ch. 1 above, pp. 3-4, 16-17, 20, 22-23; and, for further references, Iparraguirre, *Orientaciones bibliográficas,* pp. 142-144.

3 See fn. 5 on [250] above.

4 Singleness of purpose or purity of intention in serving God is another prominent characteristic of Ignatius' outlook (see [283, 288, 360] and the fnn. there; also [4]). In general, his thought can be observed to start with the Trinity and move downward toward service to men for the sake of glory to God, rather than with creatures and then upward toward God by means of the "ladder of creatures" (*scala creaturarum*). See *Autobiog,* nos. 27-30, 96; *SpEx,* [101-109, 169, and 230-237] (where the gifts and blessings move downward from God because of His love and that is why they should excite man's gratitude and love toward Him); and also, in ch. 1 above, pp. 16-17, 20. It is as a consequence of this first downward movement from God to creatures that Ignatius' thought on other occasions moves from creatures upward to God (e.g., in *SpEx,* [23] and *Cons,* [360, 361; cf. 340]). Ignatius had great esteem for natural or temporal goods and hoped that men would consecrate the temporal order to God, i.e., perfect it so that it issues in greater glory to Him than it otherwise would, much as Vatican Council II has urged (e.g., in "The Church in the Modern World," nos. 4-6, 12, 34-39, 53-62; "The Apostolate of the Laity," nos. 4-7, 13, 14). On this highly characteristic movement of Ignatius' thought, see Hugo Rahner, *Ignatius the Theologian* (New York, 1968), pp. 1-31; J. Daniélou, "La spiritualité trinitaire de saint Ignace," *Christus,* no. 3 (1956), 354-372.

5 See [161, 292], fn. 4 on [361], [814], pp. 18-19 in ch. 1 above.

6 When taken side by side, the typically Ignatian constitutions [813] and [814] make clear illustrations of his perspective and balance. He always saw the supernatural gifts, endow-

deal with his fellowmen will all be helps toward the preservation and development of this whole body, provided they are acquired and exercised for the divine service alone; employed, indeed, not that we may put our confidence in them, but that we may cooperate with the divine grace according to the arrangement of the sovereign providence of God our Lord. For He desires to be glorified both through the natural means,[7] which He gives as Creator, and through the supernatural means, which He gives as the Author of grace. Therefore the human or acquired means ought to be sought with diligence, especially well-grounded and solid learning, and a method of proposing it to the people by means of sermons, lectures,[g] and the art of dealing and conversing with men.[h]

g) 280, 402-405

h) 414

[815]—4. In similar manner, great help will be derived from maintaining the colleges in their good state and discipline, by having the superintendence over them exercised by those who cannot receive any temporal gain,[i] such as members of the professed Society, which will take care that those who possess the talent for it may receive formation in life and learning worthy of a Christian. For these students will be a seedbed[8] for the professed Society and its coadjutors.[j] Furthermore, if universities over which the Society exercises superintendence are added to the colleges, they too will aid toward the same end, as long as the method of procedure described in Part IV [440-509] is preserved.

i) 5, 326, 330, 419, 557, 763, 774, 816

j) 289, 307, 308, 333, 392, 440

[816]—5. Since poverty is like a bulwark of religious institutes which preserves them in their existence and discipline and defends them from many enemies; and since the devil uses

---

ments, and means as by far the most important. But he also esteemed the natural gifts and means, the foundation on which the supernatural builds, and desired his men to cultivate and use them for the sake of the supernatural. This perspective and balance are elements of great moment in his theory of apostolic spirituality. See pp. 22-23 in ch. 1, above.

7 For Ignatius' own exposition of the closely reasoned theological doctrine on which he based this statement, see the paragraph he wrote at the end of the first draft of the Examen, in text *a* (*Cons*MHSJ, II, 125), as edited in *DeGuiJes*, pp. 147-148.

8 *Seminario*, Latin *seminarium*: this word, which has the radical meaning of "a seedbed," took on the added meaning of "an institution to train youths." The success of the colleges founded by Ignatius to train his young men, was an influential factor in the legislation of Trent on seminaries and in its implementation. The ideas of Jay and the models furnished by the Roman and German colleges were of special moment. See also *NCathEnc*, III, 72-74; J. T. Ellis, "A Short History of Seminary Education," esp. pp. 18, 20-29, 31, 33, 39, in J. M. Lee and L. J. Putz (eds.), *Seminary Education in a Time of Change* (Notre Dame, 1965); N. D. Diaz, *San Ignacio y los seminarios* (Montevideo, 1939).

k) 287, 553

l) 567

m) 4, 554-557,
561-563

n) 4, 82, 398,
478, 499, 565,
566, 640

o) 5, 326, 330,
419, 557, 763,
774, 815

corresponding effort to destroy this bulwark in one way or another,[k] it will be highly important for the preservation and development of this whole body that every appearance of avarice should be banished afar,[l] through the Society's abstention from accepting fixed income, or any possessions,[m] or salaries for preaching, or lecturing, or Masses, or administration of sacraments, or spiritual things,[n] as is stated in Part VI [565], and also through its avoidance of converting the fixed revenue of the colleges to its own utility.[o]

[817]—6. It will also be of the highest importance toward perpetuating the Society's well-being to use great diligence in precluding from it ambition, the mother of all evils in any community or congregation whatsoever. This will be accomplished by closing the door against seeking, directly or indirectly, any

p) 390, 478, 720

dignity or prelacy[9] within the Society,[p] in such a way that all the professed should promise to God our Lord never to seek one and to expose anyone whom they observe trying to obtain one; also in such a way that one who can be proved to have sought such a prelacy becomes ineligible and disqualified for

q) 695, 696

any office.[q]

The professed should similarly promise to God our Lord not to seek any prelacy or dignity outside the Society, and, as far as in them lies, not to consent to being chosen for a similar charge unless they are compelled by an order from him who

r) 756, 771, 772,
786, 788

can command them under pain of sin.[r] Each one should desire to serve souls in conformity with our profession of humility and lowliness,[10] and to avoid having the Society deprived of the men who are necessary for its purpose.[11]

Each one should further promise to God our Lord that if some prelacy outside the Society is accepted through the aforementioned manner of compulsion, he will at any time whatsoever later on listen to the counsel of him who is the general of the Society, or of someone else whom the general substitutes for

---

9 Already in 1539 the future superior general was termed a "prelate" (*Cons*MHSJ, I, 13, no. 14; 39, no. 14; *Regimini*, [4], *Exposcit*, [3], "Praepositi Generalis seu Prelati"). Today too, clerics whether diocesan or religious who have ordinary jurisdiction in the external forum are called prelates (Canon 110).

10 Not infrequently the early Jesuits were charged with feigning humility and poverty in the hope of obtaining bishoprics or other dignities. In 1543 such a charge was made to Ignatius himself. In reply, he vowed never to accept a dignity unless compelled by the pope (*FN*, IV, 454-456).

11 In 1546 King Ferdinand I desired to have Jay made bishop of Trieste. In his efforts to dissuade the king, Ignatius wrote that until then there were only nine professed, of whom

himself; and that if he judges what has been counseled to him
to be the better thing, he will carry it out [A]. He will do this,
not because he, being a prelate, has any member of the Society
as a superior, but because he desires to oblige himself voluntarily before God our Lord to do that which he finds to be better
for His divine service, and to be happy to have someone who
presents it to him with charity and Christian freedom, to the
glory of God our Lord.[12]

[818]—A. *After observing the pressure which has been exerted
in so many ways to bring members of the Society to accept
bishoprics; and after resisting in many cases;[13] and after being
unable to resist in accepting the patriarchate and bishopric of
Ethiopia,[14] we bestowed thought upon this aid for this latter
undertaking and for other similar ones when resistance may be
impossible. However, the Society does not oblige itself to undertake this helpful activity each time one of its individual members
must accept some bishopric, but it remains free to omit this
activity or to take it up where it is judged to be of great importance for the divine service. Moreover, after the profession is
made, this simple vow will be taken along with the other vows
which have been mentioned.*[s]

s) 553, 817

[819]—7. Much aid is given toward perpetuating the well-
being of this whole body by what was said in Part I [142-144],
Part II [204], and Part V [516-523] about avoiding the admission
of a crowd, or of persons unsuitable for our Institute, even to
probation,[t] and about dismissals during the time of probation
when it is found that some persons do not turn out to be suitable.[u]
Much less ought those to be retained who are addicted to vice
or are incorrigible.[v] But even greater strictness should be

t) 142-144, 657

u) 204, 205

v) 210

four or five had already been presented for bishoprics (*EppIgn*, I, 452; *LettersIgn*,
p. 112).

12 In 1554 a meeting of the fathers living in the professed house was held about the propriety of this promise or vow. They unanimously affirmed it. See their signed opinion in
*Cons*MHSJ, I, 404-408; also *FN*, IV, 452-454.

13 The extensive measures which Ignatius took to dissuade Pope Paul III from naming Jay
bishop of Trieste are recounted in *EppIgn*, I, 450-453 and 460-466, English in *Letters-
Ign*, pp. 111-113 and 115-120. Other cases too are worthy of mention. In 1551 Julius III
determined to create Borgia a cardinal; in 1553 King Ferdinand I desired Peter Canisius
to be made bishop of Vienna; and in 1555 Paul IV decided to elevate Laynez to the cardi-
nalate (Ribadeneyra, in *FN*, IV, 448-452). Bobadilla too refused the proffered See of
Trieste (*MonBobad*, p. 105). See also Aicardo, *Comentario*, IV, 8-49, esp. 47, for Ignatius'
one exception: bishoprics in mission lands where there was no danger of ambition or gain.

14 The matter of the patriarchate of Ethiopia is recounted in *EppIgn*, VIII, Appendix, 676-
720.

w) 522, 523, 657

shown in admitting persons among the approved scholastics and formed coadjutors,^w and strictness far greater still in regard to admission to profession. The profession should be made only by persons who are selected[15] for their spirit[16] and learning, thoroughly and lengthily tested, and known with edification and satisfaction to all after various proofs of virtue and abnegation

x) 12, 308, 516, 518

of themselves.^x This procedure is used that, even though the numbers are multiplied, the spirit may not be diminished or weakened, when those who are incorporated into the Society are such as have been described.

[820]—8. Since the well-being or illness of the head has its consequences in the whole body, it is supremely important that the election of the superior general be carried out as directed in Part IX [723-735]. Next in importance is the choice of the lower superiors in the provinces, colleges, and houses of the

y) 423, 791, 797

Society.^y For in a general way, the subjects will be what these superiors are.

It is also highly important that, in addition to that choice, the individual superiors should have much authority over the

z) 206, 207, 423, 791
a) 736, 757, 759
b) 766-788

subjects,^z and the general over the individual superiors;^a and, on the other hand, that the Society have much authority over the general,^b as is explained in Part IX [736, 757, 759, 766-788]. This arrangement is made that all may have full power for good and that, if they do poorly, they may be kept under complete control.

It is similarly important that the superiors have suitable

c) 431, 432, 490-492, 798-811

ministers, as was said in the same Part [798-810], for the organization and execution of the affairs pertaining to their office.^c

[821]—9. Whatever helps toward the union of the members of this Society among themselves and with their head will also help

d) 655

much toward preserving the well-being of the Society.^d This is especially the case with the bond of wills, which is the mutual

e) 671

charity and love they have for one another.^e This bond is strengthened by their getting information and news from one

f) 673, 675

another^f and by having much intercommunication, by their following one same doctrine, and by their being uniform in every-

15 *Personas escogidas en espíritu y doctrina:* On this expression and its connection with the requirements for the profession of solemn vows, see above, fn. 18 on p. 71, [10] with fn. 20, [518] with fn. 2, [521], and supplementary Note B in the Reference matter below.
16 *Espíritu:* a word which Ignatius often uses to mean "spiritual life" or "spiritual progress" (*provecho espiritual*). See [51, 60, 81, 93, 94, 101, 243, 417, 419, 819].

thing as far as possible,[g] and above all by the link of obedience,   g) 30, 47, 136,
which unites the individuals with their superiors, and the local   273, 274, 671
superiors among themselves and with the provincials, and both
the local superiors and provincials with the general,[h] in such a   h) 424, 434, 662
way that the subordination of some to others is diligently   i) 662, 663, 666,
preserved.[i]   791

[822]—10. Temperate restraint in spiritual and bodily labors
and similar moderation in relation to the Constitutions, which
do not lean toward an extreme of rigor or toward excessive laxity[j]   j) 298, 300, 339
(and thus they can be better observed) will help this entire
body to persevere in its good state and to be maintained in it.

[823]—11. Toward the same purpose it is helpful in general
to strive to retain the good will and charity of all, even of those
outside the Society, and especially of those whose favorable or
unfavorable attitude toward it is of great importance for opening
or closing the gate leading to the service of God and the good of
souls[k] [B]. It is also helpful that in the Society there should   k) 258, 426, 489,
neither be nor be seen partiality to one side or another among   594, 626
Christian princes or rulers, but in its stead a universal love
which embraces in our Lord all parties (even though they are
adversaries to one another).

[824]—*B. First of all an effort should be made to retain the
benevolence of the Apostolic See, which the Society should
especially serve; and then that of the temporal rulers and noble
and powerful persons whose favor or disfavor does much toward
opening or closing the gate to the service of God and the good
of souls. Similarly, when an unfavorable attitude is perceived in
some persons, especially in persons of importance, prayer ought
to be offered for them and the suitable means should be employed to bring them to friendship, or at least to keep them from
being hostile.[l] This is done, not because contradictions and ill-*   l) 426
*treatment are feared, but that God our Lord may be more served
and glorified in all things through the benevolence of all these
persons.*

[825]—12. Help will also be found in a discreet and moderate
use of the favors granted by the Apostolic See, by seeking with
all sincerity nothing else than the aid of souls. For through this
God our Lord will carry forward what He has begun;[m] and the   m) 134, 812
fragrance [2 Cor. 2:15] arising from the genuineness of the   n) 89, 272, 580,
good works will increase the benevolent desire of others[n] to   595, 637

avail themselves of the Society's aid and to help the Society for the end which it seeks, the glory and service of His Divine Majesty.

[826]—13. It will also be helpful that attention should be devoted to the preservation of the health of the individual members° [C], as was stated in Part III [292-306]; and finally, that all should apply themselves to the observance of the Constitutions.ᵖ For this purpose they must know them, at least those which pertain to each one. Therefore each one should read or hear them every month.

o) 243, 292, 339, 582

p) 424, 547, 602, 746, 790

[827]—*C. For this purpose it is expedient that attention should be given to having the houses and colleges in healthy locations with pure air and not in those characterized by the opposite.*

The end

Part three

Reference matter

Reference table of important dates[1]

1491   Ignatius is born at Loyola, probably before October 23.

1506(?)   He goes to Arévalo, Castile. Is a page of Juan Velázquez de Cuéllar.

1521   He is wounded at Pamplona, May 20; receives the last sacraments, June 24. August-September: he requests books of chivalry; receives the *Life of Christ* by Ludolph and the lives of the saints by Jacobus de Voragine. Conversion. October-December: he makes excerpts from these books.

1522   He arrives at Montserrat, March 21. On March 25 he goes to Manresa and stays there until February, 1523. August-September (?), illumination beside the Cardoner. He begins to compose the Spiritual Exercises.

1523   In mid-March, he leaves Barcelona for the Holy Land. He enters Jerusalem, September 4; departs for Joppa, September 23.

1524   He reaches Venice in January, Barcelona in February.

1525   He spends the year in Barcelona, studying Latin grammar and engaging in apostolic works.

1526   In late March (?), he leaves Barcelona to study the arts at Alcalá. He studies logic, physics, and the *Sentences* of Peter Lombard. His apostolic activities lead to suspicion, trial, and prison.

---

1 This table is based on the *Conspectus chronologicus* found in *FN*, I, 26*-62*, where copious documentation is given. See also *Obras completas de san Ignacio*, pp. 35-54, which adds useful maps.

1527	He leaves Alcalá for Salamanca, about June 21. He is imprisoned and forbidden to teach theological matters before studying theology. Leaves for Paris in mid-September.
1528	He enters Paris, February 2. Studies Latin in the College of Montaigu.
1529	He enters the College of Sainte Barbe, October 1, and studies the arts. He meets Favre and Xavier.
1533	He passes his examination for the Licentiate in Arts, March 13. Begins theology under the Dominicans, April 13 (?). Meets Laynez and Salmerón.
1534	He receives degree of Master of Arts, in April. The seven companions pronounce vows at Montmartre, August 15.
1535	He meets but does not win Nadal. In March, he shows the Exercises to the Inquisitor. In early April, he leaves Paris for Azpeitia.
1536	He spends the year at Venice, visiting hospitals, studying theology, and giving the Exercises. Has an unpleasant meeting with Gian Pietro Carafa, in December.
1537	He is ordained a priest, June 24. With Favre and Laynez, leaves in July for Vicenza. Departs for Rome in late October. Mid-November (?): the vision at La Storta. His entrance into Rome.
1538	In and near Rome, the companions give the Exercises, conduct apostolic works, sustain persecutions.
1539	Mid-March to June 24, the "Deliberation of the First Fathers" about founding a new religious order dedicated to apostolic activity. None of the ancient *Rules* then insisted on, those of Sts. Basil, Augustine, Benedict, or Francis, offer precisely what they envisage. Hence they seek the pope's permission to establish a new type of religious life ("formulam vivendi" or "modus procedendi").
	May 4, the "Conclusions about the Society." After late April, the pope sends some of the companions to various places in Italy. Those in Rome compose the "First Sketch of the Institute of the Society of Jesus," which became the Formula of the Institute.
	July-August. Cardinal Contarini commends the projected new Institute to Pope Paul III. September 3, he reads the proposed Formula of the Institute to the pope at table, who verbally approves it and orders a bull to be prepared. September 28, Cardinal Ghinucci proposes alterations. December, Cardinal Guidiccioni opposes the foundation of a new order.

1540   Rodrigues departs for Portugal and India on March 4, and Xavier on March 16. September 27, the bull *Regimini* approves the Society as an institute of clerics regular but restricts its professed members to 60.

1541   March 4, as authorized by the bull, the companions in Rome meet to begin composition of the first Constitutions. They entrust the work to Ignatius and Codure, who begin on March 10. In late March or early April, signing of the "Constitutions of the Year 1541."

April 8, Ignatius unanimously elected general. He refuses, is reelected, and accepts on April 19. First solemn profession in St. Paul's-Outside-the-Walls, April 22. The first constitutions "For the Foundation of a College."

1542   Ignatius sends members to begin colleges at Coimbra and Padua. Various apostolic activities.

1543   He obtains various papal bulls. December (?), he begins the first professed house, of which some rooms still exist in Rome.

1544   January, he begins the Constitutions of the Society, starting with its poverty. His "Deliberation about Poverty." February 2—March 13, writes the part of his *Spiritual Diary* about the poverty of the professed houses.

March 14. The bull *Iniunctum nobis* confirms the Society and removes the restriction to 60 members. May 11, while continuing his *Spiritual Diary,* Ignatius deliberates over other constitutions.

1545   February 27, last entry still extant in the *Spiritual Diary.* June 3, Ignatius obtains brief *Cum inter cunctas,* granting faculties and privileges. November 29, he admits Nadal. December 25, profession of Isabel Roser and her companions. At end of year, he assigns Laynez and Salmerón to Trent, as the pope desired.

1546   He obtains the brief *Exponi nobis,* permitting reception of spiritual and temporal coadjutors into the Society. In October, Isabel Roser is freed from her vows. October 9, admits St. Francis Borgia. October 25, Province of Portugal is created. Late in the year, Ignatius composes "Constituciones de estudiantes" for Padua.

1547   He summons Polanco to be secretary of the Society. Writes the letter "On Perfection" to Coimbra, May 7; "On Humane Letters," May 21; recommends separate novitiates, late October; receives bull of November 4, founding the University of Gandía; constitutes the first spiritual coadjutors in India, Nov. 20. Last months: Polanco begins serious work on the Constitutions of the

Society; composes "Industriae" and other documents; guided by Ignatius, he completes text *a* of the Constitutions, 1547-1550.

1548   March, sends Jesuits to found the College of Messina. The *Spiritual Exercises* are approved by Paul III, July 31, and published. During the year, Ignatius writes the Declarations on the Examen.

1549   June 27, he thinks of founding the Roman College. He has Polanco compose the "Constitutiones collegiorum."

1550   July 21, he obtains the bull *Exposcit debitum*. By the end of the year, the Constitutions are ready, in text A, for examination by the professed in Rome.

1551   Early in the year, meeting of the professed to examine and discuss them. February 22, Ignatius inaugurates the Roman College. He plans many colleges throughout this year. December 19, he summons Nadal for the experimental promulgation of the Constitutions.

1552   March 25, he receives Nadal's profession and commissions him to promulgate the Constitutions in Sicily.

1553   March 26, writes the "Letter on Obedience" to Portugal. April, names Nadal commissary to promulgate the Constitutions in Spain and Portugal.
August, begins to dictate his *Autobiography*.

1554   January 7, names Borgia commissary of Spain, over three provincials.
February 1, he desires to finish the Constitutions; but he continues to work on them, in text B, the rest of his life.

1555   January 26, Jesuits in Rome number 150. May 23, Carafa elected pope as Paul IV.

1556   January-February: Paul IV authorizes the Roman College to grant any degrees.
July 31, Ignatius dies.

1558   June 6, General Congregation I convenes. July 2, Pope Paul IV orally confirms the Society's Institute. September 10, the Congregation approves the Spanish text and Polanco's Latin translation of Ignatius' Constitutions.

1583   Gregory XIII approves the Jesuit Institute, including the Constitutions, in the bull *Quanto fructuosius* (February 1, 1583), and again in *Ascendente Domino* (May 25, 1584).

1595   The processes are begun for Ignatius' beatification.

1609   December 3, his beatification by Paul V.

1622   March 12, canonization of Ignatius and Francis Xavier by Gregory XV.

Supplementary notes

Note A   The title Compañía de Jesús

Throughout the Constitutions, the words which Ignatius used as the title of his order are *Compañía de Jesús,* and *Societas Jesu* when he had occasion to use the Latin form within the Spanish text (for example, in [527, 532, 535, 540]). Polanco used *Societas Iesu* in the Latin translation of 1558. The title officially approved by the Church in 1540, in *Regimini,* [2, 5, 9], and in numerous later papal documents, is *Societas Iesu.* In Spain, Italy, and France, *compañía* and its cognates remained customary: *Compañía de Jesús, Compagnia di Gesù, Compagnie de Jésus.* In the non-Latin countries, with which correspondence from Rome was carried on in Latin, vernacular translations or cognates of *Societas* passed into legal titles and became recognized or even official usage: Society of Jesus, *Gesellschaft Jesu, Sociëteit van Jesus.*

As was noted above in footnote 3 on Examen, [1], the meaning and significance of this title *Compañía de Jesús* have been much discussed from the 1500's until today. Is it predominantly a military term? or one redolent of ascetical and mystical connotations? or one emphasizing companionship, among the members and with Christ? or something of all these? or even something haughty or sinister?

Traditional meanings of *compañía,* listed in Spanish dictionaries from Covarrubias' *Tesoro* (1611) onward, are: a group of persons united for a common end, *societas;* a companion or person accompanying another, *comes, socius;* a group of soldiers under a commander or captain, *cohors.* Cassells (1959) also lists the abstract term companionship.

In Italy in the 1500's, well before the Society of Jesus was founded, the Spanish *compañía* and the Italian *compagnia* were used frequently to denote either military groups or pious associations of great variety. Examples of the latter are the "Companies of Divine Love" in the time of St. Catherine of Genoa (d. 1510), or that formed among laymen by Favre at Parma in 1540, or the *Compagnia della Grazia (Societas de Gratia)* established by Ignatius in 1543 for his *opus Sanctae Marthae*,[1] or the religious institute of the Somaschi, begun in 1528 and officially entitled "Compagnia dei Servi dei Poveri."

In 1536 Ignatius used *compañía* in various senses then current, such as group, or group of friends. He also called the religious institutes of the Theatines, Franciscans, and Dominicans *compañías*.[2] In 1537 he and his intimate companions who shared their common apostolic ideals found their group being called *Iñiguistas* or *Ignatiani*, much as the followers of Sts. Dominic and Francis were called Dominicans and Franciscans. Ignatius in his humility was displeased by this, since he was not yet a founder or a head with any juridical authority. He proposed and his companions determined that, when asked by what name their group *(congregación, congregatio)* should be called, they should say that "since they had no head *(cabeza, caput)* except Jesus Christ, whom alone they desired to serve," they were "of the *Compañía de Jesús*" or "*Societas Iesu*."[3] Here *compañía* is a synonym which specifies *congregación* and means a group. It implies or connotes friendly companionship among the associates and with Jesus,[4] but in this context the abstract term companionship cannot be the first or direct meaning. Also, to take *compañía* here as meaning merely companions,[5] rather than a group of companions, seems to oversimplify several problems connected with this topic. The term *compañía* was not the topic of the companions' discussions but arose largely from the populace. What came from the deliberations and especially from Ignatius was the addition to it of the phrase *de Jesús*, which like a surname distinguished their group from other associations. In their group there was then neither military discipline nor even any juridical authority, but instead, a common intense loyalty to Christ under the moral leadership of Ignatius. That addition, *de Jesús*, reflected all the strong Christological aspects of his spirituality.[6]

Through many mystical experiences, especially the vision of November, 1537, at La Storta in which Ignatius saw "that God the Father was placing him with His Son," he became immovable in the choice of this title.[7] He and his associates considered themselves as a

1 See *DeGuiJes*, pp. 15, 187-188; *FN*, I, 149; Tacchi Venturi, *Storia*, I², 348-349; *Cons*MHSJ, III, 215, fn. 6.
2 *EppIgn*, I, 110, 115, 116.
3 *FN*, I, 204; cf. 313-314 and II, 10, 133, 159, 595-596; *PolChron*, I, 73, 79; *Cons*MHSJ, I, 304; *DeGuiJes*, p. 42, fn. 51.
4 Nadal in *FN*, I, 313; II, 159.
5 This seems to be done by T. Baumann in *RAM*, XXXVII (1961), 52, 60.
6 J. Iturrioz, "Compañía de Jesús," *Manresa*, XXVII (1955), 51-52; Granero, *San Ignacio* (Madrid, 1967), p. 175, fn. 42.
7 *FN*, II, 132-135.

group of companions closely united among themselves and with (as well as under) Christ as their head and chief, risen yet still living as well as suffering in the members of His Church.[8] In the *Prima Socie-tatis Jesu Instituti Summa*, [2], these companions proposed their title in its Latin form, *Societas Jesu*, to the pope for approval, which was granted in 1540.

Was the bond uniting the members of the Society companionate, or juridical, or military? These characteristics can be complementary to one another rather than exclusive; and all of them were variously stressed by early Jesuits in interpreting their title.

The bond which united the first ten companions was manifestly one of love for one another which sprang from intimate interpersonal relationship in working out and pursuing their common ideals and apostolic activities. The Deliberation of the First Fathers makes this evident. But especially after 1540 as the Society grew larger, cases arose, like that of Rodrigues and his partisans in Portugal,[9] where much more than personal love or companionship became necessary to preserve unity and cooperation. Experience showed that friendship with associates personally known had to be supplemented more and more by charity for those at a distance and unknown, and by such means as authority, obedience, and intercommunication. Consequently from 1540 to 1556 Ignatius gradually perfected directives and constitutions toward this end. It is not surprising that from their *Deliberatio* of 1539 onward he and his associates spontaneously and habitually translated their title, *Compañía*, not by terms such as *sodalitas, sodalitium,* or *amicitia* which stressed the companionship, but by *Societas,* a term which by now had juridical connotations in addition to the companionship or fellowship. The friendly charity remained always presupposed as the founders' ideal, even though they knew it to be not always possible of realization.[10] Ignatius'

8 The presence of this spirituality of the mystical body among Ignatius and the early Jesuits is manifest from Ignatius' letter of Feb. 23, 1553 (*EpplIgn,* VIII, 460-467; *LettersIgn,* pp. 367-372; and see fn. 10 on *Cons,* [137] above), and also from the words which his intimate collaborator, Nadal, used while explaining the order's title in Spain in 1554. Nadal recalled to his hearers how at La Storta God the Father had placed Ignatius with the Son to be His servant, and Jesus in turn had said to Ignatius, "It is My will that you serve Us," and how Ignatius was as a result determined to call his congregation the Society of Jesus. Then Nadal continued: ". . . God chose us to be companions (*socios*) of Jesus. . . . It is to be noted that Christ, who has risen from the dead and will never die again, still suffers in His members and bears His cross [Romans, 6:9]. . . . Therefore God calls us to this, that in this warfare (*militia*) we should follow Christ. . ." (*FN,* I, 214). In similar vein Nadal used the words "in corpore suo mystico, quod est Ecclesia" during an exhortation of 1557 in the Roman College, where many of his hearers had personally known the recently deceased Ignatius (*FN,* II, 10). See also fn. 10 on [137] above.
9 On the troubles and factions among the Jesuits in Portugal, see Astráin, *Historia,* I, 585-629.
10 See *Deliberatio primorum Patrum,* [3], in ConsMHSJ, I, 3; also *ibid.,* I, 8, 9, 10, line 8, "congregationem dictam vel Societatem"; *Prima . . . Instituti Summa,* [2-7], *ibid.,* I, 14-20; *Conclusio, ibid.,* I, 23; *Regimini,* [3, 4, 8], *ibid.,* I, 24-30; *Exposcit,* [3, 4, 5, 6], *ibid.,* 375-381; also, *Cons,* [527, 532, 535, 540].

mature ideal, involving a cooperative union of hearts joined to the appropriate means to attain it which he had learned from experience, is seen in Part IX of his Constitutions, especially in [655, 659, 662, 668, 671, 673]. His résumé is in [821].

The military aspects of the title, which connote organized activity and discipline under a commander, were not explained by Ignatius himself. But they were expounded in the interpretations of the title given by early Jesuits who knew him well. Examples are Polanco, Nadal, Ribadeneyra, Mannaerts, and others. "God has called us precisely to this," Nadal stated in his exhortation of 1554, "that we should follow Christ in this military service . . ."[11] Reflections such as theirs would be natural results from Ignatius' presentation of Christ as King *(rey)*, Lord *(Señor)*, and true Commander-in-Chief *(verdadero capitán)* in his *Spiritual Exercises*, [91, 95, 97, 138, 143, 147]. Military overtones are also prominent in the First Sketch of the Institute of the Society, [2, 3, 7], *Regimini*, [3, 4, 8], and *Exposcit*, [3, 4, 6], where we find, for example, "to serve as a soldier *(militare)* beneath the banner of the cross in our Society," and the "warfare *(militia)* of Christ." These are, however, the same metaphors which St. Paul used to describe Christian life as warfare *(militia, militare,* for example, in 2 Corinthians 10:4-6) and which have reechoed throughout the history of Christianity and of religious life. Ignatius himself neither developed nor opposed these military interpretations of his title. But he surely regarded these metaphors as less important than the underlying spiritual realities which they expressed, and which he explicitly indicated in various ways: a cooperating group of men united among themselves through charity and intimately associated with Christ as their head — the head who is still living in the members of His mystical body and inviting cooperation in His redemptive plan for them.[12]

As was natural, opponents of Ignatius or his Society focused on still other aspects of his title. In 1553 it was attacked in Toledo by Tomás de Pedroche as being "haughty and schismatic," since the whole Christian people is the society of Jesus. Nadal replied that all Christians are indeed called to be companions *(socii)* of Christ, but some in a more select way.[13] In 1553 a similar complaint came from the University of Paris against this "new Society, claiming for itself the unusual title of the name of Jesus." Polanco replied that "Society of Jesus is not used as though we were making ourselves companions of Jesus, but it is used in the customary way whereby a society or company *(cohors)* takes its name from its leader, whom we desire to follow in accordance with our Institute." Here, as later in 1574, he

---

11 *FN*, I, 314; cf. II, 158. See, for Polanco, *EppIgn*, XII, 615; *FN*, II, 597; for Ribadeneyra, *FN*, II, 377; *De ratione Instituti S.J.* (Rome, 1864), p. 47; for Manare, his *Exhortationes*, II, 4 (Brussels, 1912), p. 395.
12 See esp. *FN*, I, 204, 313-314, 496-499; II, 133-134, 159, 310, 377, 595-597; *ConsMHSJ*, I, 104; fn. 8 just above; and fn. 10 on *Cons*, [137] above.
13 *FN*, I, 320-321.

stated that the Society's members were not "companions of Jesus" *(socii)*, while Nadal stated that they were such "companions" *(socii)*.[14] This seeming discrepancy is not very serious, but a matter of varying emphasis in different circumstances. The members were companions among themselves who loved one another, but subjects of Christ as their captain for whom they had even greater love. Both Polanco and Nadal wrote repeatedly on the close union with Christ which was characteristic of the early Jesuits. In 1605 Ribadeneyra reported and argued against still later attacks on the Society's title.[15]

For Ignatius and his early followers, therefore, the title *Compañía de Jesús* meant an organized group of associates, cooperating through charity, who had Christ as their head and were totally at His service. The title was a suggestive term rich with spiritual meanings, connotations, and overtones which were overlapping and supplementary rather than contradictory or exclusive. In Ignatius' lifetime and without remonstrance from him, some of his intimate collaborators drew greater inspiration or significance from one aspect of the title and others from another. To attempt today to select some one meaning or connotation with depreciation or exclusion of the rest seems to be an oversimplifying procedure. This is particularly true of the military expressions, which were merely the traditional metaphors describing Christian or religious life.

Note B   The diversity of grades among the priests

It has long been known that Ignatius established two classes of priests in his Society, the professed of solemn vows (whether four or three) and the spiritual coadjutors with simple vows.[1] No founder of a religious order established such an arrangement before him or after his death. Students and historians of his Institute have long felt a great lack of reliable information about his reasons for doing this, the attendant circumstances which led him to it, and the manner in which his arrangement developed in practice after his death. Some recent research on this entire field carried on, at the instigation of General Congregation XXXI, by Father Ladislas Lukács in the archives of the Society in Rome, in ancient catalogues, and in other sources, has brought forth new information and statistical tables which are little short of amazing.[2] This highly documented research

14 See, for Polanco, *EppIgn*, XII, 614-615; *FN*, II, 597; for Nadal, *FN*, I, 313.
15 Ribadeneyra, *De ratione Instituti*, pp. 39-49. The Spanish original appeared in Madrid in 1605.
1 See above, *Exposcit*, [2, 6]; *Exam*, [12, 13, 112, 113]; *Cons*, [510, 511, 516-523].
2 L. Lukács, "De graduum diversitate inter sacerdotes in Societate Iesu," *AHSJ*, XXXVII (1968), 237-316 (abbreviated hereafter as Lukács).

furnishes a new vantage point enabling us to view the whole matter in fresh perspective, and it is indispensable for an accurate understanding of Ignatius' statements, in his Constitutions and elsewhere, about the two classes of priests in his Society. Father Lukács' long article was published too late to be woven evenly into the footnotes throughout this book, although some items were added at appropriate places.[3] This present supplementary Note aims to set forth its more important points, along with concrete illustration and some samples of its documentation.

One plague of the Church in that era, the widespread ignorance of priests, is a point of background necessary for an understanding of Ignatius' attitude on spiritual coadjutors. *De officio examinatoris,* a document written in about 1556 to give norms to the examiners of sacerdotal candidates in the Archdiocese of Rome, illustrates the situation concretely. After treating of the knowledge which would be ideal for a priest who will hear confessions and celebrate Mass, the document continues:

> But since not all can be men of this sort, for one to be sufficient as a confessor it is enough if he understands, in Latin or any other language, the writers who treat about the matter. . . . Wherefore, advanced *(exquisita)* knowledge in the priest is not required, . . . but sufficient *(sufficiens)* knowledge. . . . To avoid disputes among priests about these matters, at Rome we diligently observe these norms: (1) One receiving the four minor orders should at least know how to read.[4] (2) A subdeacon should be able to read, without halting, any ecclesiastical passage and understand some of what he reads. (3) A deacon should read without halting and understand more of what he reads, better than a subdeacon. (4) A priest should read and understand without halting — we mean, according to the norms of the grammarians. (5) He ought not to be ignorant of the matters pertaining to the nature of the sacraments, with account taken of the person, benefice, and other circumstances. The examiner will weigh these.[5]

It is noteworthy — as well as surprising to many today — that the document required no theological learning, such as could be gained by completing any organized curriculum with even minimal success.

Even the Council of Trent did not lay down clear and specific requirements of subject matter, proficiency, or years of study for ordination to the priesthood. The Council stipulated only that candidates should study grammar, singing, ecclesiastical computations, and some other fine arts, and then pass on to study Scripture, ecclesiastical books, homilies of the saints, and the rites and forms for administer-

---

3 A compressed summary of Lukács' article has been given in fn. 20 on *Exam,* [10] above. Other summaries are in Lukács, 235, 315-316.
4 In this context, "read" seems to mean "read aloud."
5 Lukács, 252-253.

ing the sacraments, especially those opportune for hearing confessions.[6]

Against that historical background, much of the evolution of the two grades among priests in the Society after Ignatius' death is more clearly seen to hinge on divergent interpretations of the word "conspicuous"[7] in the bulls of 1540 and 1550, *Regimini*, [8] and *Exposcit*, [6]: "this Institute requires men . . . conspicuous in the integrity of Christian life and learning."

Ignatius himself constantly understood this word "conspicuous" to mean a "sufficiency" of theological learning, such as that which anyone would possess who completed the four years of theological study which he prescribed in his Constitutions, [418, 464, 518], with the lectures based on the *Summa theologiae* of St. Thomas Aquinas. This is shown by his writings, especially the Constitutions, and by his practice. Such a sufficiency of theological knowledge would make his priests conspicuous among others of the era.[8]

The First Sketch of the Institute of the Society and the first papal approval, *Regimini* of 1540, contain nothing about the diversity of grades among the priests, although they do contain the word "conspicuous."[9] They also provide for admission of youths still unformed who are to be educated in colleges.[10] But while waiting for these youths to complete their studies, Ignatius saw that he could meanwhile admit secular priests who, although possessing little theological learning or aptitude for acquiring it (for example, because of age), could nevertheless aid the Society by exercising some sacerdotal ministries such as celebrating Mass or hearing confessions. There are 341 cases of Jesuit priests between 1540 and 1565 whose status of theological learning is known to us. Under Ignatius as general (1541-1556), there were 63 priests with theological learning and 61 without it, respectively 50.8% and 49.1%. Under Laynez (1558-1565), there were 114 with and 103 without theology, respectively 52.6% and 47.4%. By 1600 the proportion was 70% with and 30% without theology, by 1650 91.8% with and 8.2% without. Manifestly, Ignatius' prescriptions on theology in his Constitutions led to a rapid increase in the numbers of his priests who possessed theological learning. Moreover, under Ignatius, 51.8% of those admitted to the Society had the rather advanced age of 21 or over, and this was almost the same percentage as those who lacked theological learning. As the proportion of candidates 21 years or over at their entrance decreased, the proportion of those lacking theological learning also fell.[11]

In 1546, six years after the first approval of the Society as an insti-

6 *Ibid.*, 253.
7 *Ibid.*
8 *Ibid.*, 238-246.
9 *Prima . . . Instituti Summa*, [7], *Regimini*, [8], in *Cons*MHSJ, I, 20, 30.
10 *Ibid.*, [5] and [6], *Cons*MHSJ, I, 19, 29. See also fn. 2 on [160] above, where the statistics are arranged in the Tables.
11 Lukács, 239-241.

tute of clerics, Ignatius sought permission to have in it two classes
or grades of priests, the professed and the spiritual coadjutors. His
request was granted in the brief of June 5, 1546, *Exponi nobis.* The
reasons which led him to this step are not yet fully clear from primary
historical sources. In the light of the background given above, they
may well have been (1) the great cultural difference between the
priests with and without theological learning, and (2) the need,
within provincial and general congregations, to have the government
of the Society in the hands of those who possessed such learning,
the professed. "Lack of laborers" *(penuria operariorum)* was the reason which Ignatius submitted to the Holy See in his petition. This
reason would cease with the increasing percentage of those who possessed theological learning, and it seems to indicate a temporary
character of the envisaged two grades. The words of the brief, too,
seem to strengthen this indication. The coadjutors, spiritual and
temporal, were to be bound by their vows "for that time which you,
Dear Son and Superior General, judge that you must use them, and
no longer."[12] If those with theological learning had not been fewer
than desirable, the permission seemingly would not have been requested or granted; and consequently, if that fewness would decrease,
the need of spiritual coadjutors would also decrease.

Documents of Ignatius from 1541 onward carry a continual contrast, not between those priests in the Society who are conspicuous
and those merely sufficient, but between those who had "some sufficiency of learning" *(alguna suficiencia de letras)* and those who were
"less sufficient" *(menos suficientes)* in it, between the *letrados* and
the *menos letrados.* Ignatius required the professed to have philo-
sophical and theological knowledge, that is, what was acquired in the
higher faculties of university education of his day. He required the
spiritual coadjutors to have only secondary education, that is, only
grammar and humane letters, supplemented by cases of conscience.
There were 17 members living in Italy who entered the Society under
Ignatius (1541-1556) and received the vows of spiritual coadjutors
under him or Laynez (1558-1565). Of these, 2 studied only grammar, 2 also humane letters, 10 studied cases of conscience, and only
3 studied a little theology.[13]

Ignatius' understanding of the term *conspicuus* as used in the
bulls is learned also from his practice. From 1541 to 1556, he admitted 50 priests to final vows, of whom 46 (92%) were professed of
solemn vows and 4 (8%) became spiritual coadjutors.[14] He wrote
letters to various provinces, urging multiplication of the professed; and
from these letters too his norms emerge. Those who have completed
the entire course of theology with sufficient success *(sufficienter)* may
be professed with four vows. If a portion of this learning is wanting,

12 Text of *Exponi nobis* in *Cons*MHSJ, I, 170, 172. See also Lukács, 241-243.
13 Lukács, 243-244; cf. 239.
14 *Ibid.,* 296, Table I.

they should be professed with three vows. Those who have not learned theology should become spiritual coadjutors.[15]

Ignatius' mature thought which gives his official and authoritative explanation of what is stated on this matter in the bulls *Regimini* and *Exposcit*, including the words "conspicuous in the integrity of Christian life and learning," appears in the Examen and Constitutions which he left at his death, [12, 13, 112, 113, 518, 519, 521, 819].

What has been said so far raises an expectation that the proportion of spiritual coadjutors among the priests would steadily decrease and even vanish after the founder's death. But the opposite occurred. Among those admitted to final vows, the proportion of spiritual coadjutors rose slowly from 8% under Ignatius to 11.6% under Laynez and to 24.9% under Borgia (1565-1572), and then sharply to 46% under Mercurian (1573-1580) and 42% under Aquaviva (1581-1615). After him it gradually declined to 31% under Piccolomini (1649-1651), 20.9% under González (1687-1705), and 5.1% under Ricci (1758-1773).[16]

Why did this proportion, instead of decreasing after 1556, increase? and that so sharply under Mercurian? The most plausible reason so far found lies in Nadal's interpretation of "conspicuous" in the bulls, "sufficient learning" in Examen, [12] and Constitutions, [518, 519, 521], and the words "persons . . . selected for their . . . learning" in [819]. Nadal was one of the most learned men among the early Jesuits and very influential because of his knowledge of the Constitutions. Yet his opinions and administrative measures sometimes varied from those of Ignatius, to the founder's displeasure.[17]

In 1572, a year before the election of Mercurian, Nadal wrote in his *Tractatus de professione et choro:* "In accordance with the Formula of the Institute, our members professed of four vows ought to be conspicuous not only in morals but also in learning, and therefore they are employed in the more important ministries of the Society."[18] Shortly later he states: "Because of our Institute, the professed have hitherto been few and always will be."[19] The statistics now known to us, but probably not to Nadal's hearers or readers, show that his statement is erroneous in regard to the generalates of Ignatius and Laynez, who respectively assigned the profession to 92% and 88.4% of those they admitted to final vows. Nadal also states: "Our having spiritual coadjutors is necessarily bound up with our Institute; for otherwise we cannot hold to our end,"[20] apostolic ministries. Here Nadal's word "necessarily" puts him in contrast with Ignatius, who

15 *Ibid.,* 245-246.
16 *Ibid.,* 304, Table IV; cf. 296-301, Table I. In the restored Society after 1814, the percentage of spiritual coadjutors rose higher than ever, e.g., 59.3% in 1961-1963 (Lukács, 238, fn. 4).
17 See e.g., *FN,* I, 676; *DeGuiJes,* pp. 89, 93, fn. 62, 193.
18 Lukács, 249, citing *MonNad,* IV, 177.
19 Lukács, 250; *MonNad,* IV, 180.
20 Lukács, 250.

did not think that spiritual coadjutors were "necessarily bound up with" his Institute when he sought its approval. He first requested permission for spiritual coadjutors six years after that approval of the Society's basic structure in *Regimini* of 1540, and received the permission only for such time as he would need them.

Nadal's argument, based on the word *conspicuus* as found in *Regimini* of 1540 and *Exposcit* of 1550, seemed to conflict with Ignatius' explanations, in which he constantly used the term *suficiencia* of theological learning (Examen, [12, 13, 112, 113] and Constitutions, [518, 519]). To escape this difficulty, Nadal had recourse[21] to the passage in the Constitutions, [819], which states that the profession should be given only to persons "selected for their spirit and learning." He claimed that this was the norm for interpreting *conspicuus* in the papal bulls and also Ignatius' *suficiencia* of theological learning. Further still, Nadal interpreted the word *conspicuus* to mean men so outstanding in theology that they could successfully teach it; so that ordinarily they should have the doctorate in theology which required two years beyond the four prescribed by Ignatius for all (Constitutions, [476]). Very few received those extra two years. Of those admitted to the Society by Ignatius, only two received the doctorate in theology.[22]

The papal bulls of 1540 and 1550 empowered Ignatius to give further explanations or determinations of them in the Constitutions. But in this matter Nadal seemingly reversed the process and used the Constitutions as understood by himself to interpret the bulls. Neither this nor his opinion about the grades casts aspersions on his integrity or prudence. Many of his contemporary Jesuits thought as he did, but among them he was the writer and traveler through whom their opinions became more influential. He was urging what he sincerely thought to be true as well as a wise practical policy for the 1560's and 1570's. If modern research reveals his opinions on this topic to be erroneous, the blame cannot be cast on him alone.

Laynez and Borgia followed Ignatius' criteria in distributing grades.[23] But meanwhile Nadal visited almost all the provinces of the Society in Europe in 1561, and again in 1567. Thus he had many opportunities to effect a widespread dissemination of his interpretation.[24] Mercurian made it the basis of his policy. In this he was followed by Aquaviva,[25] with sanction from General Congregation V (1593-1594),[26] after which the distinction of grades was regarded as one of the substantials of the Institute.[27] Shortly after it, too, Aquaviva issued an instruction "De promovendis ad gradus," in which he clearly fol-

21 Lukács, 254, referring to Nadal, *Scholia*, p. 267.
22 Lukács, 247-257; see also 241.
23 *Ibid.*, 258.
24 *Ibid.*, 260.
25 *Ibid.*, 264.
26 *Ibid.*, 264, 281; cf. *InstSJ*, II, 271.
27 Lukács, 286; *InstSJ*, II, 162, 253, 293, 330-331.

lowed the reasoning of Nadal and set up capacity to teach theology as a requisite for profession.[28] This latter requisite became law in Decree 33 of General Congregation VII (1615-1616)[29] and remained in force until 1966. However, the distinction of grades continually gave rise to difficulties, sadness, and sometimes bitterness; and with many good and humble religious the grade of spiritual coadjutor remained a stigma.[30] After 1616 the number of scholastics admitted to the full four-year course of theology grew, and the percentage of coadjutors steadily decreased until it was only 5.1% of the priests by 1773.[31] Thus it seems that the grade of spiritual coadjutor would have disappeared after a few decades if the Society had not been suppressed.[32]

After 1814 the first members of the restored Society were laudably zealous to restore its life according to Ignatius' Institute.[33] They found this life, however, not in Ignatius' Constitutions alone, but in those Constitutions as interpreted and applied by the Fifth, Seventh, and other General Congregations and by Aquaviva's instruction "De promovendis ad gradus." They were not aware, as we are now, that this interpretation was the outgrowth of Nadal's zealous and sincere but nevertheless erroneous interpretation. Hence the policy in assigning grades has been more severe in the restored Society than it ever was before the suppression. From 1829 to 1964, a little over 60% of the priests pronouncing final vows received those of spiritual coadjutor,[34] even though the theological learning of the priests was meanwhile steadily increasing. Before 1773 scholastics in training to become spiritual coadjutors generally studied cases of conscience for two years, but little theology.[35] In 1892 General Congregation XXIV enjoined three years of training, the "cursus brevior" which added studies in canon law, history of the Church, and Scripture.[36] The new Code of Canon Law of 1917 made it necessary to extend this course to four years; and General Congregation XXVII in 1923 prescribed that this course should include a solid, complete course in dogmatic theology.[37] Hence the theological learning required for spiritual coadjutors now equalled or surpassed that for which Ignatius granted the profession. In 1966 General Congregation XXXI broadened the criteria for which profession is granted and called for extensive historical and juridical studies about the diversity of grades. Father

---

28 Lukács, 264-266; *InstSJ*, III, 302.
29 Lukács, 265-266; *InstSJ*, II, 328-329.
30 Lukács, 271, 273-280.
31 *Ibid.*, 290-292.
32 *Ibid.*, 295.
33 *DeGuiJes*, p. 464; cf. *InstSJ*, II, 468-475.
34 This, like much in this last paragraph, is from a letter of Father Lukács to the present writer. See also Lukács, 238, fn. 4.
35 *Cons*, [356, 394, 461].
36 *InstSJ*, II, 522.
37 Decree 96, in *ActRSJ*, IV (1924), 57-58.

Lukács' research is one response to that call. The entire topic will probably receive further discussion in scholarly articles. Undoubtedly, too, it will be treated anew in some future general congregation.[38]

Note C   The terms constitution, constitutions, Constitutions, *Constitutions*

The varying forms of the term constitution often present puzzling editorial problems. This present note explains the policies used in this book.

In accordance with one basic meaning, a constitution is an authoritative ordinance, decree, statute, precept, or rule, perhaps of five to fifty words. The Latin word *constitutio* often meant, from the jurist Gaius (d. 180 A.D.) onward, a decree or edict of the emperor. Hence it came to mean, in the early centuries of religious life, a short statute, rule, precept, or directive by which monks were guided. A collection of such statutes was entitled *Constitutiones*. The English word Constitution is used in a collective sense to designate the body of statutes or articles which is the fundamental law of the land, e.g., the Constitution of the United States. Consequently many Americans and Britons are so accustomed to this meaning that they are in danger of reading it into the title of Ignatius' book, printed after his death, *The Constitutions of the Society of Jesus*. But the fundamental code governing the Society of Jesus is not this book of Ignatius but rather the papal Formula of the Institute in the bull *Exposcit debitum* of 1550. Any constitution or constitutions of Ignatius are statutes which apply, refine, or further determine the various provisions in this Formula of the Institute.

Throughout the present book the words constitution or constitutions, neither capitalized nor italicized, refer to one or a few of the statutes or paragraphs comprising Ignatius' treatise. The word Constitutions, in the plural and capitalized but not italicized, means his collected constitutions or statutes taken as a whole, or a fairly large portion of them; and it often emphasizes their being still in the form of a not yet published manuscript at the time being discussed. The word *Constitutions*, italicized, always means Ignatius' treatise in the form of a published book, except that occasionally it may refer to the manuscript with emphasis on the fact that it was destined to be printed. This same policy has been followed with respect to the words

---

38 Another scholarly article on this topic has appeared, just before this book goes to press: Antonio de Aldama, S.J., "De coadiutoribus Societatis Iesu in mente et in praxi S. Ignatii," *AHSJ*, XXXVIII (1969), 389-430, with an English summary on 429-430. This study clearly, comprehensively, and objectively presents the steps by which Ignatius gradually arrived at his concepts of coadjutors both spiritual and temporal (1538-1546), and then legislatively expressed his ideas (1547-1556). Thus this copiously documented research gives valuable new background for understanding Lukács in *AHSJ*, XXXVII (1968).

Examen and Declaration. The entire procedure is shown by exemplification in the following paragraph.

The bull *Regimini militantis Ecclesiae* of 1540 contains (in [3-8]) the Formula of the Institute. Authorized by this papal document, Ignatius began to jot down now one tentative constitution, now another. As occasions arose, he assembled some of these into a list of constitutions for one or another procedure. His constitutions For the Foundation of a College *(Para fundar collegio)* were probably begun in 1541 and revised in 1545. This last sentence could also be written as 1) His constitutions *Para fundar collegio* ("For the Foundation of a College") were . . ., or 2) His constitutions "For the Foundation of a College" *(Para fundar collegio)* were . . . . By 1547 the composition of his Constitutions of the Society of Jesus was his chief occupation. His *Constitutions of the Society of Jesus* were (or was) first printed in 1558 and were (or was) read with great interest by many. In the manuscript it can be seen that he himself did not capitalize or underline or italicize constitution, constitutions, examen, or declaration. Modern editors, however, have found it more expedient to capitalize or italicize in accordance with present-day conventions. Interesting and revealing instances of Ignatius' usage of the words "constitution" or "constitutions" can be found in his *Constitutions,* [136-137]. The best known manuscript of the Constitutions is text B, the Autograph.

Note D   *The term* Spiritual Exercises

Similar editorial problems arise in connection with the term Spiritual Exercises. The procedures followed in the present book are basically those explained in De Guibert, *The Jesuits: Their Spiritual Doctrine and Practice,* page 609. They are shown by exemplification in the following paragraph.

Long before Ignatius various spiritual exercises, such as attendance at Mass or recitation of the Office, were common. He gradually composed directives for a sequence of such exercises. Before 1535 his companions Xavier and Favre made his Spiritual Exercises for a period of thirty days. Ignatius assembled his notes in his *Spiritual Exercises,* which was (or were) published at Rome in 1548. To make references easier, in modern editions since that at Turin in 1928 a number in square brackets has been added to each paragraph of the text; for example, the purpose of the Exercises is stated in *Spiritual Exercises,* [21] or, in our abbreviation, *SpEx,* [21]. The Introductory Observations *(Anotaciones)* are in [1-20]. Important meditations or other exercises in his book are the First Principle and Foundation ([23]), the Call of the King ([91-100]), which is an introduction to the second week or division of the *Exercises,* the Three Modes of Humility ([238-260]). Since 1548 the *Spiritual Exercises* have been read or made by many persons. These Exercises are often a stirring spiritual experience.

Abbreviations

AAS—*Acta Apostolicae Sedis*
ActRSJ—*Acta Romana Societatis Iesu*
AHSJ—*Archivum historicum Societatis Iesu*
ArchRSJ—Archivum Romanum Societatis Iesu
Autobiog—*The Autobiography of St. Ignatius* (dictated to Da Câmara)
BAC—Biblioteca de autores cristianos
CathEnc—The *Catholic Encyclopedia*
Colld—*Collectio decretorum Congregationum Generalium Societatis Iesu* [XXVII-XXX (1923-1957)]. Rome, 1961
Cons—The *Constitutions of the Society of Jesus*
ConsMHSJ—*Constitutiones Societatis Iesu* in the series of critically edited texts of the Monumenta historica Societatis Iesu. See MHSJ, MI, Series III
DDC—*Dictionnaire de droit canonique*
DeGuiJes—De Guibert, *The Jesuits: Their Spiritual Doctrine and Practice*
DirSpEx—*Directoria Exercitiorum Spiritualium* (1540-1599). See s.v. MHSJ
DocInd—*Documenta Indica.* See s.v. MHSJ
DTC—*Dictionnaire de théologie catholique*
EpitInstSJ—*Societatis Iesu Constitutiones et Epitome Instituti*
EppIgn—*S. Ignatii Epistolae.* See s.v. MHSJ
EppMixt—*Epistolae Mixtae.* See s.v. MHSJ
EppXav—*Epistolae S. Francisci Xaverii.* See s.v. MHSJ
EstEcl—*Estudios eclesiásticos*
Exam—The *General Examen* or *Examen Generale*
FN—*Fontes narrativi de Sancto Ignatio.* See s.v. MHSJ
Gregor—*Gregorianum*
IdeaJesUn—*St. Ignatius' Idea of a Jesuit University*, by G. E. Ganss. 2d ed., rev., Milwaukee, 1956
InstSJ—*Institutum Societatis Iesu.* 3 vols. Florence, 1892-1893
JesEdQuar—*The Jesuit Educational Quarterly*

LettersIgn—Letters of St. Ignatius, translated by W. J. Young
LitQuad—Litterae Quadrimestres. See s.v. MHSJ

MHSJ—MONUMENTA HISTORICA SOCIETATIS JESU, the Historical Records or Sources of the Society of Jesus in critically edited texts.

This scholarly series, which now contains 98 volumes, was begun in Madrid in 1894. The project was transferred to Rome in 1929. Most of the manuscripts on which these volumes are based are in the Archives of the Society of Jesus in Rome. The series is being continued by its publisher, the *Institutum Historicum Societatis Iesu,* Via dei Penitenzieri 20, 00193, Rome.

MI—Monumenta Ignatiana. The writings of St. Ignatius of Loyola.

Series I

EppIgn—S. Ignatii . . . Epistolae et Instructiones. [Edd. M. Lecina, V. Agusti, F. Cervós, D. Restrepo.] 12 vols., Madrid, 1903-1911. The letters and instructions of St. Ignatius.

Series II

SpExMHSJ—Exercitia Spiritualia S. Ignatii . . . et eorum Directoria. [Ed. A. Codina.] 1 vol. Madrid, 1919. The critical text of the *Spiritual Exercises* and of the *Directories* for conducting them.

New Series II. A revision

SpExMHSJTe—Vol. I. *Exercitia spiritualia: Textus.* [In preparation.] A revision of *SpExMHSJ.*

DirSpEx—Vol. II. *Directoria Exercitiorum Spiritualium* (1540-1599). Ed. I. Iparraguirre. 1 vol. Rome, 1955. This is a more complete edition of the *Directories* than the earlier one of **1919 in** *SpEx*MHSJ.

Series III

*Cons*MHSJ—*Constitutiones et Regulae Societatis Iesu.* 4 vols. The critically edited texts of the *Constitutions* and *Rules* of the Society of Jesus, along with copious introductions and notes.

*Cons*MHSJ, I—Vol. I. *Monumenta Constitutionum praevia.* [Ed. A. Codina.] Rome, 1934. Sources and records previous to the texts of the *Constitutions.* Historical introductions.

*Cons*MHSJ, II—Vol. II. *Textus hispanus.* [Ed. A. Codina.] Rome, 1936. Critical texts of the four chief and successive texts of the Spanish original.

*Cons*MHSJ, III—Vol. III. *Textus latinus.* [Ed. A. Codina.] Rome, 1938. The critical text of the Latin translation which was approved by the First General Congregation of the Society in 1558.

*Cons*MHSJ, IV—Vol. IV. *Regulae Societatis Jesu.* Ed. D. F. Zapico. Rome, 1948. Ancient drafts of rules or directives.

MHSJ—continued

Series IV

SdeSI—Scripta de Sancto Ignatio. [Edd. L. M. Ortiz, V. Agusti, M. Lecina, A. Macía, A. Codina, D. Fernández, D. Restrepo.] 2 vols. Madrid, 1904, 1918. Writings about St. Ignatius by his contemporaries.

Series IV, revised

FN—Fontes narrativi de S. Ignatio de Loyola et de Societatis Iesu initiis. Edd. D. Fernández Zapico, C. de Dalmases, P. Leturia. 4 vols. Rome, 1943-1960.
Vol. I—1523-1556
Vol. II—1557-1574
Vol. III—1574-1599
Vol. IV—Ribadeneyra's *Vita Ignatii Loyolae* (1572).
Narrative sources, that is, writings about Ignatius by his contemporaries. An improved edition of the documents contained in *SdeSI*.
Fontes documentales de S. Ignatio. [In preparation.]

Primary Sources from Ignatius' Contemporaries

EppMixt—Epistolae Mixtae ex variis Europae locis, 1537-1556. [Ed. V. Agusti.] 5 vols. Madrid, 1898-1901. Chiefly letters to Ignatius.

LittQuad—Litterae Quadrimestres. [Edd. M. Lecina, D. F. Zapico.] 7 vols. Madrid and Rome, 1894-1932. Quarterly reports to the central government of the Society in Rome, 1546-1562.

MonBobad—Bobadillae Monumenta. [Ed. D. Restrepo.] Madrid, 1913. 1 vol. Letters of Ignatius' companion, Nicolás Bobadilla.

MonBorg—Sanctus Franciscus Borgia. [Edd. I. Rodríguez, V. Agusti, F. Cervós.] 5 vols. Madrid, 1894-1911. Letters, diaries, and instructions of St. Francis Borgia.

MonBroet—Epistolae PP. Paschasii Broet, Claudii Jaji, Joannis Codurii et Simonis Rodericii S.J. [Ed. F. Cervós.] 1 vol. Madrid, 1903. Letters of Ignatius' companions, Paschase Broët, Claude Jay, Jean Codure, and Simão Rodrigues.

MonFabri—Fabri Monumenta. [Ed. F. Lirola.] 1 vol. Madrid, 1914. Letters and diaries of Ignatius' companion, Pierre Favre.

MonLain—Lainii Monumenta. [Ed. E. Astudillo.] 8 vols. Madrid, 1912-1917. Letters of Ignatius' companion, Diego Laynez.

MonNad—Epistolae P. Hieronymi Nadal. 6 vols. Vols. I-IV, ed. F. Cervós, 1898-1905. Vols. V, *Commentarii de Instituti S.I.,* 1962, and VI, *Orationis observationes,* 1964, ed. M. Nicolau. Letters and instructions of Ignatius' companion, Jerónimo Nadal.

MonPaed—Monumenta paedagogica. [Edd. C. Rodeles, M. Lecina, V. Agusti, F. Cervós, A. Ortiz.] 1 vol. Madrid, 1901. Pedagogical documents which antedated the first *Plan of*

Studies (Ratio Studiorum) of 1586. A revision of this volume is now in progress and will have probably four volumes.

MonPaed (1965)—*Monumenta paedagogica Societatis Iesu, I (1540-1556).* Ed. L. Lukács. Rome, 1965.

MonRib—*Ribadeneira.* [Ed. D. Restrepo, J. Vilar.] 2 vols. Madrid, 1920, 1923. Letters and notes of Ignatius' contemporary, Pedro de Ribadeneyra.

MonSalm—*Epistolae P. Alphonsi Salmeronis.* [Edd. R. Vidaurre, F. Cervós.] 2 vols. Madrid, 1906-1907. Letters of Ignatius' companion Alonso Salmerón.

MonXav—*Monumenta Xaveriana.* [Edd. M. Lecina, D. Restrepo.] 2 vols. Madrid, 1899, 1912. Writings, chiefly letters, of St. Francis Xavier.

PolChron—*Chronicon Societatis Iesu, auctore Joanne Alphonso de Polanco, S.J.* [Edd. J. M. Velez, V. Agusti.] 6 vols. Madrid, 1894-1898. Early history of the Society by Ignatius' secretary, Juan Alonso de Polanco.

PolCompl—*Polanci Complementa.* [Edd. D. Restrepo, D. F. Zapico.] 2 vols. Madrid, 1916-1917. Letters and notes by Ignatius' secretary.

MONUMENTA MISSIONUM

1. *Missiones Orientales.* (Missions Eastward from Rome.)

EppXav—*Epistolae S. Francisci Xaverii.* [Edd. G. Schurhammer, J. Wicki.] 2 vols. Rome, 1944-1945. An enlarged and improved edition of the *Monumenta Xaveriana* of 1899.

DocInd—*Documenta Indica.* [Ed. J. Wicki.] 10 vols. Rome, 1948-1960.

2. *Missiones Occidentales.* (Missions Westward from Rome.)

MonBras—*Monumenta Brasiliae.* Ed. S. Leite. 4 vols. Rome, 1956-1958. Documents pertaining to the first Jesuits in Brazil.

MonFlo—*Monumenta Antiquae Floridae (1566-1572).* Ed. F. Zubillaga. 1 vol. Rome, 1946. Documents pertaining to the first Jesuits in Florida.

MonMex—*Monumenta Mexicana.* Ed. F. Zubillaga. 3 vols. Rome, 1956-1968. Documents pertaining to establishments in Mexico, 1570-1585. Series pertaining to California, Canada, and Paraguay are in preparation.

MonNovFranc—*Monumenta Novae Franciae. Vol. I, La première mission d'Acadie (1602-1616).* Ed. L. Campeau. Rome, 1967.

MonPeru—*Monumenta Peruana.* Ed. A. de Egaña. 4 vols. Rome, 1954-1968. Documents pertaining to missions in Peru, 1565-1591.

MonBobad, or *MonBorg,* etc. See above s.v. MHSJ

NCathEnc—The *New Catholic Encyclopedia*

OxDCCh—The *Oxford Dictionary of the Christian Church*

PG—Patrologia Graeca, ed. Migne

PL—Patrologia Latina, ed. Migne

PolChron—Polanco's *Chronicon Societatis Iesu*. See s.v. MHSJ

PolCompl—*Polanci Complementa*. See s.v. MHSJ

RAM—*Revue d'ascétique et de mystique*

RazFe—*Razón y Fe*

RevRel—*Review for Religious*

SdeSI—*Scripta de Sancto Ignatio*. See s.v. MHSJ

SMV—Sommervogel, *Bibliothèque de la Compagnie de Jésus*

SpDiar—The *Spiritual Diary of St. Ignatius (1544-1545)*

SpEx—The *Spiritual Exercises* of St. Ignatius or his *Exercitia Spiritualia*

SpExMHSJ—*Exercitia Spiritualia* in the critical edition of MHSJ. See s.v. MHSJ

ST—*Summa theologiae* of St. Thomas Aquinas

WL—*Woodstock Letters*

Select bibliography

Aicardo, José Manuel, S.J. *Comentario a las Constituciones de la Compañía de Jesús.* 6 vols. Madrid, 1919-1932.

Aldama, Antonio M. de, S.J. "De coadiutoribus Societatis Iesu in mente et in praxi sancti Ignatii." *Archivum historicum Societatis Iesu,* XXXVIII (1969), 389-430.

Astráin, Antonio, S.J. *Historia de la Compañía de Jesús en la Asistencia de España.* 7 vols. Madrid, 1902-1925.

Bangert, William V., S.J. *A History of the Society of Jesus.* St. Louis: The Institute of Jesuit Sources, forthcoming.

Baumann, Theodor, S.J. "Compagnie de Jesús. Origine et sens primitif de ce nom." *Revue d'ascétique et de mystique,* XXXVII (1961), 47-60.

Benedict, St. *The Rule of St. Benedict in Latin and English.* Edited and translated by Abbot Justin McCann, O.S.B. Westminster, Md., 1963.

Blaise, A. *Dictionnaire Latin-Français des auteurs chrétiens.* Strasbourg, 1954.

Blet, Pierre, S.J. "Les fondements de l'obéissance ignatienne." *Archivum historicum Societatis Iesu,* XXV (1956), 514-538.

Braunsberger, Otto, S.J. *Beati Petri Canisii, Societatis Jesu epistulae et acta.* Collegit et adnotationibus illustravit O. Braunsberger. 8 vols. Freiburg, 1896-1923.

Broderick, J. F., S.J. "Jesuits." *New Catholic Encyclopedia,* VII, 898-909.

Brodrick, James, S.J. *St. Ignatius Loyola. The Pilgrim Years: 1491-1538.* New York, 1956.

——*The Origin of the Jesuits.* London, 1940.

——*St. Peter Canisius.* New York, 1935. Reprint, Chicago, 1962.

——*The Progress of the Jesuits,* (1556-1579). London, 1947.

——*Robert Bellarmine. Saint and Scholar.* Westminster, Md., 1961.

Brou, Alexander, S.J. Trans. W. J. Young, S.J. *The Ignatian Way to God.* Milwaukee, 1952.

Burrus, Ernest J., S.J. "Monumenta Historica Societatis Iesu (1894-1954)." *Woodstock Letters,* LXXXIII (1954), 158-168.

Carlo, Camillus de, M.I. *Jus religiosorum.* Tournai, 1950.

Chastonay, Paul de, S.J. *Les Constitutions de l'ordre des Jésuites: Leur genèse, leur contenu, leur esprit.* Paris, 1941.

Coathalem, Hervé, S.J. *Ignatian Insights.* Taichung (Taiwan), 1961.

Coemans, Augustus, S.J. *Breves notitiae de Instituto, historia, bibliographia Societatis.* 2d ed., rev. Brussels, 1937.

——*Introductio in studium Instituti et annotationes in Formulam Instituti.* 2d ed., rev. Brussels, 1937.

——Trans. M. Germing, S.J. *Commentary on the Rules.* El Paso, 1948.

Collectio decretorum Congregationum Generalium Societatis Iesu [XXVII-XXX (1923-1957)]. Rome, 1961.

Courel, François, S.J. *Constitutions,* French translation of. See below, s.v. Ignace, St.

——"La fin unique de la Compagnie de Jésus." *Archivum historicum Societatis Iesu,* XXXV (1966), 186-211.

Covarrubias, Sebastián de. *Tesoro de la Lengua Castellana o Española, según la impresión de 1611, con las adiciones de . . . 1674.* Ed. Martín de Riquer. Barcelona, 1943.

Creusen, J., S.J. Tr. A. C. Ellis, S.J., F. N. Korth, S.J. *Religious Men and Women in the Code.* Milwaukee, 1965.

Dalmases, C. de, S.J. Review of F. Roustang, *Constitutions de la Compagnie de Jésus,* II, *Introduction a une lecture. Archivum historicum Societatis Iesu,* XXXVI (1967), 300-306.

Daniélou, Jean, S.J. "The Ignatian Vision of the Universe and of Man." *Cross Currents,* IV (1954), 357-366.

Decreta Congregationis Generalis XXXI a restituta Societate XII. Annis 1965-1966. Rome, 1967.

De Guibert, Joseph, S.J. See Guibert, Joseph de.

Delchard, Antoine, S.J. "La genèse de la pauvreté ignatienne." *Christus,* VI (1959), 464-468.

Diaz, Natalio D., S.J. *San Ignacio y los seminarios.* Montevideo, 1939.

Dictionnaire de droit canonique. Paris, 1935-

Dictionnaire de Spiritualité. Ascétique et Mystique. Doctrine et histoire. Paris, 1932-

Dictionnaire de Théologie Catholique. 15 vols. Paris, 1903-1947.

Donohue, John W., S.J. *Jesuit Education. An Essay on the Foundations of its Idea.* New York, 1963.

Dudon, Paul, S.J., trans. W. J. Young, S.J. *St. Ignatius of Loyola.* Milwaukee, 1949.

Ellard, Augustine G., S.J. "Ignatian Spirituality." *Review for Religious,* XI (1952), 125-142.

Ellard, Gerald, S.J. "St. Ignatius Loyola and Public Worship." *Thought*, XIX (1944), 649-670.

Ellis, John Tracy. "A Short History of Seminary Education," pp. 1-81 in *Seminary Education in a Time of Change*. Ed. J. T. Ellis and L. J. Putz. Notre Dame, 1965.

Englander, Clara. *Ignatius von Loyola und Johannes von Polanco: der Ordensstifter und sein Sekretar*. Regensburg, 1955.

Epitome Instituti Societatis Iesu . . . See *Societatis Iesu Constitutiones et Epitome Instituti*.

Espinosa Pólit, Manuel M., S.J. Trans. W. J. Young, S.J. *Perfect Obedience*. Westminster, Md., 1947.

Farrell, Allan P., S.J. *The Jesuit Code of Liberal Education. Development and Scope of the Ratio Studiorum*. Milwaukee, 1938.

Fine, Eduardo, S.J. *Iuris regularis, tum communis tum particularis, quo regitur Societas Iesu declaratio*. Prato, 1909.

Fiorito, Miguel A., S.J. "La ley ignaciana de la oración en la Compañía de Jesús." *Stromata* (Buenos Aires), XXIII (1967), 3-89.

——Trans. A. Jacobsmeyer, S.J. "Ignatius' Own Legislation on Prayer." *Woodstock Letters*, XCVII (1968), 149-224.

——"Alianza bíblica y regla religiosa (Estudio histórico-salvífico de las Constituciones de la Compañía de Jesús)." Buenos Aires: *Ciencia y Fe*, XXI (1965), 3-36.

Fontes narrativi de Sancto Ignatio de Loyola et de Societatis Jesu initiis. Vol. I: *Narrationes scriptae ante annum 1557*. Vol. II: *1557-1574*. Vol. III: *1574-1599*. Vol. IV: *Vita Ignatii Loyolae, auctore Petro de Ribadeneyra: Textus latinus et hispanus cum censuris*. Rome, 1951-1965.

Francis of Assisi, St. *The Writings of St. Francis of Assisi*. Translated by Benen Fahy, O.F.M. London, 1964.

Futrell, John C., S.J. *Making an Apostolic Community of Love: The Role of the Superior according to St. Ignatius Loyola*. Unpublished dissertation, Institut Catholique de Paris, 1967.

——*Making an Apostolic Community of Love: The Role of the Superior according to St. Ignatius of Loyola*. St. Louis: The Institute of Jesuit Sources, forthcoming.

——"Ignatian Discernment." *Studies in the Spirituality of Jesuits*, II, no. 2 (April, 1970), 47-88. St. Louis: The American Assistancy Seminar on Jesuit Spirituality, 1970.

Ganss, George E., S.J. *Saint Ignatius' Idea of a Jesuit University: Including Part Four of the Constitutions of the Society of Jesus, Translated from the Spanish*. 2d ed., rev. Milwaukee, 1956.

——*The Jesuit Educational Tradition and Saint Louis University*. The Sesquicentennial Committee of St. Louis University, 1969.

——"'Active Life' or 'Contemplative Life'?" *Review for Religious*, XXII (1963), 53-66.

——"Education for Business in the Jesuit University: A Study in Constitutional Law." *Jesuit Educational Quarterly*, XXIII (1961), 133-150.

——"Ignatian and Jesuit Spirituality." *Proceedings of the Conference on the Total Development of the Jesuit Priest,* Santa Clara, California, 1967. Vol. IV, *Background Papers,* 1-64. St. Louis, 1967.

——"Ignatian Research and the Dialogue with the Contemporary American Mind." *Woodstock Letters,* XCIII (1964), 141-164.

——"The Origin of Jesuit Colleges for Externs and the Controversies about their Poverty, 1539-1608." *Woodstock Letters,* XCI (1962), 123-166.

——"St. Ignatius the Educator, Guide amid Contemporary Problems." *Archivum Historicum Societatis Iesu,* XXV (1956), 598-612.

——"The Authentic Spiritual Exercises of St. Ignatius: Some Facts of History and Terminology Basic to Their Functional Efficacy Today." *Studies in the Spirituality of Jesuits,* I, no. 2 (November, 1969), 1-36. St. Louis: The American Assistancy Seminar on Jesuit Spirituality, 1969.

Gill, Henry Vincent, S.J. *Jesuit Spirituality. Leading Ideas of the Spiritual Exercises of St. Ignatius.* Dublin, 1935.

Gilmont, J.-F., S.J. and Daman, P., S.J. *Bibliographie Ignatienne (1894-1957).* Louvain, 1958.

Gilmont, J.-F., S.J. *Les écrits spirituels des premiers Jésuites. Inventaire commenté.* Subsidia ad Historiam Societatis Iesus, no. 3. Rome, 1961.

Giuliani, Maurice, S.J. "Compagnons de Jésus." *Christus,* VI (1959), 221-239.

——*Finding God in All Things.* Trans. W. J. Young, S.J. Chicago, 1958.

Granero, Jesús M., S.J. *San Ignacio de Loyola: Panoramas de su vida.* Madrid, 1967.

——"Las Constituciones de la Compañía." *Manresa,* XXXIX (1967), 235-244.

——"San Ignacio al servicio de la Iglesia." *La ciencia tomista,* LXXXIII (1956), 529-572.

——"Sobre la espiritualidad ignaciana." *Manresa,* XXXI (1959), 5-34.

Guibert, Joseph de, S.J. *The Jesuits: Their Spiritual Doctrine and Practice. A Historical Study.* Trans. William J. Young, S.J. Chicago: The Institute of Jesuit Sources, 1964.

Herman, Jean Baptiste, S.J. *La pédagogie des Jésuites au xvie siècle. Ses sources, ses caractéristiques.* Louvain, 1914.

Ignace, Saint. *Constitutions de la Compagnie de Jésus.* Vol. I: *Traduction du texte officiel, notes et index par François Courel, S.J.* Vol. II: *Introduction à une lecture par François Roustang, S.J. Traduction du texte primitif par François Courel, S.J.* La Collection Christus, nos. 23, 24. Paris, 1967.

Ignacio de Loyola, S. *Constituciones de la Compañía de Jesús y sus*

Declaraciones. Reproducción fototípica del original. Rome, 1908.

Ignatius of Loyola, St. *Constitutions of the Society of Jesus.* See Abbreviations above, p. 361, s.v. MHSJ, *Cons*MHSJ; see also s.v. Courel, Iparraguirre, La Torre, Roustang, and Schoenenberger.

——*Letters of St. Ignatius of Loyola.* Selected and Translated by W. J. Young, S.J. Chicago, 1959.

——*The Spiritual Journal of St. Ignatius of Loyola.* Translated by W. J. Young, S.J. Woodstock, 1958.

——*Obras completas de san Ignacio de Loyola.* Ed. I. Iparraguirre y C. de Dalmases, S.J. Biblioteca de autores cristianos, no. 86. Madrid, 1963.

——*St. Ignatius' Own Story as Told to Luis Gonzalez de Camara.* Translated by William J. Young, S.J. Chicago, 1956. Reprint, Chicago, 1968.

Ignatius von Loyola: seine geistliche Gestalt und sein Vermächtnis (1556-1956). Ed. F. Wulf, S.J. Wurzburg, 1956.

Ignazio di Loyola, Sant'. *Costituzioni della Compagnia di Gesù. Traduzione del testo ufficiale spagnolo, note e indici e cura di Giuseppe Silvano,* S.J. Milano, 1969.

Index de l'Examen Général et des Constitutions. Paris: Christus, 1962.

Institutum Societatis Jesu. I: *Bullarium et Compendium Privilegiorum.* II: *Examen et Constitutiones. Decreta et canones Congregationum Generalium.* III: *Regulae, Ratio Studiorum, Ordinationes.* 3 vols. Florence, 1892-1893.

Iparraguirre, Ignacio, S.J. *Espíritu de san Ignacio de Loyola.* Bilbao, 1958.

——*Orientaciones bibliográficas sobre san Ignacio de Loyola.* Subsidia ad historiam Societatis Iesu, no. 1. 2d ed., rev. Rome, 1965.

——*Historia de la práctica de los Ejercicios espirituales de San Ignacio de Loyola.* Vol. I: *Práctica de los Ejercicios espirituales de San Ignacio en vida de su autor (1522-1556).* Vol. II: . . . *hasta la promulgación del Directorio oficial (1556-1599).* Bibliotheca Instituti Historici Societatis Iesu, nos. 3, 7. Rome and Bilbao, 1946, 1955.

——"Para la historia de la oración en el Colegio Romano durante la secunda mitad del siglo XVI." *Archivum Historicum Societatis Iesu,* XV (1946), 77-126.

——*Répertoire de spiritualité ignatienne (1556-1615).* Subsidia ad historiam Societatis Iesu, no. 4. Rome, 1961.

——"Perspectivas ignacianas de la obediencia." *Revista de espiritualidad,* XXI (1962), 71-93.

——"Visión ignaciana de Dios." *Gregorianum,* XXXVII (1956), 366-390.

Iturrioz, Jesús, S.J. "*Compañía de Jesús.* Sentido histórico y ascético de este nombre." *Manresa,* XXVII (1955), 43-53.

Jacobus de Voragine, O.P. *Legenda aurea.* Ed. T. Graesse. Breslau, 1890.

Janssens, Very Rev. John Baptist, S.J. "De Nostrorum in Sacra Liturgia Institutione Instructio atque Ordinatio." *Acta Romana Societatis Jesu,* XIII (1959), 636-675. This instruction is summarized by C. J. McNaspy, S.J., in *Worship,* XXXV (1961), 298-301.

Knowles, David. *From Pachomius to Ignatius: A Study in the Constitutional History of the Religious Orders.* Oxford, 1966.

Koch, Ludwig, S.J. *Jesuiten-Lexikon. Die Gesellschaft Jesu einst und jetzt.* Paderborn, 1934. Reprint, Héverlé-Louvain, 1962.

Korth, Francis N., S.J. *The Evolution of "Manifestation of Conscience" in Religious Rules, III-XVI Centuries.* Rome, 1949.

La Torre, Juan de, S.J. *Constitutiones Societatis Jesu Latinae et Hispanicae cum earum Declarationibus.* Madrid, 1892.

Leturia, Pedro de, S.J. *El gentilhombre Iñigo Lopez de Loyola en su patria y en su siglo. Estudio historico.* Montevideo, 1938.

——*Iñigo de Loyola.* Trans A. J. Owen, S.J. Syracuse, 1949. Reprint, Chicago, 1965.

——"La hora matutina de meditación en la Compañía naciente." *Archivum historicum Societatis Iesu,* III (1934), 47-86.

——"De Oratione matutina in Societate Iesu documenta selecta." *Archivum historicum Societatis Iesu,* III (1934), 87-108.

——Ed. I. Iparraguirre, S.J. *Estudios ignacianos.* 2 vols. Rome, 1957.

Lewis, Jacques, S.J. "Ignatian Spirituality." *New Catholic Encyclopedia,* VII, 349-351.

Lippert, Peter, S.J. Trans. J. Murray. *The Jesuits: A Self-Portrait.* New York, 1958.

Ludolph. *Vita Jesu Christi.* 4 vols. Paris, 1877.

Lukács, Ladislas, S.J., ed. *Monumenta Paedagogica.* Rev. and enl. Vol. I (1540-1556). Rome, 1965.

——"De graduum diversitate inter sacerdotes in Societate Iesu." *Archivum historicum Societatis Iesu,* XXXVII (1968), 237-316.

——"De origine collegiorum externorum deque controversiis circa eorum paupertatem obortis, 1539-1608." *Archivum historicum Societatis Iesu,* XXIX (1960), 189-245; XXX (1961), 4-89. English Digest by G. E. Ganss, S.J., in *Woodstock Letters,* XCI (1962), 123-166.

Maroto, P., C.M.F. *Regulae et particulares constitutiones singularum Religionum ex iure Decretalium usque ad codicem.* Rome, 1932.

Maruca, Dominic, S.J., translator. "The Deliberation of our First Fathers." *Woodstock Letters,* XCV (1966), 325-333.

Mir, Gabriel Codina, S.J. *Aux sources de la pédagogie des Jésuites: le "modus Parisiensis."* Rome, 1968.

Nadal, Jerónimo, S.J. *Scholia in Constitutiones et Declarationes S. P. Ignatii.* Prato, 1883.

New Catholic Encyclopedia. 12 vols. New York, 1967.

Olivares, Estanislao, S.J. *Los votos de los escolares de la Compañía de Jesús: Su evolución jurídica.* Rome, 1961.

Oñate, Antonio Jimenez, S.J. *El origen de la Compañía de Jesús: Carisma fundacional y génesis historica.* Rome, 1966.

Ong, Walter, S.J. *Ramus: Method, and the Decay of Dialogue.* Cambridge, Mass., 1958.

Oswald, Augustinus, S.J. *Commentarius in decem Partes Constitutionum Societatis Jesu.* Bruges, 1895.

Pastor, Ludwig F. von. Tr. by Ralph F. Kerr. *History of the Popes.* Vols. XII-XIV (1534-1559). St. Louis, 1923-1924.

Peers, Edgar Allison. "St. Ignatius of Loyola." In I, 3-24, of *Studies of the Spanish Mystics.* 3 vols. New York, 1951.

Petri Lombardi *Sententiarum libri quattuor.* Ed. Migne. Paris, 1853.

Polgár, László, S.J. *Bibliography of the History of the Society of Jesus.* Rome, 1967.

Pourrat, P. *La spiritualité chrétienne.* I: *Des origines de l'Église au Moyen Age.* II: *Le Moyen Age.* III: *Les temps moderns. 1. De la Renaissance au Jansénisme.* IV: *Les temps moderns. 2. Du Jansénisme a nos jours.* 4 vols. Paris, 1927-1931. English translation: *Christian Spirituality.* 4 vols. New York and Westminster, 1922-1955.

Puhl, Louis J. *The Spiritual Exercises of St. Ignatius. A New Translation Based on Studies in the Language of the Autograph.* Westminster, Md., 1953. Reprint, Chicago, 1968.

Rahner, Hugo, S.J. Trans. M. Barry. *Ignatius the Theologian.* New York, 1968.

——*Saint Ignatius Loyola: Letters to Women.* Trans K. Pond and S.A.H.Weetman. New York, 1960.

——*The Spirituality of St. Ignatius Loyola. An account of Its Historical Development.* Trans. F. J. Smith, S.J. Westminster, Md., 1953. Reprint, Chicago, 1968.

Ravasi, L. R., C.P. *De regulis et constitutionibus religiosorum.* Tournai, 1958.

Rey, Eusebio, S.J. "San Ignacio y el problema de los 'cristianos nuevos.'" *Razon y Fe,* CLIII (1956), 173-204.

Ribadeneyra, Pedro. *Vita Ignatii Loyolae.* See above, s.v. *Fontes narrativi,* Vol. IV.

Roustang, François, S.J. *Introduction à une lecture* . . . See above, s.v. Ignace, St.

——"Sur le rôle de Polanco dans la rédaction des *Constitutions S.J.*" *Revue d'ascétique et de mystique,* XLII (1966), 193-202.

Scaduto, Mario, S.J. *Catalago dei Gesuiti d'Italia: 1540-1565.* Subsidia ad historiam Societatis Iesu, no. 7. Rome, 1968.

Schaefer, T., O.F.M. Cap. *De religiosis: ad normam Codicis Iuris Canonici.* Rome, 1947.

Schneider, Burkhardt. "Nuestro principio y principal fundamento. Zum historischen Verständnis des Papstgehorsamgelübdes." *Archivum historicum Societatis Iesu,* XXV (1956), 488-513.

Schoenenberger, Mario, und Stalder, Robert. "Die Satzungen der Gesellschaft Jesu, aus dem Spanischen übersetzt und eingeleitet," pp. 323-412 in *Die grossem Ordensregeln*, ed. Hans Urs von Balthasar. Einsiedeln, 1961.

Schurhammer, Georg, S.J. *Franz Xaver, sein Leben und seine Zeit.* Band I. *Europa, 1506-1541.* Freiburg-im-Bresgau: Herder, 1955.

Smith, Richard F., S.J. "Religious Life" *New Catholic Encyclopedia*, XII, 287-294. New York, 1967.

Societatis Iesu Constitutiones et Epitome Instituti. 5th ed., rev. Rome, 1962.

Sommervogel, Carlos, S.J. *Bibliothèque de la Compagnie de Jésus.* Première parties: *Bibliographie*, par les PP. Augustin et Aloys de Backer, S.J. Seconde partie: *Histoire*, par A. Carayon, S.J. *Tables* . . . par P. Bliard, S.J. 12 vols. Brussels and Paris, 1890-1932. Reprint, Héverlé-Louvain, 1960.

Stierli, Josef, S.J., tr. M. Hill, S.J. "Ignatian Prayer: 'Seek God in All Things.'" *Woodstock Letters*, XC (1961), 135-166.

Tacchi Venturi, Pietro, S.J. *Storia della Compagnia di Gesù in Italia.* Vol I, Parte I: *La vita religiosa in Italia durante i primordi dell' ordine.* Parte II: *Documenti.* Vol. II, Parte I: *Dalla nascita del fondatore alla solenne approvazione dell' Ordine (1491-1540).* Parte II: *Dalla solenne approvazione dell' Ordine alla morte del fondatore (1540-1556).* 2d ed., rev. Rome, 1950-1951.

Tartaret, Pierre. *In Aristotelis philosophiam, naturalem, divinam & moralem exactissima commentaria.* Venice, 1592.

Vatican Council II, The Documents of. Ed. Walter M. Abbott, S.J. and Joseph Gallagher. New York, 1966.

Villoslada, Ricardo García, S.J. *Manual de Historia de la Compañia de Jesús.* Madrid, 1954.

Index I, to the texts

of the Formula of the Institute, General Examen, and Constitutions

Numbers **without** brackets, such as 63, 345, refer to **pages**, and those **within** brackets, such as [1,307], to **paragraphs** of the General Examen or Constitutions. Further cross-references will often be found in the margins or footnotes.

Appointment
  of superiors, [421, 490, 757, 759, 778]
  of officials, [142, 428, 760, 770, 781]
Approval, of the Institute, 64, 66, 72,
    [1]
— of appointments to offices, [421, 490,
    519, 740, 757, 759, 778]
Arabic, in universities, [447]
Arbitration in electing a general, [707]
Aristotle, [470]
Arms, [266]
Arts, the. *See* Philosophy
Assistants of the general, their
  number, [779, 803, 805]
  appointment, [779-781]
  twofold function, [677, 767, 779, 780,
    782, 799, 803, 805]
  care of the general, [766-777, 779,
    782-786]
  calling a general congregation, [681,
    773, 782-788]
  election of a temporary vicar, [773,
    786]
Assistancy, what one is, [803]
Austerities, [8, 582]. *See also* Mortifica-
    tion
Authority, of
  the Church, 66, 68, [1, 22, 165-167,
    603]
  a general congregation, 67, [677-681,
    820]
  the general and his delegates, [737-
    765, 786-789, 796]
  the hierarchy of authorities, [84, 85,
    284, 286, 424, 434, 547-552, 659,
    662, 666, 765, 791]
  See also Obedience; Superiors
Authors to be lectured on, [358, 464-470]
— to be avoided, [359, 464, 465, 468,
    469]
Avarice, avoiding it, [567, 816]

B

Banquets at graduations,]480]
Beadle, [498, 500]
Begging, alms, 67, 69, [67, 82, 331, 569,
    574, 610, 625]

See also Alms
Bell, [435, 436]
Benefactors, [309, 317, 622]
  Masses for, [309, 310, 315, 316, 638,
    640]
  See also Founders
Benefices, [59, 256]
Benevolence of externs, [593]
  of the pope, [823, 824]
  for missionaries, [626]
  toward dismissed, [225]
  of opponents, [426, 824]
Birth from non-Christian parents, [36]
Blessing before meals, [251]
Body, health of. *See* Health
  deformity of, [185, 186]. *See also* Ap-
    pearance, pleasing
Body of the Society
  the Society as a whole, head and
    members, [135, 511, 655, 671],
    and passim. *See also,* in Index II,
    Body, head, and members
  those with public vows, [219, 510,
    511, 542]
  those with last vows, [59, 510, 511]
  as the Society's exterior, distinguished
    from its spirit or soul, [813]
  organic unity of the whole body, [135-
    137, 322, 547, 591, 603, 671,
    812-817]
Books, [372, 373]. *See also* Reading
— administrative, to record
    items of candidates, [57, 200]
    names of members, [530, 545]
    names of students, [495, 496]
— read in schools. *See* Authors
— writing and censorship of. *See* Writing;
    Censors
— cautioned against, [268]. *See also*
    Authors
— publishing of, [273, 389, 653]
— as movable goods, [562]
— profane and vain, [268]
Box or cabinet, for alms, [567]
— closed to superior, [427]
Buildings, construction of, [827]
  care of, [326, 740]

Bulls and briefs, papal
to be studied in first and second probation, [18, 98, 198, 199]
before last vows, [98]
summary for the general, [792]
— specifically mentioned
Regimini militantis, 64-66, [1]
Iniunctum Nobis, 65, [1]
Licet debitum, [99, 236, 751]
Exposcit debitum, 63-73, [1, 5, 11,
119, 308, 327, 330, 419, 527-529,
532, 534, 562, 740]
Business, or things to be done, skill in,
[273, 723, 729, 806]
See also Opinions
— of the Society
the procurator general, [806]
local procurators and treasurers, [591]
— secular, forbidden to Jesuits, [591,
592]
especially to the general, [793, 794]
impediment to admission, [185, 188]
See also Institute, things foreign to

C

Candle for founders, [600]
Canon Law
training in, [351, 353]
its teaching in Jesuit schools, [464,
467]
the part on court trials, [446]
profession for proficiency in, [519]
Cases, reserved. *See* Reservation
— of conscience, [356, 394, 407, 461]
— or causes, in court, [327, 591, 593,
594]
— or works, pious, [53, 54, 57, 59, 254,
256]
Catalogue of members, [676, 792]
Catechism. *See* Doctrine, Christian
Censors of books, [273, 389, 653]
Censures, [407, 701, 704, 709, 710, 718]
Ceremonies, [110, 401, 671]
Of Holy Week, [587]
Chaldaic, [447]
Chancellor of a university, [460, 491,
493, 494, 502]

Chant, [311, 586, 587, 600]
Charity, importance of, [134, 813]
chief bond of unity, [671, 821]
measure of merit, [13]
discreet charity, norm of action, [209,
237, 269, 582, 727, 729, 735]
— toward God. *See* Love
— toward religious brethren, [624, 671,
821]
shown in humble tasks, [114, 282]
praised in exhortations, [280]
in manifesting faults, [63]
toward the dying, [595, 601]
in dismissals, [213, 225, 226]
things to be avoided, [273, 275, 823]
See also Union of hearts
— between superiors and subjects. *See*
Love
— toward one's fellowmen
toward all, [163, 572, 593, 823]
in the general, [725]
motive for studying, [361]
in dismissing students, [489]
toward founders, [318]
— works of charity, [623, 650]
Chastity
the vow, [4, 7, 13, 14, 119, 121, 527,
532, 535, 540, 547]
to be preserved perfectly, [547]
cloister, [266]
Choir, Office in, 70, [311, 586, 587, 600]
Christian doctrine. *See* Doctrine
Church, the Catholic
the Society in its service, 64, 66, 68,
[136, 638]
prayer for it, [638]
fidelity to its doctrine, [47, 174, 274,
367, 368]
in candidates, [22, 165, 167, 174]
Churches of the Society
their poverty, 69, [4, 324, 554-556,
561, 564, 566, 567, 572, 589]
and Mass foundations, [324, 325, 589,
590]
vows in them, [525, 527, 531-533]
preaching and ministries in them, [196,
281, 644-647]

— of colleges. *See* Rules
Consultations, [211, 667, 804]
Consultors of the general. *See* Assistants
— of higher superiors, [221, 810]
— of local superiors
why necessary, [810]
number and kind, [431, 490]
in faculties, [501, 502]
topics for, [431, 810]
Contemplation of Christ, [65]
Contracts, [743, 745]
Contradictions, frustrations, [728, 824]
Contributions or imposed taxes, [329, 743]
Contumacy, [208]
Contumely, injuries, [101, 102]
Convalescents, in a villa, [561]
Conversation, among members, [250]
— with externs
a Jesuit ministry, [115, 349, 648]
its manner, [414, 814]
ability in it, need of, [142, 157, 624, 729, 802, 806]
Conversation, spiritual, [46]
with candidates, [146, 190, 196, 197]
restriction in beginners, [60, 244, 247, 249, 362]
for mutual aid, [89, 115, 338, 349, 661]
apostolic means, [186, 414, 437, 461, 624, 648, 729, 814]
Cook, [84, 85, 149, 433]
Cooperation with grace, [134, 144, 814]
Corpse, as example in obedience, [547]
Correction of members
by the general, [754, 791]
manner of, [63, 269, 270, 395, 727, 754, 784, 791]
mutual. *See* Manifestation
See also Admonition; Penances
— of students
need of, and when, [395, 488]
its spirit, [395, 397, 488, 489]
through recourse to public authority, [433, 444]
Corrector of students, [395, 397, 488, 500]

— of preachers, [405]
Correspondence, official, [504, 507, 674, 790]
purpose, [673]
by whom determined, [673-675]
on ministries, [626, 629, 674]
— private, [60, 246]
Counsels, evangelical, [53, 54, 61, 254]. *See also* Poverty; Chastity; Obedience
Courses or terms, in
humanities, [471, 472]
philosophy, [473, 474]
theology, [418, 474, 476, 518]
repetitions of, [388]
See also Examinations; Humane letters; Philosophy; Theology
Court trials, [446, 593]. *See also* Lawsuits
Curacy of souls, [324, 325, 588]

D

Damage to Society, a cause for dismissal, [212]
Dead or dying of the Society, the, [595-601]. *See also* [412, 413]
Deans of faculties, [501, 502]
Debts of candidates, [38, 42, 53, 185, 188, 196, 217]
— of the Society. *See* Obligations
Deceit, in admissions, [213, 216]
Declamations, [381, 484, 485]
Declarations, the
why added, [136]
same authority as Constitutions, [136, 548, 602]
Decrees of general congregations. *See* Congregation, general
Decorum or propriety, [251, 266, 268, 271, 297, 431]
Defects, moral, manifestation to
superior or confessor, [263]
the superior's concern, [91, 92]
silence about the dismissed, [227, 228]
as impediments to admission, [30, 177, 189]
as cause of dismissal, [211]

in the assistants, [779]
in the general, [729, 735]
imparted by divine unction, [161, 414]
— in other matters
in mental exercises, [298]
in penances, [300]
in experiencing poverty, [287]
in prayer, [182, 582]
in dismissals or readmissions, [204, 205, 219, 236-238]
in ministries, [624]
in affairs of novices, [19, 285]
in the spiritual life, [279, 341, 343, 363, 583]
in corrections, [269, 270, 754]
in supplying needs, [581]
in assignments, [149, 424, 458]
in works of charity, [650, 794]
in dispensing from cloister, [267]
in common life, [301, 581]
Dismissal of students, [444, 488, 489]
— from the Society
importance, [819]
who can dismiss, [204, 205]
even of a general, [774]
order of difficulty in, [204, 205, 208]
which good prevails, [212]
Dismissal
— causes of
their justice, [120]
chief causes, [204, 211-217, 664, 665, 819]
ill health as cause, [213]
cautious weighing, [204, 205, 211, 218-222]
how far to be manifested, [227, 228]
for novices, [204, 205]
for those with simple vows, [123, 204, 205, 387]
for the professed, [205, 219]
— authority in
who has it ordinarily, [119, 120, 206, 736, 738]
provincials and local superiors, [206-208]
— manner of dismissing

the one dismissing, [204, 211, 218-222]
observances toward the dismissed, [223-226]
toward the members and externs, [227-230]
restoring possessions, [58, 224]
— ordinary
of novices, [58, 205, 208, 223, 224]
of those with simple vows, [120, 123, 204, 205, 208, 387]
of the professed, [205, 208, 219]
— extraordinary, [208]
— effects of, [119-121, 123, 223, 224, 233, 234, 536]
— readmission of dismissed, [231, 232, 241, 242]
— other manners of leaving. *See* Apostates; Fugitives; Transfer

Dispensation
who grants it, [425, 746, 747]
impediments to admission, [162, 166, 176, 178, 187]
the two years of novitiate, [515]
domestic order, [295]
in studies, [289, 290, 365, 368, 370, 416]
in observing Constitutions, [425, 746, 747]
in common life, [265, 279, 295, 592]
Disputations, [375, 378-380, 382, 455, 456, 493]
Disquiet of soul, [60, 62, 188, 219, 227, 245, 275]
Doctrine or learning
its necessity, [307, 814]
scope and measure, [351, 360, 446]
in candidates, [47, 154, 183]
in the professed, [12, 14, 518, 519, 819]
in superiors, [423]
in the secretary and assistants, [802, 803]
in the general, [729, 735, 774, 802]
— to be held in the Society
its nature, [47, 358, 464, 672, 814]

— re spiritual formation and discipline in
the novitiate, [515]
— re studies of Jesuits, 70, [358, 420, 470,
739-742]
— re schools open to the public, [392,
393, 399, 466, 491, 492, 508,
509]
— re the vows
first vows, [187, 512, 513, 523, 736]
last vows, 71, [512-526, 736, 737]
the special vows of the professed,
[617, 817]
— re poverty
the renunciation of goods, [258, 259,
744]
in administering temporalities, 70,
[322, 323, 326, 327, 420, 421,
740, 743, 744, 759, 762]
founders, [315, 319, 762]
— re ministries in general, 67, 69, [308,
325, 618, 666, 749, 751]
missions from the pope, 68, [606, 607,
617, 751]
secular business, [592]
— re union of hearts, 69
placing one under direct obedience to
himself, [663]
in congregations, [681, 682, 686, 689,
690, 691, 712, 716, 718, 755]
— re government of provinces and houses
designates and deals with superiors,
[326, 421, 490, 666, 687, 688,
740, 741, 756-761, 765, 773, 778,
780, 781, 787, 790, 791, 795,
798, 804, 805]
may visit subjects, [669]
judges reports, [516, 517, 737]
erection of houses, [320-323, 441, 442,
743, 762, 763]
communicates faculties and favors,
[511, 666, 753]
should know consciences, [764]
use of corrections, [754, 791]
and bishoprics, [756]
care for communications, [673-676,
790]
censuring of books, [273, 389, 653]

— aids for his governing well
no extraneous occupations, [789, 793,
794]
easily available documents, [676, 792]
delegated tasks, [798, 799]
delegated officials, [791, 795, 797]
consultation of others, [679, 761]
— care of the Society for the general,
[766-777, 779, 782-786]
Generosity of God
in His gifts, [282, 595, 640]
— toward God, [282]
— of an apostle, [573, 609]
in self-dedication, [282, 283]
— of benefactors, [398, 640]
Gifts, of God, [147-162, 186, 282, 624,
723-735, 813, 814]
— of men, [478, 568]
— by houses, [331, 562]
Glory of God, the greater, 72
norm of the Society's laws, [133, 508]
desire for it in place of fear, [602]
God and the Institute
His greater glory the supreme norm,
[133, 258]
everything directed to that, [305], and
passim
Society's well-being dependent on
Him, [134, 812, 825]
— and personal perfection
to be sought in all things, [250, 288]
in obedience, [84, 547]
familiarity with Him, in prayer, [288,
723, 813]
through confidence in Him, [67, 414,
555, 812, 814]
expression of His will through superior, [284, 547, 619]
prudence from His wisdom, [711, 746]
His immutability, [116]
winning His liberality, [282, 283]
— and one's fellow men
enjoins care of fellowmen, [115]
is in them as an image, [250]
knowledge of Him to be spread, [307,
446]
instrument united with God, [813]

His glory to be sought in life and death, [595, 596, 602]
the general in His service, [728]
love of Him, chief bond of union, [671]
vows bind to Him, [17]
to be seen in superiors, [85, 284, 286, 342, 424, 434, 547-552, 618, 619, 661, 765]
temporal goods belong to Him, [305]

Judgment, discretion, prudence
in scholastic candidates, [154]
in censors, [273]
in the university syndic, [504]
in the general, [729, 735]
lack of sound judgment an impediment, [29, 175]
erroneous or defective, [55, 184]
disturbed by inordinate affections, [726]
— one's own, submission of
in obedience, [284, 547]
in following spiritual direction, [263]
in difficulties of conscience, [48]
in accepting grades, [111]
in following opinions, [47, 274]
— stubborn
harmful to the community, [184]
as impediment, [216]
See also Discretion; Union of hearts

Jurisdiction, civil, in Jesuit universities, [443-445]

K

Kindness, in the general, [664, 727]
in superiors, [423]

L

Languages
purpose of their study, [351, 367]
granted to whom, [356, 368]
which taught, [447, 449]
sequence of, [460]
language of the place, [402]
in edifying letters, [675]
— classical, training of scholastics in, [351]
See also Humane letters; Latin; Greek

Latin
question candidates on, [104]
the General Examen in, [146]
training in, [351, 366, 381]
in universities, [447, 460, 461, 484]
speaking it, [381, 456]
See also Humane letters

Launderer, [149, 306, 433]

Law of the Church. *See* Canon Law
— of the Society, necessary, [134]
who can dispense, [425, 746, 747]
custom with force of law, [478]
— civil, teaching of, [452]
— interior of charity, [134, 135]

Lawsuits, [327, 572, 591-594]. *See also* Court trials

Lecturers. *See* Teachers

Lectures, sacred
proper to the Society, [402, 645]
good wider than in confessions, [623]
training scholastics for, [402-404]
how often and where, [645-647]
choosing lecturers, [624]
attracting hearers, [587]
stipends for, [4, 565, 816]
— scholastic, attendance at, [369-375]
special, in universities, [458]
accepting obligations for, [325, 442]
items to be observed in, [396, 456, 486]

Legitimacy, and candidates, [36]

Lending [257]

Letter left unfinished, [435, 547]

Letters or learning, pursuit of, 70, [289, 307, 340]
in which fields, [815]
pleasing to God, [340, 360, 361]
and temporal coadjutors, [112, 114, 117, 150]
See also Humane letters; Latin; Greek; Vernacular; Correspondence

Letters, directives for
in official letters, [674, 790]
in annual categories, [676, 792]
in historical reports, [673, 675]
See also Correspondence

Letters patent, [625, 631]

assistants for their regions, [803]

superiors for subjects, [424]

— on special occasions

assignment of ministries, [618]

deciding a dismissal, [211, 220]

electing of the general, [694, 701]

admonitions, [770, 811]

missionaries, [633]

scholastics for progress in studies, [360]

for general congregations, [692, 693, 711, 712]

upon taking up new works, [631]

before proposals to a superior, [131, 292]

before classes, [486, 487]

before and after meals, [251]

Preachers, training of, [80, 108, 251, 280, 309-312, 402, 404, 405, 437, 814]

— their function

by whom sent, [645, 749, 752]

means to be used, [402, 404, 405]

practices to be avoided, [281]

by novice priests, [70]

Preaching

a proper ministry, [113, 308, 528]

compared with confessions and Christian doctrine, [528, 623]

place and diligence, [645-647, 394]

gratuity, [4, 398, 565, 566, 816]

as experience of novices, [70, 77]

practice in, [70, 77, 80, 108, 280, 402, 404, 405]

manner, [281, 330, 394, 398, 437, 558]

attendance at by students, [395, 481, 482]

See also Exhortations

Precepts of holy obedience, [602, 765]

Prefect of health, [303, 304]

— of spiritual matters, [263, 431, 432]

— of studies, [351, 460, 471, 493]

— of library, [373]

Prelates, prayer for them, [638, 639]

Pride, [83, 101, 103, 250, 265]

Priests, Jesuit, 64, 70, [80, 276, 584]

Privileges of the Society, [511, 753, 825].

See also Indult

Probation

duration of, [16, 437, 539, 540, 544]

for those returning, [239, 240, 242]

— first and second. *See* Novitiate

— third. *See* Tertianship

Procurator, [591, 682, 683]

Procurators of civil affairs. *See* Business

Procurator general, [806, 808, 329]

appointel by whom, [760]

Professed of solemn vows, the, 66, 68, 71

firmness of bond, [205, 511]

where they live, [422, 557-559]

their teaching Christian doctrine, [528]

spiritual exercises, [551, 582]

dismissal of, [204, 205, 208]

— of four vows

are the chief members, [12, 511]

requirements, [12, 160, 187, 516, 657, 658, 819]

priesthood, 70, [12]

sufficient learning, [518, 519]

reports on, [516, 517, 737]

required for some offices, [683, 687, 688, 699, 780]

improper duties for, [421, 557]

missions from the pope, [7]

— of three vows

grade granted rarely, [11, 520]

to whom, [519-521]

See also Vows

Professed Society, the, superintends the colleges, 70, [419, 815]

Profession, religious. *See* Vows

Progress, spiritual

pursuit of it, [98, 260, 280, 289, 307, 381, 424, 484, 516]

a danger to, [60]

health to be considered, [243]

— aids to it

love of virtues, [81, 101, 284]

manifestations, [63, 91, 92]

penances, [8, 90, 291]

example of the older members, [276]

See also Virtue

Promise to enter the Society, the, in the first vows, [14, 121, 348, 511, 541]

selection and probation, [657, 658, 819]

juridical status, [121, 537, 539]

union with the Society, [204, 205, 510, 511]

required dispositions, [124, 125, 289, 307, 340]

removal from studies, [415-418]

– spiritual care of, [340-343, 439]

domestic tasks, and ministries, [362, 364, 365]

association with extern students, [349]

– care of health, [297, 339]

See also Teaching; Studies

Schools open to the public

purpose, [307, 308, 351, 360, 392, 398, 440, 446]

duties of teachers to students, [486]

– higher faculties in

establishment, [392, 440]

branches taught, [446-452]

some books not to be lectured on, [464, 465, 468, 469]

appointment of professors, [452, 457]

conferring of degrees, [478, 498, 499]

See also Universities; Faculties

– secondary

opening of, [392, 393]

works not to be lectured on, [359]

– elementary, [451]

See also Youth; Colleges

Scripture, the study of, [464]

importance, [351, 446]

versions, [367]

by preachers, [404]

lectures on, to populace, [402, 403]

See also Doctrine; Studies; Theology

Scruples, [48, 136, 235, 330, 559]

Secretary

in election of a general, [701, 703, 705, 706]

of a general congregation, [714, 717]

of a university, [495-497]

– of the Society, [800-802]

appointment, [760]

– in electing a general, [701-706, 782]

– temporal coadjutor as, [433]

Secrets, from confessions or manifestations, [93]

other secrets, [34, 92, 93, 227]

Seminaries, colleges as, 70, [289, 307, 308, 333, 392, 440, 815]

Senses, guarding of, [250]

things repugnant to sense, [83, 284]

Separation, of novices from others, [18, 21, 191, 197, 247]

Severity. *See* Rigor; Kindness

Sick, conduct of, [89, 272, 303, 304, 595]

care for them, [303, 304]

a garden for, [559]

help to the dying, [595, 596]

works of charity for them, [650]

Sickness, a gift, [272]

and admissions or dismissals, [44, 185, 196, 213, 216]

– mental, as impediment, [29, 175]

Silence, [249, 250, 702]

Simplicity, unassuming, [250]

Slavery, as impediment, [28, 173, 174, 217]

Sleep, [294, 295, 301, 339, 435, 436, 580]

Society of Jesus

origin and approval, 64-66, 72, [1, 134, 812]

– its name approved by the Holy See, [1]

called least and humble, [1, 134, 190, 638, 817]

– its spirit

love and charity, [134, 547, 551, 602, 671]

should tend toward highest love of God, [288]

– its end, [3, 156, 163, 204, 258, 307, 603, 813]

to be remembered in admissions, [163], studies, [351], schools, [446]

sought in every duty however lowly, [111, 114, 118, 132]

– its Institute. *See* Institute

– its preservation and development

on what dependent, [134, 790, 812]

aids and means, [813-826]

by whom and how, [326, 421, 490, 677, 719, 740, 757, 759, 778]

their grade, [421, 511, 683, 687, 699]

qualities of, [276, 326, 423, 434, 671, 791, 811]

duration of office, [719, 757, 758]

to be loved rather than feared, [667]

residence, [668-670]

aid from officials, [798, 811, 820]

from consultors, [431, 502, 503, 667, 770, 803, 804, 810, 811]

from documents, [792, 811]

— powers and duties in general, [206, 207, 423, 424, 631, 659-663, 666, 667, 671, 677-681, 692, 693, 789, 790, 811, 820, 821]

— powers, specific

dispensation in the Institute, [425, 746, 747]

admission and dismissals, [141, 206, 207]

admission to vows, [512, 513]

communication of encouraging news, [673-676]

official letters, [674]

and court trials, [593, 594]

hierarchical chain of command, [206, 424, 434, 626, 663, 666, 781, 821]

— and spiritual care of subjects

correction, [63, 269, 270, 291]

exercises of piety, [582]

manifestation of conscience, [91-93, 95, 97, 263, 551]

religious discipline, [80, 191, 197, 247-249, 294, 295, 428, 435]

studies, in general, [351, 355, 357, 358, 372]

obedience, [84, 85, 131, 284-286, 292, 424, 543, 547-552]

precepts of obedience, [602]

promoting union and charity, [655, 659, 661, 667, 673, 821]

poverty, [54-56, 59, 257, 571]

— and temporal administration, [740, 745]

— and aid of souls, [82, 92, 588, 603,

612-614, 618, 621-626, 629, 630, 633, 635, 645-647]

— and care of the body

health, [292, 293, 301, 304, 579, 581]

the dying and dead, [595-601]

— local superiors

appointment, [757, 759]

grade, [421, 557, 683]

consultors, [431, 490, 502, 503, 810]

powers and duties, [347, 424, 434, 662, 666]

dispensation from Institute, [425]

spiritual exhortation, [280]

right to congregations, [682, 692, 699]

officials, [424, 428]

official letters, [674]

Support of Jesuits in professed houses and residences, [4, 554-561]

Syndic, [271, 386, 431, 504-507]

T

Table, meals, [251, 436]

Talents or qualifications for admissions, [147, 163]

compensation for, [161, 162, 178]

scholastic candidates, [153-159, 161]

coadjutor candidates, [112, 114, 148-152]

scholastics for first vows, [308, 334]

temporal coadjutors for final vows, [522]

for vows of spiritual coadjutor, [112, 522]

for solemn profession, [12, 819]

for profession of three vows, [519-521]

and dismissals, [205]

Tax imposed by the general, [743]

Teachers, Jesuit,

by whom appointed, [371, 491, 740, 752]

competence in their branches, [446-450]

their number, [456-458]

— of Jesuits, their duties, [369, 377, 381, 403, 455, 456, 481, 486, 487]

their doctrine, [47, 273, 274, 358, 464]

— of externs, [486]

Vows, private
  before entrance, [45]
  novices' vows of devotion, [17, 283, 544, 545]
  juridical effects, [205, 208]
— public
  religious vows, means to the Society's end, [4]
  effects or ends, [121, 283]
  according to the Constitutions, [527, 532, 535, 540]
  documents to be kept, [530, 532, 535, 540, 545]
— first vows of the Society, [14, 121, 537, 539, 540, 544]
  not made "in hands of", [537, 546]
  meaning of this, [534, 539]
  who is admitted, [512, 513, 523, 736]
  qualifications, [14, 16, 98, 100, 121, 126, 308, 334, 336, 523, 819]
  age, [187]
  who accepts them, [526]
  what observed during, [537, 540]
  the fourth vow, [121, 511, 541]
  notanda on poverty, [348]
  union with the Society, [204, 205]
  See also Renewal of vows
— last vows of the Society
  who is admitted, [517, 522, 737]
  requisites, [582, 657, 658, 819]
  what precedes admission to, [516, 517, 737]
  who accepts, [512, 513, 525, 526]
  what precedes pronouncement, [82, 95, 98, 525]
  how taken, [525, 526, 530, 531, 533, 535]
  agenda after taking them, [530, 532, 535]
— of the solemnly professel in general
  their union with the Society, [204, 205, 511]
  on what the solemnity depends, [534]
  the five simple vows, [553, 554, 817, 818]
  their force, [553, 554, 817, 818]

— the professed of the four vows
  which vows, [4, 7, 527]
  who are admitted, [12, 516, 518, 519, 819]
  force of the fourth vow, [7, 529, 603, 605]
— the professed of three vows
  which vows, [11, 520]
  who are admitted, [11, 519-521]
— of the formed coadjutors
  which vows, [13, 119]
  juridical nature, [71, 119, 120, 205, 533-536, 539, 572]
  who admitted to them, [112, 522, 819]
  their union with the Society, [204, 205]
— freeing from the obligation of
  in those dismissed, [119-121, 123, 234, 536, 539]
  in apostates and fugitives, [235]
— *See also* Chastity; Obedience; Poverty

W

Will
  supreme rule of every good will, God, [284]
  seeking His will, [211, 220, 226, 288, 547]
  obedience of the will, [284, 516, 547, 550]
  union of wills in charity, [273, 671, 821]
  See also Affections; Union of hearts
Wills, executor of, [591, 592]
Wisdom, divine, [134, 136, 161, 243, 284, 307, 705, 708, 711]
Women, and cloister, [266, 267]
  regular confessors of religious women, [588]
Work, labors
  urged by the Institute, 64, 66, 68, 71, [308]
  superiors to be stalwart under work, [423]
— moderation in, 67, [297-299, 339, 382, 769, 822]

Works of charity, [623, 650]. *See also*
Cases, pious benefactors participate in, [317]

World, renunciation of, 64, [30, 50, 53]
in novitiate, [61, 66, 297]
spirit of the world, [101]
worldliness in externals, [576]
contempt of world as aid to union,
[671]

Writing, [373, 376, 388, 399, 433]
See also Correspondence

Writing of books
importance, [653]
textbooks, [466]
where writers may live, [558]
See also Censors; Books

Y

Youth, training of
importance, 66, [392, 394, 440]
— moral and religious training
how done, [395, 483]
for piety and good moral habits, [395,
481-489]
See also Discipline; Confessors; Christian Doctrine; Spiritual director

Z

Zeal for souls, [3, 493, 813]
embraces all men, [163]
required in candidates, [148, 153, 156]
supposed in scholastics, [340, 361]
practiced by temporal coadjutors, [114,
115]

Index II, to the Introduction and Commentary

with references to the texts added in instances necessary or helpful

Numbers **without** brackets, such as 63, 345, refer to **pages,** and those **within** brackets, such as [1,307], to **paragraphs** of the General Examen or Constitutions. Further cross-references will often be found in the margins or footnotes.

A

Abnegation, 68, 107. *See also* Lowliness

Acknowledgements, 59

Active and contemplative life, 22, 23, 183-184

Adaptation of traditions to modern times, 4, 27, 32, 47, 58, 79

— of rules, ordinances, procedures, and means to circumstances, 46, 172, 211, 251; [18, 136, 198, 395, 396, 428, 455, 585, 654, 811]

Affecto, scuela del, meaning of, 234, 309

Ages of students in colleges, 129-131, 181, 189, 190, 214, 220, 223

Aicardo, José M., S.J., 147, 149, 153, 233, 335

Aid oneself, *ayudarse,* a term meaning spiritual progress, 19, 78

Aldama, Antonio de, S.J., 59, 117, 185, 274, 356

Alienation, 67

Alms, the professed houses should live entirely on them, 166. *See also* Index I

Ambition, of
  missions, 68
  offices, a pestilence, [720, 817]

Ambrosio de Montesinos, 13

"Angelic" purity, 246

Anima, the self, person, 77, 285
  distinguished from *Animos,* hearts, 285

Apostolic character of Ignatius' Institute and spirituality, 6, 22, 23, 32, 33, 44, 50, 183. *See also* Ignatius; Institute

Aquaviva, Claudio, S.J., general policy on grades, 71, 82, 353, 354, 355

the text is left unchanged, 46, 67, 72

changes or interpretations by the Society, 46, 58, 67. *See also* General Congregation

to be studied by novices, 37, 44; [18, 98, 198, 199, 826]

the present commentary, its aim, 58

— translations of them

the Latin translation of 1558, 22, 53, 54

authentic but not definitive, 54

editions of La Torre, Codina, 53-54

vernacular translations, 56-58

the present translation, 57-58

Constitutions for Scholastics (1546), the, 46

Consultors, 330; [810]

Contarini, Cardinal, 48

Contemplación, meditación, oración, meanings of 96, 259

Contemplation, infused, or mysticism, 7, 12

source of insights into deposit of faith, 32-33

See also Ignatius, his mysticism

Contemplation, of mysteries of Christ, 13

Contemplative in action, Ignatius as a, 22-23, 183. *See also* Ignatius, his spirituality; Mysticism

Contemplative life and active life, 2-23, 183-184

Conversation and correspondence, 154

Conversations, Exercises, and other apostolic means, references to examples of, 283

Corneille, Pierre, 214

Coudret, Hannibal du, 199

Courel, François, S.J., 57, 59, 78, 82, 94, 96, 97, 120, 155, 192

Covarrubias, Horozco, Sebastián de, his dictionary (1611), 40, 78, 80, 82, 104, 209, 221, 253, 345

Creation, God's plan of

in St. Thomas, 10

in Peter Lombard, 18

Ignatius' insights on, 16

See also Redemptive

Creusen, Joseph, S.J., 105

Cristianos nuevos, 88

Cristobal de Madrid, 202

Cross, emphasis on in Ignatius' spirituality, 23-24, 66. *See also* Lowliness

Curacies of souls, 94, 178; [324, 588]

Curso, meaning of, 221

Customs, 39, 42

D

Dalmases, Candido de, S.J., 55

Daniélou, Jean, S.J., 13, 332

Dean, 227

Declaration of the Institute, power to explain is officially, 67

Declarations, the

general descriptions, 35, 37, 38, 121; [136, 548]

interwoven with texts, 53

contrasted with rules and ordinances, 121

same juridical force as Constitutions, 36; [136, 548]

Decrees and canons, of general congregations, 47

Delchard, Antoine, S.J., 251

Deliberation, dialogue, discussion, 21, 26, 47-48, 136, 147, 247-249

See also Representation

Deliberation of the First Fathers, 21, 47-48 246, 347

Democratic procedures within the monarchic structure of the Society, 11, 26. *See also* Representation

Devotion, in Ignatius' spirituality and terminology, 26, 155-156, 162, 332. *See also* Index I, Devotion

Diaz, Natalio D., S.J., 333

Difficulties, requiring long testing, 71

Discernment, discretion, prudence, 13, 14, 24, 32, 94, 104, 126, 136, 147, 156

group discernment, 147

Disciplinary theory of education, 195

G

Gandía, university of, 171

Ganss, George E., S.J., 5, 12, 107, 184, 187, 192, 216, 233

General congregation, a, 67, 294
can make or change constitutions, 67
Formula of, 296
decrees and canons of a, 47

General Congregation I and the Constitutions, 22, 36, 46, 51, 53
textual changes, 55, 179, 192, 200, 214, 215, 219, 222, 231, 258, 305, 313

— II (1565), 235, 287

— IV (1581), 53, 260

— V (1593), 354

— VI (1608), on annual Spiritual Exercises, 107

— VII (1615), policy on grades, 71, 81, 355

— XXIII (1883), 54

— XXIV (1892), 54, 355

— XXVII (1923), 47

— XXXI (1965-1966), 4, 79, 81, 178, 235, 248, 252, 253, 261, 308, 349, 355

General Examen. *See* Examen, the General

General, the superior general
his authority, 67; [736-765]
authority of Society over him, 312, 318; [766-788]
his lifelong term, 308
rules, ordinances, and instructions of, 47

Genetic study of Ignatius' world view, 4-24

Gerleman, Hugo J., S.J., 59

Gerson, John, 234

Ghinucci, Cardinal, 49, 80

Gill, H.V., S.J., 13

Gilmont, Jean François, S.J., 55

Giuliani, Maurice, S.J., 76, 184

Glory of God, the, 3, 8, 9, 10, 18, 22, 23, 24, 32, 33, 38, 72, 108, 109, 211, 248, 267, 299, 332, and passim
a pivotal point in Ignatius' thought, 8
synonymous and overlapping with praise and service of God, 8, 24, 299
in St. Thomas' synthesis, 10
— the greater, [63, 71, 72, 89, 93, 101-103, 131, 230, 343, 349, 358, 423, 431, 511, 573, 577, 579, 591, 593, 603, 609, 618, 622,a, 647, 661, 669, 779], and passim
Ignatius' basic criterion in decisions, 8, 24, 32, 38, 248, 274; [63, 71, 131, 343, 358, 511, 573, 603, 609, 618, 622,a, 647, 669, 779], and passim

God, the center of Ignatius' thoughts, 15
his total dedication to Him, 15; [17, 53, 283]
— preserves and develops the Society, 119, 331-333; [134, 812-814]
— names of in the Constitutions, 120

"God our Lord," means Christ, 7

Government, paternal but not authoritarian in manner, 250

Grace, divine, 8, 10, 23, 94; [3, 79, 93, 101, 283, 360, 547, 555, 814]. *See also* Index I, Grace

Grades or classes of members, 65, 66, 71, 81, 232, 349-356; [10, 15, 511]. *See also* Members

Grades, the diversity of among the priests
chief treatments, 65, 71, 81, 232, 349-356; [10, 12, 13, 511, 521, 819]
no founder other than Ignatius established such an arrangement, 349
background: ignorance of clergy in 1500's, 350
research of Lukács on, briefly summarized, 81; expanded, 349-356
conspicuos, divergent interpretations of, 71, 81, 336, 353-354
sufficient theology, Ignatius' criterion for profession, 71, 81, 235, 236, 336, 352, 353

410
Reference matter

Granero, Jesús M., S.J., 13, 55, 76, 247, 346

Gratuity of ministries, 67, 79, 226, 251, 256; [4, 398, 478, 495, 499, 565-567, 640, 816]

of instruction, 200, 222, 226; [398, 478, 495]

dispensation from, 226

Gregory X, pope, 40, 48, 49

Gregory XIII, pope, 56, 65

Guibert, Joseph de, S.J., 5, 8, 13, 17, 153

Guidiccioni, Cardinal, 49

H

Hands, received into the, 163, 233, 240; [283, 534, 539]

Head of the Society. *See* Body

Health in the early Society, incidences of poor, 107

Herman, Jean Baptiste, S.J., 161, 192

Hierarchy of beings and values, Ignatius', 18, 33, 172, 213, 214

— or channel of authorities, his, 3, 11, 22, 32, 66, 80, 102, 247, 289, 346. *See also* Body; Authority; Subordination

Historical Records S.J., 292, 359-361

Hours of Our Lady, the, 184

House, technical meaning of, 76, 165

professed houses, 166, 254

colleges preferred to them, 166

— of first probation, 76, 127

Humility, 69. *See also* Lowliness

three kinds of, and Ignatius' world view, 107

concrete examples, references to, 108

I

Ignatius, **his life and character**

his place in history of salvation, 3, 32-33

his *Autobiography,* 13-26, 332

receives Master of Arts, 19, 20

studies theology, 19, 20

Ignatius, his character, continued

in the school of experience, 20

associated with Christ, 3, 332. *See also* Association

totally dedicated to Him, 15, 16, 64, 163, 165; [283, 288, 813]

a self-portrait, 309; [723-725]

prudence or discretion, his, 23, 126. *See also* Discernment

his practical character, 7, 12, 27, 32, 38

his large perspective, 6, 22-23, 332

needs, alertness to contemporary, 27, 32

a link between the past and future, 32

his character as a leader who consulted and dialogued much, 26. *See also* Representation; Deliberation

functioning of his mind, 58, 165, 317

originality of his new Institute, 6, 22, 23, 32, 33, 44, 50, 246

aided by Polanco in composing the Constitutions, 49-53

his role and Polanco's, 54-55. *See also* Polanco

as superior, 49, 103, 250, 309

inspired more than he commanded, 103, 250

See also Obedience

— **and greater glory to God,** 3, 8, 18, 23, 24, 25, 33, 107, 108, 109, 172, 211, 267, 332, and passim

context in God's redemptive plan, 8

the norm in his decisions, 8, 274, 299; [622,a]

glory, praise, and service of God are overlapping concepts, 8, 24, 299

their place in his apostolic spirituality, 8

all things are means to God's glory, but he did not always explicitate this, 24

See also Glory

— **his spirituality,** 6

syntheses of it, 4, 13

genetic approach, benefits of, 4

Ignatius, his spirituality, continued

is Christian spirituality, with special emphases, 6

Trinitarian, 16, 22, 26

his thought moves downward from the Trinity, 332

mediators in his spirituality, 17, 20, 22, 25

Christocentric character of, 22, 26, 107-108; [101]

balance a characteristic of it, 23, 24, 25, 332

his desire to be associated with Christ in God's redemptive plan, 3, 7, 16-17, 20, 22, 25, 33, 76, 80, 102, 247, 332, 346, 347, 348, 349. *See also* Redemptive

stresses virtues opposite to vices, 23-24, 108, 159, 234, 251, 320-321

esteemed material creatures and natural gifts, 19, 23, 127, 167, 190; [147, 151-162, 300, 339, 728-734, 813-814]

but valued supernatural gifts above them, 23, 127, 167, 332, 333; [812-814]

lowliness, virtues of, in his spirituality, 20, 23, 27, 48, 69, 107, 235; [101, 516]

his concept of apostolic spirituality, 6, 22-23, 183-184

a spirituality for superiors, 103, 309

on prayer for those in formation, 183, 260-261; [340-345]

on prayer for the formed, 183, 260-261; [582-584]

actions can be prayer, 183-184

formal and virtual prayer, 183-184

prayer in time of retreat, and of daily living, 183-184

post-Ignatian legislation, 260-261

ecclesiology of, 123

and the mystical body of Christ, 3, 21, 22, 123, 247, 347

and the glorified Christ, 3, 21, 22, 347

at service of the pope and Church, 3,

Ignatius, his spirituality, continued

22, 32, 33, 66, 68, 79, 123, 239, 246, 247; [7, 529, 603, 612]

desired to have a group ready for any task of the pope, 247

loyalty to ecclesiastical authority, 32, 247

and thinking rightly within the Church 32

his message of service through love, 3, 7, 22, 25

and finding God in all things, 22-23, 26, 156, 183. *See also* Finding

a contemplative in action, 22-23, 183

contemplative love to be manifested by deeds, 22, 183

— his mysticism or infused contemplation

his mystical favors, 16, 17, 20, 22-26

a source of his world view, 7, 12

gave new insights into the deposit of faith, 32-33

similarity and dissimilarity with inspired Scriptural writers, 32-33

impells to apostolic service, 25, 183-184

applied to practical decisions, 24

"devotion," 26, 155, 162. *See also* Devotion; Finding God; Contemplative

— his world view, 3, 4

centered about God's redemptive plan, 3, 20

influenced by his mystic prayer, 7, 12

its dynamic apostolic character, 6, 32, 33, 50

steps of its gradual formation, 4, 12-24

expressed through the Constitutions, 6, 33, 299, 331

is the key to interpreting them, 7, 9

the Constitutions seen in perspective of it, 6, 33

in it all things are seen as means to greater glory of God, 33, 107, 108, 299

is a framework of reference, 7, 9, 33

applied to educational activities, 172

the English text of *Exposcit debitum*, 63-73

the term, strictly taken, means *Exposcit*, [3-6], 64

authorizes the Constitutions, 36, 64, 67

printed as a preface, 36, 63

numbering of the paragraphs, 66

to be studied by novices, 44; [18, 98, 134, 198, 199]

approved "in specific form," 45

Instrument in God's hands, 4, 22, 322; [813]

Intellectual powers, exercise of, 195; [379]

Intention, a right or pure, 165, 183, 190, 273, 332; [288, 340, 360, 618, 814]

Iparraguirre, Ignacio, S.J., 13, 53, 59, 89, 108, 120, 121, 247, 332

Iturrioz, Jesús, S.J., 76, 346

J

Jacobus de Voragine, *Legenda aurea*, 9, 13, 14, 15, 251

Jacobsmeyer, Aloysius A., S.J., 261

Janssens, Very Rev. John B., S.J., 59

Jay, Claude, early companion of Ignatius, 19, 64, 248, 333, 334, 335

Jesus Christ

Head of the Society, 76, 123, 346

Head of the mystical body, 3, 9, 21, 22, 123, 347

association and cooperation with Him. *See* Association

Ignatius' devotion was to the glorified Christ, 3, 21, 22, 347. *See also* Mystical body

is in the superior, 69, 102, 247. *See also* Authority

more like to Him by putting on His uniform, 108

John Baptist de la Salle, St., F.S.C., 172

John of the Cross, St., O.C.D., 33

Julius III, pope, 21, 36, 45, 50, 63, 76, 335. *See also Exposcit;* Constitutions; Formula

K

Korth, Francis N., S.J., 105

L

La Storta, Ignatius' vision at, 3, 20, 21, 22, 76, 80, 247, 346, 347

Latin, used in all instruction, 195. *See also* Style

preaching in Latin, 196, 209

La Torre, Juan José de, S.J., 54, 143, 187

Law or constitutions, interior and exterior, 119-120

did Ignatius hope for a Society without laws? 120

Law, faculties of, 215

Laynez, Diego, early companion of Ignatius, 19, 20, 21, 50, 54, 56, 64, 75, 85, 260, 335

Lección, leer, 209. *See also Praelectio*

Lectures, sacred, 201, 209, 256, 276, 280, 282

speculative or practical? 201

Leo XIII, pope, 56, 247

Lessius, Leonard, S.J., 214

Letter left unfinished, 208, 247

Letters *(letras)*, means education in general, 82

Letters, inspection of, 94

Leturia, Pedro de, S.J., 175, 184, 261

Lewis, Jacques, S.J., 13

Libraries, were small in 1500's, 193

Lippert, Peter, S.J., 13

Liturgy, the, 9, 261-262

Lowliness, virtues of, in Ignatius' spirituality, 20, 23, 27, 48, 69, 107, 234; [101, 516]

means to inspiring ends, but he did not always explicitate their being means, 24

Ludolph the Carthusian, 9, 13, 23, 251

Lukács, Ladislas, S.J.

research on the diversity of grades, 71, 81, 232, 349-356

compressed summary of it, 81

statistics on education had by early Jesuits, 129-131

how he mirrored them, 309

aimed to produce men of the Church, 32

application of Ignatius' world view, 33

and discernment of spirits, 126. *See also* Discernment

approved by the pope, 50, 66

a proper ministry of the Society, 66

annual obligation since 1608, 107

and selection of ministries, 203

rules for thinking rightly within the Church, 245

prayer in time of retreat, 260

making "some of the former Exercises or others," 107; [98]

the authentic Exercises, in *Studies*, 107

Spirituality, Christian

an application of the deposit of faith, 5, 33

schools of, 5, 6, 13

Ignatian spirituality, an application of Christian spirituality, 6, 33

Stalder, Robert, S.J., 57

Standards, the Two, 15, 20

Statistics, on:

qualifications of early candidates, 129-131, 351

professed anl spiritual coadjutors, 81-82, 349-356

illiteracy, 89

colleges and professed houses, 166

number of Jesuits in 1556, 232

priests with and without theology, 130, 351

professed and spiritual coadjutors in 1556, 232, 352-353

Stierli, Josef, S.J., 184

Stipends, dispensation to accept them, 79, 226. *See also* Gratuity

Study, earnest application to, 218

Style, Ignatius' literary, 27, 55

doublets and triplets in it, 8, 24, 44, 82, 94, 104, 143, 165, 299

personal usages of words, 24, 58, 78, 83, 94, 104, 187, 279, 317

difficult ellipses, 79, 163, 239, 247, 268

his attitude on style, elegance, Latin, and Greek, 188, 195, 196, 216; [456]

— Ignatius' opinions on, 172, 216

Subordination of superiors, 3, 11, 22, 32, 66-69, 80, 102, 247, 289, 346; [206, 284, 286, 424, 434, 547, 626, 662, 663, 666, 765, 791, 821]. *See also* Authority; Hierarchy; Obedience

Sufficiency of theological learning, Ignatius' criterion for profession, 71, 81, 235, 236, 336, 352, 353; [518, 521]

See also Lukács; *Conspicuos*

Summary of the Constitutions, replaced by *Readings from . . .* , 85

Superior, the

seeing Christ present in him, 69. *See also* Authority, presence of Christ

Superior, Ignatius' ideal of a, 206, 250, 309; [423-427, 723-735]

a self-portrait, 309; [723-735]

Superiors' manner of governing, 250, 290; [270, 551, 667]

Swain, Very Rev. John L., S.J., 59

Syndic, 160, 197, 228

T

Tartaret, Pierre, 188

Tempesta, Antonio, 28-31, 59

Temporal order, consecration of the to God, 332. *See also* Ignatius, his spirituality

Tertianship or "third probation," 84

original with Ignatius, 233

test and apprenticeship, 233, 235

ministerial training in, 233-235

at first not made in separate house, 235

history of, 234-235

Textbooks, rare in Ignatius' day, 913, 197

Theatines, 44

Theology, most important branch in the curriculum, 211, 213; [446]

scholastic and positive, 188